AN ESSAY ON THE FOUNDATIONS OF GEOMETRY

AN ESSAY ON THE FOUNDATIONS OF GEOMETRY

BY

BERTRAND A W RUSSELL, M.A.

FELLOW OF TRINITY COLLEGE, CAMBRIDGE.

KALPAZ

ISBN: 978-93-5128-841-1(HB)

First Published in 1897
Indian Reprint in 2017

Published by

Kalpaz Publications
C-30, Satyawati Nagar,
Delhi – 110052
E-mail: kalpaz@hotmail.com
Website: kalpazpublications.com
Ph.: +91-9212142040

Cataloging in Publication Data—DK
Courtesy: D.K. Agencies (P) Ltd. <docinfo@dkagencies.com>

Russell, Bertrand, 1872-1970, **author.**
An essay on the foundations of geometry / by Bertrand AW Russell (M.A.).
pages cm
"First published in 1897"—Title page verso.
ISBN 9789351288411

1. Geometry—Foundations. I. Title.

QA681.E87 2017 DDC 516 23

PREFACE.

THE present work is based on a dissertation submitted at the Fellowship Examination of Trinity College, Cambridge, in the year 1895. Section B of the third chapter is in the main a reprint, with some serious alterations, of an article in *Mind* (New Series, No. 17). The substance of the book has been given in the form of lectures at the Johns Hopkins University, Baltimore, and at Bryn Mawr College, Pennsylvania.

My chief obligation is to Professor Klein. Throughout the first chapter, I have found his "Lectures on non-Euclidean Geometry" an invaluable guide; I have accepted from him the division of Metageometry into three periods, and have found my historical work much lightened by his references to previous writers. In Logic, I have learnt most from Mr Bradley, and next to him, from Sigwart and Dr Bosanquet. On several important points, I have derived useful suggestions from Professor James's "Principles of Psychology."

My thanks are due to Mr G. F. Stout and Mr A. N. Whitehead for kindly reading my proofs, and helping me by many useful criticisms. To Mr Whitehead I owe, also, the inestimable assistance of constant criticism and suggestion throughout the course of construction, especially as regards the philosophical importance of projective Geometry.

HASLEMERE.
May, 1897.

TO

JOHN McTAGGART ELLIS McTAGGART

TO WHOSE DISCOURSE AND FRIENDSHIP IS OWING

THE EXISTENCE OF THIS BOOK.

TABLE OF CONTENTS.

INTRODUCTION.

OUR PROBLEM DEFINED BY ITS RELATIONS TO LOGIC, PSYCHOLOGY AND MATHEMATICS.

CHAPTER I.

A SHORT HISTORY OF METAGEOMETRY.

CHAPTER II.

CRITICAL ACCOUNT OF SOME PREVIOUS PHILOSOPHICAL THEORIES OF GEOMETRY.

CHAPTER III.

SECTION A. THE AXIOMS OF PROJECTIVE GEOMETRY.

SECTION B. THE AXIOMS OF METRICAL GEOMETRY.

I. *The Axiom of Free Mobility.*

CHAPTER IV.

PHILOSOPHICAL CONSEQUENCES.

INTRODUCTION.

OUR PROBLEM DEFINED BY ITS RELATIONS TO LOGIC, PSYCHOLOGY AND MATHEMATICS.

1. GEOMETRY, throughout the 17th and 18th centuries, remained, in the war against empiricism, an impregnable fortress of the idealists. Those who held—as was generally held on the Continent—that certain knowledge, independent of experience, was possible about the real world, had only to point to Geometry: none but a madman, they said, would throw doubt on its validity, and none but a fool would deny its objective reference. The English Empiricists, in this matter, had, therefore, a somewhat difficult task; either they had to ignore the problem, or if, like Hume and Mill, they ventured on the assault, they were driven into the apparently paradoxical assertion that Geometry, at bottom, had no certainty of a different *kind* from that of Mechanics—only the perpetual presence of spatial impressions, they said, made our experience of the truth of the axioms so wide as to *seem* absolute certainty.

Here, however, as in many other instances, merciless logic drove these philosophers, whether they would or no, into glaring opposition to the common sense of their day. It was only through Kant, the creator of modern Epistemology, that the geometrical problem received a modern form. He reduced the question to the following hypotheticals: If Geometry has apodeictic certainty, its matter, *i.e.* space, must be *à priori*, and as such must be purely subjective; and conversely, if space is purely subjective, Geometry must have apodeictic certainty. The latter hypothetical has more weight with Kant, indeed it is ineradicably bound up with his whole Epistemology; nevertheless it has, I think, much less force than the former. Let us accept, however, for the moment, the Kantian formulation, and endeavour to give precision to the terms *à priori* and *subjective*.

2. One of the great difficulties, throughout this controversy, is the extremely variable use to which these words, as well as the word *empirical*, are put by different authors. To Kant, who was nothing of a psychologist, *à priori* and *subjective* were almost interchangeable terms[1]; in modern usage there is, on the whole, a tendency to confine the word *subjective* to Psychology, leaving *à priori* to do duty for Epistemology. If we accept this differentiation, we may set up, corresponding to the problems of these two sciences, the following provisional definitions: *à priori* applies to any piece of knowledge which, though perhaps elicited by experience, is *logically* presupposed in experience: *subjective* applies to any mental state whose immediate cause lies, not in the external world, but within the limits of the subject. The latter definition, of course, is framed exclusively for Psychology: from the point of view of physical Science all mental states are subjective. But for a Science whose matter, strictly speaking, is *only* mental states, we require, if we are to use the word to any purpose, some differentia among mental states, as a mark of a more special subjectivity on the part of those to which this term is applied.

Now the only mental states whose immediate causes lie in the external world are *sensations*. A pure sensation is, of course, an impossible abstraction—we are never wholly passive under the action of an external stimulus—but for the purposes of Psychology the abstraction is a useful one. Whatever, then, is not sensation, we shall, in Psychology, call subjective. It is in sensation alone that we are directly affected by the external world, and only here does it give us direct information about itself.

3. Let us now consider the epistemological question, as to the sort of knowledge which can be called *à priori*. Here we have nothing to do—in the first instance, at any rate—with the cause or genesis of a piece of knowledge; we accept knowledge as a datum to be analysed and classified. Such analysis will reveal a formal and a material element in

[1] Cf. Erdmann, Axiome der Geometrie, p. 111: "Für Kant sind Apriorität und ausschliessliche Subjectivität allerdings Wechselbegriffe."

knowledge. The formal element will consist of postulates which are required to make knowledge possible at all, and of all that can be deduced from these postulates; the material element, on the other hand, will consist of all that comes to fill in the form given by the formal postulates—all that is contingent or dependent on experience, all that might have been otherwise without rendering knowledge impossible. We shall then call the formal element *à priori*, the material element empirical.

4. Now what is the connection between the subjective and the *à priori*? It is a connection, obviously—if it exists at all—from the outside, *i.e.* not deducible directly from the nature of either, but provable—if it can be proved—only by a general view of the conditions of both. The question, what knowledge is *à priori*, must, on the above definition, depend on a logical analysis of knowledge, by which the conditions of possible experience may be revealed; but the question, what elements of a cognitive state are subjective, is to be investigated by pure Psychology, which has to determine what, in our perceptions, belongs to sensation, and what is the work of thought or of association. Since, then, these two questions belong to different sciences, and can be settled independently, will it not be wise to conduct the two investigations separately? To decree that the *à priori* shall always be subjective, seems dangerous, when we reflect that such a view places our results, as to the *à priori*, at the mercy of empirical psychology. How serious this danger is, the controversy as to Kant's pure intuition sufficiently shows.

5. I shall, therefore, throughout the present Essay, use the word *à priori* without any psychological implication. My test of apriority will be purely logical: Would experience be impossible, if a certain axiom or postulate were denied? Or, in a more restricted sense, which gives apriority only within a particular science: Would experience as to the subject-matter of that science be impossible, without a certain axiom or postulate? My results also, therefore, will be purely logical. If Psychology declares that some things, which I have declared *à priori*, are not subjective, then, failing an error of detail in my proofs, the connection of the *à priori* and the subjective,

so far as those things are concerned, must be given up. There will be no discussion, accordingly, throughout this Essay, of the relation of the *à priori* to the subjective—a relation which cannot determine what pieces of knowledge are *à priori*, but rather depends on that determination, and belongs, in any case, rather to Metaphysics than to Epistemology.

6. As I have ventured to use the word *à priori* in a slightly unconventional sense, I will give a few elucidatory remarks of a general nature.

The *à priori*, since Kant at any rate, has generally stood for the necessary or apodeictic element in knowledge. But modern logic has shown that necessary propositions are always, in one aspect at least, hypothetical. There may be, and usually is, an implication that the connection, of which necessity is predicated, has some existence, but still, necessity always points beyond itself to a *ground* of necessity, and asserts this ground rather than the actual connection. As Bradley points out, "arsenic poisons" remains true, even if it is poisoning no one. If, therefore, the *à priori* in knowledge be primarily the necessary, it must be the necessary on some hypothesis, and the *ground* of necessity must be included as *à priori*. But the ground of necessity is, so far as the necessary connection in question can show, a mere fact, a merely categorical judgment. Hence necessity alone is an insufficient criterion of apriority.

To supplement this criterion, we must supply the hypothesis or ground, on which alone the necessity holds, and this ground will vary from one science to another, and even, with the progress of knowledge, in the same science at different times. For as knowledge becomes more developed and articulate, more and more necessary connections are perceived, and the merely categorical truths, though they remain the foundation of apodeictic judgments, diminish in relative number. Nevertheless, in a fairly advanced science such as Geometry, we can, I think, pretty completely supply the appropriate ground, and establish, within the limits of the isolated science, the distinction between the necessary and the merely assertorical.

7. There are two grounds, I think, on which necessity may be sought within any science. These may be (very roughly) distinguished as the ground which Kant seeks in the

Prolegomena, and that which he seeks in the *Pure Reason*. We may start from the existence of our science as a fact, and analyse the reasoning employed with a view to discovering the fundamental postulate on which its logical possibility depends; in this case, the postulate, and all which follows from it alone, will be *à priori*. *Or* we may accept the existence of the subject-matter of our science as our basis of fact, and deduce dogmatically whatever principles we can from the essential nature of this subject-matter. In this latter case, however, it is not the whole empirical nature of the subject-matter, as revealed by the subsequent researches of our science, which forms our ground; for if it were, the whole science would, of course, be *à priori*. Rather it is that element, in the subject-matter, which makes *possible* the branch of experience dealt with by the science in question[1]. The importance of this distinction will appear more clearly as we proceed[2].

8. These two grounds of necessity, in ultimate analysis, fall together. The *methods* of investigation in the two cases differ widely, but the *results* cannot differ. For in the first case, by analysis of the science, we discover the postulate on which alone its reasonings are possible. Now if reasoning in the science is impossible without some postulate, this postulate must be essential to experience of the subject-matter of the science, and thus we get the second ground. Nevertheless, the two methods are useful as supplementing one another, and the first, as starting from the actual science, is the safest and easiest method of investigation, though the second seems the more convincing for exposition.

9. The course of my argument, therefore, will be as follows: In the first chapter, as a preliminary to the logical analysis of Geometry, I shall give a brief history of the rise and development of non-Euclidean systems. The second chapter will prepare the ground for a constructive theory of Geometry, by a criticism of some previous philosophical views; in this chapter, I shall

[1] I use "experience" here in the widest possible sense, the sense in which the word is used by Bradley.

[2] Where the branch of experience in question is essential to all experience, the resulting apriority may be regarded as absolute; where it is necessary only to some special science, as relative to that science.

endeavour to exhibit such views as partly true, partly false, and so to establish, by preliminary polemics, the truth of such parts of my own theory as are to be found in former writers. A large part of this theory, however, cannot be so introduced, since the whole field of projective Geometry, so far as I am aware, has been hitherto unknown to philosophers. Passing, in the third chapter, from criticism to construction, I shall deal first with projective Geometry. This, I shall maintain, is necessarily true of any form of externality, and is, since some such form is necessary to experience, completely *à priori*. In metrical Geometry, however, which I shall next consider, the axioms will fall into two classes: (1) Those common to Euclidean and non-Euclidean spaces. These will be found, on the one hand, essential to the possibility of measurement in any continuum, and on the other hand, necessary properties of any form of externality with more than one dimension. They will, therefore, be declared *à priori*. (2) Those axioms which distinguish Euclidean from non-Euclidean spaces. These will be regarded as wholly empirical. The axiom that the number of dimensions is three, however, though empirical, will be declared, since small errors are here impossible, exactly and certainly true of our actual world; while the two remaining axioms, which determine the value of the space-constant, will be regarded as only approximately known, and certain only within the errors of observation[1]. The fourth chapter, finally, will endeavour to prove, what was assumed in Chapter III., that some form of externality is necessary to experience, and will conclude by exhibiting the logical impossibility, if knowledge of such a form is to be freed from contradictions, of wholly abstracting this knowledge from all reference to the matter contained in the form.

I shall hope to have touched, with this discussion, on all the main points relating to the Foundations of Geometry.

[1] I have given no account of these empirical proofs, as they seem to be constituted by the whole body of physical science. Everything in physical science, from the law of gravitation to the building of bridges, from the spectroscope to the art of navigation, would be profoundly modified by any considerable inaccuracy in the hypothesis that our actual space is Euclidean. The observed truth of physical science, therefore, constitutes overwhelming empirical evidence that this hypothesis is very approximately correct, even if not rigidly true.

CHAPTER I.

A SHORT HISTORY OF METAGEOMETRY.

10. When a long established system is attacked, it usually happens that the attack begins only at a single point, where the weakness of the established doctrine is peculiarly evident. But criticism, when once invited, is apt to extend much further than the most daring, at first, would have wished.

> "First cut the liquefaction, what comes last,
> But Fichte's clever cut at God himself?"

So it has been with Geometry. The liquefaction of Euclidean orthodoxy is the axiom of parallels, and it was by the refusal to admit this axiom without proof that Metageometry began. The first effort in this direction, that of Legendre[1], was inspired by the hope of deducing this axiom from the others—a hope which, as we now know, was doomed to inevitable failure. Parallels are defined by Legendre as lines in the same plane, such that, if a third line cut them, it makes the sum of the interior and opposite angles equal to two right angles. He proves without difficulty that such lines would not meet, but is unable to prove that non-parallel lines in a plane must meet. Similarly he can prove that the sum of the angles of a triangle cannot exceed two right angles, and that if any one triangle has a sum equal to two right angles, all triangles have the same sum; but he is unable to prove the existence of this one triangle.

11. Thus Legendre's attempt broke down; but mere failure

[1] V. Mémoires de l'Académie royale des Sciences de l'Institut de France, T. XII. 1833, for a full statement of his results, with references to former writings.

could prove nothing. A bolder method, suggested by Gauss, was carried out by Lobatchewsky and Bolyai[1]. If the axiom of parallels is logically deducible from the others, we shall, by denying it and maintaining the rest, be led to contradictions. These three mathematicians, accordingly, attacked the problem indirectly: they denied the axiom of parallels, and yet obtained a logically consistent Geometry. They inferred that the axiom was logically independent of the others, and essential to the Euclidean system. Their works, being all inspired by this motive, may be distinguished as forming the first period in the development of Metageometry.

The second period, inaugurated by Riemann, had a much deeper import: it was largely philosophical in its aims and constructive in its methods. It aimed at no less than a logical analysis of all the essential axioms of Geometry, and regarded space as a particular case of the more general conception of a *manifold*. Taking its stand on the methods of analytical metrical Geometry, it established two non-Euclidean systems, the first that of Lobatchewsky, the second—in which the axiom of the straight line, in Euclid's form, was also denied—a new variety, by analogy called spherical. The leading conception in this period is the *measure of curvature*, a term invented by Gauss, but applied by him only to surfaces. Gauss had shown that free mobility on surfaces was only possible when the measure of curvature was constant; Riemann and Helmholtz extended this proposition to n dimensions, and made it the fundamental property of space.

In the third period, which begins with Cayley, the philosophical motive, which had moved the first pioneers, is less apparent, and is replaced by a more technical and mathematical spirit. This period is chiefly distinguished from the second, in a mathematical point of view, by its method, which is projective instead of metrical. The leading mathematical conception here

[1] This bolder method, it appears, had been suggested, nearly a century earlier, by an Italian, Saccheri. His work, which seems to have remained completely unknown until Beltrami rediscovered it in 1889, is called "Euclides ab omni naevo vindicatus, etc." Mediolani, 1733. (See Veronese, Grundzüge der Geometrie, German translation, Leipzig, 1894, p. 636.) His results included spherical as well as hyperbolic space; but they alarmed him to such an extent that he devoted the last half of his book to disproving them.

is the Absolute (*Grundgebild*), a figure by relation to which all metrical properties become projective. Cayley's work, which was very brief, and attracted little attention, has been perfected and elaborated by F. Klein, and through him has found general acceptance. Klein has added to the two kinds of non-Euclidean Geometry already known, a third, which he calls elliptic; this third kind closely resembles Helmholtz's spherical Geometry, but is distinguished by the important difference that, in it, two straight lines meet in only one point[1]. The distinctive mark of the spaces represented by both is that, like the surface of a sphere, they are finite but unbounded. The reduction of metrical to projective properties, as will be proved hereafter, has only a technical importance; at the same time, projective Geometry is able to deal directly with those purely descriptive or qualitative properties of space which are common to Euclid and Metageometry alike. The third period has, therefore, great philosophical importance, while its method has, mathematically, much greater beauty and unity than that of the second; it is able to treat all kinds of space at once, so that every symbolic proposition is, according to the meaning given to the symbols, a proposition in whichever Geometry we choose. This has the advantage of proving that further research cannot lead to contradictions in non-Euclidean systems, unless it at the same moment reveals contradictions in Euclid. These systems, therefore, are logically as sound as that of Euclid himself.

After this brief sketch of the characteristics of the three periods, I will proceed to a more detailed account. It will be my aim to avoid, as far as possible, all technical mathematics, and bring into relief only those fundamental points in the

[1] Klein's first account of elliptic Geometry, as a result of Cayley's projective theory of distance, appeared in two articles entitled "Ueber die sogenannte Nicht-Euklidische Geometrie, I, II," Math. Annalen 4, 6 (1871—2). It was afterwards independently discovered by Newcomb, in an article entitled "Elementary Theorems relating to the geometry of a space of three dimensions, and of uniform positive curvature in the fourth dimension," Crelle's Journal für die reine und angewandte Mathematik, Vol. 83 (1877). For an account of the mathematical controversies concerning elliptic Geometry, see Klein's "Vorlesungen über Nicht-Euklidische Geometrie," Göttingen 1893, I. p. 284 ff. A bibliography of the relevant literature up to the year 1878 was given by Halsted in the American Journal of Mathematics, Vols. 1, 2.

mathematical development, which seem of logical or philosophical importance.

First Period.

12. The originator of the whole system, *Gauss*, does not appear, as regards strictly non-Euclidean Geometry, in any of his hitherto published papers, to have given more than results; his proofs remain unknown to us. Nevertheless he was the first to investigate the consequences of denying the axiom of parallels[1], and in his letters he communicated these consequences to some of his friends, among whom was Wolfgang Bolyai. The first mention of the subject in his letters occurs when he was only 18; four years later, in 1799, writing to W. Bolyai, he enunciates the important theorem that, in hyperbolic Geometry, there is a maximum to the area of a triangle. From later writings it appears that he had worked out a system nearly, if not quite, as complete as those of Lobatchewsky and Bolyai[2].

It is important to remember, however, that Gauss's work on curvature, which *was* published, laid the foundation for the whole method of the second period, and was undertaken, according to Riemann and Helmholtz[3], with a view to an (unpublished) investigation of the foundations of Geometry. His work in this direction will, owing to its method, be better treated of under the second period, but it is interesting to observe that he stood, like many pioneers, at the head of two tendencies which afterwards diverged.

13. *Lobatchewsky*, a professor in the University of Kasan, first published his results, in their native Russian, in the proceedings of that learned body for the years 1829—1830. Owing to this double obscurity of language and place, they attracted little attention, until he translated them into French[4]

[1] Veronese (op. cit. p. 638) denies the priority of Gauss in the invention of a non-Euclidean system, though he admits him to have been the first to regard the axiom of parallels as indemonstrable. His grounds for the former assertion seem scarcely adequate: on the evidence against it, see Klein, Nicht-Euklid, I. pp. 171–174.

[2] V. Briefwechsel mit Schumacher, Bd. II. p. 268.

[3] Cf. Helmholtz, Wiss. Abh. II. p. 611.

[4] Crelle's Journal, 1837.

and German[1]: even then, they do not appear to have obtained the notice they deserved, until, in 1868, Beltrami unearthed the article in Crelle, and made it the theme of a brilliant interpretation.

In the introduction to his little German book, Lobatchewsky laments the slight interest shown in his writings by his compatriots, and the inattention of mathematicians, since Legendre's abortive attempt, to the difficulties in the theory of parallels. The body of the work begins with the enunciation of several important propositions which hold good in the system proposed as well as in Euclid: of these, some are in any case independent of the axiom of parallels, while others are rendered so by substituting, for the word "parallel," the phrase "not intersecting, however far produced." Then follows a definition, intentionally framed so as to contradict Euclid's: With respect to a given straight line, all others in the same plane may be divided into two classes, those which cut the given straight line, and those which do not cut it; a line which is the limit between the two classes is called *parallel* to the given straight line. It follows that, from any external point, two parallels can be drawn, one in each direction. From this starting-point, by the Euclidean synthetic method, a series of propositions are deduced; the most important of these is, that in a triangle the sum of the angles is always less than, or always equal to two right angles, while in the latter case the whole system becomes orthodox. A certain analogy with spherical Geometry—whose meaning and extent will appear later—is also proved, consisting roughly in the substitution of hyperbolic for circular functions.

14. Very similar is the system of *Johann Bolyai*, so similar, indeed, as to make the independence of the two works, though a well-authenticated fact, seem all but incredible. Johann Bolyai first published his results in 1832, in an appendix to a work by his father Wolfgang, entitled; "Appendix, scientiam spatii absolute veram exhibens: a veritate aut falsitate Axiomatis XI. Euclidei (a priori haud unquam decidenda) independentem; adjecta ad casum falsitatis, quadratura circuli geometrica." Gauss, whose bosom friend he became at college

[1] Theorie der Parallellinien, Berlin, 1840. Republished, Berlin, 1887. Translated by Halsted, Austin, Texas, U.S.A. 4th edition, 1892.

and remained through life, was, as we have seen, the inspirer of Wolfgang Bolyai, and used to say that the latter was the only man who appreciated his philosophical speculations on the axioms of Geometry; nevertheless, Wolfgang appears to have left to his son Johann the detailed working out of the hyperbolic system. The works of both the Bolyai are very rare, and their method and results are known to me only through the renderings of Frischauf and Halsted[1]. Both as to method and as to results, the system is very similar to Lobatchewsky's, so that neither need detain us here. Only the initial postulates, which are more explicit than Lobatchewsky's, demand a brief attention. Frischauf's introduction, which has a philosophical and Newtonian air, begins by setting forth that Geometry deals with absolute (empty) space, obtained by abstracting from the bodies in it, that two figures are called congruent when they differ only in position, and that the axiom of Congruence is indispensable in all determination of spatial magnitudes. Congruence was to refer to geometrical bodies, with none of the properties of ordinary bodies except impenetrability (Erdmann, Axiome der Geometrie, p. 26). A straight line is defined as determined by two of its points[2], and a plane as determined by three. These premisses, with a slight exception as to the straight line, we shall hereafter find essential to every Geometry. I have drawn attention to them, as it is often supposed that non-Euclideans deny the axiom of Congruence, which, here and elsewhere, is never the case. The stress laid on this axiom by Bolyai is probably due to the influence of Gauss, whose work on the curvature of surfaces laid the foundation for the use made of congruence by Helmholtz.

15. It is important to remember that, throughout the period we have just reviewed, the purpose of hyperbolic Geometry is indirect: not the truth of the latter, but the logical independence of the axiom of parallels from the rest, is

[1] Frischauf, Absolute Geometrie, nach Johann Bolyai, Leipzig, 1872. Halsted, The Science Absolute of Space, translated from the Latin, 4th edition, Austin, Texas, U.S.A. 1896.

[2] Both Lobatchewsky and Bolyai, as Veronese remarks, start rather from the point-pair than from distance. See Frischauf, Absolute Geometrie, Anhang.

the guiding motive of the work. If, by denying the axiom of parallels while retaining the rest, we can obtain a system free from logical contradictions, it follows that the axiom of parallels cannot be implicitly contained in the others. If this be so, attempts to dispense with the axiom, like Legendre's, cannot be successful; Euclid must stand or fall with the suspected axiom. Of course, it remained possible that, by further development, latent contradictions might have been revealed in these systems. This possibility, however, was removed by the more direct and constructive work of the second period, to which we must now turn our attention.

Second Period.

16. The work of Lobatchewsky and Bolyai remained, for nearly a quarter of a century, without issue—indeed, the investigations of Riemann and Helmholtz, when they came, appear to have been inspired, not by these men, but rather by Gauss[1] and Herbart. We find, accordingly, very great difference, both of aim and method, between the first period and the second. The former, beginning with a criticism of one point in Euclid's system, preserved his synthetic method, while it threw over one of his axioms. The latter, on the contrary, being guided by a philosophical rather than a mathematical spirit, endeavoured to classify the conception of space as a species of a more general conception: it treated space algebraically, and the properties it gave to space were expressed in terms, not of intuition, but of algebra. The aim of Riemann and Helmholtz was to show, by the exhibition of logically possible alternatives, the empirical nature of the received axioms. For this purpose, they conceived space as a particular case of a manifold, and showed that various relations of magnitude (*Massverhältnisse*) were mathematically possible in an extended manifold. Their philosophy, which seems to me not always irreproachable, will be discussed in Chapter II.; here, while it is important to remember the philosophical motive of Riemann and Helmholtz, we shall confine our attention to the mathematical side of their work. In so doing, while we shall, I fear, somewhat maim the system of their thoughts, we shall secure a closer unity of subject, and

[1] Compare Stallo, Concepts of Modern Physics, p. 248.

a more compact account of the purely mathematical development. But there is, in my opinion, a further reason for separating their philosophy from their mathematics. While their philosophical purpose was, to prove that all the axioms of Geometry are empirical, and that a different content of our experience might have changed them all, the unintended result of their mathematical work was, if I am not mistaken, to afford material for an *à priori* proof of certain axioms. These axioms, though they believed them to be unnecessary, were always introduced in their mathematical works, before laying the foundations of non-Euclidean systems. I shall contend, in Chapter III., that this retention was logically inevitable, and was not merely due, as they supposed, to a desire for conformity with experience. If I am right in this, there is a divergence between Riemann and Helmholtz the philosophers, and Riemann and Helmholtz the mathematicians. This divergence makes it the more desirable to trace the mathematical development apart from the accompanying philosophy.

17. *Riemann's* epoch-making work, "*Ueber die Hypothesen, welche der Geometrie zu Grunde liegen*[1]", was written, and read to a small circle, in 1854; owing, however, to some changes which he desired to make in it, it remained unpublished till 1867, when it was published by his executors. The two fundamental conceptions, on whose invention rests the historic importance of this dissertation, are that of a *manifold*, and that of the *measure of curvature* of a manifold. The former conception serves a mainly philosophical purpose, and is designed, principally, to exhibit space as an instance of a more general conception. On this aspect of the manifold, I shall have much to say in Chapter II.; its mathematical aspect, which alone concerns us here, is less complicated and less fruitful of controversy. The latter conception also serves a double purpose, but its mathematical use is the more prominent. We will consider these two conceptions successively.

18. (1) *Conception of a manifold*[2]. The general purpose of Riemann's dissertation is, to exhibit the axioms as successive

[1] Gesammelte Werke, pp. 255–268.

[2] On the history of this word, see Stallo, Concepts of Modern Physics, p. 258. It was used by Kant, and adapted by Herbart to almost the same

steps in the classification of the species space. The axioms of Geometry, like the marks of a scholastic definition, appear as successive determinations of class-conceptions, ending with Euclidean space. We have thus, from the analytical point of view, about as logical and precise a formulation as can be desired—a formulation in which, from its classificatory character, we seem certain of having nothing superfluous or redundant, and obtain the axioms explicitly in the most desirable form, namely as adjectives of the conception of space. At the same time, it is a pity that Riemann, in accordance with the metrical bias of his time, regarded space as primarily a magnitude[1], or assemblage of magnitudes, in which the main problem consists in assigning quantities to the different elements or points, without regard to the qualitative nature of the quantities assigned. Considerable obscurity thus arises as to the whole nature of magnitude[2]. This view of Geometry underlies the definition of the manifold, as the general conception of which space forms a special case. This definition, which is not very clear, may be rendered as follows.

19. Conceptions of magnitude, according to Riemann, are possible there only, where we have a general conception, capable of various determinations (*Bestimmungsweisen*). The various determinations of such a conception together form a *manifold*, which is continuous or discrete, according as the passage from one determination to another is continuous or discrete. Particular bits of a manifold, or quanta, can be compared by counting when discrete, and by measurement when continuous. "Measurement consists in a superposition of the magnitudes to be compared. If this be absent, magnitudes can only be compared when one is part of another, and then only the more or less, not the how much, can be decided" (p. 256). We thus reach the general conception of a manifold of several dimensions, of which space and colours are mentioned as special cases.

meaning as it bears in Riemann. Herbart, however, also uses the word *Reihenform* to express a similar idea. See Psychologie als Wissenschaft, I. § 100 and II. § 139, where Riemann's analogy with colours is also suggested.

[1] Compare Erdmann's "Grössenbegriff vom Raum."

[2] Compare Veronese. op. cit. p. 642: "Riemann ist in seiner Definition des Begriffs Grösse dunkel." See also Veronese's whole following criticism.

To the absence of this conception Riemann attributes the "obscurity" which, on the subject of the axioms, "lasted from Euclid to Legendre" (p. 254). And Riemann certainly has succeeded, from an algebraic point of view, in exhibiting, far more clearly than any of his predecessors, the axioms which distinguish spatial quantity from other quantities with which mathematics is conversant. But by the assumption, from the start, that space can be regarded as a quantity, he has been led to state the problem as: What sort of magnitude is space? rather than: What must space be in order that we may be able to regard it as a magnitude at all? He does not realise, either—indeed in his day there were few who realized—that an elaborate Geometry is possible which does not deal with space as a quantity at all. His definition of space as a species of manifold, therefore, though for analytical purposes it defines, most satisfactorily, the nature of spatial magnitudes, leaves obscure the true ground for this nature, which lies in the nature of space as a system of relations, and is anterior to the possibility of regarding it as a system of magnitudes at all.

But to proceed with the mathematical development of Riemann's ideas. We have seen that he declared measurement to consist in a superposition of the magnitudes to be compared. But in order that this may be a possible means of determining magnitudes, he continues, these magnitudes must be independent of their position in the manifold (p. 259). This can occur, he says, in several ways, as the simplest of which, he assumes that the lengths of lines are independent of their position. One would be glad to know what other ways are possible: for my part, I am unable to imagine any other hypothesis on which magnitude would be independent of place. Setting this aside, however, the problem, owing to the fact that measurement consists in superposition, becomes identical with the determination of the most general manifold in which magnitudes are independent of place. This brings us to Riemann's other fundamental conception, which seems to me even more fruitful than that of a manifold.

20. (2) *Measure of curvature.* This conception is due to Gauss, but was applied by him only to surfaces; the novelty in Riemann's dissertation was its extension to a manifold of n

dimensions. This extension, however, is rather briefly and obscurely expressed, and has been further obscured by Helmholtz's attempts at popular exposition. The term *curvature*, also, is misleading, so that the phrase has been the source of more misunderstanding, even among mathematicians, than any other in Pangeometry. It is often forgotten, in spite of Helmholtz's explicit statement[1], that the "measure of curvature" of an *n*-dimensional manifold is a purely analytical expression, which has only a symbolic affinity to ordinary curvature. As applied to three-dimensional space, the implication of a four-dimensional "plane" space is wholly misleading; I shall, therefore, generally use the term space-constant instead[2]. Nevertheless, as the conception grew, historically, out of that of curvature, I will give a very brief exposition of the historical development of theories of curvature.

Just as the notion of *length* was originally derived from the straight line, and extended to other curves by dividing them into infinitesimal straight lines, so the notion of *curvature* was derived from the circle, and extended to other curves by dividing them into infinitesimal circular arcs. Curvature may be regarded, originally, as a measure of the amount by which a curve departs from a straight line; in a circle, which is similar throughout, this amount is evidently constant, and is measured by the reciprocal of the radius. But in all other curves, the amount of curvature varies from point to point, so that it cannot be measured without infinitesimals. The measure which at once suggests itself is, the curvature of the circle most nearly coinciding with the curve at the point considered. Since a circle is determined by three points, this circle will pass through three consecutive points of the curve. We have thus defined the curvature of any curve, plane or tortuous; for, since any three points lie in a plane, such a circle can always be described.

If we now pass to a surface, what we want is, by analogy, a measure of its departure from a plane. The curvature, as above defined, has become indeterminate, for through any point of the surface we can draw an infinite number of arcs, which

[1] Vorträge und Reden, Vol. II. p. 18.
[2] Cf. Klein. Nicht-Euklid, I. p. 160.

will not, in general, all have the same curvature. Let us, then, draw all the geodesics joining the point in question to neighbouring points of the surface in all directions. Since these arcs form a singly infinite manifold, there will be among them, if they have not all the same curvature, one arc of maximum, and one of minimum curvature[1]. The product of these maximum and minimum curvatures is called the *measure of curvature* of the surface at the point under consideration. To illustrate by a few simple examples: on a sphere, the curvatures of all such lines are equal to the reciprocal of the radius of the sphere, hence the measure of curvature everywhere is the square of the reciprocal of the radius of the sphere. On any surface, such as a cone or a cylinder, on which straight lines can be drawn, these have no curvature, so that the measure of curvature is everywhere zero—this is the case, in particular, with the plane. In general, however, the measure of curvature of a surface varies from point to point.

Gauss, the inventor of this conception[2], proved that, in order that two surfaces may be developable upon each other —*i.e.* may be such that one can be bent into the shape of the other without stretching or tearing—it is necessary that the two surfaces should have equal measures of curvature at corresponding points. When this is the case, every figure which is possible on the one is, in general, possible on the other, and the two have practically the same Geometry[3]. As a corollary, it follows that a necessary condition, for the free mobility of figures on any surface, is the constancy of the

[1] Since we are considering the curvature at a point, we are only concerned with the first infinitesimal elements of the geodesics that start from such a point.

[2] Disquisitiones generales circa superficies curvas, Werke, Bd. IV. SS. 219–258, 1827.

[3] Nevertheless, the Geometries of different surfaces of equal curvature are liable to important differences. For example, the cylinder is a surface of zero curvature, but since its lines of curvature in one direction are finite, its Geometry coincides with that of the plane only for lengths smaller than the circumference of its generating circle (see Veronese, op. cit. p. 644). Two geodesics on a cylinder may meet in many points. For surfaces of zero curvature on which this is not possible, the identity with the plane may be allowed to stand. Otherwise, the identity extends only to the properties of figures not exceeding a certain size.

measure of curvature[1]. This condition was proved to be sufficient, as well as necessary, by Minding[2].

21. So far, all has been plain sailing—we have been dealing with purely geometrical ideas in a purely geometrical manner —but we have not, as yet, found any sense of the measure of curvature, in which it can be extended to space, still less to an n-dimensional manifold. For this purpose, we must examine Gauss's method, which enables us to determine the measure of curvature of a surface at any point as an inherent property, quite independent of any reference to the third dimension.

The method of determining the measure of curvature from within is, briefly, as follows: If any point on the surface be determined by two coordinates, u, v, then small arcs of the surface are given by the formula

$$ds^2 = Edu^2 + 2Fdu\,dv + Gdv^2,$$

where E, F, G are, in general, functions of u, v.[3] From this formula alone, without reference to any space outside the surface, we can determine the measure of curvature at the point u, v, as a function of E, F, G and their differentials with respect to u and v. Thus we may regard the measure of curvature of a surface as an inherent property, and the above geometrical definition, which involved a reference to the third dimension, may be dropped. But at this point a caution is necessary. It will appear in Chap. III. (§ 176), that it is logically impossible to set up a precise coordinate system, in which the coordinates represent spatial magnitudes, without the axiom of Free Mobility, and this axiom, as we have just seen, holds on surfaces only when the measure of curvature is constant. Hence our definition of the measure of curvature will only be *really* free from reference to the third dimension, when we are dealing with a surface of constant measure of curvature—a point which

[1] For we may consider two different parts of the same surface as corresponding parts of different surfaces; the above proposition then shows that a figure can be reproduced in one part when it has been drawn in another, if the measures of curvature correspond in the two parts.

[2] Crelle, Vols. XIX., XX., 1839–40.

[3] In this formula, u, v may be the lengths of lines, or the angles between lines, drawn on the surface, and having thus no necessary reference to a third dimension.

Riemann entirely overlooks. This caution, however, applies only in space, and if we take the coordinate system as presupposed in the conception of a manifold, we may neglect the caution altogether—while remembering that the possibility of a coordinate system in space involves axioms to be investigated later. We can thus see how a meaning might be found, without reference to any higher dimension, for a constant measure of curvature of three-dimensional space, or for any measure of curvature of an n-dimensional manifold in general.

22. Such a meaning is supplied by Riemann's dissertation, to which, after this long digression, we can now return. We may define a continuous manifold as any continuum of elements, such that a single element is defined by n continuously variable magnitudes. This definition does not really include space, for coordinates in space do not define a point, but its relations to the origin, which is itself arbitrary. It includes, however, the analytical conception of space with which Riemann deals, and may, therefore, be allowed to stand for the moment. Riemann then assumes that the difference—or distance, as it may be loosely called—between any two elements is comparable, as regards magnitude, to the difference between any other two. He assumes further, what it is Helmholtz's merit to have proved, that the difference ds between two consecutive elements can be expressed as the square root of a quadratic function of the differences of the coordinates: *i.e.*

$$ds^2 = \Sigma_1^n \, \Sigma_1^n \, a_{ik} \, dx_i \, . \, dx_k,$$

where the coefficients a_{ik} are, in general, functions of the coordinates $x_1 \, x_2 \ldots x_n$.[1] The question is: How are we to obtain a definition of the measure of curvature out of this formula? It is noticeable, in the first place, that, just as in a surface we found an infinite number of *radii* of curvature at a point, so in a manifold of three or more dimensions we must find an infinite number of *measures* of curvature at a point, one for every two-dimensional manifold passing through the point, and contained in the higher manifold. What we have first to do, therefore, is

[1] In what follows, I have given rather Klein's exposition of Riemann, than Riemann's own account. The former is much clearer and fuller, and not substantially different in any way. V. Klein, Nicht-Euklid, I. pp. 206 ff.

to define such two-dimensional manifolds. They must consist, as we saw on the surface, of a singly infinite series of geodesics through the point. Now a geodesic is completely determined by one point and its direction at that point, or by one point and the next consecutive point. Hence a geodesic through the point considered is determined by the ratios of the increments of coordinates, $dx_1\, dx_2 \ldots dx_n$. Suppose we have two such geodesics, in which the i'th increments are respectively $d'x_i$ and $d''x_i$. Then all the geodesics given by

$$dx_i = \lambda' d'x_i + \lambda'' d''x_i$$

form a singly infinite series, since they contain one parameter, namely $\lambda' : \lambda''$. Such a series of geodesics, therefore, must form a two-dimensional manifold, with a measure of curvature in the ordinary Gaussian sense. This measure of curvature can be determined from the above formula for the elementary arc, by the help of Gauss's general formula alluded to above. We thus obtain an infinite number of

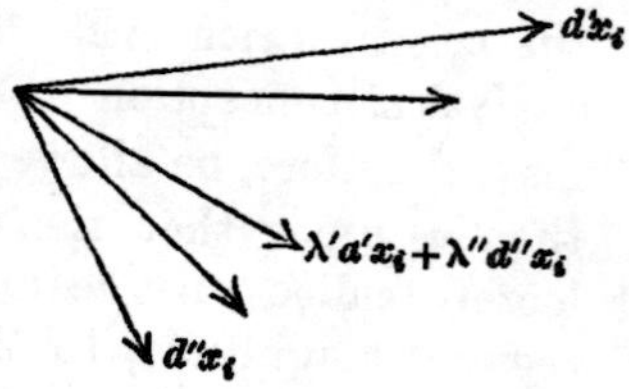

measures of curvature at a point, but from $\frac{n.(n-1)}{2}$ of these, the rest can be deduced (Riemann, Gesammelte Werke, p. 262). When all the measures of curvature at a point are constant, and equal to all the measures of curvature at any other point, we get what Riemann calls a manifold of constant curvature. In such a manifold free mobility is possible, and positions do not differ intrinsically from one another. If a be the measure of curvature, the formula for the arc becomes, in this case,

$$ds^2 = \Sigma dx^2 \Big/ \left(1 + \frac{a}{4}\Sigma x^2\right)^2.$$

In this case only, as I pointed out above, can the term "measure of curvature" be properly applied to space without reference to a higher dimension, since free mobility is logically indispensable to the existence of quantitative or metrical Geometry.

23. The mathematical result of Riemann's dissertation

may be summed up as follows. Assuming it possible to apply magnitude to space, *i.e.* to determine its elements and figures by means of algebraical quantities, it follows that space can be brought under the conception of a manifold, as a system of quantitatively determinable elements. Owing, however, to the peculiar nature of spatial measurement, the quantitative determination of space demands that magnitudes shall be independent of place—in so far as this is not the case, our measurement will be necessarily inaccurate. If we now assume, as the quantitative relation of distance between two elements, the square root of a quadratic function of the coordinates—a formula subsequently proved by Helmholtz and Lie—then it follows, since magnitudes are to be independent of place, that space must, within the limits of observation, have a constant measure of curvature, or must, in other words, be homogeneous in all its parts. In the infinitesimal, Riemann says (p. 267), observation could not detect a departure from constancy on the part of the measure of curvature; but he makes no attempt to show how Geometry could remain possible under such circumstances, and the only Geometry he has constructed is based entirely on Free Mobility. I shall endeavour to prove, in Chapter III., that any metrical Geometry, which should endeavour to dispense with this axiom, would be logically impossible. At present I will only point out that Riemann, in spite of his desire to prove that all the axioms can be dispensed with, has nevertheless, in his mathematical work, retained three fundamental axioms, namely, Free Mobility, the finite integral number of dimensions, and the axiom that two points have a unique relation, namely distance. These, as we shall see hereafter, are retained, in actual mathematical work, by all metrical Metageometers, even when they believe, like Riemann and Helmholtz, that no axioms are philosophically indispensable.

24. *Helmholtz*, the historically nearest follower of Riemann, was guided by a similar empirical philosophy, and arrived independently at a very similar method of formulating the axioms. Although Helmholtz published nothing on the subject until after Riemann's death, he had then only just seen Riemann's dissertation (which was published posthumously), and had worked out his results, so far as they were then

completed, in entire independence both of Riemann and of Lobatchewsky. Helmholtz is by far the most widely read of all writers on Metageometry, and his writings, almost alone, represent to philosophers the modern mathematical standpoint on this subject. But his importance is much greater, in this domain, as a philosopher than as a mathematician; almost his only original mathematical result, as regards Geometry, is his proof of Riemann's formula for the infinitesimal arc, and even this proof was far from rigid, until Lie reformed it by his method of continuous groups. In this chapter, therefore, only two of his writings need occupy us, namely the two articles in the *Wissenschaftliche Abhandlungen*, Vol. II., entitled respectively "Ueber die thatsächlichen Grundlagen der Geometrie," 1866 (p. 610 ff.), and "Ueber die Thatsachen, die der Geometrie zum Grunde liegen," 1868 (p. 618 ff.).

25. In the first of these, which is chiefly philosophical, Helmholtz gives hints of his then uncompleted mathematical work, but in the main contents himself with a statement of results. He announces that he will prove Riemann's quadratic formula for the infinitesimal arc; but for this purpose, he says, we have to *start* with Congruence, since without it spatial measurement is impossible. Nevertheless, he maintains that Congruence is proved by experience. How we could, without the help of measurement, discover lapses from Congruence, is a point which he leaves undiscussed. He then enunciates the four axioms which he considers essential to Geometry, as follows:

(1) *As regards continuity and dimensions.* In a space of n dimensions, a point is uniquely determined by the measurement of n continuous variables (coordinates).

(2) *As regards the existence of moveable rigid bodies.* Between the $2n$ coordinates of any point-pair of a rigid body, there exists an equation which is the same for all congruent point-pairs. By considering a sufficient number of point-pairs, we get more equations than unknown quantities: this gives us a method of determining the form of these equations, so as to make it possible for them all to be satisfied.

(3) *As regards free mobility.* Every point can pass freely and continuously from one position to another. From (2) and

(3) it follows, that if two systems A and B can be brought into congruence in any one position, this is also possible in every other position.

(4) *As regards independence of rotation in rigid bodies* (Monodromy). If $(n-1)$ points of a body remain fixed, so that every other point can only describe a certain curve, then that curve is closed.

These axioms, says Helmholtz, suffice to give, with the axiom of three dimensions, the Euclidean and non-Euclidean systems as the only alternatives. That they *suffice*, mathematically, cannot be denied, but they seem, in some respects, to go too far. In the first place, there is no necessity to make the axiom of Congruence apply to actual rigid bodies—on this subject I have enlarged in Chapter II.[1] Again, Free Mobility, as distinct from Congruence, hardly needs to be specially formulated: what barrier could empty space offer to a point's progress? The axiom is involved in the homogeneity of space, which is the same thing as the axiom of Congruence. Monodromy, also, has been severely criticized; not only is it evident that it might have been included in Congruence, but even from the purely analytical point of view, Sophus Lie has proved it to be superfluous[2]. Thus the axiom of Congruence, rightly formulated, includes Helmholtz's third and fourth axioms and part of his second axiom. All the four, or rather, as much of them as is relevant to Geometry, are consequences, as we shall see hereafter, of the one fundamental principle of the relativity of position.

26. The second article, which is mainly mathematical, supplies the promised proof of the arc-formula, which is Helmholtz's most important contribution to Geometry. Riemann had *assumed* this formula, as the simplest of a number of alternatives: Helmholtz proved it to be a necessary consequence of his axioms. The present paper begins with a short repetition of the first, including the statement of the axioms, to which, at the end of the paper, two more are added, (5) that space has three dimensions, and (6) that space is infinite. It

[1] See §§ 69–73.

[2] Grundlagen der Geometrie, I. and II., Leipziger Berichte, 1890; v. end of present chapter, § 45.

is supposed in the text, as also in the first paper, that the measure of curvature cannot be negative, and, consequently, that an infinite space must be Euclidean. This error in both papers is corrected in notes, added after the appearance of Beltrami's paper on negative curvature. It is a sample of the slightly unprofessional nature of Helmholtz's mathematical work on this subject, which elicits from Klein the following remarks[1]: "Helmholtz is not a mathematician by profession, but a physicist and physiologist....From this non-mathematical quality of Helmholtz, it follows naturally that he does not treat the mathematical portion of his work with the thoroughness which one would demand of a mathematician by trade (*von Fach*)." He tells us himself that it was the physiological study of vision which led him to the question of the axioms, and it is as a physicist that he makes his axioms refer to actual rigid bodies. Accordingly, we find errors in his mathematics, such as the axiom of Monodromy, and the assumption that the measure of curvature must be positive. Nevertheless, the proof of Riemann's arc-formula is extremely able, and has, on the whole, been substantiated by Lie's more thorough investigations.

27. Helmholtz's other writings on Geometry are almost wholly philosophical, and will be discussed at length in Chapter II. For the present, we may pass to the only other important writer of the second period, *Beltrami*. As his work is purely mathematical, and contains few controverted points, it need not, despite its great importance, detain us long.

The "Saggio di Interpretazione della Geometria non-Euclidea[2]," which is principally confined to two dimensions, interprets Lobatchewsky's results by the characteristic method of the second period. It shows, by a development of the work of Gauss and Minding[3], that all the propositions in plane Geometry, which Lobatchewsky had set forth, hold, within ordinary Euclidean space, on surfaces of constant negative

[1] Nicht-Euklid, I. pp. 258–9.

[2] Giornale di Matematiche, Vol. VI., 1868. Translated into French by J. Hoüel in the "Annales Scientifiques de l'École Normale Supérieure," Vol. VI. 1869.

[3] Crelle's Journal, Vols. XIX. XX., 1839–40.

curvature. It is strange, as Klein points out[1], that this interpretation, which was known to Riemann and perhaps even to Gauss, should have remained so long without explicit statement. This is the more strange, as Lobatchewsky's "Géométrie Imaginaire" had appeared in Crelle, Vol. XVII.[2], and Minding's article, from which the interpretation follows at once, had appeared in Crelle, Vol. XIX. Minding had shewn that the Geometry of surfaces of constant negative curvature, in particular as regards geodesic triangles, could be deduced from that of the sphere by giving the radius a purely imaginary value ia[3]. This result, as we have seen, had also been obtained by Lobatchewsky for his Geometry, and yet it took thirty years for the connection to be brought to general notice.

28. In Beltrami's Saggio, straight lines are, of course, replaced by geodesics; his coordinates are obtained through a point-by-point correspondence with an auxiliary plane, in which straight lines correspond to geodesics on the surface. Thus geodesics have linear equations, and are always uniquely determined by two points. Distances on the surface, however, are not equal to distances on the plane; thus while the surface is infinite, the corresponding portion of the plane is contained within a certain finite circle. The distance of two points on the surface is a certain function of the coordinates, not the ordinary function of elementary Geometry. These relations of plane and surface are important in connection with Cayley's theory of distance, which we shall have to consider next. If we were to define distance on the plane as that function of the coordinates which gives the corresponding distance on the surface, we should obtain what Klein calls "a plane with a hyperbolic system of measurement (*Massbestimmung*)," in which Cayley's theory of distance would hold. It is evident, however, that the ordinary notion of distance has been presupposed in setting up the coordinate system, so that we do not really

[1] Nicht-Euklid, I. p. 190.

[2] This article is more trigonometrical and analytical than the German book, and therefore makes the above interpretation peculiarly evident.

[3] Such surfaces are by no means particularly remote. One of them, for example, is formed by the revolution of the common Tractrix

$$x = a \sin\phi, \qquad y = a\left(\log\tan\frac{\phi}{2} + \cos\phi\right).$$

get alternative Geometries on one and the same plane. The bearing of these remarks will appear more fully when we come to consider Cayley and Klein.

29. The value of Beltrami's Saggio, in his own eyes, lies in the intelligible Euclidean sense which it gives to Lobatchewsky's planimetry: the corresponding system of Solid Geometry, since it has no meaning for Euclidean space, is barely mentioned in this work. In a second paper[1], however, almost contemporaneous with the first, he proceeds to consider the general theory of *n*-dimensional manifolds of constant negative curvature. This paper is greatly influenced by Riemann's dissertation; it begins with the formula for the linear element, and proves from this first, that Congruence holds for such spaces, and next, that they have, according to Riemann's definition, a constant negative measure of curvature. (It is instructive to observe, that both in this and in the former Essay, great stress is laid on the necessity of the Axiom of Congruence.)

This work has less philosophical interest than the former, since it does little more than repeat, in a general form, the results which the Saggio had obtained for two dimensions—results which sink, when extended to *n* dimensions, to the level of mere mathematical constructions. Nevertheless, the paper is important, both as a restoration of negative curvature, which had been overlooked by Helmholtz, and as an analytical treatment of Lobatchewsky's results—a treatment which, together with the Saggio, at last restored to them the prominence they deserved.

Third Period.

30. The third period differs radically, alike in its methods and aims, and in the underlying philosophical ideas, from the period which it replaced. Whereas everything, in the second period, turned on measurement, with its apparatus of Congruence, Free Mobility, Rigid Bodies, and the rest, these vanish completely in the third period, which, swinging to the opposite extreme, regards quantity as a perfectly irrelevant

[1] "Teoria fondamentale degli spazii di curvatura costanta," Annali di Matematica, II. Vol. 2, 1868–9. Also translated by J. Hoüel, *loc. cit.*

category in Geometry, and dispenses with congruence and the method of superposition. The ideas of this period, unfortunately, have found no exponent so philosophical as Riemann or Helmholtz, but have been set forth only by technical mathematicians. Moreover the change of fundamental ideas, which is immense, has not brought about an equally great change in actual procedure; for though spatial quantity is no longer a part of projective Geometry, quantity is still employed, and we still have equations, algebraic transformations, and so on. This is apt to give rise to confusion, especially in the mind of the student, who fails to realise that the quantities used, so far as the propositions are really projective, are mere names for points, and not, as in metrical Geometry, actual spatial magnitudes.

Nevertheless, the fundamental difference between this period and the former must strike any one at once. Whereas Riemann and Helmholtz dealt with metrical ideas, and took, as their foundations, the measure of curvature and the formula for the linear element—both purely metrical—the new method is erected on the formulae for transformation of coordinates required to express a given collineation. It begins by reducing all so-called metrical notions—distance, angle, etc.—to projective forms, and obtains, from this reduction, a methodological unity and simplicity before impossible. This reduction depends, however, except where the space-constant is negative, upon imaginary figures—in Euclid, the circular points at infinity; it is moreover purely symbolic and analytical, and must be regarded as philosophically irrelevant. As the question concerning the import of this reduction is of fundamental importance to our theory of Geometry, and as Cayley, in his Presidential Address to the British Association in 1883, formally challenged philosophers to discuss the use of imaginaries, on which it depends, I will treat this question at some length. But first let us see how, as a matter of mathematics, the reduction is effected.

31. We shall find, throughout this period, that almost every important proposition, though misleading in its obvious interpretation, has nevertheless, when rightly interpreted, a wide philosophical bearing. So it is with the work of *Cayley*, the pioneer of the projective method.

The projective formula for angles, in Euclidean Geometry, was first obtained by Laguerre, in 1853. This formula had, however, a perfectly Euclidean character, and it was left for Cayley to generalize it so as to include both angles and distances in Euclidean and non-Euclidean systems alike[1].

Cayley was, to the last, a staunch supporter of Euclidean *space*, though he believed that non-Euclidean *Geometries* could be applied, within Euclidean space, by a change in the definition of distance[2]. He has thus, in spite of his Euclidean orthodoxy, provided the believers in the possibility of non-Euclidean spaces with one of their most powerful weapons. In his "Sixth Memoir upon Quantics" (1859), he set himself the task of "establishing the notion of distance upon purely descriptive principles." He showed that, with the ordinary notion of distance, it can be rendered projective by reference to the circular points and the line at infinity, and that the same is true of angles[3]. Not content with this, he suggested a new definition of distance, as the inverse sine or cosine of a certain function of the coordinates; with this definition, the properties usually known as metrical become projective properties, having reference to a certain conic, called by Cayley the Absolute. (The circular points are, analytically, a degenerate conic, so that ordinary Geometry forms a particular case of the above.) He proves that, when the Absolute is an *imaginary* conic, the Geometry so obtained for two dimensions is spherical Geometry. The correspondence with Lobatchewsky, in the case where the Absolute is *real*, is not worked out: indeed there is, throughout, no evidence of acquaintance with non-Euclidean systems. The importance of the memoir, to Cayley, lies entirely in its proof that metrical is only a branch of descriptive Geometry.

32. The connection of Cayley's Theory of Distance with Metageometry was first pointed out by Klein[4]. Klein showed in detail that, if the Absolute be real, we get Lobatchewsky's

[1] See Klein, Nicht-Euklid, I. p. 47 ff., and the references there given.

[2] See quotation below, from his British Association Address.

[3] Compare the opening sentence, due to Cayley, of Salmon's Higher Plane Curves.

[4] V. Nicht-Euklid, I. Chaps. I. and II.

(hyperbolic) system; if it be imaginary, we get either spherical Geometry or a new system, analogous to that of Helmholtz, called by Klein elliptic; if the Absolute be an imaginary point-pair, we get parabolic Geometry, and if, in particular, the point-pair be the circular points, we get ordinary Euclid. In elliptic Geometry, two straight lines in the same plane meet in only one point, not two as in Helmholtz's system. The distinction between the two kinds of Geometry is difficult, and will be discussed later.

33. Since these systems are all obtained from a Euclidean plane, by a mere alteration in the definition of distance, Cayley and Klein tend to regard the whole question as one, not of the nature of space, but of the definition of distance. Since this definition, on their view, is perfectly arbitrary, the philosophical problem vanishes—Euclidean *space* is left in undisputed possession, and the only problem remaining is one of convention and mathematical convenience[1]. This view has been forcibly expressed by Poincaré: "What ought one to think," he says, "of this question: Is the Euclidean Geometry true? The question is nonsense." Geometrical axioms, according to him, are mere conventions: they are "definitions in disguise[2]." Thus Klein blames Beltrami for regarding his auxiliary plane as merely auxiliary, and remarks that, if he had known Cayley's Memoir, he would have seen the relation between the plane and the pseudosphere to be far more intimate than he supposed[3]. A view which removes the problem entirely from the arena of philosophy demands, plainly, a full discussion. To this discussion we will now proceed.

34. The view in question has arisen, it would seem, from a natural confusion as to the nature of the coordinates employed. Those who hold the view have not adequately realised, I believe, that their coordinates are not *spatial* quantities, as in metrical Geometry, but mere conventional signs, by which different points can be distinctly designated. There is no reason, therefore, until we already have metrical Geometry,

[1] See p. 9 of Cayley's address to the Brit. Ass. 1883. Also a quotation from Klein in Erdmann's Axiome der Geometrie, p. 124 note.

[2] Nature, Vol. XLV. p. 407.

[3] Nicht-Euklid, I. p. 200.

for regarding one function of the coordinates as a better expression of distance than another, so long as the fundamental addition-equation[1] is preserved. Hence, if our coordinates are regarded as adequate for all Geometry, an indeterminateness arises in the expression of distance, which can only be avoided by a convention. But projective coordinates—so our argument will contend—though perfectly adequate for all projective properties, and entirely free from any metrical presupposition, are inadequate to express metrical properties, just because they have no metrical presupposition. Thus where metrical properties are in question, Beltrami remains justified as against Klein; the reduction of metrical to projective properties is only apparent, though the independence of these last, as against metrical Geometry, is perfectly real.

35. But what are projective coordinates, and how are they introduced? This question was not touched upon in Cayley's Memoir, and it seemed, therefore, as if a logical error were involved in using coordinates to define distance. For coordinates, in all previous systems, had been deduced from distance; to use any existing coordinate system in defining distance was, accordingly, to incur a vicious circle. Cayley mentions this difficulty in a note, where he only remarks, however, that he had regarded his coordinates as numbers arbitrarily assigned, on some system not further investigated, to different points. The difficulty has been treated at length by Sir R. Ball (Theory of the Content, Trans. R. I. A. 1889), who urges that if the values of our coordinates already involve the usual measure of distance, then to give a new definition, while retaining the usual coordinates, is to incur a contradiction. He says (op. cit. p. 1): "In the study of non-Euclidean Geometry I have often felt a difficulty which has, I know, been shared by others. In that theory it seems as if we try to replace our ordinary notion of distance between two points by the logarithm of a certain anharmonic ratio[2]. But this ratio itself involves the notion of distance measured in the ordinary way. How, then,

[1] I.e. the equation $AB + BC = AC$, for three points in one straight line.

[2] The formula substituted by Klein for Cayley's inverse sine or cosine. The two are equivalent, but Klein's is mathematically much the more convenient.

can we supersede our old notion of distance by the non-Euclidean notion, inasmuch as the very definition of the latter involves the former?"

36. This objection is valid, we must admit, so long as anharmonic ratio is defined in the ordinary metrical manner. It would be valid, for example, against any attempt to found a new definition of distance on Cremona's account of anharmonic ratio[1], in which it appears as a metrical property unaltered by projective transformation. If a logical error is to be avoided, in fact, all reference to spatial magnitude of any kind must be avoided; for all spatial magnitude, as will be shown hereafter[2], is logically dependent on the fundamental magnitude of distance. Anharmonic ratio and coordinates must alike be defined by purely descriptive properties, if the use afterwards made of them is to be free from metrical presuppositions, and therefore from the objections of Sir R. Ball.

Such a definition has been satisfactorily given by Klein[3], who appeals, for the purpose, to v. Staudt's quadrilateral construction[4]. By this construction, which I have reproduced in outline in Chapter III. Section A, § 112 ff., we obtain a purely descriptive definition of harmonic and anharmonic ratio, and, given a pair of points, we can obtain the harmonic conjugate to any third point on the same straight line. On this construction, the introduction of projective coordinates is based. Starting with any three points on a straight line, we assign to them arbitrarily the numbers 0, 1, ∞. We then find the harmonic conjugate to the first with respect to 1, ∞, and assign to it the number 2. The object of assigning this number rather than any other, is to obtain the value −1 for the anharmonic ratio of the four numbers corresponding to the four points[5]. We then find the harmonic conjugate to the point 1, with respect to 2, ∞, and assign to it the number 3; and so on. Klein has shown that by this construction, we can obtain any number of points, and

[1] Elements of Projective Geometry, Second Edition, Oxford, 1893, Chap. IX.

[2] Chap. III. Section B.

[3] See Nicht-Euklid, I. p. 338 ff.

[4] See his Geometrie der Lage, § 8, Harmonische Gebilde.

[5] The anharmonic ratio of four numbers, p, q, r, s, is defined as

$$(p-q).(r-s)/(p-r).(q-s).$$

can construct a point corresponding to any given number, fractional or negative. Moreover, when two sets of four points have the same anharmonic ratio, descriptively defined[1], the corresponding numbers also have the same anharmonic ratio. By introducing such a numerical system on two straight lines, or on three, we obtain the coordinates of any point in a plane, or in space. By this construction, which is of fundamental importance to projective Geometry, the logical error, upon which Sir R. Ball bases his criticism, is satisfactorily avoided. Our coordinates are introduced by a purely descriptive method, and involve no presupposition whatever as to the measurement of distance.

37. With this coordinate system, then, to define distance as a certain function of the coordinates is not to be guilty of a vicious circle. But it by no means follows that the definition of distance is arbitrary. All reference to distance has been hitherto excluded, to avoid metrical ideas; but when distance is introduced, metrical ideas inevitably reappear, and we have to remember that our coordinates give no information, *primâ facie*, as to any of these metrical ideas. It is open to us, of course, if we choose, to continue to exclude distance in the ordinary sense, as the quantity of a finite straight line, and to define the *word* distance in any way we please. But the conception, for which the word has hitherto stood, will then require a new name, and the only result will be a confusion between the *apparent* meaning of our propositions, to those who retain the associations belonging to the old sense of the word, and the *real* meaning, resulting from the new sense in which the word is used.

This confusion, I believe, has actually occurred, in the case of those who regard the question between Euclid and Metageometry as one of the definition of distance. Distance is a quantitative relation, and as such presupposes identity of quality. But projective Geometry deals only with quality—for which reason it is called descriptive—and cannot distinguish between two figures which are qualitatively alike. Now the meaning of qualitative likeness, in Geometry, is the possibility

[1] *I.e.* as transformable into each other by a collineation. See Chap. III. Sec. A, § 110.

of mutual transformation by a collineation[1]. Any two pairs of points on the same straight line, therefore, are qualitatively alike; their only qualitative relation is the straight line, which both pairs have in common; and it is exactly the qualitative identity of the relations of the two pairs, which enables the difference of their relations to be exhaustively dealt with by quantity, as a difference of distance. But where quantity is excluded, any two pairs of points on the same straight line appear as alike, and even any two sets of three: for any three points on a straight line can be projectively transformed into any other three. It is only with *four* points in a line that we acquire a projective property distinguishing them from other sets of four, and this property is anharmonic ratio, descriptively defined. The projective Geometer, therefore, sees no reason to give a name to the relation between two points, in so far as this relation is anything over and above the unlimited straight line on which they lie; and when he introduces the notion of distance, he defines it, in the only way in which projective principles allow him to define it, as a relation between *four* points. As he nevertheless wishes the word to give him the power of distinguishing between different *pairs* of points, he agrees to take two out of the four points as fixed. In this way, the only variables in distance are the two remaining points, and distance appears, therefore, as a function of *two* variables, namely the coordinates of the two variable points. When we have further defined our function so that distance may be additive, we have a function with many of the properties of distance in the ordinary sense. This function, therefore, the projective Geometer regards as the only proper definition of distance.

We can see, in fact, from the manner in which our projective coordinates were introduced, that *some* function of these coordinates must express distance in the ordinary sense. For they were introduced serially, so that, as we proceeded from the zero-point towards the infinity-point, our coordinates continually grew. To every point, a definite coordinate corresponded: to the distance between two variable points, therefore, as a function dependent on no other variables, must correspond

[1] See Chap. III. Sec. A.

some definite function of the coordinates, since these are themselves functions of their points. The function discussed above, therefore, must certainly include distance in the ordinary sense.

But the arbitrary and conventional nature of distance, as maintained by Poincaré and Klein, arises from the fact that the two fixed points, required to determine our distance in the projective sense, may be arbitrarily chosen, and although, when our choice is once made, any two points have a definite distance, yet, according as we make that choice, distance will become a different function of the two variable points. The ambiguity thus introduced is unavoidable on projective principles; but are we to conclude, from this, that it is really unavoidable? Must we not rather conclude that projective Geometry cannot adequately deal with distance? If A, B, C, be three different points on a line, there must be *some* difference between the relation of A to B and of A to C, for otherwise, owing to the qualitative identity of all points, B and C could not be distinguished. But such a difference involves a relation, between A and B, which is independent of other points on the line; for unless we have such a relation, the other points cannot be distinguished as different. Before we can distinguish the two fixed points, therefore, from which the projective definition starts, we must already suppose some relation, between any two points on our line, in which they are independent of other points; and this relation is distance in the ordinary sense[1]. When we have measured this quantitative relation by the ordinary methods of metrical Geometry, we can proceed to decide what base-points must be chosen, on our line, in order that the projective function discussed above may have the same value as ordinary distance. But the choice of these base-points, when we are discussing distance in the ordinary sense, is not arbitrary, and their introduction is only a technical device. Distance, in the ordinary sense, remains a relation between *two* points, not between *four*; and it is the failure to perceive that the projective sense differs from, and cannot

[1] It follows from this, that the reduction of metrical to projective properties, even when, as in hyperbolic Geometry, the Absolute is real, is only apparent, and has a merely technical validity.

supersede, the ordinary sense, which has given rise to the views of Klein and Poincaré. The question is not one of convention, but of the irreducible metrical properties of space. To sum up: Quantities, as used in projective Geometry, do not stand for spatial magnitudes, but are conventional symbols for purely qualitative spatial relations. But distance, *quâ* quantity, presupposes identity of quality, as the condition of quantitative comparison. Distance in the ordinary sense is, in short, that quantitative relation, between two points on a line, by which their difference from other points can be defined. The projective definition, however, being unable to distinguish a collection of less than four points from any other on the same straight line, makes distance depend on two other points besides those whose relation it defines. No name remains, therefore, for distance in the ordinary sense, and many projective Geometers, having abolished the name, believe the thing to be abolished also, and are inclined to deny that *two* points have a unique relation at all. This confusion, in projective Geometry, shows the importance of a name, and should make us chary of allowing new meanings to obscure one of the fundamental properties of space.

38. It remains to discuss the manner in which non-Euclidean Geometries result from the projective definition of distance, as also the true interpretation to be given to this view of Metageometry. It is to be observed that the projective methods which follow Cayley deal throughout with a Euclidean plane, on which they introduce different measures of distance. Hence arises, in any interpretation of these methods, an apparent subordination of the non-Euclidean spaces, as though these were less self-subsistent than Euclid's. This subordination is not intended in what follows; on the contrary, the correlation with Euclidean space is regarded as valuable, first, because Euclidean space has been longer studied and is more familiar, but secondly, because this correlation proves, when truly interpreted, that the other spaces are self-subsistent. We may confine ourselves chiefly, in discussing this interpretation, to distances measured along a single straight line. But we must be careful to remember that the metrical definition of distance—which, according to the view here advocated, is the only adequate definition—is the same in Euclidean and in non-Euclidean spaces; to argue in its favour is not, therefore, to argue in favour of Euclid.

The projective scheme of coordinates consists of a series of numbers, of which each represents a certain anharmonic ratio and denotes one and only one point, and which increase uniformly with the distance from a fixed origin, until they become infinite on reaching a certain point. Now Cayley showed that, in Euclidean Geometry, distance may be expressed as the limit of the logarithm of the anharmonic ratio of the two points and the (coincident) points at infinity on their straight line; while, if we assumed that the points at infinity were distinct, we obtained the formula for distance in hyperbolic or spherical Geometry, according as these points were real or imaginary. Hence it follows that, with the projective definition of distance, we shall obtain precisely the formulae of hyperbolic, parabolic or spherical Geometry, according as we choose the point, to which the value $+\infty$ is assigned, at a finite, infinite or imaginary distance (in the ordinary sense) from the point to which we assign the value 0. Our straight line remains, all the while, an ordinary Euclidean straight line. But we have seen that the projective definition of distance fits with the true definition only when the two fixed points to which it refers are suitably chosen. Now the ordinary meaning of distance is required in non-Euclidean as in Euclidean Geometries—indeed, it is only in metrical properties that these Geometries differ. Hence our *Euclidean* straight line, though it may serve to illustrate other Geometries than Euclid's, can only be dealt with correctly by Euclid. Where we give a different definition of distance from Euclid's, we are still in the domain of purely projective properties, and derive no information as to the metrical properties of our straight line. But the importance, to Metageometry, of this new interpretation, lies in the fact that, having independently established the metrical formulae of non-Euclidean spaces, we find, as in Beltrami's Saggio, that these spaces can be related, by a homographic correspondence, with the points of Euclidean space; and that this can be effected in such a manner as to give, for the distance between two points of our non-Euclidean space, the hyperbolic or spherical measure of distance for the corresponding points of Euclidean space.

39. On the whole, then, a modification of Sir R. Ball's view, which is practically a generalized statement of Beltrami's method, seems the most tenable. He imagines what, with Grassmann, he calls a Content, *i.e.* a perfectly general three-dimensional manifold, and then correlates its elements, one by one, with points in Euclidean space. Thus every element of the Content acquires, as its coordinates, the ordinary Euclidean coordinates of the corresponding point in Euclidean space. By means of this correlation, our calculations, though they refer to the Content, are carried on, as in Beltrami's Saggio, in ordinary Euclidean space. Thus the confusion disappears, but with it, the supposed Euclidean interpretation also disappears. Sir R. Ball's Content, if it is to be a space at all, must be a space radically different from Euclid's[1]; to speak, as Klein does, of ordinary planes with hyperbolic or elliptic measures of distance, is either to incur a contradiction, or to forego any metrical meaning of distance. Instead of ordinary planes, we have surfaces like Beltrami's, of constant measure of curvature; instead of Euclid's space, we have hyperbolic or spherical space. At the same time, it remains true that we can, by Klein's method, give a Euclidean meaning to every symbolic proposition in non-Euclidean Geometry. For by substituting, for distance, the logarithm above alluded to, we obtain, from the non-Euclidean result, a result which follows from the ordinary Euclidean axioms. This correspondence removes, once for all, the possibility of a lurking contradiction in Metageometry, since, to a proposition in the one, corresponds one and only one proposition in the other, and contradictory results in one system, therefore, would correspond to contradictory results in the other. Hence Metageometry cannot lead to contradictions, unless Euclidean Geometry, at the same moment, leads to corresponding contradictions. Thus the Euclidean plane with hyperbolic or elliptic measure of distance, though either contradictory or not metrical

[1] Sir R. Ball does not regard his non-Euclidean content as a possible space (*v. op. cit.* p. 151). In this important point I disagree with his interpretation, holding such a content to be a space as possible, *à priori*, as Euclid's, and perhaps actually true within the margin due to errors of observation.

as an independent notion, has, as a help in the interpretation of non-Euclidean results, a very high degree of utility.

40. We have still to discuss Klein's third kind of non-Euclidean Geometry, which he calls elliptic. The difference between this and spherical Geometry is difficult to grasp, but it may be illustrated by a simpler example. A plane, as every one knows, can be wrapped, without stretching, on a cylinder, and straight lines in the plane become, by this operation, geodesics on the cylinder. The Geometries of the plane and the cylinder, therefore, have much in common. But since the generating circle of the cylinder, which is one of its geodesics, is finite, only a portion of the plane is used up in wrapping it once round the cylinder. Hence, if we endeavour to establish a point-to-point correspondence between the plane and the cylinder, we shall find an infinite series of points on the plane for a single point on the cylinder. Thus it happens that geodesics, though on the plane they have only one point in common, may on the cylinder have an infinite number of intersections. Somewhat similar to this is the relation between the spherical and elliptic Geometries. To any one point in elliptic space, two points correspond in spherical space. Thus geodesics, which in spherical space may have two points in common, can never, in elliptic space, have more than one intersection.

But Klein's method can only prove that elliptic Geometry holds of the ordinary Euclidean plane with elliptic measure of distance. Klein has made great endeavours to enforce the distinction between the spherical and elliptic Geometries[1], but it is not immediately evident that the latter, as distinct from the former, is valid.

In the first place, Klein's elliptic Geometry, which arises as one of the alternative metrical systems on a Euclidean plane or in a Euclidean space, does not by itself suffice, if the above discussion has been correct, to prove the possibility of an elliptic space, *i.e.* of a space having a point-to-point correspondence with the Euclidean space, and having as the ordinary distance between two of its points the elliptic definition of the distance between corresponding points of the Euclidean space. To prove this possibility, we must adopt the direct method of

[1] See Nicht-Euklid, I. p. 97 ff. and p. 292 ff.

Newcomb (Crelle's Journal, Vol. 83). Now in the first place Newcomb has not proved that his postulates are self-consistent; he has only failed to prove that they are contradictory[1]. This would leave elliptic space in the same position in which Lobatchewsky and Bolyai left hyperbolic space. But further there seems to be, at first sight, in *two*-dimensional elliptic space, a positive contradiction. To explain this, however, some account of the peculiarities of the elliptic plane will be necessary.

The elliptic plane, regarded as a figure in three-dimensional elliptic space, is what is called a double surface[2], *i.e.* as Newcomb says (*loc. cit.* p. 298): "The two sides of a complete plane are not distinct, as in a Euclidean surface.... If...a being should travel to distance $2D$, he would, on his return, find himself on the opposite surface to that on which he started, and would have to repeat his journey in order to return to his original position without leaving the surface." Now if we imagine a

[1] Newcomb says (*loc. cit.* p. 293): "The system here set forth is founded on the following three postulates.

"1. I assume that space is triply extended, unbounded, without properties dependent either on position or direction, and possessing such planeness in its smallest parts that both the postulates of the Euclidean Geometry, and our common conceptions of the relations of the parts of space are true for every indefinitely small region in space.

"2. I assume that this space is affected with such curvature that a right line shall always return into itself at the end of a finite and real distance $2D$ without losing, in any part of its course, that symmetry with respect to space on all sides of it which constitutes the fundamental property of our conception of it.

"3. I assume that if two right lines emanate from the same point, making the indefinitely small angle a with each other, their distance apart at the distance r from the point of intersection will be given by the equation

$$s = \frac{2aD}{\pi} \sin \frac{r\pi}{2D}.$$

The right line thus has this property in common with the Euclidean right line that two such lines intersect only in a single point. It may be that the number of points in which two such lines can intersect admit of being determined from the laws of curvature, but not being able so to determine it, I assume as a postulate the fundamental property of the Euclidean right line."

It is plain that in the absence of the determination spoken of, the possibility of elliptic space is not established. It may be possible, for example, to prove that, in a space where there is a maximum to distance, there must be an infinite number of straight lines joining two points of maximum distance. In this event, elliptic space would become impossible.

[2] For an elucidation of this term, see Klein, Nicht-Euklid, I. p. 99 ff.

two-dimensional elliptic space, the distinction between the sides of a plane becomes unmeaning, since it only acquires significance by reference to the third dimension. Nevertheless, some such distinction would be forced upon us. Suppose, for example, that we took a small circle provided with an arrow, as in the figure, and moved this circle once round the universe. Then the sense of the arrow would be reversed. We should thus be forced, either to regard the new position as distinct from the former, which transforms our plane into a spherical plane, or to attribute the reversal of the arrow to the action of a motion which restores our circle to its original place. It is to be observed that nothing short of moving round the universe would suffice to reverse the sense of the arrow. This reversal *seems* like an action of empty space, which would force us to regard the points which, from a three-dimensional point of view, are coincident though opposite, as really distinct, and so reduce the elliptic to the spherical plane. But motion, not space, really causes the change, and the elliptic plane is therefore not proved to be impossible. The question is not, however, of any great philosophic importance.

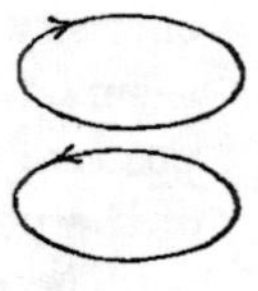

41. In connection with the reduction of metrical to projective Geometry, we have one more topic for discussion. This is the geometrical use of imaginaries, by means of which, except in the case of hyperbolic space, the reduction is effected. I have already contended, on other grounds, that this reduction, in spite of its immense technical importance, and in spite of the complete logical freedom of projective Geometry from metrical ideas, is *purely* technical, and is not philosophically valid. The same conclusion will appear, if we take up Cayley's challenge at the British Association, in his Presidential Address of 1883.

In this address, Professor Cayley devoted most of his time to non-Euclidean systems. Non-Euclidean *spaces*, he declared, seemed to him mistaken *à priori*[1]; but non-Euclidean *Geometries*,

[1] Cf. p. 9 of Report: "My own view is that Euclid's twelfth axiom, in Playfair's form of it, does not need demonstration, but is part of our notion of space, of the physical space of our experience, but which is the representation lying at the bottom of all external experience."

here as in his mathematical works, were accepted as flowing from a change in the definition of distance. This view has been already discussed, and need not, therefore, be further criticised here. What I wish to speak about, is the question with which Cayley himself opened his address, namely, the geometrical use and meaning of imaginary quantities. From the manner in which he spoke of this question, it becomes imperative to treat it somewhat at length. For he said (pp. 8–9):

"...The notion which is the really fundamental one (and I cannot too strongly emphasize the assertion) underlying and pervading the whole notion of modern analysis and Geometry, [is] that of imaginary magnitude in analysis, and of imaginary space (or space as the *locus in quo* of imaginary points and figures) in Geometry: I use in each case the word imaginary as including real.... Say even the conclusion were that the notion belongs to mere technical mathematics, or has reference to nonentities in regard to which no science is possible, still it seems to me that (as a subject of philosophical discussion) the notion ought not to be thus ignored; it should at least be shown that there is a right to ignore it."

42. This right it is now my purpose to demonstrate. But for fear non-mathematicians should miss the point of Cayley's remark (which has sometimes been erroneously supposed to refer to non-Euclidean spaces), I may as well explain, at the outset, that this question is radically distinct from, and only indirectly connected with, the validity or import of Metageometry. An imaginary quantity is one which involves $\sqrt{-1}$: its most general form is $a+\sqrt{-1}\,b$ where a and b are real; Cayley uses the word imaginary so as to include real, in order to cover the special case where $b=0$. It will be convenient, in what follows, to exclude this wider meaning, and assume that b is not zero. An imaginary point is one whose coordinates involve $\sqrt{-1}$, *i.e.* whose coordinates are imaginary quantities. An imaginary curve is one whose points are imaginary—or, in some special uses, one whose equation contains imaginary coefficients. The mathematical subtleties to which this notion leads need not be here discussed; the reader who is interested in them will find an excellent elementary account of their geometrical uses in Klein's Nicht-Euklid, II. pp. 38–46.

But for our present purpose, we may confine ourselves to imaginary points. If these are found to have a merely technical import, and to be destitute of any philosophical meaning, then the same will hold of any collection of imaginary points, *i.e.* of any imaginary curve or surface.

That the notion of imaginary points is of supreme importance in Geometry, will be seen by any one who reflects that the circular points are imaginary, and that the reduction of metrical to projective Geometry, which is one of Cayley's greatest achievements, depends on these points. But to discuss adequately their philosophical import is difficult to me, since I am unacquainted with any satisfactory philosophy of imaginaries in pure Algebra. I will therefore adopt the most favourable hypothesis, and assume that no objection can be successfully urged against this use. Even on this hypothesis, I think, no case can be made out for imaginary points in Geometry.

In the first place, we must exclude, from the imaginary points considered, those whose coordinates are only imaginary with certain special systems of coordinates. For example, if one of a point's coordinates be the tangent from it to a sphere, this coordinate will be imaginary for any point inside the sphere, and yet the point is perfectly real. A point, then, is only to be called imaginary, when, whatever real system of coordinates we adopt, one or more of the quantities expressing these coordinates remains imaginary. For this purpose, it is mathematically sufficient to suppose our coordinates Cartesian—a point whose Cartesian coordinates are imaginary, is a true imaginary point in the above sense.

To discuss the meaning of such a point, it is necessary to consider briefly the fundamental nature of the correspondence between a point and its coordinates. Assuming that elementary Geometry has proved—what I think it does satisfactorily prove—that spatial relations are susceptible of quantitative measurement, then a given point will have, with a suitable system of coordinates, in a space of n dimensions, n quantitative relations to the fixed spatial figure forming the axes of coordinates, and these n quantitative relations will, under certain reservations, be unique—*i.e.*, no other point will have the same quantities assigned to it. (With many possible coordinate systems, this latter condition is not realized: but for that very reason they are inconvenient, and employed only in special problems.) Thus given a coordinate system, and given any set of quantities, these quantities, *if they determine a point at all*, determine it uniquely. But, by a natural extension of the method, the above reservation is dropped, and it is assumed that to *every* set of quantities some point must correspond. For this assumption there seems to me no vestige of evidence. As well might a postman assume that, because every house in a street is uniquely determined by its number, therefore there must be a house for every imaginable number. We must know, in fact, that a given set of quantities can be the coordinates of some point in space, before it is legitimate to give any spatial significance to these quantities: and this knowledge, obviously, cannot be derived from operations with coordinates alone, on pain of a vicious circle. We must, to return to the above analogy, know the number of houses in Piccadilly, before we know whether a given number has a corresponding house or not; and arithmetic alone, however subtly employed, will never give us this information.

Thus the distinction which is important is, not the distinction between real and imaginary quantities, but between quantities to which points correspond and quantities to which no points correspond. We can conventionally agree to denote real points by imaginary coordinates, as in the Gaussian method of denoting by the single quantity $(a + \sqrt{-1}\, b)$ the point whose ordinary coordinates are a, b. But this does not touch Cayley's meaning. Cayley means that it is of great utility in mathematics to regard, as points with a real existence in space, the assumed spatial correlates of quantities which, with the coordinate system employed, have no correlates in every-day space; and that this utility is supposed, by many mathematicians, to indicate the validity of so fruitful an assumption. To fix our ideas, let us consider Cartesian axes in three-dimensional Euclidean space. Then it appears, by inspection, that a point may be situated at any distance to right or left of any of the three coordinate planes; taking this distance as a coordinate, therefore, it appears that real points correspond to all quantities from $-\infty$ to $+\infty$. The same appears for the other two coordinates; and since elementary Geometry proves their variations mutually independent, we know that one and only one real point corresponds to any three real quantities. But we also know, from the exhaustive method pursued, that all space is covered by the range of these three variable quantities: a fresh set of quantities, therefore, such as is introduced by the use of imaginaries, possesses no spatial correlate, and can be supposed to possess one only by a convenient fiction.

43. The fact that the fiction *is* convenient, however, may be thought to indicate that it is more than a fiction. But this presumption, I think, can be easily explained away. For all the fruitful uses of imaginaries, in Geometry, are those which begin and end with real quantities, and use imaginaries only for the intermediate steps. Now in all such cases, we have a real spatial interpretation at the beginning and end of our argument, where alone the spatial interpretation is important: in the intermediate links, we are dealing in a purely algebraical manner with purely algebraical quantities, and may perform any operations which are algebraically permissible. If the quantities with which we end are capable of spatial interpretation, then, and only then, our result may be regarded as geometrical. To use geometrical language, in any other case, is only a convenient help to the imagination. To speak, for example, of projective properties which refer to the circular points, is a mere *memoria technica* for purely algebraical properties; the circular points are not to be found in space, but only in the auxiliary quantities by which geometrical equations are transformed. That no contradictions arise from the geometrical interpretation of imaginaries, is not wonderful: for they are interpreted solely by the rules of Algebra, which we may admit as valid in their application to imaginaries. The perception of space being wholly absent, Algebra rules supreme, and no inconsistency can arise. Wherever, for a moment, we allow our ordinary spatial notions to intrude, the grossest absurdities do arise—every one can see that a circle, being a closed curve, cannot get to infinity. The metaphysician, who should invent anything so preposterous as the circular points, would be hooted from the field. But the mathematician may steal the horse with impunity.

Finally, then, only a knowledge of space, not a knowledge of Algebra, can assure us that any given set of quantities will have a spatial correlate, and in the absence of such a correlate, operations with these quantities have no geometrical import. This is the case with imaginaries in Cayley's sense, and their use in Geometry, great as are its technical advantages, and rigid as is its technical validity, is wholly destitute of philosophical importance.

44. We have now, I think, discussed most of the questions concerning the scope and validity of the projective method. We have seen that it is independent of all metrical presuppositions, and that its use of coordinates does not involve the assumption that spatial magnitudes are measured or expressed by them. We have seen that it is able to deal, by its own methods alone, with the question of the qualitative likeness of geometrical figures, which is logically prior to any comparison as to quantity, since quantity presupposes qualitative likeness. We have seen also that, so far as its legitimate use extends, it applies equally to all homogeneous spaces, and that its criterion of an independently possible space—the determination of a straight line by two points[1]—is not subject to the qualifications and limitations which belong, as we have seen in the case of the cylinder, to the metrical criterion of constant curvature. But we have also seen that, when projective Geometry endeavours to grapple with spatial magnitude, and bring distance and the measurement of angles beneath its sway, its success, though technically valid and important, is philosophically an apparent success only. Metrical Geometry, therefore, if quantity is to be applied to space at all, remains a separate, though logically subsequent branch of Mathematics.

45. It only remains to say a few words about *Sophus Lie*. As a mathematician, as the inventor of a new and immensely powerful method of analysis, he cannot be too highly praised. Geometry is only one of the numerous subjects to which his

[1] The exception to this axiom, in spherical space, presupposes metrical Geometry, and does not destroy the validity of the axiom for projective Geometry. See Chap. III. Sec. B. § 171.

theory of continuous groups applies, but its application to Geometry has made a revolution in method, and has rendered possible, in such problems as Helmholtz's, a treatment infinitely more precise and exhaustive than any which was possible before.

The general definition of a group is as follows: If we have any number of independent variables $x_1\ x_2 \ldots x_n$, and any series of transformations of these into new variables—the transformations being defined by equations of specified forms, with parameters varying from one transformation to another—then the series of transformations form a *group*, if the successive application of any two is equivalent to a single member of the original series of transformations. The group is *continuous*, when we can pass, by infinitesimal gradations within the group, from any one of the transformations to any other.

Now, in Geometry, the result of two successive motions or collineations of a figure can always be obtained by a single motion or collineation, and any motion or collineation can be built up of a series of infinitesimal motions or collineations. Moreover the analytical expression of either is a certain transformation of the coordinates of all the points of the figure[1]. Hence the transformations determining a motion or a collineation are such as to form a continuous group. But the question of the projective equivalence of two figures, to which all projective Geometry is reducible, must always be dealt with by a collineation; and the question of the equality of two figures, to which all metrical Geometry is reducible, must always be decided by a motion such as to cause superposition; hence the whole subject of Geometry may be regarded as a theory of the continuous groups which define all possible collineations and motions.

Now Sophus Lie has developed, at great length, the purely analytical theory of groups; he has therefore, by this method of formulating the problem, a very powerful weapon ready for

[1] Mathematicians of Lie's school have a habit, at first somewhat confusing, of speaking of motions of space instead of motions of bodies, as though space as a whole could move. All that is meant is, of course, the equivalent motion of the coordinate axes, *i.e.* a change of axes in the usual elementary sense.

the attack. In two papers "On the foundations of Geometry[1]," undertaken at Klein's urgent request, he takes premisses which roughly correspond to those of Helmholtz, omitting Monodromy, and applies the theory of groups to the deduction of their consequences[2]. Helmholtz's work, he says, can hardly be looked upon as *proving* its conclusions, and indeed the more searching analysis of the group-theory reveals several possibilities unknown to Helmholtz. Nevertheless, as a pioneer, devoid of Lie's machinery, Helmholtz deserves, I think, more praise than Lie is willing to give him[3].

Lie's method is perfectly exhaustive; omitting the premiss of Monodromy, the others show that a body has six degrees of freedom, *i.e.* that the group giving all possible motions of a body will have six independent members; if we keep one point fixed, the number of independent members is reduced to three. He then, from his general theory, enumerates all the groups which satisfy this condition. In order that such a group should

[1] "Ueber die Grundlagen der Geometrie," Leipziger Berichte, 1890. The problem of these two papers is really metrical, since it is concerned, not with collineations in general, but with motions. The problem, however, is dealt with by the projective method, motions being regarded as collineations which leave the Absolute unchanged. It seemed impossible, therefore, to discuss Lie's work, until some account had been given of the projective method.

[2] Lie's premisses, to be accurate, are the following:

Let

$$x_1 = f(x, y, z, a_1, a_2 \ldots)$$
$$x_2 = \phi(x, y, z, a_1, a_2 \ldots)$$
$$x_3 = \psi(x, y, z, a_1, a_2 \ldots)$$

give an infinite family of real transformations of space, as to which we make the following hypotheses:

A. The functions f, ϕ, ψ, are *analytical* functions of

$$x, y, z, a_1, a_2 \ldots.$$

B. Two points $x_1y_1z_1$, $x_2y_2z_2$ possess an invariant, *i.e.*

$$\Omega(x_1, y_1, z_1, x_2, y_2, z_2) = \Omega(x_1', y_1', z_1', x_2', y_2', z_2')$$

where $x_1' \ldots$, $x_2', \ldots$ are the transformed coordinates of the two points.

C. Free Mobility: *i.e.*, any point can be moved into any other position; when one point is fixed, any other point of general position can take up ∞^2 positions; when two points are fixed, any other of general position can take up ∞^1 positions; when three, no motion is possible—these limitations being results of the equations given by the invariant Ω.

[3] On this point, cf. Klein, Höhere Geometrie, Göttingen, 1893, II. pp. 225–244, especially pp. 230–1.

give possible motions, it is necessary, by Helmholtz's second axiom, that it should leave invariant some function of the coordinates of any two points. This eliminates several of the groups previously enumerated, each of which he discusses in turn. He is thus led to the following results:

I. *In two dimensions,* if free mobility is to hold *universally,* there are no groups satisfying Helmholtz's first three axioms, except those which give the ordinary Euclidean and non-Euclidean motions; but if it is to hold only *within a certain region,* there is also a possible group in which the curve described by any point in a rotation is not closed, but an equiangular spiral. To exclude this possibility, Helmholtz's axiom of Monodromy is required.

II. *In three dimensions,* the results go still more against Helmholtz. Assuming free mobility only *within a certain region,* we have to distinguish two cases: *Either* free mobility holds, within that region, absolutely without exception, *i.e.* when one point is held fast, *every* other point within the region can move freely over a surface: in this case the axiom of Monodromy is unnecessary, and the first three axioms suffice to define our group as that of Euclidean and non-Euclidean motions. *Or* free mobility, within the specified region, holds only of every point *of general position,* while the points of a certain line, when one point is fixed, are only able to move on that line, not on a surface; when this is the case, other groups are possible, and can only be excluded by Helmholtz's fourth axiom.

Having now stated the purely mathematical results of Lie's investigations, we may return to philosophical considerations, by which Helmholtz's work was mainly motived. It becomes obvious, not only that exceptions within a certain region, but also that limitation to a certain region, of the axiom of Free Mobility, are philosophically quite impossible and inconceivable. How can a certain line, or a certain surface, form an impassable barrier in space, or have any mobility different in kind from that of all other lines or surfaces? The notion cannot, in philosophy, be permitted for a moment, since it destroys that most fundamental of all the axioms, the homogeneity of space. We not only may, therefore, but must take Helmholtz's axiom of Free Mobility in its very strictest sense; the axiom of Monodromy thus becomes mathematically, as well as philosophically, superfluous. This is, from a philosophical standpoint, the most important of Lie's results.

46. I have now come to the end of my history of Metageometry. It has not been my aim to give an exhaustive account of even the important works on the subject—in the third period, especially, the names of Poincaré, Pasch, Cremona, Veronese, and others who might be mentioned, would have cried shame upon me, had I had any such object. But I have tried to set forth, as clearly as I could, the principles at work in the various periods, the motives and results of successive theories. We have seen how the philosophical motive, at first predominant, has been gradually extruded by the purely mathematical and technical spirit of most recent Geometers. At first, to discredit the Transcendental Aesthetic seemed, to Metageometers, as important as to advance their science; but from the works of Cayley, Klein or Lie, no reader could gather that Kant had ever lived. We have also seen, however, that as the interest *in* philosophy waned, the interest *for* philosophy increased: as the mathematical results shook themselves free from philosophical controversies, they assumed gradually a stable form, from which further development, we may reasonably hope, will take the form of growth, rather than transformation. The same gradual development out of philosophy might, I believe, be traced in the infancy of most branches of mathematics; when philosophical motives cease to operate, this is, in general, a sign that the stage of uncertainty as to premisses is past, so that the future belongs entirely to mathematical technique. When this stable stage has been attained, it is time for Philosophy to borrow of Science, accepting its final premisses as those imposed by a real necessity of fact or logic.

47. Now in discussing the systems of Metageometry, we have found two kinds, radically distinct and subject to different axioms. The historically prior kind, which deals with metrical ideas, discusses, to begin with, the conditions of Free Mobility, which is essential to all measurement of space. It finds the analytical expression of these conditions in the existence of a space-constant, or constant measure of curvature, which is equivalent to the homogeneity of space. This is its first axiom.

Its second axiom states that space has a finite integral number of dimensions, *i.e.* in metrical terms, that the position of a point, relative to any other figure in space, is uniquely determined by a finite number of spatial magnitudes, called coordinates.

The third axiom of metrical Geometry may be called, to distinguish it from the corresponding projective axiom, the axiom of distance. There exists one relation, it says, between any two points, which can be preserved unaltered in a combined motion of both points, and which, in any motion of a system as one rigid body, is always unaltered. This relation we call distance.

The above statement of the three essential axioms of metrical Geometry is taken from Helmholtz as amended by Lie. Lie's own statement of the axioms, as quoted above, has been too much influenced by projective methods to give a historically correct rendering of the spirit of the second period; Helmholtz's statement, on the other hand, requires, as Lie has shewn, very considerable modifications. The above compromise may, therefore, I hope be taken as accepting Lie's corrections while retaining Helmholtz's spirit.

48. But metrical Geometry, though it is historically prior, is logically subsequent to projective Geometry. For projective Geometry deals directly with that qualitative likeness, which the judgment of quantitative comparison requires as its basis. Now the above three axioms of metrical Geometry, as we shall see in Chapter III. Section B, do not presuppose measurement, but are, on the contrary, the conditions presupposed by measurement. Without these axioms, which are common to all three spaces, measurement would be impossible; with them, so I shall contend, measurement is able, though only empirically, to decide approximately which of the three spaces is valid of our actual world. But if these three axioms themselves express, not results, but conditions, of measurement, must they not be equivalent to the statement of that qualitative likeness on which quantitative comparison depends? And if so, must we

4—2

not expect to find the same axioms, though perhaps under a different form, in projective Geometry?

49. This expectation will not be disappointed. The above three axioms, as we shall see hereafter, are one and all philosophically equivalent to the homogeneity of space, and this in turn is equivalent to the axioms of projective Geometry. The axioms of projective Geometry, in fact, may be roughly stated thus:

I. Space is continuous and infinitely divisible; the zero of extension, resulting from infinite division, is called a Point. All points are qualitatively similar, and distinguished by the mere fact that they lie outside one another.

II. Any two points determine a unique figure, the straight line; two straight lines, like two points, are qualitatively similar, and distinguished by the mere fact that they are mutually external.

III. Three points not in one straight line determine a unique figure, the plane, and four points not in one plane determine a figure of three dimensions. This process may, so far as can be seen *à priori*, be continued, without in any way interfering with the possibility of projective Geometry, to five or to n points. But projective Geometry requires, as an axiom, that the process should stop with some positive integral number of points, after which, any fresh point is contained in the figure determined by those already given. If the process stops with $(n+1)$ points, our space is said to have n dimensions.

These three axioms, it will be seen, are the equivalents of the three axioms of metrical Geometry[1], expressed without reference to quantity. We shall find them to be deducible, as before, from the homogeneity of space, or, more generally still, from the possibility of experiencing externality. They will therefore appear as *à priori*, as essential to the existence of any Geometry and to experience of an external world as such.

50. That some logical necessity is involved in these axioms might, I think, be inferred as probable, from their historical development alone. For the systems of Metageometry have not, in general, been set up as more likely to fit facts than the

[1] Axiom II. of the metrical triad corresponds to Axiom III. of the projective, and *vice versâ*.

system of Euclid; with the exception of Zöllner, for example, I know of no one who has regarded the fourth dimension as required to explain phenomena. As regards the space-constant again, though a *small* space-constant is regarded as empirically possible, it is not usually regarded as probable; and the finite space-constants, with which Metageometry is equally conversant, are not usually thought even possible, as explanations of empirical fact[1]. Thus the motive has been throughout not one of fact, but one of logic. Does not this give a strong presumption, that those axioms which are retained, are retained because they are logically indispensable? If this be so, the axioms common to Euclid and Metageometry will be *à priori*, while those peculiar to Euclid will be empirical. After a criticism of some differing theories of Geometry, I shall proceed, in Chapters III. and IV., to the proof and consequences of this thesis, which will form the remainder of the present work.

[1] Cf. Helmholtz, Wiss. Abh. Vol. II. p. 640, note: "Die Bearbeiter der Nicht-Euklidischen Geometrie (haben) deren objective Wahrheit nie behauptet."

CHAPTER II.

CRITICAL ACCOUNT OF SOME PREVIOUS PHILOSOPHICAL THEORIES OF GEOMETRY.

51. We have now traced the mathematical development of the theory of geometrical axioms, from the first revolt against Euclid to the present day. We may hope, therefore, to have at our command the technical knowledge required for the philosophy of the subject. The importance of Geometry, in the theories of knowledge which have arisen in the past, can scarcely be exaggerated. In Descartes, we find the whole theory of method dominated by analytical Geometry, of whose fruitfulness he was justly proud. In Spinoza, the paramount influence of Geometry is too obvious to require comment. Among mathematicians, Newton's belief in absolute space was long supreme, and is still responsible for the current formulation of the laws of motion. Against this belief on the one hand, and against Leibnitz's theory of space on the other, and not, as Caird has pointed out[1], against Hume's empiricism, was directed that keystone of the Critical Philosophy, the Kantian doctrine of space. Thus Geometry has been, throughout, of supreme importance in the theory of knowledge.

But in a criticism of representative modern theories of Geometry, which is designed to be, not a history of the subject, but an introduction to, and defence of, the views of the author, it will not be necessary to discuss any more ancient theory than that of Kant. Kant's views on this subject, true or false, have so dominated subsequent thought, that whether they were

[1] The Critical Philosophy of Kant, Vol. I. p. 287.

accepted or rejected, they seemed equally potent in forming the opinions, and the manner of exposition, of almost all later writers.

Kant.

52. It is not my purpose, in this chapter, to add to the voluminous literature of Kantian criticism, but only to discuss the bearing of Metageometry on the argument of the Transcendental Aesthetic, and the aspect under which this argument must be viewed in a discussion of Geometry[1]. On this point several misunderstandings seem to me to have had wide prevalence, both among friends and foes, and these misunderstandings I shall endeavour, if I can, to remove.

In the first place, what does Kant's doctrine mean for Geometry? Obviously not the aspect of the doctrine which has been attacked by psychologists, the "Kantian machine-shop" as James calls it—at any rate, if this can be clearly separated from the logical aspect. The question whether space is given in sensation, or whether, as Kant maintained, it is given by an intuition to which no external matter corresponds, may for the present be disregarded. If, indeed, we held the view which seems crudely to sum up the standpoint of the Critique, the view that all certain knowledge is self-knowledge, then we should be committed, if we had decided that Geometry was apodeictic, to the view that space is subjective. But even then, the psychological question could only arise when the epistemological question had been solved, and could not, therefore, be taken into account in our first investigation. The question before us is precisely the question whether, or how far, Geometry is apodeictic, and for the moment we have only to investigate this question, without fear of psychological consequences.

53. Now on this question, as on almost all questions in the Aesthetic or the Analytic, Kant's argument is twofold. On the one hand, he says, Geometry is known to have apodeictic certainty: therefore space must be *à priori* and subjective. On the other hand, it follows, from grounds independent of

[1] For a discussion of Kant from a less purely mathematical standpoint, see Chap. IV.

Geometry, that space is subjective and *à priori*; therefore Geometry must have apodeictic certainty. These two arguments are not clearly distinguished in the Aesthetic, but a little analysis, I think, will disentangle them. Thus in the first edition, the first two arguments deduce, from non-geometrical grounds, the apriority of space; the third deduces the apodeictic certainty of Geometry, and maintains, conversely, that no other view can account for this certainty[1]; the last two arguments only maintain that space is an intuition, not a concept. In the second edition, the double argument is clearer, the apriority of space being proved independently of Geometry in the metaphysical deduction, and deduced from the certainty of Geometry, as the only possible explanation of this, in the transcendental deduction. In the Prolegomena, the latter argument alone is used, but in the Critique both are employed.

54. Now it must be admitted, I think, that Metageometry has destroyed the legitimacy of the argument from Geometry to space; we can no longer affirm, on purely geometrical grounds, the apodeictic certainty of Euclid. But unless Metageometry has done more than this—unless it has proved, what I believe it alone cannot prove, that Euclid has *not* apodeictic certainty—then Kant's other line of argument retains what force it may ever have had. The actual space we know, it may say, is admittedly Euclidean, and is proved, without any reference to Geometry, to be *à priori; hence* Euclid has apodeictic certainty, and non-Euclid stands condemned. To this it is no answer to urge, with the Metageometers, that non-Euclidean systems are *logically* self-consistent; for Kant is careful to argue that geometrical reasoning, by virtue of our intuition of space, is synthetic, and cannot, though *à priori*, be upheld by the principle of contradiction alone[2]. Unless non-Euclideans can prove, what they have certainly failed to prove up to the present, that we can frame an *intuition* of non-Euclidean spaces,

[1] Cf. Vaihinger's Commentar, II. pp. 202, 265. Also p. 336 ff.

[2] E.g. second edition, p. 39: "So werden auch alle geometrischen Grundsätze, z. B. dass in einem Triangel zwei Seiten zusammen grösser sind als die dritte, niemals aus allgemeinen Begriffen von Linie und Triangel, sondern aus der Anschauung, und zwar *à priori* mit apodiktischer Gewissheit abgeleitet."

Kant's position cannot be upset by Metageometry alone, but must also be attacked, if it is to be successfully attacked, on its purely philosophical side.

55. For such an attack, two roads lie open: either we may disprove the first two arguments of the Aesthetic, or we may criticize, from the standpoint of general logic, the Kantian doctrine of synthetic *à priori* judgments and their connection with subjectivity. Both these attacks, I believe, could be conducted with some success; but if we are to disprove the apodeictic certainty of Geometry, one or other is essential, and both, I believe, will be found only partially successful. It will be my aim to prove, in discussing these two lines of attack, (1) that the distinction of synthetic and analytic judgments is untenable, and further, that the principle of contradiction can only give fruitful results on the assumption that experience in general, or, in a particular science, some special branch of experience, is to be formally possible; (2) that the first two arguments of the Transcendental Aesthetic suffice to prove, not Euclidean space, but *some* form of externality—which may be sensational or intuitional, but not merely conceptual—a necessary prerequisite of experience of an external world. In the third and fourth chapters, I shall contend, as a result of these conclusions, that those axioms, which Euclid and Metageometry have in common, coincide with those properties of any form of externality which are deducible, by the principle of contradiction, from the possibility of experience of an external world. These properties, then, may be said, though not quite in the Kantian sense, to be *à priori* properties of space, and as to these, I think, a modified Kantian position may be maintained. But the question of the subjective or objective nature of space may be left wholly out of account during the course of this discussion, which will gain by dealing exclusively with logical, as opposed to psychological points of view.

56. (1) *Kant's logical position.* The doctrine of synthetic and analytic judgments—at any rate if this is taken as the corner-stone of Epistemology—has been so completely rejected by most modern logicians[1], that it would demand little attention

[1] Cf. Bradley's Logic, Bk. III. Pt. I. Chap. VI.; Bosanquet's Logic, Bk. I. Chap. I. pp. 97–103.

here, but for the fact that an enthusiastic French Kantian, M. Renouvier, has recently appealed to it, with perfect confidence, on the very question of Geometry[1]. And it must be owned, with M. Renouvier, that if such judgments existed, in the Kantian sense, non-Euclidean Geometry, which makes no appeal to intuition, could have nothing to say against them. M. Renouvier's contention, therefore, forces us briefly to review the arguments against Kant's doctrine, and briefly to discuss what logical canon is to replace it.

Every judgment—so modern logic contends—is both synthetic and analytic; it combines parts into a whole, and analyses a whole into parts[2]. If this be so, the distinction of analysis and synthesis, whatever may be its importance in pure Logic, can have no value in Epistemology. But such a doctrine, it must be observed, allows full scope to the principle of contradiction: this criterion, since all judgments, in one aspect at least, are analytic, is applicable to all judgments alike. On the other hand, the whole which is analysed must be supposed already given, before the parts can be mutually contradictory: for only by connection in a given whole can two parts or adjectives be incompatible. Thus the principle of contradiction remains barren until we already have some judgments, and even some inference: for the parts may be regarded, to some extent, as an inference from the whole, or *vice versâ*. When once the arch of knowledge is constructed, the parts support one another, and the principle of contradiction is the keystone: but until the arch is built, the keystone remains suspended, unsupported and unsupporting, in the empty air. In other words, knowledge once existent can be analysed, but knowledge which should have to win every inch of the way against a critical scepticism, could never begin, and could never attain that circular condition in which alone it can stand.

But Kant's doctrine, if true, is designed to restrain a critical scepticism even where it might be effective. Certain fundamental propositions, he says, are not deducible from logic,

[1] Philosophie de la Règle et du Compas, Année Philosophique, II. pp. 1–66.

[2] I have stated this doctrine dogmatically, as a proof would require a whole treatise on Logic. I accept the proofs offered by Bradley and Bosanquet, to which the reader is referred.

i.e. their contradictories are not self-contradictory; they combine a subject and predicate which cannot, in any purely logical way, be shewn to have any connection, and yet these judgments have apodeictic certainty. But concerning such judgments, Kant is generally careful not to rely upon the mere subjective conviction that they are undeniable: he proves, with every precaution, that without them experience would be impossible. Experience consists in the combination of terms which formal logic leaves apart, and presupposes, therefore, certain judgments by which a framework is made for bringing such terms together. Without these judgments—so Kant contends—all synthesis and all experience would be impossible. If, therefore, the detail of the Kantian reasoning be sound, his results may be obtained by the principle of contradiction *plus* the possibility of experience, as well as by his distinction of synthetic and analytic judgments.

Logic, at the present day, arrogates to itself at once a wider and a narrower sphere than Kant allowed to it. Wider, because it believes itself capable of condemning any false principle or postulate; narrower, because it believes that its law of contradiction, without a given whole or a given hypothesis, is powerless, and that two terms, *per se*, though they may be different, cannot be contradictories, but acquire this relation only by combination in a whole about which something is known, or by connection with a postulate which, for some reason, must be preserved. Thus no judgment, *per se*, is either analytic or synthetic, for the severance of a judgment from its context robs it of its vitality, and makes it not truly a judgment at all. But in its proper context it is neither purely synthetic nor purely analytic; for while it is the further determination of a given whole, and thus in so far analytic, it also involves the emergence of *new* relations within this whole, and is so far synthetic.

57. We may retain, however, a distinction roughly corresponding to the Kantian *à priori* and *à posteriori*, though less rigid, and more liable to change with the degree of organisation of knowledge. Kant usually endeavoured to prove, as observed above, that his synthetic *à priori* propositions were necessary prerequisites of experience; now although we cannot retain the term synthetic, we can retain the term *à priori*, for those assumptions, or those postulates, from which alone the possibility of experience follows. Whatever can be deduced from these postulates, without the aid of the matter of experience, will also, of course, be *à priori*. From the standpoint of general logic, the laws of thought and the categories, with the indispensable conditions of their applicability, will be alone *à priori*; but from the standpoint of any special science, we may call *à priori* whatever renders possible the experience which forms the subject-matter of our science. In Geometry, to particularize, we may call *à priori* whatever renders possible experience of externality as such.

It is to be observed that this use of the term is at once more rationalistic and less precise than that of Kant. Kant would seem to have supposed himself immediately aware, by inspection, that some knowledge was apodeictic, and its subject-matter, therefore, *à priori*: but he did not always deduce its apriority from any further principle. Here, however, it is to be shown, before admitting apriority, that the falsehood of the judgment in question would not be effected by a mere change in the *matter* of experience, but only by a change which should render some branch of experience formally impossible, *i.e.* inaccessible to our methods of cognition. The above use is also less precise, for it varies according to the specialization of the experience we are assuming possible, and with every progress of knowledge some new connection is perceived, two previously isolated judgments are brought into logical relation, and the *à priori* may thus, at any moment, enlarge its sphere, as more is found deducible from fundamental postulates.

58. (2) *Kant's arguments for the apriority of space.* Having now discussed the logical canon to be used as regards the *à priori*, we may proceed to test Kant's arguments as regards space. The argument from Geometry, as remarked above, is upset by Metageometry, at least so far as those properties are concerned, which belong to Euclid but not to non-Euclidean spaces; as regards the common properties of both kinds of space, we cannot decide on their apriority till we have discussed the consequences of denying them, which will be done in Chapter III. As regards the two arguments which prove that space is an intuition, not a concept, they would call for much discussion in a special criticism of Kant, but here they may be passed by with the obvious comment that infinite homogeneous Euclidean space is a concept, not an intuition—a concept invented to explain an intuition, it is true, but still a pure concept[1]. And it is this pure concept which, in all discussions of Geometry, is primarily to be dealt with; the intuition need only be referred to where it throws light on the functions or the nature of the concept. The second of Kant's arguments, that we can imagine empty space, though not the absence of space, is false if it means a space without matter anywhere, and irrelevant if it merely means a space between matters and regarded as empty[2]. The only argument of importance, then, is the first argument. But I must insist, at the outset, that our problem is purely logical, and that all psychological implications must be excluded to the utmost possible extent. Moreover, as will be proved in Chapter IV., the proper function of space is to distinguish between different presented things, not between the Self and the object of sensation or perception. The argument then becomes the following: consciousness of a world of mutually external things demands, in presentations, a cognitive but non-inferential element leading to the discrimination of the objects presented. This element must be non-inferential, for from whatever number or combination of presentations, which did not of themselves demand diversity in their objects, I could never be led to infer the mutual externality of their objects. Kant says: "In order that sensations may be ascribed to something external to me...and similarly in order that I may be able to present them as outside and beside one another,... the presentation of space must be already present." But this goes rather too far: in the first place, the question should be only as to the mutual externality of presented things, not as to their externality to the Self[3]; and in the second place, things will appear mutually external if I have the presentation of *any* form of externality, whether Euclidean

[1] For a further discussion of this point, see Chaps. III. and IV.

[2] See Chap. IV. for a discussion of this argument.

[3] See Chap. IV. § 185.

or non-Euclidean. Whatever may be true of the *psychological* scope of this argument—whose validity is here irrelevant—the *logical* scope extends, not to Euclidean space, but only to any form of externality which could exist intuitively, and permit knowledge, in beings with our laws of thought, of a world of diverse but interrelated things.

Moreover externality, to render the scope of the argument wholly logical, must not be left with a sensational or intuitional meaning, though it must be supposed given in sensation or intuition. It must mean, in this argument, the fact of Otherness[1], the fact of being different from some other thing: it must involve the distinction between different things, and must be that element, in a cognitive state, which leads us to discriminate constituent parts in its object. So much, then, would appear to result from Kant's argument, that experience of diverse but interrelated things demands, as a necessary prerequisite, some sensational or intuitional element, in perception, by which we are led to attribute complexity to objects of perception[2]; that this element, in its isolation may be called a form of externality; and that those properties of this form, if any such be found, which can be deduced from its mere function of rendering experience of interrelated diversity possible, are to be regarded as *à priori*. What these properties are, and how the various lines of argument here suggested converge to a single result, we shall see in Chapters III. and IV.

59. In the philosophers who followed Kant, Metaphysics, for the most part, so predominated over Epistemology, that little was added to the theory of Geometry. What was added, came indirectly from the one philosopher who stood out against the purely ontological speculations of his time, namely *Herbart*. Herbart's actual views on Geometry, which are to be found chiefly in the first section of his *Synechologie*, are not of any great value, and have borne no great fruit in the development of the subject. But his psychological theory of space, his construction of extension out of series of points, his comparison of space with the tone and colour-series, his general preference

[1] An Otherness of substance, rather than of attribute, is here intended; an Otherness which may perhaps be called real as opposed to logical diversity.

[2] This proposition will be argued at length in Chap. IV.

for the discrete above the continuous, and finally his belief in the great importance of classifying space with other forms of series (*Reihenformen*[1]), gave rise to many of Riemann's epoch-making speculations, and encouraged the attempt to explain the nature of space by its analytical and quantitative aspect alone[2]. Through his influence on Riemann, he acquired, indirectly, a great importance in geometrical philosophy. To Riemann's dissertation, which we have already discussed in its mathematical aspect, we must now return, considering, this time, only its philosophical views.

Riemann.

60. The aim of Riemann's dissertation, as we saw in Chapter I., was to define space as a species of manifold, *i.e.* as a particular kind of collection of magnitudes. It was thus assumed, to begin with, that spatial figures could be regarded as magnitudes, and the axioms which emerged, accordingly, determined only the particular place of these among the many algebraically possible varieties of magnitudes. The resulting formulation of the axioms—while, from the mathematical standpoint of metrical Geometry, it was almost wholly laudable—must, from the standpoint of philosophy, be regarded, in my opinion, as a *petitio principii*. For when we have arrived at regarding spatial figures as magnitudes, we have already traversed the most difficult part of the ground. The axioms of metrical Geometry—and it is metrical Geometry, exclusively, which is considered in Riemann's Essay—will appear, in Chapter III., to be divisible into two classes. Of these, the first class—which contains the axioms common to Euclid and Metageometry, the only axioms seriously discussed by Riemann—are not the results of measurement, nor of any conception of magnitude, but are conditions to be fulfilled before measurement becomes possible. The second class only—those which express the difference between Euclidean and non-

[1] See Psychologie als Wissenschaft, I. Section III. Chap. VII.; II. Section I. Chap. III. and Section II. Chap. III. Compare also Synechologie, Section I. Chaps. II. and III.

[2] On the influence of Herbart on Riemann, compare Erdmann, Die Axiome der Geometrie, p. 30.

Euclidean spaces—can be deduced as results of measurement or of conceptions of magnitude. As regards the first class, on the contrary, we shall see that the relativity of position—by which space is distinguished from all other known manifolds, except time—leads logically to the necessity of three of the most distinctive axioms of Geometry, and yet this relativity cannot be called a deduction from conceptions of magnitude. In analytical Geometry, owing to the fact that coordinate systems start from points, and hence build up lines and surfaces, it is easy to suppose that points can be given independently of lines and of each other, and thus the relativity of position is lost sight of. The error thus suggested by mathematics was probably reinforced by Herbart's theory of space, which, by its serial character, as we have seen, appeared to him to facilitate a construction out of successive points, and to which Riemann acknowledges his indebtedness both in his Dissertation and elsewhere. The same error reappears in Helmholtz, in whom it is probably due wholly to the methods of analytical Geometry. It is a striking fact that, throughout the writings of these two men, there is not, so far as I know, one allusion to the relativity of position, that property of space from which, as our next chapter will shew, the richest quarry of consequences can be extracted. This is not a result of any conception of magnitude, but follows from the nature of our space-intuition; yet no one, surely, could call it empirical, since it is bound up in the very possibility of locating things *there* as opposed to *here*.

61. Indeed we can see, from a purely logical consideration of the judgment of quantity, that Riemann's manner of approaching the problem can never, by legitimate methods, attain to a philosophically sound formulation of the axioms. For quantity is a result of comparison of two qualitatively similar objects, and the judgment of quantity neglects altogether the qualitative aspect of the objects compared. Hence a knowledge of the essential properties of space can never be obtained from judgments of quantity, which neglect these properties, while they yet presuppose them. As well might one hope to learn the nature of man from a census. Moreover, the judgment of quantity is the result of comparison, and therefore presupposes the possibility of comparison. To know whether, or by what means, comparison is possible, we must know the qualities of the things compared and of the medium in which comparison is effected; while to know that *quantitative* comparison is possible, we must know that there is a qualitative identity between the things compared, which again involves a previous qualitative knowledge. When spatial figures have once been reduced to quantity, their quality has already been neglected, as known and similar to the quality of other figures. To hope, therefore, for the qualities of space, from a comparison of its expression as pure quantity with other pure quantities, is an error natural to an analytical geometer, but an error, none the less, from which there is no return to the qualitative basis of spatial quantity.

62. We must entirely dissent, therefore, from the disjunction which underlies Riemann's philosophy of space. Either the axioms must be consequences of general conceptions of magnitude, he thinks, or else they can only be proved by experience (p. 255). Whatever *can* be derived from general conceptions of magnitude, we may retort, cannot be an *à priori* adjective of space: for all the necessary adjectives of space are presupposed in any judgment of spatial quantity, and cannot, therefore, be consequences of such a judgment. Riemann's disjunction, accordingly, since one of its alternatives is obviously impossible, really begs the question. In formulating the axioms of metrical Geometry, our question should be: What axioms, *i.e.* what adjectives of space, must be presupposed, in order that quantitative comparison of the parts of space may be possible at all? And only when we have determined these conditions, which are *à priori* necessary to any quantitative science of space, does the second question arise: what inferences can we draw, as to space, from the observed results of this quantitative science, *i.e.* of this measurement of spatial figures? The conditions of measurement themselves, though not results of any conception of magnitude, will be *à priori*, if it can be shown that, without them, experience of externality would be impossible.

After this initial protest against Riemann's general philosophical position, let us proceed to examine, in detail, his use of the notion of a manifold.

63. In the first place there is, if I am not mistaken, considerable obscurity in the definition of a manifold, of which an almost verbal rendering was given in Chapter I. What is meant, to begin with, by a general conception capable of various determinations? Does not this property belong to all conceptions? It affords, certainly, a basis for counting, but if continuous quantity is to arise, we must, surely, have some less discrete formulation. It might afford a basis, for example, for the distinction of points in projective Geometry, but projective Geometry has nothing to do with quantity. Something more fluid and flexible than a conception, one would think, is necessary as the basis of continua. Then, again, what is meant by a quantum of a manifold? In space, the answer is obvious: what is meant is a piece of volume. But how about Riemann's other continuous manifold, colour? Does a quantum of colour mean a single line in the spectrum, or a band of finite thickness? In either case, what are the magnitudes to be compared? And how is superposition necessary, or even possible? A colour is fixed by its position in the spectrum: two lines in the same spectrum cannot be superposed, and two lines in different spectra need not be—their positions in their respective spectra suffice, or even, roughly, their immediate sense-quality. The fact is, Riemann had space in his mind from the start, and many of the properties, which he enunciates as belonging to all manifolds, belong, as a matter of fact, only to space. It is far from clear what the magnitudes are which the various determinations make possible. Do these magnitudes measure the elements of the manifold, or the relations between elements? This is surely a very fundamental point, but it is one which Riemann never touches on. In the former case, the superposition which he speaks of becomes unnecessary, since the magnitude is inherent in the element considered. We do not require superposition to measure quantities corresponding to different tones or colours; these can be discovered by analysis of single tones or colours. With space, on the other hand, if we seek for elements, we can find none except points, and no analysis of a point will find magnitudes inherent in it—such magnitudes are a fiction of coordinate Geometry. The magnitudes which space deals with, as we shall see in Chapter III.,

are relations between points, and it is for this reason that superposition is essential to space-measurement. There is no inherent quality in a single point, as there is in a single colour, by which it can be quantitatively distinguished from another. Thus the conception of a manifold, as defined by Riemann, either does not include colours, or does not involve superposition as the only means of measurement. From this dilemma there is no escape.

64. But if "measurement *consists* in a superposition of the magnitudes compared" (p. 256), does it not follow immediately that measurement is logically possible *only* where such superposition leaves the magnitudes unchanged? And therefore that measurement, as above defined, involves, as an *à priori* condition, that magnitudes are unchanged by motion? This consequence is not drawn by Riemann; indeed he proceeds immediately (pp. 256–7) to consider what he calls a general portion of the doctrine of magnitude (*Grössenlehre*), independent of measurement. But how is any doctrine of magnitude possible, in which the magnitudes cannot be measured? The reason of the confusion is, that Riemann's definition of measurement is applicable to no single manifold except space, since it depends on the noteworthy property that what we measure in Geometry is not points, but relations between points, and the latter, though not the former, may of course be unaltered by motion. Let us try, in illustration, to apply Riemann's definition of measurement to colours. We must remember that motion, in dealing with the colour manifold, means—not motion in space but—motion in the colour manifold itself. Now since every point of the colour manifold is completely determined by three magnitudes, which are given in fact, and cannot be arbitrarily chosen, it is plain that measurement by superposition—involving, as it does, motion, and therefore change in these determining magnitudes—is totally out of the question. The superposition of one colour on another, as a means of measurement, is sheer nonsense. And yet measurement is possible in the colour-manifold, by means of Helmholtz's law of mixture (*Mischungsgesetz*); but the measurement is of every separate element, not of the relations between elements, and is thus radically different from space-measurement[1]. The elements are not, like points in space, qualitatively

[1] I do not mean that measurement of colours is effected without reference to

alike, and distinguished by the mere fact of their mutual externality. What we have, in colours, is three fundamental qualitatively distinct elements, out of certain proportions of which we can build up all the other elements of the manifold—each of the resulting elements having the same combination of qualitative diversity and similarity as the three original elements. But in space, what could we make of such a procedure? Given three points, how are we to combine them in certain proportions? The phrase is meaningless. If some one makes the obvious retort, that we have to combine lines, not points, my rejoinder is equally obvious. To begin with, lines are not elements. Metaphysically, space has *no* elements, being, as the sequel will show, mere relations between non-spatial elements. Mathematically, this fact exhibits itself in the self-contradictory notion of the point, or zero magnitude in space, as the limit in our vain search for spatial elements. But even if we allow the line to pass as the spatial element, what does the combination of three lines in definite proportions give us? It gives us, simply, the coordinates of a *point*. Here again we see a great difference between the colour and space-manifolds. In colours, the combination of magnitudes gives a new magnitude of the same kind; in space, it defines, not a magnitude at all, but a would-be element of a different kind from the defining magnitudes. In the tone-manifold, we should find still different conditions. Here, no one of the measuring magnitudes can vanish without the tone vanishing too, and all three are so bound up together, in the single resulting sensation, that none can exist without a finite quantity of the others. They are all qualitatively different, both from each other, and from any possible tone, being constituents of it, as mass and velocity are constituents of momentum. All these different conditions require to be examined, before a manifold can be completely defined; and until we have conducted such an examination in detail, we cannot pronounce as to the *à priori* or empirical nature of the laws of the manifold. As regards space, I have attempted such an examination in the third and fourth chapters of this Essay.

their relations, since all measurement is essentially comparison. But in colours, it is the elements which are compared, while in space, it is the relations between elements.

65. I do not wish to deny, however, the great value of the conception of space as a manifold. On the contrary, this conception seems to have become essential to any treatment of the question. I only wish to urge that the purely algebraical treatment of any manifold, important as it may be in deducing fresh consequences from known premisses, tends rather to conceal than to make clear the basis of the premisses themselves, and is therefore misleading in a philosophical investigation. For mathematics, where quantity reigns supreme, Riemann's conception has proved itself abundantly fruitful; for philosophy, on the contrary, where quantity appears rather as a cloak to conceal the qualities it abstracts from, the conception seems to me more productive of error and confusion than of sound doctrine.

We are thus brought back to the point from which we started, namely, the falsity of Riemann's initial disjunction, and the consequent fallacy in his proof of the empirical nature of the axioms. His philosophy is chiefly vitiated, to my mind, by this fallacy, and by the uncritical assumption that a metrical coordinate system can be set up independently of any axioms as to space-measurement[1]. Riemann has failed to observe, what I have endeavoured to prove in the next chapter, that, unless space had a strictly constant measure of curvature, Geometry would become impossible; also that the absence of constant measure of curvature involves absolute position, which is an absurdity. Hence he is led to the conclusion that all geometrical axioms are empirical, and may not hold in the infinitesimal, where observation is impossible. Thus he says (p. 267): "Now the empirical conceptions, on which spatial measurements are based, the conceptions of the rigid body and the light-ray, appear to lose their validity in the infinitesimal: it is therefore quite conceivable that the relations of spatial magnitudes in the infinitesimal do not correspond to the presuppositions of Geometry, and this would, in fact, have to be assumed, as soon as it would enable us to explain the phenomena more simply." From this conclusion I must entirely dissent. In very large spaces, there might be a departure from Euclid; for they depend upon the axiom of

[1] For a discussion of this point, see Chap. III. Sec. B, § 176.

parallels, which is not contained in the axiom of Free Mobility; but in the infinitesimal, departures from Euclid could only be due to the absence of Free Mobility, which, as I hope my third chapter will show, is once for all impossible.

Helmholtz.

66. Helmholtz, like Riemann, was important both in the mathematics and in the philosophy of Geometry. From the mathematical point of view, his work has been already considered in Chapter I.; the consideration of his philosophy, which must occupy us here, will be a more serious task. Like Riemann, he endeavoured to prove that all the axioms are empirical, and like Riemann, he based his proof chiefly on Metageometry. He had an additional resource, however, in the physiology of the senses, which first led him to reject the Transcendental Aesthetic, and enabled him to attack Kant from the psychological as well as the mathematical side[1].

The principal topics, for a criticism of Helmholtz, are three: First, his criterion of the *à priori*; second, his discussion with Land as to the "imaginability" of non-Euclidean spaces; third —and this is by far the most important of the three—his

[1] The works of Helmholtz on geometrical philosophy comprise, in addition to the articles quoted in Chap. I., the following articles: "Ursprung und Sinn der geometrischen Axiome, gegen Land," Wiss. Abh. Vol. II. p. 640, 1878. (Also Mind, Vol. III.: an answer to Land in Mind, Vol. II.) "Ursprung und Bedeutung der geometrischen Axiome," 1870, Vorträge und Reden, Vol. II. p. 1. (Also Mind, Vol. I.) Two Appendices to "Die Thatsachen in der Wahrnehmung," entitled: II. "Der Raum kann transcendental sein, ohne dass es die Axiome sind"; and III. "Die Anwendbarkeit der Axiome auf die physische Welt," 1878, Vorträge und Reden, Vol. II. p. 256 ff.

The two Appendices last mentioned are popularizings and expansions of the article in Mind, Vol. III. The most widely read, though also, to my mind, the least valuable, of all Helmholtz's writings on Geometry, is the article in Mind, Vol. I. This contains the famous and much misunderstood analogies of Flatland and Sphereland, which will be discussed, and as far as possible defended, in answering Lotze's attack on Metageometry—an attack based, apparently, almost entirely on this one popular article. The present discussion, therefore, may be confined almost entirely to Mind, Vol. III., and the philosophical portions of the two papers quoted in Chap. I., *i.e.* to the articles in Wiss. Abh. Vol. II. pp. 610–660. His other works are popular, and important only because of the large public to which they appeal.

theory of the dependence of Geometry on Mechanics. Let us discuss these three points successively.

67. Helmholtz's criterion of apriority is difficult to discover, as he never, to my knowledge, gives a precise statement of it. From his discussion of physical and transcendental Geometry[1], however, it would appear that he regards as empirical whatever applies to empirical matter. For he there maintains, that even if space were an *à priori* form, yet any Geometry, which aimed at an application to Physics, would, since the actual places of bodies are not known *à priori*, be necessarily empirical[2]. It seems the more probable that he regards this as a possible criterion, as it is adopted, in several passages, by his disciple Erdmann[3], and so strange a test could hardly be accepted by a philosopher, unless he had found it in his master. I have called this a strange test, because it seems to me completely to ignore the work of the Critical Philosophy. For if there is one thing which, one might have hoped, had been made sufficiently clear by Kant's Critique, it is this, that knowledge which is *à priori*, being itself the condition of possible experience, applies—and in Kant's view, applies only—to empirical matter. Helmholtz and Erdmann, therefore, in setting up this test without discussion, simply ignore the existence of Kant and the possibility of a transcendental argument. Helmholtz assumes always that empirical knowledge must be wholly empirical, that there can be no *à priori* conditions of the experience in question, that experience will always be possible, and may give any kind of result. Thus in discussing "physical" Geometry, he assumes that the possibility of empirical measurement involves no *à priori* axioms, and that no *à priori* element can be contained in the process. This assumption, as we shall see in Chapter III., is quite unwarrantable: certain properties of *space*, in fact, are involved in the possibility of measuring *matter*. In spite of the fact, therefore, that we apply measurement to empirical matter, and that our results are therefore empirical, there

[1] In the answer to Land, Mind, Vol. III. and Wiss. Abh. II. p. 640.

[2] See also Die Thatsachen in der Wahrnehmung, Zusatz II., Der Raum kann transcendental sein, ohne dass es die Axiome sind. Vorträge und Reden, Vol. II.

[3] See below, criticism of Erdmann, § 84.

may well be an *à priori* element in measurement, which is presupposed in its possibility. Such a criterion, therefore, must pronounce everything empirical, but must itself be pronounced worthless.

Another and a better criterion, it is true, is also to be found in Helmholtz, and has also been adopted by Erdmann. Whatever might, by a different experience, have been rendered different—so this criterion contends—must itself be dependent on experience, and so empirical. This criterion seems perfectly sound, but Helmholtz's use of it is usually vitiated by his neglecting to prove the possibility of the different experience in question. He says, for example, that if our experience showed us only bodies which changed their shapes in motion, we should not arrive at the axiom of Congruence, which he pronounces accordingly to be empirical. But I shall endeavour to prove, in Chapter III., that without the axiom of Congruence, experience of spatial magnitude would be impossible. If my proof be correct, it follows that no experience can ever reveal spatial magnitudes which contradict this axiom—a possibility which Helmholtz nowhere discusses, in setting up his hypothetical experience. Thus this second criterion, though perfectly sound, requires always an accompanying transcendental argument, as to the conditions of possible experience. But this accompaniment is seldom to be found in Helmholtz.

68. One of the few cases, in which Helmholtz has attempted such an accompaniment, occurs in connection with our second point, the imaginability of non-Euclidean spaces. The argument on this point was elicited by Helmholtz's Kantian opponents, who maintained that the merely logical possibility of these spaces was irrelevant, since the basis of Geometry was not logic, but intuition. The axioms, they said, are synthetic propositions, and their contraries are, therefore, not self-contradictory; they are nevertheless apodeictic propositions, since no other *intuition* than the Euclidean is possible to us[1]. I have already criticized this line of argument in the beginning of the present chapter. Helmholtz's criticism, however, was different: admitting the internal consistency of the argument, he denied one of its premisses. We *can* imagine non-Euclidean spaces,

[1] See Prof. Land, in Mind, Vol. II.

he said, though their unfamiliarity makes this difficult. From this view it followed, of course, that Kant's argument, even if it were formally valid, could not prove the apriority of Euclidean space in particular, but only of that general space which included Euclid and non-Euclid alike[1].

Although I agree with Helmholtz in thinking the distinction between Euclidean and non-Euclidean spaces empirical, I cannot think his argument on the "imaginability" of the latter a very happy one. The validity of any proof must turn, obviously, on the definition of imaginability. The definition which Helmholtz gives in his answer to Land is as follows: Imaginability requires "die vollständige Vorstellbarkeit derjenigen Sinneseindrücke, welche das betreffende Object in uns nach den bekannten Gesetzen unserer Sinnesorgane unter allen denkbaren Bedingungen der Beobachtung erregen, und wodurch es sich von anderen ähnlichen Objecten unterscheiden würde" (Wiss. Abh. II. p. 644). This definition is not very clear, owing to the ambiguity of the word "*Vorstellbarkeit.*" The following definition seems less ambiguous: "Wenn die Reihe der Sinneseindrücke vollständig und eindeutig angegeben werden kann, muss man m. E. die Sache für *anschaulich vorstellbar* erklären" (Vorträge und Reden, II. p. 234). This makes clear, what also appears from his manner of proof, that he regards things as imaginable which can be *described* in conceptual terms. Such, as Land remarks (Mind, Vol. II. p. 45), "is not the sense required for argumentation in this case." That Land's criticism is just, is shown by Helmholtz's proof for non-Euclidean spaces, for it consists only in an analogy to the volume inside a sphere, which is mathematically obtained thus: We take the symbols representing magnitudes in "pseudo-spherical" (hyperbolic) space, and give them a new Euclidean meaning; thus all our symbolic propositions become capable of two interpretations, one for pseudo-spherical space, and one for the volume inside a sphere. It is, however, sufficiently obvious that this procedure, though it enables us to *describe* our new space, does not enable us to *imagine* it, in the sense of calling up images of the way things would look in it. We really derive, from this analogy, no more knowledge than a man born blind may derive, as to light, from

[1] See concluding paragraph of Helmholtz's article in Mind, Vol. III.

an analogy with heat. The dictum "Nihil est in intellectu quod non fuerit ante in sensu," would unquestionably be true, if for *intellect* we were to substitute *imagination*; it is vain, therefore, *if* our actual space be Euclidean, to hope for a power of *imagining* a non-Euclidean space. What Helmholtz might, I believe with perfect truth, have urged against Land, is that the image we actually have of space is not sufficiently accurate to exclude, in the actual space we know, all possibility of a slight departure from the Euclidean type. But in maintaining that we cannot imagine, though we can conceive and describe, a space different from that we actually have, Land is, in my opinion, unquestionably in the right. For a pure Kantian, who maintains, with Land, that none of the axioms can be proved, this question is of great importance. But if, as I have maintained, some of the axioms are susceptible of a transcendental proof, while the others can be verified empirically, the question is freed from psychological implications, and the imaginability or non-imaginability of metageometrical spaces becomes unimportant.

69. We come now to the third and most important question, the relation of Geometry to Mechanics. There are three senses in which Helmholtz's appeal to rigid bodies may be taken: the first, I think, is the sense in which he originally intended it; the second seems to be the sense which he adopted in his defence against Land; while the third is admitted by Land, and will be admitted in the following argument. These three senses are as follows:

(1) It may be asserted that the actual meaning of the axiom of Free Mobility lies in the assertion of empirical rigid bodies, and that the two propositions are equivalent to one another. This is certainly false.

(2) The axiom of Free Mobility, it may be said, is logically distinguishable from the assertion of rigid bodies, and may even be not empirical; but it is barren, even for pure Geometry, without the aid of measures, which must themselves be empirical rigid bodies. This sense is more plausible than the first, but I believe we can show that, in this sense also, the proposition is false.

(3) For pure Geometry and the abstract study of space,

it may be said, Free Mobility, as applied to an abstract geometrical matter, gives a sufficient possibility of quantitative comparison; but the moment we extend our results to mixed mathematics, and apply them to empirically given matter, we require also, as measures, empirically given rigid bodies, or bodies, at least, whose departures from rigidity are empirically known. In this sense, I admit, the proposition is correct[1].

In discussing these three meanings, I shall not confine myself strictly to the text of Helmholtz or Land: if I endeavoured to do so, I should be met by the difficulty that neither of them defines the *à priori*, and that each is too much inclined, in my opinion, to test it by psychological criteria. I shall, therefore, take the three meanings in turn, without laying stress on their historical adequacy to the views of Land or Helmholtz.

70. (1) Congruence may be taken to mean—as Helmholtz would certainly seem to desire—that we find actual bodies, in our mechanical experience, to preserve their shapes with approximate constancy, and that we infer, from this experience, the homogeneity of space. This view, in my opinion, radically misconceives the nature of measurement, and of the axioms involved in it. For what is meant by the non-rigidity of a body? We mean, simply, that it has changed its shape. But this involves the possibility of comparison with its former shape, in other words, of measurement. In order, therefore, that there may be any question of rigidity or non-rigidity, the measurement of spatial magnitudes must be already possible. It follows that measurement cannot, without a vicious circle, be itself derived from experience of rigid bodies. Geometrical measurement, in fact, is the comparison of spatial magnitudes, and such comparison involves, as will be proved at length in Chapter III., the homogeneity of space. This is, therefore, the logical prerequisite of all experience of rigid bodies, and cannot be the result of such experience. Without the homogeneity of space, the very notion of rigidity or non-rigidity could not exist, since these mean, respectively, the constancy or inconstancy of spatial magnitude in pieces of

[1] Cf. Veronese, Grundzüge der Geometrie (German translation), p. ix. Also pp. xxxiv, 304, and Note II. pp. 692–4.

matter, and both alike, therefore, presuppose the possibility of spatial measurement. From the homogeneity of space, we learn that a body, when it moves, will not change its shape without some physical cause; that it actually does not change its shape, is never asserted, and is indeed known to be false. As soon as measurement is possible, actual changes of shape can be estimated, and their empirical causes can be sought. But if space were not homogeneous, measurement would be impossible, constant shape would be a meaningless phrase, and rigidity could never be experienced. Congruence asserts, in short, that a body can, so far as mere space is concerned, move without change of shape; rigidity asserts that it actually does so move—a very different proposition, involving obviously, as its logical prius, the former geometrical proposition.

This argument may be summed up by the following disjunction: If bodies change their shapes in motion—and to some extent, since no body is perfectly rigid, they must all do so—then one of two cases must occur. *Either* the changes of shape, as bodies move from place to place, follow no geometrical law, are not, for instance, functions of the amount or direction of motion; in which case the law of causation requires that they should not be effects of the change of place, but of some simultaneous non-geometrical change, such as temperature. *Or* the changes are regular, and the shape S becomes, in a new position p, $Sf(p)$. In this case, the law of concomitant variations leads us to attribute the change of shape to the mere motion, and shape thus becomes a function of absolute position. But this is absurd, for position *means* merely a relation or set of relations; it is impossible, therefore, that mere position should be able to effect changes in a body. Position is one term in a relation, not a thing *per se*; it cannot, therefore, act on a thing, nor exist by itself, apart from the other terms of the relation. Thus Helmholtz's view, that Congruence depends on the existence of rigid bodies, must, since it involves absolute position, be condemned as a logical fallacy. Congruence, in fact, as I shall prove more fully in Chapter III., is an *à priori* deduction from the relativity of position.

71. (2) The above argument seems to me to answer satisfactorily Helmholtz's contention in the precise form which he first gave it. The axiom of Congruence, we must agree, is logically distinguishable from the existence of rigid bodies. Nevertheless some reference to matter is logically involved in Geometry[1], but whether this reference makes Geometry empirical, or does not, rather, show an *à priori* element in dynamics, is a further question.

The reference to matter is necessitated by the homogeneity of empty space. For so long as we leave matter out of account, one position is perfectly indistinguishable from another, and a science of the relations of positions is impossible. Indeed, before spatial relations can arise at all, the homogeneity of empty space must be destroyed, and this destruction must be effected by matter. The blank page is useless to the geometer until he defaces its homogeneity by lines in ink or pencil. No spatial figures, in short, are conceivable, without a reference to a not purely spatial matter. Again, if Congruence is ever to be used, there must be motion: but a purely geometrical point, being defined solely by its spatial attributes, cannot be supposed to move without a contradiction in terms. What moves, therefore, must be matter. Hence, in order that motion may afford a test of equality, we must have some *matter* which is known to be unaffected throughout the motion, that is, we must have some rigid bodies. And the difficulty is, that these bodies must not only undergo no change due solely to the nature of space, but must, further, be unchanged by their changing relation to other bodies. And here we have a requisite which can no longer be fulfilled *à priori*: which, indeed, we know to be, in strictness, untrue. For the forces acting on a body depend upon its spatial relations to other bodies, and changing forces are liable to produce changing configuration. Hence, it would seem, actual measurement must be purely empirical, and must depend on the degree of rigidity to be obtained, during the process of measurement, in the bodies with which we are conversant.

This conclusion, I believe, is valid of all actual measurement. But the possibility of such empirical and approximate rigidity, I must insist, depends on the *à priori* law that *mere* motion, apart from the action of other matter, cannot effect a change

[1] See Chap. IV. § 197 ff.

of shape. For without this law, the effect of other matter would not be discoverable; the laws of motion would be absurd, and Physics would be impossible. Consider the second law, for example: How could we measure the change of motion, if motion itself produced a change in our measures? Or consider the law of gravitation: How could we establish the inverse square, unless we were able, independently of Dynamics, to measure distances? The whole science of Dynamics, in short, is fundamentally dependent on Geometry, and but for the independent possibility of measuring spatial magnitudes, none of the magnitudes of Dynamics could be measured. Time, force, and mass are alike measured by spatial correlates: these correlates are given, for time, by the first law, for force and mass, by the second and third. It is true, then, that an empirical element appears unavoidably in all actual measurement, inasmuch as we can only know empirically that a given piece of matter preserves its shape throughout the necessary change of dynamical relations to other matter involved in motion; but it is further true that, for Geometry—which regards matter simply as supplying the necessary breach in the homogeneity of space, and the necessary term for spatial relations, not as the bearer of forces which change the configuration of other material systems—for Geometry, which deals with this abstract and merely kinematical matter, rigidity is *à priori*, in so far as the only changes with which it is cognizant—changes of mere position, namely—are incapable of affecting the shapes of the imaginary and abstract bodies with which it deals. To use a scholastic distinction, we may say that matter is the *causa essendi* of space, but Geometry is the *causa cognoscendi* of Physics. Without a Geometry independent of Physics, Physics itself, which necessarily assumes the results of Geometry, could never arise; but when Geometry is used in Physics, it loses some of its *à priori* certainty, and acquires the empirical and approximate character which belongs to all accounts of actual phenomena.

72. (3) This argument leads us to Land's distinction of physical and geometrical rigidity. The distinction may be expressed—and I think it is better expressed—by distinguishing between the conceptions of matter proper to Dynamics and to Geometry respectively. In Dynamics, we are concerned with matter as subject to and as causing motion, as affected by and as exerting *force*. We are therefore concerned with the changes of spatial configuration to which material systems are liable: the description and explanation of these changes is the proper subject-matter of all Dynamics. But in order that such a science may exist, it is obviously necessary that spatial configuration should be already measurable. If this were not the case, motion, acceleration and force would remain perfectly indeterminate. Geometry, therefore, must already exist before Dynamics becomes possible: to make Geometry dependent for its possibility on the laws of motion or any of their consequences, is a gross *ὕστερον πρότερον*. Nevertheless, as we have seen, some sort of matter is essential to Geometry. But this geometrical matter is a more abstract and wholly different matter from that of Dynamics. In order to study space by itself, we reduce the properties of matter to a bare minimum: we avoid entirely the category of causation, so essential to Dynamics, and retain nothing, in our matter, but its spatial adjectives[1]. The kind of rigidity affirmed of this abstract matter—a kind which suffices for the theory of our science, though not for its application to the objects of daily life—is purely geometrical, and asserts no more than this: That since our matter is devoid, *ex hypothesi*, of causal properties, there remains nothing, in mere empty space, which is capable of changing the configuration of any geometrical system. A change of absolute position, it asserts, is nothing; therefore the only real change involved in motion is a change of relation to other matter; but such other matter, for the purposes of our science, is regarded as destitute of causal powers; hence no change can occur, in the configuration of our system, by the mere effect of motion through empty space. The necessity of such a principle may be shown by a simple *reductio ad absurdum*, as follows. A motion of translation of the universe as a whole, with constant direction and velocity, is dynamically negligeable; indeed it is, philosophically, no motion at all, for it involves no change in the condition or mutual relations of the things in the universe. But if our geometrical rigidity were denied, the change in the parameter of space might cause all bodies to

[1] Cf. the opinion of Bolyai, quoted by Erdmann, Axiome, p. 26; cf. also ib. p. 60.

change their shapes owing to the mere change of absolute position, which is obviously absurd.

To make quite plain the function of rigid bodies in Geometry, let us suppose a liquid geometer in a liquid world. We cannot suppose the liquid perfectly homogeneous and undifferentiated, in the first place because such a liquid would be indistinguishable from empty space, in the second place because our geometer's body—unless he be a disembodied spirit—will itself constitute a differentiation for him. We may therefore assume

"dim beams,
Which amid the streams
Weave a network of coloured light,"

and we may suppose this network to form the occasion for our geometer's reflections. Then he will be able to imagine a network in which the lines are straight, or circular, or parabolic, or any other shape, and he will be able to infer that such a network, if it can be woven in one part of the fluid, can be woven in another. This will form sufficient basis for his deductions. The superposition he is concerned with—since not actual equality, but only the formal conditions of equality, are the subject-matter of Geometry—is purely ideal, and is unaffected by the impossibility of congealing any actual network. But in order to apply his Geometry to the exigencies of life, he would need some standard of comparison between actual networks, and here, it is true, he would need either a rigid body, or a knowledge of the conditions under which similar networks arose. Moreover these conditions, being necessarily empirical, could hardly be known apart from previous measurement. Hence for applied, though not for pure Geometry, one rigid body at least seems essential.

73. The utility, for Dynamics, of our abstract geometrical matter, is sufficiently evident. For having, by its means, a power of determining the configurations of material systems in whatever part of space, and knowing that changes of configuration are not due to mere change of place, we are able to attribute these changes to the action of other matter, and thus to establish the notion of force, which would be impossible if change of shape might be due to empty space.

Thus, to conclude: Geometry requires, if it is to be *practically* possible, some body or bodies which are either rigid (in the dynamical sense), or known to undergo some definite changes of shape according to some definite law. (These changes, we may suppose, are known by the laws of Physics, which have been experimentally established, and which throughout assume the truth of Geometry.) One or more such bodies are necessary to applied Geometry—but only in the sense in which rulers and compasses are necessary. They are necessary as, in making the Ordnance Survey, an elaborate apparatus was necessary for measuring the base line on Salisbury Plain. But for the *theory* of Geometry, geometrical rigidity suffices, and geometrical rigidity means only that a shape, which is possible in one part of space, is possible in any other. The empirical element in practice, arising from the purely empirical nature of physical rigidity, is comparable to the empirical inaccuracies arising from the failure to find straight lines or circles in the world—which no one but Mill has regarded as rendering Geometry itself empirical or inaccurate. But to make Geometry await the perfection of Physics, is to make Physics, which depends throughout on Geometry, forever impossible. As well might we leave the formation of numbers until we had counted the houses in Piccadilly.

Erdmann.

74. In connection with Riemann and Helmholtz, it is natural to consider Erdmann's philosophical work on their theories[1]. This is certainly the most important book on the subject which has appeared from the philosophical side, and in spite of the fact that, like the whole theory of Riemann and Helmholtz, it is inapplicable to projective Geometry, it still deserves a very full discussion.

Erdmann agrees throughout with the conclusions of Riemann and Helmholtz, except on a few points of minor importance; and his views, as this agreement would lead one to expect, are ultra-empirical. Indeed his logic seems—though I say this with

[1] Die Axiome der Geometrie: Eine philosophische Untersuchung der Riemann-Helmholtz'schen Raumtheorie, Leipzig, 1877.

hesitation—to be incompatible with any system but that of Mill: there is apparently no distinction, to him, between the general and the universal, and consequently no concept not embodied in a series of instances. Such a theory of logic, to my mind, vitiates most of his work, as it vitiated Riemann's philosophy[1]. This general criticism will find abundant illustration in the course of our account of Erdmann's views.

75. After a general introduction, and a short history of the development of Metageometry, Erdmann proceeds, in his second chapter, to discuss what are the axioms of Euclidean Geometry. The arithmetical axioms, as they are called, he leaves aside, as applying to magnitude in general; what we want here, he says, is a definition of space, for which the geometrical axioms are alone relevant. But a definition of space, he says—following Riemann—demands a genus of which space shall be a species, and this, since our space is psychologically unique, can only be furnished by analytical mathematics (p. 36). Now the space-forms dealt with by Geometry are magnitudes, and conceptions of magnitude are everywhere applied in Geometry. But before Riemann, only particular determinations of space could be exhibited as magnitudes, and thus the desired definition was impossible to obtain. Now, however, we can subsume space as a whole under a general conception of magnitude, and thus obtain, besides the space-intuition and the space-conception, a third form, namely, the conception of space as a magnitude (*Grössenbegriff vom Raum*, pp. 38–39). The definition of this will give us the complete, but not redundant, system of axioms, which could not be obtained by transforming the general intuition of space into the space-conception, for want of a plurality of instances (p. 40).

76. Before considering the subsequent method of definition, let us reflect on the theories involved in the above account of the conception of space as a magnitude. In the first place, it is assumed that conceptions cannot be formed unless we have a series of separate objects from which to abstract a common property—in other words, that the universal is always the general. In the second place, it is assumed that all

[1] On the influence of Mill, cf. Stallo, Concepts of Modern Physics, p. 216.

definition is classification under a genus. In the third place, the conception of magnitude, if I am not mistaken, is fundamentally misunderstood when it is supposed applicable to space as a whole. But in the fourth place, even if such a conception existed, it could give none of the essential properties of space. Let us consider these four points successively.

77. As regards the first point, it is to be observed that people certainly had some conception of space before Riemann invented the notion of a manifold, and that this conception was certainly something other than the common qualities of all the points, lines or figures in space. In the second place, Erdmann's view would make it impossible to conceive God, unless one were a polytheist, or the universe—unless, like Leibnitz, one imagined a series of possible worlds, set over against God, and none of them, therefore, a true Universe—or, to take an instance more likely to appeal to an empiricist, the necessarily unique centre of mass of the material universe. Any universal, in short, which is a bond or unity between things, and not merely a common property among independent objects, becomes impossible on Erdmann's view. We cannot, therefore, unless we adopt Mill's philosophy intact, regard the conception of space as demanding a series of instances from which to abstract. But even if we did so regard it, Riemann's manifolds would leave us without resources. For Euclidean space still appears as unique, at the end of his series of determinations. We have instances of manifolds, but not instances of Euclidean space. Thus if Erdmann's theory of conceptions were correct, he would still be left searching in vain for the conception of Euclidean space.

78. The second point, the view that all definition is classification, is closely allied to the first, and the two together plunge us into the depths of scholastic formal logic. The same instances of things which could not, on Erdmann's view, be conceived, may now be adduced as things which cannot be defined. Whatever was said above applies here also, and the point need not, therefore, be further discussed[1].

[1] This view seems to be derived, through Riemann, from Herbart. See Psych. als Wiss. ed. Hart. Vol. v. p. 262.

79. As regards the third point, the impossibility of applying conceptions of magnitude to space as a whole, a longer argument will be necessary, for we are concerned, here, with the whole question of the logical nature of judgments of magnitude. As we had before too much comparison for our needs, so we have now too little. I will endeavour to explain this point, which is of great importance, and underlies, I think, most of the philosophical fallacies of Riemann's school.

A judgment of magnitude is always a judgment of comparison, and what is more, the comparison is never concerned with quality, but only with quantity. Quality, in the judgment of magnitude, is supposed identical, in the object whose magnitude is stated, and in the unit with which it is compared. But quality, except in pure number, and in pure quantity as dealt with by the Calculus, is always present, and is partly absorbed into quantity, partly untouched by the judgment of magnitude. As Bosanquet says (Logic, Vol. I. p. 124); "Quantitative comparison is not *prima facie* coordinate with qualitative, but rather stands in its place as the *effect of comparison on quality*, which so far as comparable *becomes quantity*, and so far as incomparable furnishes the distinction of parts essential to the quantitative whole" (italics in the original). Thus, if we are to regard space as a magnitude, we must be able to adduce all those series of instances of which Erdmann speaks, and which, for the conception of space, seemed irrelevant. But it remains to be proved that the comparison, which we *can* institute between various spaces, is capable of expression in a quantitative form. Rather it would seem that the difference of quality is such as to preclude quantitative comparison between different spaces, and therefore also to preclude all judgments of magnitude about space as a whole. Here an exception might seem to be demanded by non-Euclidean spaces, whose space-constants give a definite magnitude, inherent in space as a whole, and therefore, one might think, characterizing space as a magnitude. But this is a mistake. For the space-constant, in such spaces, is the ultimate unit, the fixed term in all quantitative comparison; it is itself, therefore, destitute of quantity, since there is no independently given magnitude with which to compare it. A non-Euclidean world, in which the space-constant and all lines and figures were suddenly multiplied in a constant ratio, would be wholly unchanged; the lines, as measured against the space-constant, would have the same magnitude as before, and the space-constant itself, having no outside standard of comparison, would be destitute of quantity, and therefore not subject to change of quantity. Such an enlargement of a non-Euclidean world, in other words, is unmeaning; and this proves how inapplicable is the notion of quantity to space as a whole.

It might be objected that this only proves the absence of quantitative difference between different spaces of positive space-constant, or between those of negative space-constant: the quantitative difference persists, it might be said, between those of positive curvature in general and those of negative curvature in general, or between both together and Euclidean space. This I entirely deny. There is no qualitatively similar unit, in the three kinds of space, by which quantitative comparison could be effected. The straight lines of one space cannot be put into the other: the two straight lines, in one space, whose product is the reciprocal of the measure of curvature, have no corresponding curves in the other space, and the measures of curvature cannot, therefore, be quantitatively compared with each other. That the one may be regarded as positive, the other negative, I admit, but their values are indeterminate, and the units in the two cases are qualitatively different. A debt of £300 may be represented as the asset of − £300, and the height of the Eiffel Tower is + 300 metres; but it does not follow that the two are quantitatively comparable. So with space-constants: the space-constant is itself the unit for magnitudes in its own space, and differs qualitatively from the space-constant of another kind of space.

Again, to proceed to a more philosophical argument, two different spaces cannot co-exist in the same world: we may be unable to decide between the alternatives of the disjunction, but they remain, none the less, absolutely incompatible alternatives. Hence we cannot get that coexistence of two spaces which is essential to comparison. The fact seems to be that Erdmann, in his admiration for Riemann and Helmholtz, has fallen in with their mathematical bias, and assumed, as mathematicians naturally tend to assume, that quantity is everywhere and always applicable and adequate, and can deal with more than the mere comparison of things whose qualities are already known as similar[1].

80. This suggests the fourth and last of the above points, that the *qualities* of space, even if space could be successfully regarded as a magnitude, would have to be entirely omitted in such a manner of regarding it, and that, therefore, none of its important or essential properties would emerge from such treatment. For to regard space as a magnitude involves, as we saw, a comparison with something qualitatively similar, and an abstraction from the similar qualities. To some extent and by the help of certain doubtful arguments, such a comparison is instituted by Riemann and Erdmann; but when they have instituted it, they forget all about the common qualities on which its possibility depends. But these are precisely the fundamental properties of space, and those from which, as I shall endeavour to prove in Chapter III., the axioms common to Euclid and Metageometry follow *à priori*. Such are the dangers of the quantitative bias.

81. After this protest against the initial assumptions in Erdmann's deduction of space, let us return to consider the manner in which this deduction is carried out. Here there will be less ground for criticism, as the deduction, given its presuppositions, is, I think, as good as such a deduction can be. To define space as a magnitude, he says, let us start with two of its most obvious properties, continuity and the three dimensions. Tones and colours afford other instances of a manifold with these two properties, but differ from space in that their dimensions are not homogeneous and interchangeable. To designate this difference, Erdmann introduces a useful pair of terms: in the general case, he calls a manifold *n*-determined (n-*bestimmt*); in the case where, as in space, the dimensions are homogeneous, he calls the manifold *n*-extended (n-*ausgedehnt*). Manifolds of the latter sort he calls extents (*Ausgedehntheiten*).

[1] The same irreducibility of space to mere magnitude is proved by Kant's hands and spherical triangles, in which a difference persists in spite of complete quantitative equality.

That the difference between the two kinds is one of quality, not of quantity, he seems not to perceive; he also overlooks the fact that, in the second kind, from its very definition, the axiom of Congruence must hold, on account of the qualitative similarity of different parts. In spite of this fact, he defines space as an extent, and then regards Congruence as empirical, and as possibly false in the infinitesimal. This is the more strange, as he actually proves (p. 50) that measurement is impossible, in an extent, unless the parts are independent of their place, and can be carried about unaltered as measures. In spite of this, he proceeds immediately to discuss whether the measure of curvature is constant or variable, without investigating how, in the latter case, Geometry could exist. We cannot know, he says, from geometrical superposition, that geometrical bodies are independent of place, for if their dimensions altered in motion according to any fixed law, two bodies which could be superposed in one place could be superposed in any other. That such a hypothesis involves absolute position, and denies the qualitative similarity of the parts of space, which he declares (p. 171) to be the principle of his theory of Geometry, is nowhere perceived. But what is more, his notion that magnitude is something absolute, independent of comparison, has prevented him from seeing that such a hypothesis is unmeaning. He says himself that, even on this hypothesis, a geometrical body can be defined as one whose points retain constant distances from each other, for, since we have no absolute measure, measurement could not reveal to us the change of absolute magnitude (p. 60). But is not this a *reductio ad absurdum?* For magnitude is nothing apart from comparison, and the comparison here can only be effected by superposition; if, then, as on the above hypothesis, superposition always gives the same result, by whatever motion it is effected, there is no sense in speaking of magnitudes as no longer equal when separated: absolute magnitude is an absurdity, and the magnitude resulting from comparison does not differ from that which would result if the dimensions of bodies were unchanged in motion. Therefore, since magnitude is only intelligible as the result of comparison, the dimensions of bodies *are* unchanged in motion, and the suggested hypothesis is unmeaning. On this subject I shall have more to say in Chapter III.[1]

82. This hypothesis, however, is not introduced for its own sake, but only to usher in the Helmholtzian *deus ex machina*, Mechanics. For Mechanics proves—so Erdmannn confidently continues—that rigidity must hold, not merely as to ratios, in the above restricted geometrical sense, but as to absolute magnitudes (p. 62). Hence we get at last true Congruence, empirical as Mechanics is empirical, and impossible to prove apart from Mechanics. I have already criticized Helmholtz's view of the dependence of Geometry on Mechanics, and need not here speak of it at length. It is a pity that Erdmann has in no way specified the procedure by which Mechanics decides the geometrical alternatives—indeed he seems to rely on the *ipse dixit* of Helmholtz. How, if Geometry would be totally unable to discover a change in dimensions of the kind suggested, the Laws of Motion, which throughout depend on Geometry, should be able to discover it if it existed, I am wholly at a loss to understand. Uniform motion in a straight line, for example, presupposes geometrical measurement; if this measurement is mistaken, what Mechanics imagines to be uniform motion is not really such, but Mechanics can never discover the discrepancy. If the Laws of Motion had been regarded as *à priori*, Geometry might possibly have been reinforced by them; but so long as they are empirical, they presuppose geometrical measurement, and cannot therefore condition or affect it.

Erdmann's conclusion, in the second chapter, is that Congruence is probable, but cannot be verified in the infinitesimal; that its truth involves the actual existence of rigid bodies (though, by the way, we know these to be, strictly speaking, non-existent), that rigid bodies are freely moveable, and do not alter their size in rotation (Helmholtz's Monodromy); that the axiom of three dimensions is certain, since small errors are impossible; and that the remaining axioms of Euclid—those of the straight line and of parallels—are approximately, if not accurately, true of our actual space (pp. 78, 83). He does not

[1] See §§ 146–7.

discuss how Congruence, on the above view, is compatible with the atomic theory, or even with the observed deformations of approximately rigid bodies; nor how, if space, as he assumes, is homogeneous, rigid bodies can fail to be freely moveable through space. The axioms are all lumped together as empirical, and it appears, in the following chapters, that Erdmann regards their empirical nature as sufficiently proved by their applicability to empirical material (cf. pp. 159, 165)—a strange criterion, which would prove the same conclusion, with equal facility, of Arithmetic and of the laws of thought.

83. The third chapter, on the philosophical consequences of Metageometry, need not be discussed at length, since it deals rather with space than with Geometry. At the same time, it will be worth while to treat briefly of Erdmann's criterion of apriority. On this subject it is very difficult to discover his meaning, since it seems to vary with the topic he is discussing. Thus at one time (p. 147) he rejects most emphatically the Kantian connection of the *à priori* and the subjective[1], and yet at another time (p. 96) he regards every presentation of external things as partly *à priori*, partly empirical, merely because such a presentation is due to an interaction between ourselves and things, and is therefore partly due to subjective activity, partly due to outside objects. Hence, he says, the distinction is not between different presentations, but between different aspects of one and the same presentation. This seems to return wholly to the Kantian psychological criterion of subjectivity, with the added disadvantage that it makes the distinction, like that of analytic and synthetic, epistemologically worthless. And yet he never hesitates to pronounce every piece of knowledge in turn empirical. The fact seems to be, that where he wants a more logical criterion, he adopts a modification of Helmholtz's criterion for sensations. If space be an *à priori* form, he says, no experience could possibly change it (p. 108); but this Metageometry has proved not to be the case, since we can intuit the perceptions which non-Euclidean space would give us (p. 115).

[1] "Jeder Versuch, Kant's Lehre von der Apriorität als des subjectiven, von aller Erfahrung absolut unabhängigen Erkenntnissfactors, trotzdem zu halten, ist deshalb von vornherein aussichtslos."

I have criticised this argument in discussing Helmholtz; at present we are concerned with Erdmann's criterion of apriority. The subjectivity-criterion—though he certainly uses it in discussing the apriority of space, and solemnly decides, by its means, that space is both *à priori* and empirical, since a change either in us or in the outer world could change it (p. 97)—would seem, like several of his other tests, to be a lapse on his part: the criterion which he means to use is Helmholtz's. This criterion, I think, with a slight change of wording, might be accepted; it seems to me a necessary, but not a sufficient condition. The *à priori*, we may say, is not only that which no experience can change, but that without which experience would become impossible. It is the omission to discuss the conditions which render geometrical (and mechanical) experience possible, to my mind, which vitiates the empirical conclusions of Helmholtz and Erdmann. Why certain conditions should be necessary for experience—whether on account of the constitution of the mind, or for some other reason—is a further question, which introduces the relation of the *à priori* to the subjective. But in discussing the question as to what knowledge is *à priori*, as opposed to the question concerning the further consequences of apriority, it is well to keep to the purely logical criterion, and so preserve our independence of psychological controversies. The fact, if it be a fact, that the world might be such as to defy our attempts to know it, will not, with the above criterion, invalidate the conclusion that certain elements in knowledge are *à priori*; for whether fulfilled or not, they remain necessary conditions for the existence of any knowledge at all.

84. With this caution as to the meaning of apriority, we shall find, I think, that the conclusions of Erdmann's final chapter, on the principles of a theory of Geometry, are largely invalidated by the diversity and inadequacy of his tests of the *à priori*. He begins by asserting, in conformity with the quantitative bias noticed above, that the question as to the nature of geometrical axioms is completely analogous to the corresponding question of the foundations of pure mathematics (p. 138). This is, I think, a radical error: for the function of the axioms seems to be, to establish that qualitative basis on which, as we saw, all qualitative comparison must rest. But in pure mathematics, this qualitative basis is irrelevant, for we deal there with pure quantity, *i.e.* with the merely quantitative result of quantitative comparison, wherever it is possible, independently of the qualities underlying the comparison. Geometry, as Grassmann insists[1], ought not to be classed with pure mathematics, for it deals with a matter which is given to the intellect, not created by it. The axioms give the means by which this matter is made amenable to quantity, and cannot, therefore, be themselves deduced from purely quantitative considerations.

Leaving this point aside, however, let us return to Erdmann. He distinguishes, within space, a form and a matter: the form is to contain the properties common to all extents, the matter the properties which distinguish space from other extents. This distinction, he says, is purely logical, and does not correspond with Kant's: matter and form, for Erdmann, are alike empirical. The axioms and definitions of Geometry, he says, deal exclusively with the matter of space. It seems a pity, having made this distinction, to put it to so little use: after a few pages, it is dropped, and no epistemological consequences are drawn from it. The reason is, I think, that Erdmann has not perceived how much can be deduced from his definition of an extent, as a manifold in which the dimensions are homogeneous and interchangeable. For this property suffices to prove the complete homogeneity of an extent, and hence—from the absence of qualitative differences among elements—the relativity of position and the axiom of Congruence. This deduction will be made at length in the sequel[2]; at present, I have only to observe that every extent, on this view, possesses all the properties (except the three dimensions) common to Euclidean and non-Euclidean spaces. The axioms which express these properties, therefore, apply to the form of space, and follow from homogeneity alone, which Erdmann allows (p. 171) as the principle of any theory of space. The above distinction of form and matter, therefore, corresponds, when its full consequences are deduced, to the distinction between the axioms which follow from the

[1] Ausdehnungslehre von 1844, 2nd edition, pp. xxii. xxiii.

[2] See § 129 ff.

homogeneity of space and those which do not. Since, then, homogeneity is equivalent to the relativity of position, and the relativity of position is of the very essence of a form of externality, it would seem that his distinction of form and matter can also be made coextensive with the distinction of the *à priori* and empirical in Geometry. On this subject, I shall have more to say in Chapter III.

In the remainder of the chapter, Erdmann insists that the straight line, etc., though not abstracted from experience, which nowhere presents straight lines, must yet, as applicable to admittedly empirical sciences, be empirical (p. 159)—a criterion which he appears to employ only when all other grounds for an empirical opinion fail, and one which, obviously, can never refuse to do its work, since all elements of knowledge are susceptible of employment on some empirical material. He also defines the straight line (p. 155) as a line of constant curvature zero, as though curvature could be measured independently of the straight line. Even the arithmetical axioms are declared empirical (p. 165), since in a world where things were all hopelessly different from one another, these axioms could not be applied. After this reminder of Mill, we are not surprised, a few pages later (p. 172), at a vague appeal to "English logicians" as having proved Geometry to be an inductive science. Nevertheless, Erdmann declares, almost on the last page of his book (p. 173), that Geometry is distinguished from all other sciences by the homogeneity of its material: a principle of which no single application occurs throughout his book, and which, as we shall see in Chapter III., flatly contradicts the philosophical theories advocated throughout his preceding pages.

On the whole, then, it cannot be said that Erdmann has done much to strengthen the philosophical position of Riemann and Helmholtz. I have criticized him at length, because his book has the appearance of great thoroughness, and because it is undoubtedly the best defence extant of the position which it takes up. We shall now have the opposite task to perform, in defending Metageometry, on its mathematical side, from the attacks of Lotze and others, and in vindicating for it that measure of philosophical importance—far inferior, indeed, to the hopes of Erdmann—which it seems really to possess.

Lotze.

85. Lotze's argument as regards Geometry[1]—which follows a metaphysical argument as to the ontological nature of space, and assumes the results of this argument—consists of two parts: the first discusses the various meanings logically assignable (pp. 233–247) to the proposition that other spaces than Euclid's are possible, and the second criticizes, in detail, the procedure of Metageometry. The first of these questions is very important, and demands considerable care as to the logical import of a judgment of possibility. Although Lotze's discussion is excellent in many respects, I cannot persuade myself that he has hit on the only true sense in which non-Euclidean spaces are possible. I shall endeavour to make good this statement in the following pages.

86. Lotze opens with a somewhat startling statement, which, though philosophically worthy to be true, does not appear to be historically borne out. Euclidean Geometry has been chiefly shaken, he says, by the Kantian notion of the exclusive subjectivity of space—if space is only our private form of intuition, to which there exists no analogue in the objective world, then other beings may have other spaces, without supposing any difference in the world which they arrange in these spaces (p. 233). This certainly seems a legitimate deduction from the subjectivity of space, which, so far from establishing the universal validity of Euclid, establishes his validity only after an empirical investigation of the nature of space as intuited by Tom, Dick or Harry. But as a matter of fact, those who have done most to further non-Euclidean Geometry—with the exception of Riemann, who was a disciple of Herbart—have usually inherited from Newton a naïve realism as regards absolute space. I might instance the passage quoted from Bolyai in Chapter I., or Clifford, who seems to have thought that we actually see the images of things on the retina[2], or again Helmholtz's belief in the dependence of Geometry on the behaviour of rigid bodies. This belief led to the view that

[1] Metaphysik, Book II. Chap. II. My references are to the original.

[2] See Lectures and Essays, Vol. I. p. 261.

Geometry, like Physics, is an experimental science, in which objective truth can be attained, it is true, but only by empirical methods. However, Lotze's ground for uncertainty about Euclid is a philosophically tenable ground, and it will be instructive to observe the various possibilities which arise from it.

If space is only a subjective form—so Lotze opens his argument—other beings may have a different form. If this corresponds to a different world, the difference, he says, is uninteresting: for our world alone is relevant to any metaphysical discussion. But if this different space corresponds to the same world which we know under the Euclidean form, then, in his opinion, we get a question of genuine philosophic interest. And here he distinguishes two cases: *either* the relations between things, which are presented to these hypothetical beings under the form of some different space, are relations which do not appear to us, or at any rate do not appear spatial; *or* they are the same relations which appear to us as figures in Euclidean space (p. 235). The first possibility would be illustrated, he says, by beings to whom the tone or colour-manifolds appeared extended; but we cannot, in his opinion, imagine a manifold, such as is required for this case, to have its dimensions homogeneous and comparable *inter se*, and therefore the contents of the various presentations constituting such a manifold could not be combined into a single content containing them all. But the possibility of such a combination is of the essence of anything worth calling a space: therefore the first of the above possibilities is unmotived and uninteresting. Lotze's conclusion on this point, I think, is undeniable, but I doubt whether his argument is very cogent. However, as this possibility has no connection with that contemplated by non-Euclideans, it is not worth while to discuss it further.

The second possibility also, Lotze thinks, is not that of Metageometry, but in truth it comes nearer to it than any of the other possibilities discussed. If a non-Euclidean were at the same time a believer in the subjectivity of space, he would have to be an adherent of this view. Let us see more precisely what the view is. In Book II., Chapter I., Lotze has accepted the argument of the Transcendental Aesthetic, but rejected that of the mathematical antinomies: he has decided that space is, as Kant believed, subjective, but possesses nevertheless, what Kant denied it, an objective counterpart. The relation of presented space to its objective counterpart, as conceived by Lotze, is rather hard to understand. It seems scarcely to resemble the relation of sensation to its object—*e.g.* of light to ether-vibrations—for if it did, space would not be in any peculiar sense subjective. It seems rather to resemble the relation of a perceived bodily motion to the state of mind of the person willing the motion. However this may be, the objective counterpart of space is supposed to consist of certain immediate interactions of monads, who experience the interactions as modifications of their internal states. Such interactions, it is plain, do not form the subject-matter of Geometry, which deals only with our resulting perceptions of spatial figures. Now if Lotze's construction of space be correct, there seems certainly no reason why these resulting perceptions should not, for one and the same interaction between monads, be very different in beings differently constituted from ourselves. But if they were different, says Lotze, they would have to be utterly different—as different, for example, as the interval between two notes is from a straight line. The possibility is, therefore, in his opinion, one about which we can know nothing, and one which must remain always a mere empty idea. This seems to me to go too far: for whatever the objective counterpart may be, any argument which gives us information about it must, when reversed, give us information about any possible form of intuition in which this counterpart is presented. The argument which Lotze has used in his former chapter, for example, deducing, from the relativity of position, the merely relational nature of the objective counterpart, allows us, conversely, to infer, from this relational nature, the complete relativity of position in any possible space-intuition—unless, indeed, it bore a wholly deceitful relation to those interactions of monads which form its objective counterpart. But the complete relativity of position, as I shall endeavour to establish in Chapter III., suffices to prove that our Geometry must be Euclidean, elliptic, spherical or pseudo-spherical. We have, therefore, it would seem, very considerable knowledge, on Lotze's theory of space, of the manner in which what appears to us as space *must* appear to any beings with our laws of thought. We cannot know, it is true, what *psychological* theory of space-perception would apply to such beings: they might have a sense different from any of ours, and they might have no sense in any way resembling ours, but yet their Geometry would have points of resemblance to ours, as that of the blind coincides with that of the seeing. If space has any objective counterpart whatever, in short, and if any inference is possible, as Lotze holds it to be, from space to its counterpart, then a converse argument is also possible, though it may give some only of the qualities of Euclidean space, since some only of these qualities may be found to have a necessary analogue in the counterpart.

87. Admitting, then, in Lotze's sense, the subjectivity of space, the above possibility does not seem so empty as he imagines. He discusses it briefly, however, in order to pass on to what he regards as the real meaning of Metageometry. In this he is guilty of a mathematical mistake, which causes much irrelevant reasoning. For he believes that Metageometry constructs its spaces out of straight lines and angles in all respects similar to Euclid's, whence he derives an easy victory in proving that these elements can lead only to the one space. In this he has been misled by the phraseology of non-Euclideans, as well as by Euclid's separation of definitions and axioms. For the fact is, of course, that straight lines are only fully defined when we add to the formal definition the axioms of the straight line and of parallels. Within Euclidean space, Euclid's definition suffices to distinguish the straight line from all other curves; the two axioms referred to are then absorbed into the definition of space. But apart from the restriction to Euclidean space, the definition has to be supplemented by the two axioms, in order to define completely the Euclidean straight line. Thus Lotze has misconceived the bearing of non-Euclidean constructions, and has simply missed the point in arguing as he does. The possibility contemplated by a non-Euclidean, if it fell under any of Lotze's cases, would fall under the second case discussed above.

88. But the bearing of Metageometry is really, I think, different from anything imagined by Lotze; and as few writers seem clear on this point, I will enter somewhat fully into what I conceive to be its purpose.

In the first place, there are some writers—notably Clifford—who, being naïve realists as regards space, hold that our evidence is wholly insufficient, as yet, to decide as to its nature in the infinite or in the infinitesimal (cf. Essays, Vol. I. p. 320): these writers are not concerned with any possibility of beings different from ourselves, but simply with the everyday space we know, which they investigate in the spirit of a chemist discussing whether hydrogen is a metal, or an astronomer discussing the nebular hypothesis.

But these are a minority: most, more cautious, admit that our space, so far as observation extends, is Euclidean, and if not accurately Euclidean, must be only slightly spherical or pseudo-spherical. Here again, it is the space of daily life which is under discussion, and here further the discussion is, I think, independent of any philosophical assumption as to the nature of our space-intuition. For even if this be purely subjective, the translation of an intuition into a conception can only be accomplished approximately, within the errors of observation incident to self-analysis; and until the intuition of space has become a conception, we get no scientific Geometry. The apodeictic certainty of the axiom of parallels shrinks to an unmotived subjective conviction, and vanishes altogether in those who entertain non-Euclidean doubts. To reinforce the Euclidean faith, reason must now be brought to the aid of intuition; but reason, unfortunately, abandons us, and we are left to the mercy of approximate observations of stellar triangles —a meagre support, indeed, for the cherished religion of our childhood.

89. But the possibility of an inaccuracy so slight, that our finest instruments and our most distant parallaxes show no trace of it, would trouble men's minds no more than the analogous chance of inaccuracy in the law of gravitation, were it not for the philosophical import of even the slenderest possibility in this sphere. And it is the philosophical bearing of Metageometry alone, I think, which constitutes its real importance. Even if, as we will suppose for the moment, observation had established, beyond the possibility of doubt, that our space might be safely regarded as Euclidean, still Metageometry would have shown a philosophical possibility, and on this ground alone it could claim, I think, very nearly all the attention which it at present deserves.

But what is this possibility? A thing is possible, according to Bradley (Logic, p. 187), when it would follow from a certain number of conditions, some of which are known to be realized. Now the conditions to which a form of externality must conform, in order to be affirmed, are: first, of course, that it should be experienced, or legitimately inferred from something experienced; but secondly, that it should conform to certain logical conditions, detailed in Chapter III., which may be summed up in the relativity of position. Now what Metageometry has done, in any case, is to suggest the proof that the second of these conditions is fulfilled by non-Euclidean spaces. Euclid is affirmed, therefore, on the ground of immediate experience alone, and his truth, as unmediated by logical necessity, is merely assertorical, or, if we prefer it, empirical. This is the most important sense, it seems to me, in which non-Euclidean spaces are possible. They are, in short, a step in a philosophical argument, rather than in the investigation of fact: they throw light on the nature of the grounds for Euclid, rather than on the actual conformation of space[1]. This import of Metageometry is denied by Lotze, on the ground that non-Euclidean logic is faulty, a ground which he endeavours, by much detail and through many pages, to make good—with what success, we will now proceed to examine.

90. Lotze's attack on Metageometry—although it remains, so far as I know, the best hostile criticism extant, and although its arguments have become part of the regular stock-in-trade of Euclidean philosophers—contains, if I am not mistaken, several misunderstandings due to insufficient mathematical knowledge of the subject. As these misunderstandings have been widely spread among philosophers, and cannot be easily removed except by a critic who has gone into non-Euclidean Geometry with some care, it seems desirable to discuss Lotze's strictures point by point.

[1] On the meaning of geometrical possibility, cf. Veronese, Grundzüge der Geometrie (German translation), pp. xi.–xiii.

91. The mathematical criticism begins (§ 131) with a somewhat question-begging definition of parallel straight lines. Two straight lines $a\alpha$, $b\beta$, according to this definition, are

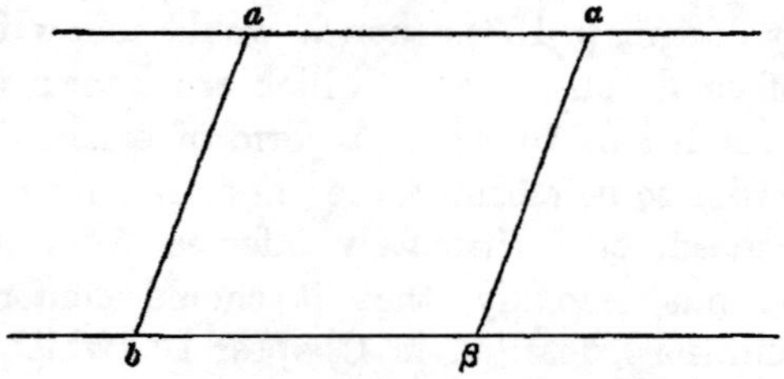

parallel when—a and b being arbitrary points on the two lines—if $a\alpha = b\beta$, then $ab = \alpha\beta$, where α, β are two other points on the two straight lines respectively. This definition—which contains Euclid's axiom and definition combined in a very convenient and enticing form—is of course thoroughly suitable to Euclidean Geometry, and leads immediately to all the Euclidean propositions about parallels. But it is perhaps more honest to follow Euclid's course; when an axiom is thus buried in a definition, it is apt to seem, since definitions are supposed to be arbitrary, as though the difficulty had been overcome, while in reality, the possibility of parallels, as above defined, involves the very point in question, namely, the disputed axiom of parallels. For what this axiom asserts is simply the existence of lines conforming to Lotze's definition. The deduction of the principal propositions on parallels, with which Lotze follows up his definition, is of course a very simple proceeding—a proceeding, however, in which the first step begs the question.

92. The next argument for the apriority of Euclidean Geometry has, oddly enough, an exactly opposite bearing, although it is a great favourite with opponents of Metageometry. Measurements of stellar triangles, and all similar attempts at an empirical determination of the space-constant are, according to Lotze, beside the mark; for any observed departure from two right angles, or any finite annual parallax for distant stars, would be attributed to some new kind of refraction, or, as in the case of aberration, to some other physical cause, and never to the geometrical nature of space. This is a

7—2

strong argument for the empirical validity of Euclid, but as an argument for the apodeictic certainty of the orthodox system, it has an opposite tendency. For observations of the kind contemplated would have to be due to departures from Euclidean straightness, hitherto unknown, on the part of stellar light-rays. Such departure could, in certain cases, be accounted for by a finite space-constant, but it could also, probably, be accounted for by a change in Optics, for example, by attributing refractive properties to the ether. Such properties could only exist if ether were of varying density, if (say) it were denser in the neighbourhood of any of the heavenly bodies. But such an assumption would, I believe, destroy the utility of ether for Physics; a slight alteration in our Geometry, so slight as not appreciably to affect distances within the Solar System, would probably be in the end, therefore, should such errors ever be discovered, a simpler explanation than any that Physics could offer. But this is not the point of my contention. The point is that, if the physical explanation, as Lotze holds, be possible in the above case, the converse must also hold: it must be possible to explain the present phenomena by supposing ether refractive and space non-Euclidean. From this conclusion there is no escape. If every conceivable behaviour of light-rays can be explained, within Euclid, by physical causes, it must also be possible, by a suitable choice of hypothetical physical causes, to explain the actual phenomena as belonging to a non-Euclidean space. Such a hypothesis would be rightly rejected by Science, for the present, on account of its unnecessary complexity. Nevertheless it would remain, for philosophy, a possibility to be reckoned with, and the choice could only be decided upon empirical grounds of simplicity. It may well be doubted whether, in the world we know, the phenomena could be attributed to a distinctly non-Euclidean space, but this conclusion follows inevitably from the contention that no phenomena could force us to assume such a space. Lotze's argument, therefore, if pushed home, disproves his own view, and puts Euclidean space, as an empirical explanation of phenomena, on a level with luminiferous ether[1].

[1] Compare Calinon, "Sur l'Indétermination géométrique de l'Univers," Revue Philosophique, 1893, Vol. XXXVI. pp. 595–607.

93. Lotze now proceeds (§ 132) to a detailed criticism of Helmholtz, whom he regards as a typical exponent of Metageometry. It is possible that, at the time when he wrote, Helmholtz really did occupy this position; but it is unfortunate that, in the minds of philosophers, he should still continue to do so, after the very material advances brought about by the projective treatment of the subject. It is also unfortunate that his somewhat careless attempts to popularise mathematical results have so often been disposed of, without due attention to his more technical and solid contributions. Thus his romances about Flatland and Sphereland—at best only fairy-tale analogies of doubtful value—have been attacked as if they formed an essential feature of Metageometry.

But to proceed to particulars: Lotze readily allows that the Flatlanders would set up Plane Geometry, as we know it, but refuses to admit that the Spherelanders could, without inferring the third dimension, set up a two-dimensional spherical Geometry which should be free from contradictions. I will endeavour to give a free rendering of Lotze's argument on this point.

Suppose, he says, a north and south pole, *N* and *S*, arbitrarily fixed, and an equator *EW*. Suppose a being, *B*, capable of impressions only from things on the surface of the sphere, to move in a meridian *NBS*. Let *B* start from some point *a*, and finally, after describing a great circle, return to the same point *a*. If *a* is known only by the quality of the impression it makes on *B*, *B* may imagine he has not reached the same point *a*, but another similar point *a'*, bearing a relation to *a* similar to that of the octave in singing: he might even not arrange his impressions spatially at all. In order that this may occur, we require the further assumption, that every difference in the above-mentioned feelings (as he describes the meridian) may be presented as a spatial distance between two places. Even now, *B* may think he is describing a Euclidean straight line, containing similar points at certain intervals. Allowing, however, that he realizes the identity of *a* with his initial position,

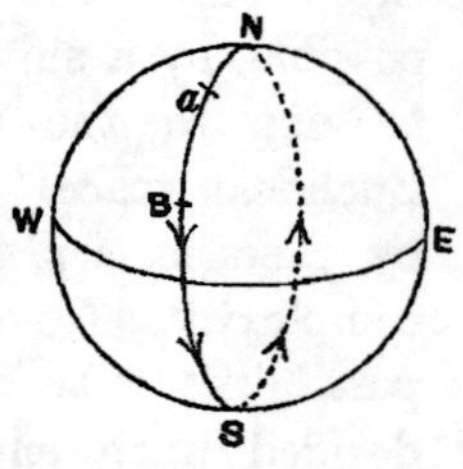

he will now seem, by motion in a straight line, to have returned to the point from which he started, for his motion cannot, without the third dimension, seem to him other than rectilinear.

Up to this point, there seems little ground for objection, except, perhaps, to the idea of a straight line with periodical similar points—if *B* were as philosophical as, in these discussions, we usually suppose him to be, he would probably object to this interpretation of his experiences, on the ground that it regards empty space as something independent of the objects in it. It is worth pointing out, also, that *B* would not need to describe the whole circle, in order suddenly to find himself home again with his old friends. Accurate measurements of small triangles would suffice to determine his space-constant, and show him the length of a great circle (or straight line, as he would call it). We must admit, also, that so hypothetical a being as *B* might form no space-intuition at all, but as he is introduced solely for the purposes of the analogy, it is convenient to allow him all possible qualifications for his post. But these points do not touch the kernel of the argument, which lies in the statement that such a straight line, returning into itself after a finite time, would appear to *B* as an "unendurable contradiction," and thus force him, for logical though not for sensational purposes, into the assumption of a third dimension. This assertion seems to me quite unwarranted: the whole of Metageometry is a solid array in disproof of it. Helmholtz's argument is, it must be remembered, only an analogy, and the contradiction would exist *only* for a Euclidean. A complete *three*-dimensional Geometry has, we have seen in Chapter I., been developed on the assumption that straight lines are of finite length. A *constant* value for the measure of curvature, as our discussion of Riemann showed, involves neither reference to the fourth dimension, nor any kind of internal contradiction. This fact disproves Lotze's contention, which arises solely from inability to divest his imagination of Euclidean ideas.

Lotze next attacks Helmholtz for the assertion that *B* would know nothing of parallel lines—parallel *straight* lines, as the context shows, he meant to say[1]. Lotze, however, takes him

[1] Vorträge und Reden, Vol. II. p. 9: "Parallele Linien würden die

as meaning, apparently, mere curves of constant distance from a given straight line, which are part of the regular stock-in-trade of Metageometry. Parallels of latitude, in the geographical sense, would not—with the exception of the equator—appear to B as straight lines, but as circles. *Great* circles he *would* call straight, and this fact seems to have misled Lotze into thinking *all* circles were to be treated as straight lines. Parallels of latitude, therefore, though B might call them parallels, would not invalidate Helmholtz's contention, which applies only to straight lines.

The argument that such small circles would be parallel, which we have just disposed of, is only the preface to another proof that B would need a third dimension. Let us call two of these parallels of latitude l_n and l_s, and let them be equidistant from the equator, one in the northern, one in the southern hemisphere. Consecutive tangent planes, along these parallels, converge, in the one case northwards, in the other southwards. Either B could become aware of their difference, says Lotze, or he could not. In the former case, which he regards as the more probable, he easily proves that B would infer a third dimension. But this alternative is, I think, wholly inadmissible. Tangent planes, like Euclidean planes in general, would have no meaning to B; unless, indeed, he were a metageometrician, which, with all his metaphysical and mathematical subtlety, the argument supposes him not to be—and to such a supposition Lotze, surely, is the last person who has a right to object. Lotze's attempted proof that this is the right alternative rests, if I understand him aright, on a sheer error in ordinary spherical Geometry. B would observe, he says, that the meridians made smaller angles with his path towards the nearer than towards the further pole—as a matter of fact, they would be simply perpendicular to his path in both directions. What Lotze means is, perhaps, that all the meridians would meet sooner in one direction than in the other, and this, of course, is true.

Bewohner der Kugel gar nicht kennen. Sie würden behaupten, dass jede beliebige zwei *geradeste* Linien, gehörig verlängert, sich schliesslich nicht nur in einem, sondern in zwei Punkten schneiden müssten." (The italics are mine.) The omission of *straight* in such phrases is a frequent laxity of mathematicians.

But the poles, in which the meridians meet, would appear to *B* as the centres of the respective parallels, while the parallels themselves would appear to be circles. Now I am at a loss to see what difficulty would arise, to *B*, in supposing two different circles to have different centres[1]. We must, therefore, take the first alternative, that *B* would have no sort of knowledge as to the direction in which the tangent planes converged. Here Lotze attempts, if I have not misunderstood him, to prove a *reductio ad absurdum*: *B* would think, he says, that he was describing two paths wholly the same in direction, and then he *might* regard both paths as circles in a plane. It may be observed that direction, when applied to a circle as a whole, is meaningless; indeed direction, in all Metageometry, can only mean, even when applied to straight lines, direction towards a point. To speak of two lines, which do not meet, as having the same direction, is a surreptitious introduction of the axiom of parallels. Apart from this, I cannot conceive any objection, on *B*'s part, to such a view—one should say *must*, not *might*. The whole argumentation, therefore, unless its obscurity has led me astray, must be pronounced fruitless and inconclusive.

94. After this preliminary discussion of Sphereland, Lotze proceeds to the question of a fourth dimension, and thence to spherical and pseudo-spherical space. As before, he appears to know only the more careless and popular utterances of Helmholtz and Riemann, and to have taken no trouble to understand even the foundations of mathematical Metageometry. By this neglect, much of what he says is rendered wholly worthless. To begin with, he regards, as the purpose of Helmholtz's fairy tale, the suggestion of a possible fourth dimension, whereas the real purpose was quite the opposite—to make intelligible a purely three-dimensional non-Euclidean space. Helmholtz introduced Flatland only because its relation to Sphereland is analogous to the relation of ours to spherical space[2]. But

[1] It has been suggested to me that Lotze regards the meridians as projected on to a plane, as in a map. If this be so, there is an obviously illegitimate introduction of the third dimension.

[2] This is proved by Helmholtz's remark at the end of a detailed attempt to make spherical and pseudo-spherical spaces imaginable (l.c. p. 28): "Anders ist es mit den drei Dimensionen des Raumes. Da alle unsere Mittel sinnlicher Anschauung sich nur auf einen Raum von drei Dimensionen erstrecken, und

Lotze says: The Flatlanders would find no difficulty in a third dimension, since it would in no way contradict their own Geometry, while the people in Sphereland, from the contradictions in their two-dimensional system, would already have been led to it. The latter contention I have already tried to answer; the former has an odd sound, in view of the attempt, a few pages later, to prove *à priori* that all forms of intuition, in any way analogous to space, *must* have three dimensions. One cannot help suspecting that the Flatlanders, with two instead of three dimensions, would make a similar attempt. But to return to Lotze's argument: Neither analogy can be used, he says, to prove that we ought perhaps to set up a fourth dimension, since, for us, no contradictions or otherwise inexplicable phenomena exist. The only people, so far as I know, who have used this analogy, are Dr Abbot and a few Spiritualists—the former in joke, the latter to explain certain phenomena more simply explained, perhaps, by Maskelyne and Cooke. But although Lotze's conclusion in this matter is sound, and one with which Helmholtz might have agreed, his arguments, to my mind, are irrelevant and unconvincing. There is this difference, he says, between us and the Spherelanders: the latter were logically forced to a new dimension, and found it possible; we are not forced to it, and find it, in our space, impossible. I have contended that, on the contrary, nothing would force the Spherelanders to assume a third dimension, while they would find it impossible exactly as we find a fourth impossible—not logically, that is to say, but only as a presentable construction in given space.

After a somewhat elephantine piece of humour, about socialistic whales in a four-dimensional sea of Fourrier's *eau sucrée*, Lotze proceeds to a proof, by logic, that every form of intuition, which embraces the whole system of ordered relations of a coexisting manifold, *must* have three dimensions. One might object, on *à priori* grounds, to any such attempt: what belongs to pure intuition could hardly, one would have

die vierte Dimension nicht bloss eine Abänderung von Vorhandenem, sondern etwas vollkommen Neues wäre, so befinden wir uns schon wegen unserer körperlichen Organisation in der absoluten Unmöglichkeit, uns eine Anschauungsweise einer vierten Dimension vorzustellen."

thought, be determined by *à priori* reasoning[1]. I will not, however, develop this argument here, but endeavour to point out, as far as its obscurity will allow, the particular fallacy of the proof in question.

Lotze's argument is as follows. In this discussion, though our terminology is necessarily taken from space, we are really concerned with a much more general conception. We assume, in order to preserve the homogeneity of dimensions, that the difference (distance) between any two elements (points) of our manifold—to borrow Riemann's word—is of the same kind as, and commensurable with, the difference between any other two elements. Let us take a series of elements at successive distances x such that the distance between any two is the sum of the distances between intermediate elements. Such a series corresponds to a straight line, which is taken as the x-axis. Then a series OY is called perpendicular to the x-axis OX,

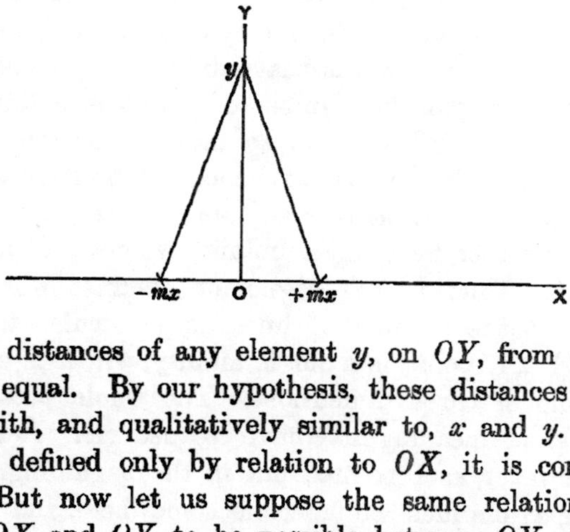

when the distances of any element y, on OY, from $+mx$ and $-mx$ are equal. By our hypothesis, these distances are comparable with, and qualitatively similar to, x and y. So long as OY is defined only by relation to OX, it is conceptually unique. But now let us suppose the same relation as that between OX and OY, to be possible between OY and a new series OZ; we then get a third series OZ, perpendicular to OY, and again conceptually unique, so long as it is defined by relation to OY alone. We might proceed, in the same way, to a fourth line OU perpendicular to OZ. But it is necessary, for our purposes, that OZ should be perpendicular to OX as well as OY. Without this condition, OZ might extend into

[1] Cf. Grassmann, Ausdehnungslehre von 1844, 2nd Edition, p. xxiii.

another world, and have no corresponding relation to *OX*—this is a possibility only excluded by our unavoidable spatial images. At this point comes the crux of the argument. *That OZ*, says Lotze, which, besides being perpendicular to *OY*, is also perpendicular to *OX*, must be among the series of *OY*'s, for these were defined only by perpendicularity to *OX*. *Hence*, he concludes, there can only be even a third dimension if *OZ* coincides with one, and—as soon as *OX* is considered fixed—with *only* one, of the many members of the *OY* series.

In this argument it is difficult—to me at any rate—to see any force at all. The only way I can account for it is, to suppose that Lotze has neglected the possibility of any but single infinities. On this interpretation, the argument might be stated thus: There is an infinite series of continuously varying *OY*'s; to the common property of these, we add another property, which will divide their total number by infinity. The remaining *OZ*, therefore, must be uniquely determined. The same form of argument, however, would prove that two surfaces can only cut one another in a single point, and numberless other absurdities. The fact is, that infinities may be of different orders. For example, the number of points in a line may be taken as a single infinity, and so may the number of lines in a plane through any point; hence, by multiplication, the number of points in a plane is a double infinity, ∞^2, and if we divide this number by a single infinity, we get still an infinite number left. Thus Lotze's argument assumes what he has to prove, that the number of lines perpendicular to a given line, through any point, is a single infinity, which is equivalent to the axiom of three dimensions. The whole passage is so obscure, that its meaning may have escaped me. It is obvious *à priori*, however, as I pointed out in the beginning, that any proof of the axiom must be fallacious somewhere, and the above interpretation of the argument is the only one I have been able to find.

95. The rest of the Chapter is devoted to an attack on spherical and pseudo-spherical space, on the ground that they interfere with the homogeneity of the three dimensions, and with the similarity of all parts of space. This is simply false. Such spaces, like the surface of a sphere, *are* exactly alike throughout. Lotze shows, here and elsewhere, that he has not taken the pains to find out what Metageometry really is. I hold myself, and have tried to prove in this Essay, that Congruence is an *à priori* axiom, without which Geometry would be impossible; but the wish to uphold this axiom is, as Lotze ought to have known, the precise motive which led Metageometry to limit itself to spaces of constant measure of curvature. We see here the importance of distinguishing between Helmholtz the philosopher and Helmholtz the mathematician. Though the philosopher wished to dispense with Congruence, the mathematician, as we saw in Chapter I., retained and strongly emphasized it. A little later Lotze shows, again, how he has been misled by the unfortunate analogy of Sphereland. A spherical *surface*, he says, he can understand; but how are we to pass from this to a spherical space? Either this surface is the whole of our space, as in Sphereland, or it generates space by a gradually growing radius. Such concentric spheres, as Lotze triumphantly points out, of course generate Euclidean space. His disjunction, however, is utterly and entirely false, and could never have been suggested by any one with even a superficial knowledge of Metageometry. This point is less laboured than the former, which, in all its nakedness, is thus re-stated in the last sentence of the Chapter: "I cannot persuade myself that one could, without the elements of homogeneous space, even form or define the presentation of heterogeneous spaces, or of such as had variable measures of curvature." As though such spaces were ever set up by non-Euclidean mathematics!

In conclusion, Lotze expresses a hope that Philosophy, on this point, will not allow itself to be imposed upon by Mathematics. I must, instead, rejoice that Mathematics has not been imposed upon by Philosophy, but has developed freely an important and self-consistent system, which deserves, for its subtle analysis into logical and factual elements, the gratitude of all who seek for a philosophy of space.

96. The objections to non-Euclidean Geometry which have just been discussed fall under four heads:

I. Non-Euclidean spaces are not homogeneous; Metageometry therefore unduly reifies space.

II. They involve a reference to a fourth dimension.

III. They cannot be set up without an implicit reference to Euclidean space, or to the Euclidean straight line, on which they are therefore dependent.

IV. They are self-contradictory in one or more ways.

The reader who has followed me in regarding these four objections as fallacious, will have no difficulty in disposing of any other critic of Metageometry, as these are the only mathematical arguments, so far as I know, ever urged against non-Euclideans[1]. The logical validity of Metageometry, and the mathematical possibility of three-dimensional non-Euclidean spaces, will therefore be regarded, throughout the remainder of the work, as sufficiently established.

97. Two other objections may, indeed, be urged against Metageometry, but these are rather of a philosophical than of a strictly mathematical import. The first of these, which has been made the base of operations by Delbœuf, applies equally to all non-Euclidean spaces. The second, which has not, so far as I know, been much employed, but yet seems to me deserving of notice, bears directly against spaces of positive curvature alone; but if it could discredit these, it might throw doubt on the method by which all alike are obtained. The two objections are:

I. Space must be such as to allow of similarity, *i.e.* of the increase or diminution, in a constant ratio, of all the lines in a figure, without change of angles; whereas in non-Euclid, lines, like angles, have absolute magnitude.

II. Space must be infinite, whereas spherical and elliptic spaces are finite.

I will discuss the first objection in connection with Delbœuf's articles referred to above. The second, which has not, to my knowledge, been widely used in criticism, will be better deferred to Chapter III.

[1] See especially Stallo, Concepts of Modern Physics, International Science Series, Vol. XLII. Chaps. XIII. and XIV.; Renouvier, "Philosophie de la règle et du compas," Année Philosophique, II.; Delbœuf, "L'ancienne et les nouvelles géométries," Revue Philosophique, Vols. XXXVI.–XXXIX.

Delbœuf.

98. M. Delbœuf's four articles in the Revue Philosophique contain much matter that has already been dealt with in the criticism of Lotze, and much that is irrelevant for our present purpose. The only point, which I wish to discuss here, is the question of absolute magnitude, as it is called—the question, that is, whether the possibility of similar but unequal geometrical figures can be known *à priori*[1].

In discussing this question, it is important, to begin with, to distinguish clearly the sense in which absolute magnitude *is* required in non-Euclidean Geometry, from another sense, in which it would be absurd to regard any magnitude as absolute. Judgments of magnitude can only result from comparison, and if Metageometry required magnitudes which could be determined without comparison, it would certainly deserve condemnation. But this is not required. All we require is, that it shall be impossible, while the rest of space is unaffected, to alter the magnitude of any figure, as compared with other figures, while leaving the relative internal magnitudes of its parts unchanged. This construction, which is possible in Euclid, is impossible in Metageometry. We have to discuss whether such an impossibility renders non-Euclidean spaces logically faulty.

M. Delbœuf's position on this axiom—which he calls the postulate of homogeneity[2]—is, that all Geometry must presuppose it, and that Metageometry, consequently, though logically sound, is logically subsequent to Euclid, and can only make its constructions within a Euclidean "homogeneous" space (Rev. Phil. Vol. XXXVII., pp. 380–1). He would appear to think, nevertheless, that homogeneity (in his sense) is learnt from experience, though on this point he is not very explicit. (See Vol. XXXVIII., p. 129.) No *à priori* proof, at any rate, is offered

[1] M. Delbœuf deserves credit for having based Euclid, already in 1860, in his "Prolégomènes Philosophiques de la Géométrie," on this axiom—certainly a better basis, at first sight, than the axiom of parallels.

[2] This meaning of homogeneity must not be confounded with the sense in which I have used the word. In Delbœuf's sense, it means that figures may be similar though of different sizes; in my sense it means that figures may be similar though in different places. This property of space is called by Delbœuf isogeneity.

in his articles. As a result of experience, every one would admit, similarity is known to be possible within the limits of observation; but the fact that this possibility extends to Ordnance maps, which deal with a spherical surface, should make us chary of inferring, from such a datum, the certainty of Euclid for large spaces. Moreover if homogeneity be empirical, Metageometry, which dispenses with it, is not necessarily in *logical* dependence upon Euclid, since homogeneity and isogeneity are *logically* separable. I shall assume, therefore, as the only contention which can be interesting to our argument, that homogeneity is regarded as *à priori*, and as logically essential to Geometry.

99. Now we saw, in discussing Erdmann's views of the judgment of quantity, that in non-Euclidean space, as in Euclidean, a change of all spatial magnitudes, in the same ratio, would be no change at all; the ratios of all magnitudes to the space-constant would be unchanged, and the space-constant, as the ultimate standard of comparison, cannot, in any intelligible sense, be said to have any particular magnitude. The absolute magnitudes of Metageometry, therefore, are absolute only as against any other *particular* magnitude, not as against other magnitudes in general. If this were not the case, the comparative nature of the judgment of magnitude would be contradicted, and metrical Metageometry would become absurd. But as it is, the difference from Euclid consists only in this: that in Metageometry we have, while in Euclid we have not, a standard of comparison involved in the nature of our space as a whole, which we call the space-constant. We have to discuss whether the assertion of such a standard involves an undue reification of space.

I do not believe that this is the case. For an undue reification of space would only arise, if we were no longer able to regard position as wholly relative, and as geometrically definable only by departure from other positions. But the relativity of position, as we have abundantly seen, is preserved by all spaces of constant curvature—in all of these, positions can only be defined, geometrically, by relations to fresh positions[1]. This series of definitions may lead to an infinite regress, but it may

[1] For a full proof of this proposition, see Chap. III.

also, as in spherical space, form a vicious circle, and return again to the position from which it started. No reification of space, no independent existence of mere relations, seems involved in such a procedure. The whole of Metageometry, in short, is a proof that the relativity of position is compatible with absolute magnitude, in the only sense required by non-Euclidean spaces. We must conclude, therefore, that there is nothing incompatible, in a denial of homogeneity (in Delbœuf's sense), either with the relational nature of space, or with the comparative nature of magnitude. This last *à priori* objection to Metageometry, therefore, cannot be maintained, and the issue must be decided on empirical grounds alone.

100. The foundations of Geometry have been the subject of much recent speculation in France, and this seems to demand some notice. But in spite of the splendid work which the French have done on the allied question of number and continuous quantity, I cannot persuade myself that they have succeeded in greatly advancing the subject of geometrical philosophy. The chief writers have been, from the mathematical side, *Calinon* and *Poincaré*, from the philosophical, *Renouvier* and *Delbœuf*; as a mediator between mathematics and philosophy, *Lechalas*.

Calinon, in an interesting article on the geometrical indeterminateness of the universe, maintains that any Geometry may be applied to the actual world by a suitable hypothesis as to the course of light-rays. For the earth only is known to us otherwise than by Optics, and the earth is an infinitesimal part of the universe. This line of argument has been already discussed in connection with Lotze, but Calinon adds a new suggestion, that the space-constant may perhaps vary with the time. This would involve a causal connection between space and other things, which seems hardly conceivable, and which, if regarded as possible, must surely destroy Geometry, since Geometry depends throughout on the irrelevance of Causation[1]. Moreover, in all operations of measurement, some time is spent; unless we knew that space was unchanging throughout the operation, it is hard to see how our results could be trustworthy, and how, consequently, a change in the parameter could be

[1] See Chap. III., especially § 133.

discovered. The same difficulties would arise, in fact, as those which result from supposing space not homogeneous.

Poincaré maintains that the question, whether Euclid or Metageometry should be accepted, is one of convenience and convention, not of truth; axioms are definitions in disguise, and the choice between definitions is arbitrary. This view has been discussed in Chapter I., in connection with Cayley's theory of distance, on which it depends.

Lechalas is a philosophical disciple of Calinon. He is a rationalist of the pre-Kantian type, but a believer in the validity of Metageometry. He holds that Geometry can dispense with all purely spatial postulates, and work with axioms of magnitude alone[1], which, in his opinion, are purely analytic. The principle of contradiction, to him, is the sole and only test of truth; we make long chains of reasoning from our premisses to see if contradictions will emerge. It might be objected that this view, though it saves general Geometry from being logically empirical, leaves it only empirically logical; this must, in fact, be the fate of every piece of *à priori* knowledge, if M. Lechalas's were the only test of truth. However, he concludes that general Geometry is apodeictic, while the space of our actual world, like all other phenomena, is contingent.

Delbœuf criticizes non-Euclidean space from an ultra-realist standpoint: he holds that *real* space is neither homogeneous nor isogeneous, but that *conceived* space, as abstracted from real space, has both these properties. He offers no justification for his real space, which seems to be maintained in the spirit of naïve realism, nor does he show how he has acquired his intimate knowledge of its constitution[2]. His arguments against Metageometry, in so far as they are not repetitions of Lotze, have been discussed above.

Renouvier, finally, is a pure Kantian, of the most orthodox type. His views as to the importance, for Geometry, of the distinction between synthetic and analytic judgments, have

[1] For a criticism of this view, see the above discussions on Riemann and Erdmann.

[2] Cf. Couturat, "De l'Infini Mathématique," Paris, Félix Alcan, 1896, p. 544.

been discussed, in connection with Kant, at the beginning of the present Chapter[1].

101. Before beginning the constructive argument of the next Chapter, let us endeavour briefly to sum up the theories which have been polemically advocated throughout the criticisms we have just concluded. We agreed to accept, with Kant, necessity for any possible experience as the test of the *à priori*, but

[1] The following is a list of the most important recent French philosophical writings on Geometry, so far as I am acquainted with them.

Andrade: "Les bases expérimentales de la géométrie euclidienne"; Rev. Phil. 1890, II., and 1891, I.

Bonnel: "Les hypothèses dans la géométrie"; Gauthier-Villars, 1897.

L'Abbé de Broglie: "La géométrie non-euclidienne," two articles; Annales de Phil. Chrét. 1890.

Calinon: "Les espaces géométriques"; Rev. Phil. 1889, I., and 1891, II.
"Sur l'indétermination géométrique de l'univers"; ib. 1893, II.

Couturat: "L'Année Philosophique de F. Pillon," Rev. de Mét. et de Morale, Jan. 1893.
"Note sur la géométrie non-euclidienne et la relativité de l'espace"; ib., May, 1893.
"Études sur l'espace et le temps," ib. Sep. 1896.

Delbœuf: "L'ancienne et les nouvelles géométries," four articles; Rev. Phil. 1893—5.

Lechalas: "La géométrie générale"; Crit. Phil. 1889.
"La géométrie générale et les jugements synthétiques à priori" and "Les bases expérimentales de la géométrie"; Rev. Phil. 1890, II.
"M. Delbœuf et Le problème des mondes semblables"; ib. 1894, I.
"Note sur la géométrie non-euclidienne et le principe de similitude"; Rev. de Mét. et de Morale, March, 1893.
"La courbure et la distance en géométrie générale"; ib., March, 1896.
"La géométrie générale et l'intuition"; Annales de Phil. Chrét., 1890.
"Étude sur l'espace et le temps"; Paris, Alcan, 1896.

Liard: "Des définitions géométriques et des définitions empiriques," 2nd ed.; Paris, Alcan, 1888.

Mansion: "Premiers principes de la métagéométrie"; two articles in Rev. Néo-Scholastique, 1896. Separately published, Gauthier-Villars, 1896.

Milhaud: "La géométrie non-euclidienne et la théorie de la connaissance"; Rev. Phil. 1888, I.

Poincaré: "Non-Euclidian Geometry"; Nature, Vol. XLV., 1891—2.
"L'espace et la géométrie"; Rev. de Mét. et de Morale, Nov. 1895.
"Réponse à quelques critiques," ib. Jan. 1897.

Renouvier: "Philosophie de la règle et du compas"; Crit. Phil., 1889, and L'Année Phil., IIme année, 1891.

Sorel: "Sur la géométrie non-euclidienne"; Rev. Phil., 1891, I.

Tannery: "Théorie de la connaissance mathématique"; Rev. Phil., 1894, II.

we refused, for the present, to discuss the connection of the *à priori* with the subjective, regarding the purely logical test as sufficient for our immediate purpose. We also refused to attach importance to the distinction of analytic and synthetic, since it seemed to apply, not to different judgments, but only to different aspects of any judgment.

We then discussed Riemann's attempt to identify the empirical element in Geometry with the element not deducible from ideas of magnitude, and we decided that this identification was due to a confusion as to the nature of magnitude. For judgments of magnitude, we said, require always some qualitative basis, which is not quantitatively expressible.

In criticizing Helmholtz, we decided that Mechanics logically presupposes Geometry, though space presupposes matter; but that the matter which space presupposes, and to which Geometry indirectly refers, is a more abstract matter than that of Mechanics, a matter destitute of force and of causal attributes, and possessed only of the purely spatial attributes required for the possibility of spatial figures. But we conceded that Geometry, when applied to mixed mathematics or to daily life, demands more than this, demands, in fact, some means of discovering, in the more concrete matter of Mechanics, either a rigid body, or a body whose departure from rigidity follows some empirically discoverable law. *Actual* measurement, therefore, we agreed to regard as empirical.

Our conclusions, as regards the empiricism of Riemann and Helmholtz, were reinforced by a criticism of Erdmann. We then had an opposite task to perform, in defending Metageometry against Lotze. Here we saw that there are two senses in which Metageometry is possible. The first concerns our actual space, and asserts that it may have a very small space-constant; the second concerns philosophical theories of space, and asserts a purely logical possibility, which leaves the decision to experience. We saw also that Lotze's mathematical strictures arose from insufficient knowledge of the subject, and could all be refuted by a better acquaintance with Metageometry.

Finally, we discussed the question of absolute magnitude, and found in it no logical obstacle to non-Euclidean spaces. Our conclusion, then, in so far as we are as yet entitled to a conclusion, is that all spaces with a space-constant are *à priori* justifiable, and that the decision between them must be the work of experience. Spaces without a space-constant, on the other hand, spaces, that is, which are not homogeneous throughout, we found logically unsound and impossible to know, and therefore to be condemned *à priori*. The constructive proof of this thesis will form the argument of the following chapter.

CHAPTER III.

Section A.

THE AXIOMS OF PROJECTIVE GEOMETRY.

102. PROJECTIVE Geometry proper, as we saw in Chapter I., does not employ the conception of magnitude, and does not, therefore, require those axioms which, in the systems of the second or metrical period, were required solely to render possible the application of magnitude to space. But we saw, also, that Cayley's reduction of metrical to projective properties was purely technical and philosophically irrelevant. Now it is in metrical properties alone—apart from the exception to the axiom of the straight line, which itself, however, presupposes metrical properties[1]—that non-Euclidean and Euclidean spaces differ. The properties dealt with by projective Geometry, therefore, in so far as these are obtained without the use of imaginaries, are properties common to all spaces. Finally, the differences which appear between the Geometries of different spaces of the same curvature—*e.g.* between the Geometries of the plane and the cylinder—are differences in projective properties[2]. Thus the necessity which arises, in metrical Geometry, for further qualifications besides those of constant curvature, disappears when our general space is defined by purely projective properties.

103. We have good ground for expecting, therefore, that the axioms of projective Geometry will be the simplest and most complete expression of the indispensable requisites of

[1] See infra, Axiom of Distance, in Sec. B. of this Chapter.

[2] Thus on a cylinder, two geodesics, *e.g.* a generator and a helix, may have any number of intersections—a very important difference from the plane.

any geometrical reasoning: and this expectation, I hope, will not be disappointed. Projective Geometry, in so far as it deals only with the properties common to all spaces, will be found, if I am not mistaken, to be wholly *à priori*, to take nothing from experience, and to have, like Arithmetic, a creature of the pure intellect for its object. If this be so, it is that branch of pure mathematics which Grassmann, in his *Ausdehnungslehre* of 1844, felt to be possible, and endeavoured, in a brilliant failure, to construct without any appeal to the space of intuition.

104. But unfortunately, the task of discovering the axioms of projective Geometry is far from easy. They have, as yet, found no Riemann or Helmholtz to formulate them philosophically. Many geometers have constructed systems, which they intended to be, and which, with sufficient care in interpretation, really are, free from metrical presuppositions. But these presuppositions are so rooted in all the very elements of Geometry, that the task of eliminating them demands a reconstruction of the whole geometrical edifice. Thus Euclid, for example, deals, from the start, with spatial equality—he employs the circle, which is necessarily defined by means of equality, and he bases all his later propositions on the congruence of triangles as discussed in Book I.[1] Before we can use any elementary proposition of Euclid, therefore, even if this expresses a projective property, we have to prove that the property in question can be deduced by projective methods. This has not, in general, been done by projective geometers, who have too often assumed, for example, that the quadrilateral construction—by which, as we saw in Chap. I., they introduce projective coordinates—or anharmonic ratio, which is *primâ facie* metrical, could be satisfactorily established on their principles. Both these assumptions, however, can be justified, and we may admit, therefore, that the claims of projective Geometry to logical independence of measurement or congruence are valid. Let us see, then, how it proceeds.

105. In the first place, it is important to realize that

[1] Cf. Cremona, Projective Geometry (Clarendon Press, 2nd ed. 1893) p. 50: "Most of the propositions in Euclid's Elements are metrical, and it is not easy to find among them an example of a purely descriptive theorem."

when coordinates are used, in projective Geometry, they are not coordinates in the ordinary metrical sense, *i.e.* the numerical measures of certain spatial magnitudes. On the contrary, they are a set of numbers, arbitrarily but systematically assigned to different points, like the numbers of houses in a street, and serving only, from a philosophical standpoint, as convenient designations for points which the investigation wishes to distinguish. But for the brevity of the alphabet, in fact, they might, as in Euclid, be replaced by letters. How they are introduced, and what they mean, has been discussed in Chapter I. Here we have only to repeat a caution, whose neglect has led to much misunderstanding.

106. The distinction between various points, then, is not a result, but a condition, of the projective coordinate system. The coordinate system is a wholly extraneous, and merely convenient, set of marks, which in no way touches the essence of projective Geometry. What we must begin with, in this domain, is the possibility of distinguishing various points from one another. This may be designated, with Veronese, as the first axiom of Geometry[1]. How we are to define a point, and how we distinguish it from other points, is for the moment irrelevant; for here we only wish to discover the nature of projective Geometry, and the kind of properties which it uses and demonstrates. How, and with what justification, it uses and demonstrates them, we will discuss later.

107. Now it is obvious that a mere collection of points, distinguished one from another, cannot found a Geometry: we must have some idea of the manner in which the points are interrelated, in order to have an adequate subject-matter for discussion. But since all ideas of quantity are excluded, the relations of points cannot be relations of distance in the ordinary sense, nor even, in the sense of ordinary Geometry, anharmonic ratios, for anharmonic ratios are usually defined as the ratios of four distances, or of four sines, and are thus quantitative. But since all quantitative comparison presupposes an identity of quality, we may expect to find, in projective Geometry, the qualitative substrata of the metrical superstructure.

And this, we shall see, is actually the case. We have not

[1] Op. cit. p. 226.

distance, but we *have* the straight line; we have not quantitative anharmonic ratio, but we *have* the property, in any four points on a line, of being the intersections with the rays of a given pencil. And from this basis, we can build up a qualitative science of abstract externality, which is projective Geometry. How this happens, I shall now proceed to show.

108. All geometrical reasoning is, in the last resort, circular: if we start by assuming points, they can only be defined by the lines or planes which relate them; and if we start by assuming lines or planes, they can only be defined by the points through which they pass. This is an inevitable circle, whose ground of necessity will appear as we proceed. It is, therefore, somewhat arbitrary to start either with points or with lines, as the eminently projective principle of duality mathematically illustrates; nevertheless we will elect, with most geometers, to start with points[1]. We suppose, therefore, as our datum, a set of discrete points, for the moment without regard to their interconnections. But since connections are essential to any reasoning about them as a system, we introduce, to begin with, the axiom of the straight line. Any two of our points, we say, lie on a line which those two points completely define. This line, being determined by the two points, may be regarded as a relation of the two points, or an adjective of the system formed by both together. This is the only purely qualitative adjective—as will be proved later—of a system of two points. Now projective Geometry can only take account of qualitative adjectives, and can distinguish between different points only by their relations to other points, since all points, *per se*, are qualitatively similar. Hence it comes that, for projective Geometry, when two points only are given, they are qualitatively indistinguishable from any two other points on the same straight line, since any two such other points have the same qualitative relation. Reciprocally, since one straight line is a figure determined by any two of its points, and all points are qualitatively similar, it follows that all straight lines are qualitatively similar. We may regard a point, therefore, as determined by two straight lines which meet in it, and the

[1] Some ground for this choice will appear when we come to metrical Geometry.

point, on this view, becomes the only qualitative relation between the two straight lines. Hence, if the point only be regarded as given, the two straight lines are qualitatively indistinguishable from any other pair through the point.

109. The extension of these two reciprocal principles is the essence of all projective transformations, and indeed of all projective Geometry. The fundamental operations, by which figures are projectively transformed, are called projection and section. The various forms of projection and section are defined in Cremona's "Projective Geometry," Chapter I., from which I quote the following account.

"*To project from a fixed point S* (the *centre of projection*) a figure (*ABCD...abcd...*) composed of points and straight lines, is to construct the straight lines or *projecting rays SA, SB, SC, SD*,...and the planes (*projecting planes*) *Sa, Sb, Sc, Sd*,.... We thus obtain a new figure composed of straight lines and planes which all pass through the centre *S*.

"*To cut by a fixed plane σ* (*transversal plane*) a figure ($\alpha\beta\gamma\delta$ ...*abcd*...) made up of planes and straight lines, is to construct the straight lines or *traces* $\sigma\alpha$, $\sigma\beta$, $\sigma\gamma$... and the points or *traces* σa, σb, σc...[1]. By this means we obtain a new figure composed of straight lines and points lying in the plane σ.

"*To project from a fixed straight line s* (the *axis*) a figure *ABCD* composed of points, is to construct the planes *sA, sB, sC*.... The figure thus obtained is composed of planes which all pass through the axis *s*.

"*To cut by a fixed straight line s* (a *transversal*) a figure $\alpha\beta\gamma\delta$... composed of planes, is to construct the points $s\alpha$, $s\beta$, $s\gamma$.... In this way a new figure is obtained, composed of points all lying on the fixed transversal *s*.

"If a figure is composed of straight lines *a, b, c*... which all pass through a fixed point or *centre S*, it can be *projected* from a straight line or *axis s* passing through *S*; the result is a figure composed of planes *sa, sb, sc*....

"If a figure is composed of straight lines *a, b, c*... all lying in a fixed plane, it may be cut by a straight line (transversal)

[1] The straight line $\sigma\alpha$ denotes the straight line common to the planes σ and α, the point σa denotes the point common to the plane σ and the straight line a, and similarly for the rest of the notation.

s lying in the same plane; the figure which results is formed by the points *sa*, *sb*, *sc*...."

110. The successive application, to any figure, of two reciprocal operations of projection and section, is regarded as producing a figure projectively indistinguishable from the first, provided only that the dimensions of the original figure were the same as those of the resulting figure, that, for example, if the second operation be section by a plane, the original figure shall have been a plane figure. The figures obtained from a given figure, by projection or section alone, are related to that figure by the principle of duality, of which we shall have to speak later on.

I shall endeavour to show, in what follows, first, in what sense figures obtained from each other by projective transformation are qualitatively alike; secondly, what axioms, or adjectives of space, are involved in the principle of projective transformation; and thirdly, that these adjectives must belong to any form of externality with more than one dimension, and are, therefore, *à priori* properties of any possible space.

For the sake of simplicity, I shall in general confine myself to two dimensions. In so doing, I shall introduce no important difference of principle, and shall greatly simplify the mathematics involved.

111. The two mathematically fundamental things in projective Geometry are anharmonic ratio, and the quadrilateral construction. Everything else follows mathematically from these two. Now what is meant, in projective Geometry, by anharmonic ratio?

If we start from anharmonic ratio as ordinarily defined, we are met by the difficulty of its quantitative nature[1]. But among the properties deduced from this definition, many, if not most, are purely qualitative. The most fundamental of these is that, if through any four points in a straight line we draw four straight lines which meet in a point, and if we then draw a new straight line meeting these four, the four new

[1] Cremona (op. cit. Chap. IX. p. 50) defines anharmonic ratio as a metrical property which is unaltered by projection. This, however, destroys the logical independence of projective Geometry, which can only be maintained by a purely descriptive definition.

points of intersection have the same anharmonic ratio as the four points we started with. Thus, in the figure, *abcd*, *a′b′c′d′*, *a″b″c″d″*, all have the same anharmonic ratio. The reciprocal

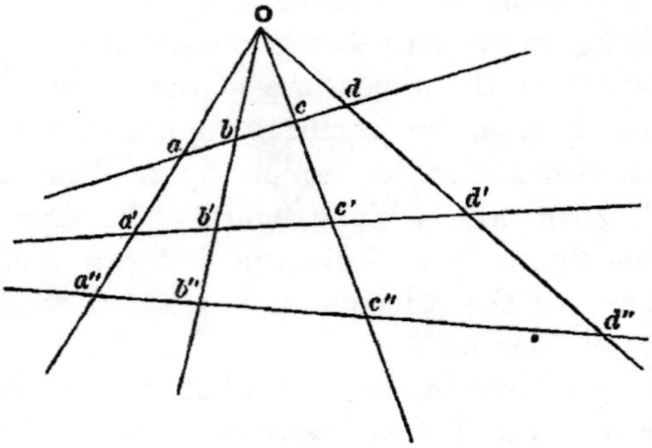

relation holds for the anharmonic ratio of four straight lines. Here we have, plainly, the required basis for a qualitative definition. The definition must be as follows:

Two sets of four points each are defined as having the same anharmonic ratio, when (1) each set of four lies in one straight line, and (2) corresponding points of different sets lie two by two on four straight lines through a single point, or when both sets have this relation to any third set[1]. And reciprocally: Two sets of four straight lines are defined as having the same anharmonic ratio when (1) each set of four passes through a single point, and (2) corresponding lines of different sets pass, two by two, through four points in one straight line, or when both sets have this relation to any third set.

Two sets of points or of lines, which have the same anharmonic ratio, are treated by projective Geometry as equivalent: this qualitative equivalence replaces the quantitative equality of metrical Geometry, and is obviously included, by its definition, in the above account of projective transformations in general.

112. We have next to consider the quadrilateral con-

[1] There is no corresponding property of *three* points on a line, because they can be projectively transformed into any other three points on the same line. See § 120.

struction[1]. This has a double purpose: first, to define the important special case known as a harmonic range; and secondly, to afford an unambiguous and exhaustive method of assigning different numbers to different points. This last method has, again, a double purpose: first, the purpose of giving a convenient symbolism for describing and distinguishing different points, and of thus affording a means for the introduction of analysis; and secondly, of so assigning these numbers that, if they had the ordinary metrical significance, as distances from some point on the numbered straight line, they would yield -1 as the anharmonic ratio of a harmonic range, and that, if four points have the same anharmonic ratio as four others, so have the corresponding numbers. This last purpose is due to purely technical motives: it avoids the confusion with our preconceptions which would result from any other value for a harmonic range; it allows us, when metrical interpretations of projective results are desired, to make these interpretations without tedious numerical transformations, and it enables us to perform projective transformations by algebraical methods. At the same time, from the strictly projective point of view, as observed above, the numbers introduced have a purely conventional meaning; and until we pass to metrical Geometry, no reason can be shown for assigning the value -1 to a harmonic range. With this preliminary, let us see in what the quadrilateral construction consists.

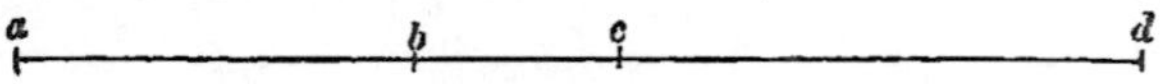

113. A harmonic range, in elementary Geometry, is one whose anharmonic ratio is -1, or one in which the three segments formed by the four points are in harmonic progression, or again, one in which the ratio of the two internal segments is equal to the ratio of the two external segments. If a, b, c, d be the four points, it is easily seen that these definitions are equivalent to one another: they give respectively:

$$\frac{ab}{bc}\Big/\frac{ad}{dc}=-1,\quad \frac{1}{ab}-\frac{1}{ac}=\frac{1}{ac}-\frac{1}{ad},\ \text{and}\ \frac{ab}{bc}=\frac{ad}{cd}.$$

[1] Due to v. Staudt's "Geometrie der Lage."

But as they are all quantitative, they cannot be used for our present purpose. Nor are any definitions which involve bisection of lines or angles available. We must have a definition which proceeds entirely by the help of straight lines and points, without measurement of distances or angles. Now from the above definitions of a harmonic range, we see that *a, b, c, d* have the same anharmonic ratio as *c, b, a, d*. This gives us the property we require for our definition. For it shows that, in a harmonic range, we can find a projective transformation which will interchange *a* and *c*. This is a necessary and sufficient condition for a harmonic range, and the quadrilateral construction is the general method for giving effect to it.

Given any three points *A, B, D* in one straight line, the quadrilateral construction finds the point *C* harmonic to *A* with respect to *B, D* by the following method: Take any point *O* outside the straight line *ABD*, and join it to *B* and *D*. Through *A* draw any straight line cutting *OD, OB* in *P* and *Q*.

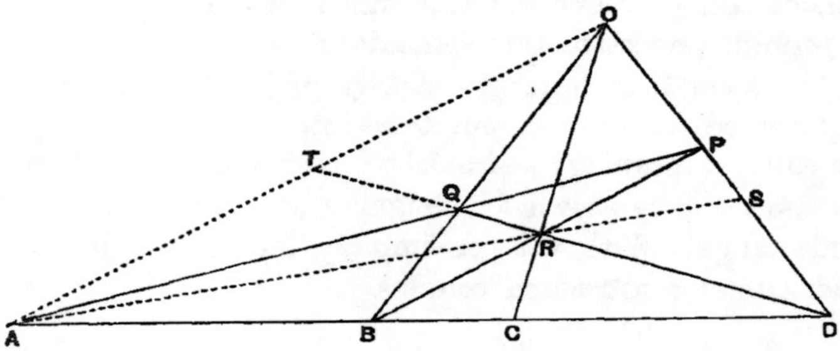

Join *DQ, BP*, and let them intersect in *R*. Join *OR*, and let *OR* meet *ABD* in *C*. Then *C* is the point required.

To prove this, let *DRQ* meet *OA* in *T*, and draw *AR*, meeting *OD* in *S*. Then a projective transformation of *A, B, C, D* from *R* on to *OD* gives the points *S, P, O, D*, which, projected from *A* on to *DQ*, give *R, Q, T, D*. But these again, projected from *O* on to *ABD*, give *C, B, A, D*. Hence *A, B, C, D* can be projectively transformed into *C, B, A, D*, and therefore form a harmonic range. From this point, the proof that the construction is unique and general follows simply[1].

[1] See Cremona, op. cit. Chapter VIII.

The introduction of numbers, by this construction, offers no difficulties of principle—except, indeed, those which always attend the application of number to continua—and may be studied satisfactorily in Klein's Nicht-Euklid (I. p. 337 ff.). The principle of it is, to assign the numbers 0, 1, ∞ to A, B, D and therefore the number 2 to C, in order that the differences AB, AC, AD may be in harmonic progression. By taking B, C, D as a new triad corresponding to A, B, D, we find a point harmonic to B with respect to C, D and assign to it the number 3, and so on. In this way, we can obtain any number of points, and we are sure of having no number and no point twice over, so that our coordinates have the essential property of a unique correspondence with the points they denote, and *vice versa.*

114. The point of importance in the above construction, however, and the reason why I have reproduced it in detail, is that it proceeds entirely by means of the general principles of transformation enunciated above. From this stage onwards, everything is effected by means of the two fundamental ideas we have just discussed, and everything, therefore, depends on our general principle of projective equivalence. This principle, as regards two dimensions, may be stated more simply than in the passage quoted from Cremona. It starts, in two dimensions, from the following definitions:

To project the points $A, B, C, D\ldots$ from a centre O, is to construct the straight lines OA, OB, OC, $OD\ldots$.

To cut a number of straight lines $a, b, c, d\ldots$ by a transversal s, is to construct the points sa, sb, sc, $sd\ldots$[1].

The successive application of these two operations, provided the original figure consisted of points on one straight line or of straight lines through one point, gives a figure projectively indistinguishable from the former figure; and hence, by extension, if any points in one straight line in the original figure lie in one straight line in the derived figure, and reciprocally for straight lines through points, the two operations have given projectively similar figures. This general principle may be regarded as consisting of two parts, according to the order of the operations: if we begin with projection and end with

[1] The corresponding definitions, for the two-dimensional manifold of lines through a point, follow by the principle of duality.

section, we transform a figure of points into another figure of points; by the converse order, we transform a figure of lines into another figure of lines.

115. Before we can be clear as to the meaning of our principle, we must have some notion as to our definition of points and straight lines. But this definition, in projective Geometry, cannot be given without some discussion of the principle of duality, the mathematical form of the philosophical circle involved in geometrical definitions.

Confining ourselves for the moment to two dimensions, the principle asserts, roughly speaking, that any theorem, dealing with lines through a point and points on a line, remains true if these two terms, wherever they occur, are interchanged. Thus: two points lie on one straight line which they completely determine; and two straight lines meet in one point, which they completely determine. The four points of intersection of a transversal with four lines through a point have an anharmonic ratio independent of the particular transversal; and the four lines joining four points on one straight line to a fifth point have an anharmonic ratio independent of that fifth point. So also our general principle of projective transformation has two sides: one in which points move along fixed lines, and one in which lines turn about fixed points.

This duality suggests that any definition of points must be effected by means of the straight line, and any definition of the straight line must be effected by means of points. When we take the third dimension into account, it is true, the duality is no longer so simple; we have now to take account also of the plane, but this only introduces a circle of three terms, which is scarcely preferable to a circle of two terms. We now say: Three points, or a line and a point, determine a plane: but conversely, three planes, or a line and plane, determine a point. We may regard the straight line as a relation between two of its points, but we may also regard the point as a relation between two straight lines through it. We may regard the plane as a relation between three points, or between a point and a line, but we may also regard the point as a relation between three planes, or between a line and a plane, which meet in it.

116. How are we to get outside this circle? The fact is that, in pure Geometry, we cannot get outside it. For space, as we shall see more fully hereafter, is nothing but relations; if, therefore, we take any spatial figure, and seek for the terms between which it is a relation, we are compelled, in Geometry, to seek these terms within space, since we have nowhere else to seek them, but we are doomed, since anything purely spatial is a mere relation, to find our terms melting away as we grasp them.

Thus the relativity of space, while it is the essence of the principle of duality, at the same time renders impossible the expression of that principle, or of any other principle of pure Geometry, in a manner which shall be free from contradictions. Nevertheless, if we are to advance at all with our analysis of geometrical reasoning and with our definitions of lines and points, we must, for a while, ignore this contradiction; we must argue as though it did not exist, so as to free our science from any contradictions which are not inevitable.

117. In accordance with this procedure, then, let us define our points as the terms of spatial relations, regarding whatever is not a point as a relation between points. What, on this view, must our points be taken to be? Obviously, if extension is mere relativity, they must be taken to contain no extension; but if they are to supply the terms for spatial relations, *e.g.* for straight lines, these relations must exhibit them as the terms of the figures they relate. In other words, since what can really be taken, without contradiction, as the term of a spatial relation, is unextended, we must take, as the term to be used in Geometry, where we cannot go outside space, the least spatial thing which Geometry can deal with, the thing which, though *in* space, *contains* no space; and this thing we define as the point[1].

Neglecting, then, the fundamental contradiction in this definition, the rest of our definitions follow without difficulty.

[1] It is important to observe that this definition of the Point introduces metrical ideas. Without metrical ideas, we saw, nothing appears to give the Point precedence of the straight line, or indeed to distinguish it conceptually from the straight line. A reference to quantity is therefore inevitable in defining the Point, if the definition is to be geometrical. A non-metrical definition would have to be also non-geometrical. See Chap. IV. §§ 196–199.

The straight line is the relation between two points, and the plane is the relation between three. These definitions will be argued and defended at length in section B of this Chapter[1], where we can discuss at the same time the alternative metrical definitions; for our present purpose, it is sufficient to observe that projective Geometry, from the first, regards the straight line as determined by two points, and the plane as determined by three, from which it follows, if we take points as possible terms for spatial relations, that the straight line and the plane may be regarded as relations between two and three points respectively. If we agree on these definitions, we can proceed to discuss the fundamental principle of projective Geometry, and to analyse the axioms implicated in its truth.

118. Projective Geometry, we have seen, does not deal with quantity, and therefore recognizes no difference where the difference is purely quantitative. Now quantitative comparison depends on a recognized identity of quality; the recognition of qualitative identity, therefore, is logically prior to quantity, and presupposed by every judgment of quantity. Hence all figures, whose differences can be exhaustively described by quantity, *i.e.* by pure measurement, must have an identity of quality, and this must be recognizable without appeal to quantity. It follows that, by defining the word quality in geometrical matters, we shall discover what sets of figures are projectively indiscernible. If our definition is correct, it ought to yield the general projective principle with which we set out.

119. We agreed to regard points as the terms of spatial relations, and we agreed that different points could be distinguished. But we postponed the discussion of the conditions under which this distinction could be effected. This discussion will yield us the definition of quality and the proof of our general projective principle.

Points, to begin with, have been defined as nothing but the terms for spatial relations. They have, therefore, no intrinsic properties; but are distinguished solely by means of their relations. Now the relation between two points, we said,

[1] §§ 163–175.

is the straight line on which they lie. This gives that identity of quality for all pairs of points on the same straight line, which is required both by our projective principle and by metrical Geometry. (For only where there is identity of quality can quantity be properly applied.) If only two points are given, they cannot, without the use of quantity, be distinguished from any two other points on the same straight line; for the qualitative relation between any two such points is the same as for the original pair, and only by a difference of relation can points be distinguished from one another.

But conversely, one straight line is nothing but the relation between two of its points, and all points are qualitatively alike. Hence there can be nothing to distinguish one straight line from another except the points through which it passes, and these are distinguished from other points only by the fact that it passes through them. Thus we get the reciprocal transformation: if we are given only one point, any pair of straight lines through that point is qualitatively indistinguishable from any other. This again is, on the one hand, the basis of the second part of our general projective principle, and on the other hand the condition of applying quantity, in the measurement of angles, to the departure of two intersecting straight lines.

120. We can now see the reason for what may have hitherto seemed a somewhat arbitrary fact, namely, the necessity of *four* collinear points for anharmonic ratio. Recurring to the quadrilateral construction and the consequent introduction of number, we see that anharmonic ratio is an intrinsic projective relation of four collinear points or concurrent straight lines, such that given three terms and the relation, the fourth term can be uniquely determined by projective methods. Now consider first a pair of points. Since all straight lines are projectively equivalent, the relation between one pair of points is precisely equivalent to that between another pair. Given one point only, therefore, no projective relation, to any second point, can be assigned, which shall in any way limit our choice of the second point. Given two points, however, there is such a relation—the third point may be given collinear with the first two. This limits its position to one straight line, but since two points determine nothing but one straight line, the third point cannot be further limited. Thus we see why no intrinsic projective relation can be found between three points, which shall enable us, from two, uniquely to determine the third. With three given collinear points, however, we have more given than a mere straight line, and the quadrilateral construction enables us uniquely to determine any number of fresh collinear points. This shows why anharmonic ratio must be a relation between four points, rather than between three.

121. We can now prove, I think, that two figures, which are projectively related, are qualitatively similar. Let us begin with a collection of points on a straight line. So long as these are considered without reference to other points or figures, they are all qualitatively similar. They can be distinguished by immediate intuition, but when we endeavour, without quantity, to distinguish them conceptually, we find the task impossible, since the only qualitative relation of any two of them, the straight line, is the same for any other two. But now let us choose, at hap-hazard, some point outside the straight line. The points of our line now acquire new adjectives, namely their relations to the new point, *i.e.* the straight lines joining them to this new point. But these straight lines, reciprocally, alone define our external point, and all straight lines are qualitatively similar. If we take some other external point, therefore, and join it to the same points of our original straight line, we obtain a figure in which, so long as quantity is excluded, there is no conceptual difference from the former figure. Immediate intuition can distinguish the two figures, but qualitative discrimination cannot do so. Thus we obtain a projective transformation of four lines into four other lines, as giving a figure qualitatively indistinguishable from the original figure. A similar argument applies to the other projective transformations. Thus the only reason, within projective Geometry, for not regarding projective figures as actually identical, is the intuitive perception of difference of position. This is fundamental, and must be accepted as a *datum*. It is presupposed in the distinction of various points, and forms the very life of Geometry. It is, in fact, the essence of the notion of a form of externality, which notion forms the subject-matter of projective Geometry.

122. We may now sum up the results of our analysis of projective Geometry, and state the axioms on which its reasoning is based. We shall then have to prove that these axioms are necessary to any form of externality, with which we shall pass, from mere analysis, to a transcendental argument.

The axioms which have been assumed in the above analysis, and which, it would seem, suffice to found projective Geometry, may be roughly stated as follows:

I. We can distinguish different parts of space, but all parts are qualitatively similar, and are distinguished only by the immediate fact that they lie outside one another.

II. Space is continuous and infinitely divisible; the result of infinite division, the zero of extension, is called a *point*[1].

III. Any two points determine a unique figure, called a straight line, any three in general determine a unique figure, the plane. Any four determine a corresponding figure of three dimensions, and for aught that appears to the contrary, the same may be true of any number of points. But this process comes to an end, sooner or later, with some number of points which determine the whole of space. For if this were not the case, no number of relations of a point to a collection of given points could ever determine its relation to fresh points, and Geometry would become impossible[2].

This statement of the axioms is not intended to have any exclusive precision: other statements equally valid could easily be made. For all these axioms, as we shall see hereafter, are philosophically interdependent, and may, therefore, be enunciated in many ways. The above statement, however, includes, if I am not mistaken, everything essential to projective Geometry, and everything required to prove the principle of projective transformation. Before discussing the apriority of these axioms, let us once more briefly recapitulate the ends which they are intended to attain.

123. From the exclusively mathematical standpoint, as we

[1] On this axiom, however, compare § 131.

[2] For the proof of this proposition, see Chap. III. Sec. B, Axiom of Dimensions.

have seen, projective Geometry discusses only what figures can be obtained from each other by projective transformations, *i.e.* by the operations of projection and section. These operations, in all their forms, presuppose the point, straight line, and plane[1], whose necessity for projective Geometry, from the purely mathematical point of view, is thus self-evident from the start. But philosophically, projective Geometry has, as we saw, a wider aim. This wider aim, which gives, to the investigation of projectively equivalent figures, its chief importance, consists in the determination of qualitative spatial similarity, in the determination, that is, of all the figures which, when any one figure is given, can be distinguished from the given figure, so long as quantity is excluded, only by the mere fact that they are external to it.

124. Now when we consider what is involved in such absolute qualitative equivalence, we find at once, as its most obvious prerequisite, the perfect homogeneity of space. For it is assumed that a figure can be completely defined by its internal relations, and that the external relations, which constitute its position, though they suffice to distinguish it from other figures, in no way affect its internal properties, which are regarded as qualitatively identical with those of figures with quite different external relations. If this were not the case, anything analogous to projective transformation would be impossible. For such transformation always alters the position, *i.e.* the external relations, of a figure, and could not, therefore, if figures were dependent on their relations to other figures or to empty space, be studied without reference to other figures, or to the absolute position of the original figure. We require for our principle, in short, what may be called the mutual passivity and reciprocal independence of two parts or figures of space.

This passivity and this independence involve the homogeneity of space, or its equivalent, the relativity of position.

[1] The straight line and plane, in all discussions of general Geometry, are not necessarily Euclidean. They are simply figures determined, in general, by two and by three points respectively; whether they conform to the axiom of parallels and to Euclid's form of the axiom of the straight line, is not to be considered in the general definition.

For if the internal properties of a figure are the same, whatever its external relations may be, it follows that all parts of space are qualitatively similar, since a change of external relation is a change in the part of space occupied. It follows, also, that all position is relative and extrinsic, *i.e.*, that the position of a point, or the part of space occupied by a figure, is not, and has no effect upon, any intrinsic property of the point or figure, but is exclusively a relation to other points or figures in space, and remains without effect except where such relations are considered.

125. The homogeneity of space and the relativity of position, therefore, are presupposed in the qualitative spatial comparison with which projective Geometry deals. The latter, as we saw, is also the basis of the principle of duality. But these properties, as I shall now endeavour to prove, belong of necessity to any form of externality, and are thus *à priori* properties of all possible spaces. To prove this, however, we must first define the notion of a form of externality in general.

Let us observe, to begin with, that the distinction between Euclidean and non-Euclidean Geometries, so important in metrical investigations, disappears in projective Geometry proper. This suggests that projective Geometry, though originally invented as the science of Euclidean space, and subsequently of non-Euclidean spaces also, deals really with a wider conception, a conception which includes both, and neglects the attributes in which they differ. This conception I shall speak of as a form of externality.

126. In Grassmann's profound philosophical introduction to his *Ausdehnungslehre* of 1844, he suggested that Geometry, though improperly regarded as pure, was really a branch of applied mathematics, since it dealt with a subject-matter not created, like number, by the intellect, but given to it, and therefore not wholly subject to its laws alone. But it must be possible —so he contended—to construct a branch of pure mathematics, a science, that is, in which our object should be wholly a creature of the intellect, which should yet deal, as Geometry does, with extension—extension as conceived, however, not as empirically perceived in sensation or intuition.

From this point of view, the controversy between Kantians

and anti-Kantians becomes wholly irrelevant, since the distinction between pure and mixed mathematics does not lie in the distinction between the subjective and the objective, but between the purely intellectual on the one hand, and everything else on the other. Now Kant had contended, with great emphasis, that space was not an intellectual construction, but a subjective intuition. Geometry, therefore, with Grassmann's distinction, belongs to mixed mathematics as much on Kant's view as on that of his opponents. And Grassmann's distinction, I contend, is the more important for Epistemology, and the one to be adopted in distinguishing the *à priori* from the empirical. For what is merely intuitional can change, without upsetting the laws of thought, without making knowledge formally impossible: but what is purely intellectual cannot change, unless the laws of thought should change, and all our knowledge simultaneously collapse. I shall therefore follow Grassmann's distinction in constructing an *à priori* and purely conceptual form of externality.

127. The pure doctrine of extension, as constructed by Grassmann, need not be discussed—it included much empirical material, and was philosophically a failure. But his principles, I think, will enable us to prove that projective Geometry, abstractly interpreted, is the science which he foresaw, and deals with a matter which can be constructed by the pure intellect alone. If this be so, however, it must be observed that projective Geometry, for the moment, is rendered purely hypothetical[1]. All necessary truth, as Bradley has shown, is hypothetical[2], and asserts, *primâ facie*, only the ground on which rests the necessary connection of premisses and conclusion. If we construct a mere conception of externality, and thus abandon our actually given space, the result of our construction, until we return to something actually given, remains without existential import—if there *be* experienced externality, it asserts, then there must be a form of externality with such and such properties. That there must be experienced externality, Kant's first argument about space proves, I think, to

[1] That projective Geometry must have existential import, I shall attempt to prove in Chapter IV.

[2] Logic, Book I. Chapter II.

those who admit experience of a world of diverse but interrelated things. But this is a question which belongs to the next Chapter.

What we have to do here is, not to discuss whether there is a form of externality, but whether, if there be such a form, it must possess the properties embodied in the axioms of projective Geometry. Now first of all, what do we mean by such a form?

128. In any world in which perception presents us with various things, with discriminated and differentiated contents, there must be, in perception, at least one "principle of differentiation[1]," an element, that is, by which the things presented are distinguished as various. This element, taken in isolation, and abstracted from the content which it differentiates, we may call a form of externality. That it must, when taken in isolation, appear as a form, and not as a mere diversity of material content, is, I think, fairly obvious. For a diversity of material content cannot be studied apart from that material content; what we wish to study here, on the contrary, is the bare possibility of such diversity, which forms the residuum, as I shall try to prove hereafter[2], when we abstract from any sense-perception all that is distinctive of its particular matter. This possibility, then, this principle of bare diversity, is our form of externality. How far it is necessary to assume such a form, as distinct from interrelated things, I shall consider later on[3]. For the present, since space, as dealt with by Geometry, is certainly a form of this kind, we have only to ask: What properties must such a form, when studied in abstraction, necessarily possess?

129. In the first place, externality is an essentially relative conception—nothing can be external to itself. To be external to something is to be another with some relation to that thing. Hence, when we abstract a form of externality from all material content, and study it in isolation, position will appear, of

[1] Cf. Bradley's Logic, p. 63. It will be seen that the sense in which I have spoken of space as a principle of differentiation is not the sense of a "principle of individuation" which Bradley objects to.

[2] Chap. IV. §§ 186–191.

[3] Chap. IV. § 201 ff.

necessity, as purely relative—a position can have no intrinsic quality, for our form consists of pure externality, and externality contains no shadow or trace of an intrinsic quality. Thus we obtain our fundamental postulate, the relativity of position, or, as we may put it, the complete absence, on the part of our form, of any vestige of thinghood.

The same argument may also be stated as follows: If we abstract the conception of externality, and endeavour to deal with it *per se*, it is evident that we must obtain an object alike destitute of elements and of totality. For we have abstracted from the diverse matter which filled our form, while any element, or any whole, would retain some of the qualities of a matter. Either an element or a whole, in fact, would have to be a thing not external to itself, and would thus contain something not pure externality. Hence arise infinite divisibility, with the self-contradictory notion of the point, in the search for elements, and unbounded extension, with the contradiction of an infinite regress or a vicious circle, in the search for a completed whole. Thus again, our form contains neither elements nor totality, but only endless relations—the terms of these relations being excluded by our abstraction from the matter which fills our form.

130. In like manner we can deduce the homogeneity of our form. The diversity of content, which was possible only within the form of externality, has been abstracted from, leaving nothing but the bare possibility of diversity, the bare principle of differentiation, itself uniform and undifferentiated. For if diversity presupposes such a form, the form cannot, unless it were contained in a fresh form, be itself diverse or differentiated.

Or we may deduce the same property from the relativity of position. For any quality in one position, by which it was marked out from another, would be necessarily more or less intrinsic, and would contradict the pure relativity. Hence all positions are qualitatively alike, *i.e.* the form is homogeneous throughout.

131. From what has been said of homogeneity and relativity, follows one of the strangest properties of a form of externality. This property is, that the relation of externality between any two things is infinitely divisible, and may be regarded, consequently, as made up of an infinite number of the would-be elements of our form, or again as the sum of two relations of externality[1]. To speak of dividing or adding relations may well sound absurd—indeed it reveals the impropriety of the word relation in this connexion. It is difficult, however, to find an expression which shall be less improper. The fact seems to be, that externality is not so much a relation as bare relativity, or the bare possibility of a relation. On this subject, I shall enlarge in Chapter IV.[2] At this point it is only important to realize, what the subsequent argument will assume, that the relation—if we may so call it—of externality between two or more things must, since our form is homogeneous, be capable of continuous alteration, and must, since our infinitely divisible form is constituted by such relations, be capable of infinite division. But the result of infinite division is defined as the element of our form. (Our form has no elements, but we have to imagine elements in order to reason about it, as will be shown more fully in Chapter IV.) Hence it follows, that every relation of externality may be regarded, for scientific purposes, as an infinite congeries of elements, though philosophically, the relations alone are valid, and the elements are a self-contradictory result of hypostatizing the form of externality. This way of regarding relations of externality is important in understanding the meaning of such ideas as three or four collinear points.

As this point is difficult and important, I will repeat, in somewhat greater detail, the explanation of the manner in which straight lines and planes come to be regarded as congeries of points. From the strictly projective standpoint, though all other figures *are* merely a collection of any required number of points, lines or planes, given by some projective construction, straight lines and planes themselves are given integrally, and are not to be considered as divisible or composed of parts. To

[1] It is important to observe, however, that this way of regarding spatial relations is metrical; from the projective standpoint, the relation between two points is the whole unbounded straight line on which they lie, and need not be regarded as divisible into parts or as built up of points.

[2] §§ 207, 208. Cf. Hegel, Naturphilosophie, § 254.

say that a point lies on a straight line means, for projective Geometry proper, that the straight line is a relation between this and some other point. Here the points concerned, if our statement is to be freed from contradictions, must be regarded, if I may use such an expression, as *real* points—*i.e.* as unextended material centres[1]. Straight lines and planes are then relations between these material atoms. They are relations, however, which may undergo a metrical alteration while remaining projectively unchanged. When the projective relation between the two points *A*, *B* is the same as that between the two points *A*, *C*, while the metrical relation (distance) is different, the three points *A*, *B*, *C* are said to be collinear. Now the metrical manner of regarding spatial figures demands that they should be hypostatized, and no longer regarded as mere relations. For when we regard a quantity as extensive, *i.e.* as divisible into parts, we necessarily regard it as more than a mere relation or adjective, since no mere relation or adjective can be divided. For quantitative treatment, therefore, spatial relations must be hypostatized[2]. When this is done, we obtain, as we saw above, a homogeneous and infinitely divisible form of externality. We find now that distance, for example, may be continuously altered without changing the straight line on which it is measured. We thus obtain, on the straight line in question, a continuous series of points, which, since it is continuous, we regard as constituting our straight line. It is thus solely from the hypostatizing of relations, which metrical Geometry requires, that the view of straight lines and planes as *composed* of points arises, and it is from this hypostatizing that the difficulties of metrical Geometry spring.

132. The next step, in defining a form of externality, is obtained from the idea of *dimensions*. Positions, we have seen, are defined solely by their relations to other positions. But in order that such definition may be possible, a finite number of relations must suffice, since infinite numbers are philosophically inadmissible. A position must be definable, therefore, if knowledge of our form is to be possible at all, by some finite integral

[1] See Chap. IV. §§ 196–199.

[2] See a forthcoming article on "The relations of number and quantity" by the present writer in *Mind*, July, 1897.

number of relations to other positions. Every relation thus necessary for definition we call a dimension. Hence we obtain the proposition: *Any form of externality must have a finite integral number of dimensions.*

133. The above argument, it may be urged, has overlooked a possibility. It has used a transcendental argument, so an opponent may contend, without sufficiently proving that knowledge about externality must be possible without reference to the matters external to each other. The definition of a position may be impossible, so long as we neglect the matter which fills the form, but may become possible when this matter is taken into account. Such an objection can, I think, be successfully met, by a reference to the passivity and homogeneity of our form. For any dependence of the definition of a position on the particular matter filling that position, would involve some kind of interaction between the matter and its position, some effect of the diverse content on the homogeneous form. But since the form is totally destitute of thinghood, perfectly impassive, and perfectly void of differences between its parts, any such effect is inconceivable. An effect on a position would have to alter it in some way, but how could it be altered? It has no qualities except those which make it the position it is, as opposed to other positions; it cannot change, therefore, without becoming a different position. But such a change contradicts the law of identity. Hence it is not the position which has changed, but the content which has moved in the form. Thus it must be possible, if knowledge of our form can be obtained at all, to obtain this knowledge in logical independence of the particular matter which fills it. The above argument, therefore, granted the possibility of knowledge in the department in question, shows the necessity of a finite integral number of dimensions.

134. Let us repeat our original argument in the light of this elucidation. A position is completely defined when, and only when, enough relations are known to enable us to determine its relation to any fresh known position. Only by relations within the form of externality, as we have just seen, and never by relations which involve a reference to the particular matter filling the form, can such a definition be effected. But the possibility of such a definition follows from the Law of Excluded Middle, when this law is interpreted to mean, as Bosanquet makes it mean, that "Reality...is a system of reciprocally determinate parts[1]." For this implies that, given the relations of a part A to other parts B, C..., a sufficient wealth of such relations throws light on the relations of B to C, etc. If this were not the case, the parts A, B, C...could not be said to form such a system; for in such a system, to define A is to define, at the same time, all the other members, and to give an adjective to A, is to give an adjective to B and C. But the relations between positions are, when we restore the matter from which the positions were abstracted, relations between the things occupying those positions, and these relations, we have seen, can be studied without reference to the particular nature, in other respects, of the related things. It follows that, when we apply the general principle of systematic unity to these relations in particular, we find these relations to be dependent on each other, since they are not dependent, for their definition, on anything else. This gives the axiom of dimensions, in the above general form, as the result, on our abstract geometrical level, of the relativity of position and the law of excluded middle.

135. Before proceeding further, it is necessary to discuss the important special case where a form of externality has only one dimension. Of the two such forms, given in experience, one, namely time, presents an instance of this special case. But it may be shown, I think, that the function, in constituting the possibility of experience, which we demand of such forms, could not be accomplished by a one-dimensional form alone. For in a one-dimensional form, the various contents may be arranged in a series, and cannot, without interpenetration, change the order of contents in the series. But interpenetration is impossible, since a form of externality is the mere expression of diversity among things, from which it follows that things cannot occupy the same position in a form, unless there is another form by which to differentiate them. For without externality, there is no diversity[2]. Thus two bodies

[1] Logic, Vol. II. Chap. VII. p. 211.

[2] Real, as opposed to logical, diversity is throughout intended. Diverse

may occupy the same space, but only at different times: two things may exist simultaneously, but only at different places. A form of one dimension, therefore, could not, by itself, allow that change of the relations of externality, by which alone a varied world of interrelated things can be brought into consciousness. In a one-dimensional space, for example, only a single object, which must appear as a point, or two objects at most, one in front and one behind, could ever be perceived. Thus two or more dimensions seem an essential condition of anything worth calling an experience of interrelated things.

136. It may be objected, to this argument, that its validity depends upon the assumption that the change of a relation of externality must be continuous. Both to make and to meet this objection, in a manner which shall not imply time, seems almost impossible. For we cannot speak of change, whether continuous or discrete, without imagining time. Let us, therefore, allow time to be known, and discuss whether the temporal change, in any other form of externality, is necessarily continuous[1]. We must reply, I think, that continuity is necessary. The change of relation, in our non-temporal form, may be safely described as motion, and the law of Causality—since we have already assumed time—may be applied to this motion. It then follows that discrete motion would involve a finite effect from an infinitesimal cause, for a cause acting only for a moment of time would be infinitesimal. It involves, also, a validity in the point of time, whereas what is valid in any form of externality is not, as we have already seen, the infinitesimal and self-contradictory element resulting from infinite division, but the finite relation which mathematics analyzes into vanishing elements. Hence change must be continuous, and the possibility of serial arrangement holds good.

In a one-dimensional form other than time, the same argument must hold. For something analogous to Causality would be necessary to experience, and the relativity of the form would still necessarily hold. Hence, since only these two

aspects may coexist in a thing at one time and place, but two diverse real things cannot so coexist.

[1] On the insufficiency of time alone, see Chapter IV. § 191.

properties of time have been assumed, the above contention would remain valid of any second form whose relations were correlated with those of the first, as the analogue of Causality would require them to be.

137. The next step in the argument, which assumes two or more dimensions, is concerned with the general analogues of straight lines and planes, *i.e.* with figures—which may be regarded either as relations between positions or as series of positions—uniquely determined by two or by three positions. If this step can be successfully taken, our deduction of the above projective axioms will be complete, and descriptive Geometry will be established as the abstract *à priori* doctrine of forms of externality.

To prove this contention, consider of what nature the relations can be by which positions are defined. We have seen already that our form is purely relational and infinitely divisible, and that positions (points) are the self-contradictory outcome of the search for something other than relations. What we really mean, therefore, by the relations defining a position, is, when we undo our previous abstraction, the relations of externality by which some thing is related to other things. But how, when we remain in the abstract form, must such relations appear?

138. We have to prove that two positions must have a relation independent of any reference to other positions. To prove this, let us recur to what was said, in connection with dimensions, as to the passivity and homogeneity of our form. Since positions are defined only by relations, there must be relations, within the form, between positions. But if there are such relations, there must be a relation which is intrinsic to two positions. For to suppose the contrary, is to attribute an interaction or causal connection, of some kind, between those two positions and other positions—a supposition which the perfect homogeneity of our form renders absurd, since all positions are qualitatively similar, and cannot be changed without losing their identity. We may put this argument thus: since positions are only defined by their relations, such definition could never begin, unless it began with a relation between only two positions. For suppose three positions A,

B, *C* were necessary, and gave rise to the relation *abc* between the three. Then there would remain no means of defining the different pairs *BC*, *CA*, *AB*, since the only relation defining them would be one common to all three pairs. Nothing would be gained, in this case, by reference to fresh points, for it follows, from the homogeneity and passivity of the form, that these fresh points could not affect the internal relations of our triad, which relations, if they can give definiteness at all, must give it without the aid of external reference. Two positions must, therefore, if definition is to be possible, have some relation which they by themselves suffice to define. Precisely the same argument applies to three positions, or to four; the argument loses its scope only when we have exhausted the dimensions of the form considered. Thus, in three dimensions, five positions have no fresh relation, not deducible from those already known, for by the definition of dimensions, all the relations involved can be deduced from those of the fourth point to the first three, together with those of the fifth to the first three.

We may give the argument a more concrete, and perhaps a more convincing shape, by considering the matter arranged in our form. If two things are mutually external, they must since they belong to the same world, have some relation of externality; there is, therefore, a relation of externality between two things. But since our form is homogeneous, the same relation of externality may subsist in other parts of the form, *i.e.* while the two things considered alter their relations of externality to other things. The relation of externality between two things is, therefore, independent of other things. Hence, when we return to the abstract language of the form, two positions have a relation determined by those two positions alone, and independent of other positions.

Precisely the same argument applies to the relations of three positions, and in each case the relation must appear in the form as not a mere inference from the positions it relates. For relations, as we have seen, actually constitute a form of externality, and are not mere inferences from terms, which are nowhere to be found in the form[1].

[1] Geometrically, the axiom of the plane is, not that three points determine a figure at all, which follows from the axiom of the straight line, but that the

To sum up: Since position is relative, two positions must have *some* relation to each other; and since our form of

straight line joining two casual points of the plane lies wholly in the plane. This axiom requires a projective method of constructing the plane, *i.e.* of finding all the triads of points which determine the same projective figure as the given triad. The required construction will be obtained if we can find any projective figure determined by three points, and any projective method of reaching other points which determine the same figure.

Let *O, P, Q* be the three points whose projective relation is required. Then we have given us the three straight lines *PQ, QO, OP*. Metrically, the

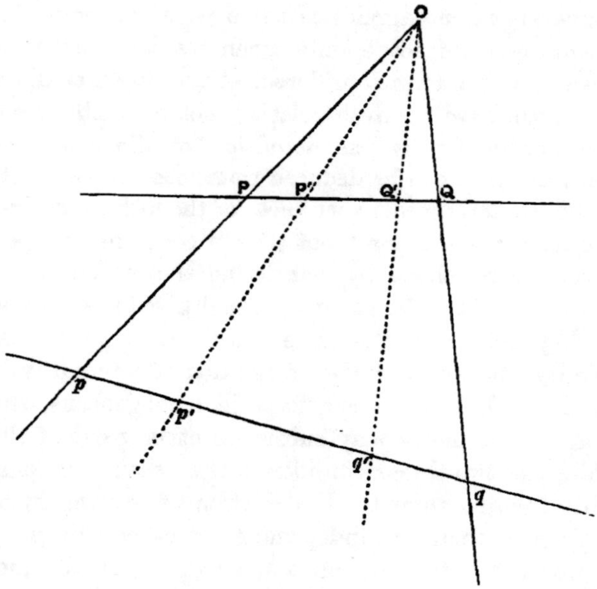

relation between these points is made up of the area, and the magnitude of the sides and angles, of the triangle *OPQ*, just as the relation between two points is distance. But projectively, the figure is unchanged when *P* and *Q* travel along *OP* and *OQ*, or when *OP* and *OQ* turn about *O* in such a way as still to meet *PQ*. This is a result of the general principle of projective equivalence enunciated above (§§ 108, 109). Hence the projective relation between *O, P, Q* is the same as that between *O, p, q* or *O, P', Q'*; that is, *p, q* and *P', Q'* lie in the plane *OPQ*. In this way, any number of points on the plane may be obtained, and by repeating the construction with fresh triads, every point of the plane can be reached. We have to prove that, when the plane is so constructed, the straight line joining any two points of the plane lies wholly in the plane.

It is evident, from the manner of construction, that any point of *PQ, OP, OQ, OP'* or *OQ'* lies in the plane. If we can prove that any point of *pq* lies in externality is homogeneous, this relation can be kept unchanged while the two positions change their relations to other positions. Hence their relation is intrinsic, and independent of other positions. Since the form is a mere complex of relations, the relation in question must, if the form is sensuous or intuitive, be itself sensuous or intuitive, and not a mere inference. In this case, a unique relation must be a unique figure—in spatial terms, the straight line joining the two points.

139. With this, our deduction of projective Geometry from the *à priori* conceptual properties of a form of externality is completed. That such a form, when regarded as an independent thing, is self-contradictory, has been abundantly evident throughout the discussion. But the science of the form has been founded on the opposite way of regarding it: we have held it throughout to be a mere complex of relations, and have deduced its properties exclusively from this view of it. The many difficulties, in applying such an *à priori* deduction to intuitive space, and in explaining, as logical necessities, properties which appear as sensuous or intuitional data, must be postponed to Chapter IV. For the present, I wish to point out that projective Geometry is wholly *à priori*; that it deals with an object whose properties are logically deduced from its definition, not empirically discovered from data; that its definition, again, is founded on the possibility of experiencing diversity in relation, or multiplicity in unity; and that our whole science, therefore, is logically implied in, and deducible from, the possibility of such experience.

140. In metrical Geometry, on the contrary, we shall find a very different result. Although the geometrical conditions which render spatial measurement possible, will be found identical, except for slight differences in the form of statement, with the *à priori* axioms discussed above, yet the actual

the plane, we shall have proved all that is required, since pq may be transformed, by successive repetitions of the same construction, into any straight line joining two points of the plane. But we have seen that the same plane is determined by O, p, q and by O, P, Q. The straight lines PQ, pq have, therefore, the same relation to the plane. But PQ lies wholly in the plane; therefore pq also lies wholly in the plane. Hence our axiom is proved.

measurement—which deals with actually given space, not the mere intellectual construction we have been just discussing—gives results which can only be known empirically and approximately, and can be deduced by no necessity of thought. The Euclidean and non-Euclidean spaces give the various results which are *à priori* possible; the axioms peculiar to Euclid—which are properly not axioms, but empirical results of measurement—determine, within the errors of observation, which of these *à priori* possibilities is realized in our actual space. Thus measurement deals throughout with an empirically given matter, not with a creature of the intellect, and its *à priori* elements are only the conditions presupposed in the possibility of measurement. What these conditions are, we shall see in the second section of this chapter.

Section B.

THE AXIOMS OF METRICAL GEOMETRY.

141. We have now reviewed the axioms of projective Geometry, and have seen that they are *à priori* deductions from the fact that we can experience externality, *i.e.* a co-existent multiplicity of different but interrelated things. But projective Geometry, in spite of its claims, is not the whole science of space, as is sufficiently proved by the fact that it cannot discriminate between Euclidean and non-Euclidean spaces[1]. For this purpose, spatial measurement is required: metrical Geometry, with its quantitative tests, can alone effect the discrimination. For all application of Geometry to physics, also, measurement is required; the law of gravitation, for example, requires the determination of actual distances. For many purposes, in short, projective Geometry is wholly insufficient: thus it is unable to distinguish between different kinds of conics, though their distinction is of fundamental importance in many departments of knowledge.

[1] A detailed proof has been given above, Chap. I. 3rd period. It is to be observed that any reference to infinitely distant elements involves metrical ideas.

Metrical Geometry is, then, a necessary part of the science of space, and a part not included in descriptive Geometry. Its *à priori* element, nevertheless, so far as this is spatial and not arithmetical, is the same as the postulate of projective Geometry, namely, the homogeneity of space, or its equivalent, the relativity of position. We can see, in fact, that the *à priori* element in both is likely to be the same. For the *à priori* in metrical Geometry will be whatever is presupposed in the possibility of spatial measurement, *i.e.* of quantitative spatial comparison. But such comparison presupposes simply a known identity of quality, the determination of which is precisely the problem of projective Geometry. Hence the conditions for the possibility of measurement, in so far as they are not arithmetical, will be precisely the same as those for projective Geometry.

142. Metrical Geometry, therefore, though distinct from projective Geometry, is not independent of it, but presupposes it, and arises from its combination with the extraneous idea of *quantity*. Nevertheless the mathematical form of the axioms, in metrical Geometry, is slightly different from their form in projective Geometry. The homogeneity of space is replaced by its equivalent, the axiom of Free Mobility. The axiom of the straight line is replaced by the axiom of distance: Two points determine a unique quantity, distance, which is unaltered in any motion of the two points as a single figure. This axiom, indeed, will be found to involve the axiom of the straight line—such a quantity could not exist unless the two points determined a unique curve—but its mathematical form is changed. Another important change is the collapse of the principle of duality: quantity can be applied to the straight line, because it is divisible into similar parts, but cannot be applied to the indivisible point. We thus obtain a reason, which was wanting in descriptive Geometry, for preferring points, as spatial elements, to straight lines or planes[1]. Finally, an entirely new idea is introduced with quantity, namely, the idea of *Motion*. Not that we study motion, or that any of our results have reference to motion, but that they cannot, though in projective

[1] Cf. Section A, §§ 115—117.

Geometry they could, be obtained without at least an ideal motion of our figures through space.

Let us now examine in detail the prerequisites of spatial measurement. We shall find three axioms, without which such measurement would be impossible, but with which it is adequate to decide, empirically and approximately, the Euclidean or non-Euclidean nature of our actual space. We shall find, further, that these three axioms can be deduced from the conception of a form of externality, and owe nothing to the evidence of intuition. They are, therefore, like their equivalents the axioms of projective Geometry, *à priori*, and deducible from the conditions of spatial experience. This experience, accordingly, can never disprove them, since its very existence presupposes them.

I. *The Axiom of Free Mobility.*

143. Metrical Geometry, to begin with, may be defined as the science which deals with the comparison and relations of spatial magnitudes. The conception of magnitude, therefore, is necessary from the start. Some of Euclid's axioms, accordingly, have been classed as arithmetical, and have been supposed to have nothing particular to do with space. Such are the axioms that equals added to or subtracted from equals give equals, and that things which are equal to the same thing are equal to one another. These axioms, it is said, are purely arithmetical, and do not, like the others, ascribe an adjective to space. As regards their use in arithmetic, this is of course true. But if an arithmetical axiom is to be applied to spatial magnitudes, it must have some spatial import[1], and thus even this class is not, in Geometry, *merely* arithmetical. Fortunately, the geometrical element is the same in all the axioms of this class—we can see at once, in fact, that it can amount to no more than a definition of spatial magnitude[2]. Again, since the space with which Geometry deals is infinitely divisible, a definition of spatial magnitude

[1] Contrast Erdmann, op. cit. p. 138.

[2] Cf. Erdmann, op. cit. p. 164.

reduces itself to a definition of spatial equality, for, as soon as we have this last, we can compare two spatial magnitudes by dividing each into a number of equal units, and counting the number of such units in each[1]. The ratio of the number of units is, of course, the ratio of the two magnitudes.

144. We require, then, at the very outset, some criterion of spatial equality: without such a criterion metrical Geometry would become wholly impossible. It might appear, at first sight, as though this need not be an axiom, but might be a mere definition. In part this is true, but not wholly. The part which is merely a definition is given in Euclid's eighth axiom: "Magnitudes which exactly coincide are equal." But this gives a sufficient criterion only when the magnitudes to be compared already occupy the same position. When, as will normally be the case, the two spatial magnitudes are external to one another —as, indeed, must be the case, if they are distinct, and not whole and part—the two magnitudes can only be made to coincide by a motion of one or both of them. In order, therefore, that our definition of spatial magnitude may give unambiguous results, coincidence when superposed, if it can ever occur, must occur always, whatever path be pursued in bringing it about. Hence, if mere motion could alter shapes, our criterion of equality would break down. It follows that the application of the conception of magnitude to figures in space involves the following axiom[2]: *Spatial magnitudes can be moved from place to place without distortion;* or, as it may be put, *Shapes do not in any way depend upon absolute position in space.*

The above axiom is the axiom of Free Mobility[3]. I propose to prove (1) that the denial of this axiom would involve logical and philosophical absurdities, so that it must be classed as

[1] Strictly speaking, this method is only applicable where the two magnitudes are commensurable. But if we take infinite divisibility rigidly, the units can theoretically be taken so small as to obtain any required degree of approximation. The difficulty is the universal one of applying to continua the essentially discrete conception of number.

[2] Cf. Erdmann, op. cit. p. 50.

[3] Also called the axiom of congruence. I have taken congruence to be the *definition* of spatial equality by superposition, and shall therefore generally speak of the *axiom* as Free Mobility.

wholly *à priori*; (2) that metrical Geometry, if it refused this axiom, would be unable, without a logical absurdity, to establish the notion of spatial magnitude at all. The conclusion will be, that the axiom cannot be proved or disproved by experience, but is an *à priori* condition of metrical Geometry. As I shall thus be maintaining a position which has been much controverted, especially by Helmholtz and Erdmann, I shall have to enter into the arguments at some length.

145. A. *Philosophical Argument.* The denial of the axiom involves absolute position, and an action of mere space, *per se*, on things. For the axiom does not assert that real bodies, as a matter of empirical fact, never change their shape in any way during their passage from place to place; on the contrary, we know that such changes do occur, sometimes in a very noticeable degree, and always to some extent. But such changes are attributed, not to the change of place as such, but to physical causes: changes of temperature, pressure, etc. What our axiom has to deal with is not actual material bodies, but geometrical figures[1], and it asserts that a figure which is possible in any one position in space is possible in every other. Its meaning will become clearer by reference to a case where it does not hold, say the space formed by the surface of an egg. Here, a triangle drawn near the equator cannot be moved without distortion to the point, as it would no longer fit the greater curvature of the new position; a triangle drawn near the point cannot be fitted on to the flatter end, and so on. Thus the method of superposition, such as Euclid employs in Book I. Prop. IV., becomes impossible; figures cannot be freely moved about, indeed, given any figure, we can determine a certain series of possible positions for it on the egg, outside which it becomes impossible. What I assert is, then, that there is a philosophic absurdity in supposing space in general to be of this nature. On the egg we have marked points, such as the two ends; the space formed by its surface is not homogeneous, and if things are moved about in it, it must of itself exercise a distorting effect upon them, quite independently of physical causes; if it did not exercise such an effect, the things

[1] For the sense in which these figures are to be regarded as material, see criticism of Helmholtz, Chapter II. §§ 69 ff.

could not be moved. Thus such a space would not be homogeneous, but would have marked points, by reference to which bodies would have absolute position, quite independently of any other bodies. Space would no longer be passive, but would exercise a definite effect upon things, and we should have to accommodate ourselves to the notion of marked points in empty space; these points being marked, not by the bodies which occupied them, but by their effects on any bodies which might from time to time occupy them. This want of homogeneity and passivity is, however, absurd; space must, since it is a form of externality, allow only of relative, not of absolute, position, and must be completely homogeneous throughout. To suppose it otherwise, is to give it a thinghood which no form of externality can possibly possess. We must, then, on purely philosophical grounds, admit that a geometrical figure which is possible anywhere is possible everywhere, which is the axiom of Free Mobility.

146. B. *Geometrical Argument.* Let us see next what sort of Geometry we could construct without this axiom. The ultimate standard of comparison of spatial magnitudes must, as we saw in introducing the axiom, be equality when superposed; but need we, from this equality, infer equality when separated? It has been urged by Erdmann that, for the more immediate purposes of Geometry, this would be unnecessary[1]. We might construct a new Geometry, he thinks, in which sizes varied with motion on any definite law. Such a view, as I shall show below, involves a logical error as to the nature of magnitude. But before pointing this out, let us discuss the geometrical consequences of assuming its truth. Suppose the length of an infinitesimal arc in some standard position were ds; then in any other position p its length would be $ds \,.\, f(p)$, where the form of the function $f(p)$ must be supposed known. But how are we to determine the position p? For this purpose, we require p's coordinates, *i.e.*, some measurement of distance from the origin. But the distance from the origin could only be measured if we assumed our law $f(p)$ to measure it by. For suppose the origin to be O, and Op to be a straight line whose length is required. If we have a measuring rod with which we travel

[1] Op. cit. p. 60.

along the line and measure successive infinitesimal arcs, the measuring rod will change its size as we move, so that an arc which appears by the measure to be ds will really be $f(s) . ds$, where s is the previously traversed distance. If, on the other hand, we move our line Op slowly through the origin, and measure each piece as it passes through, our measure, it is true, will not alter, but now we have no means of discovering the law by which any element has changed its length in coming to the origin. Hence, until we assume our function $f(p)$, we have no means of determining p, for we have just seen that distances from the origin can only be estimated by means of the law $f(p)$. It follows that experience can neither prove nor disprove the constancy of shapes throughout motion, since, if shapes were not constant, we should have to *assume* a law of their variation before measurement became possible, and therefore measurement could not itself reveal that variation to us[1].

Nevertheless, such an arbitrarily assumed law *does*, at first sight, give a mathematically possible Geometry. The fundamental proposition, that two magnitudes which can be superposed in any one position can be superposed in any other, still holds. For two infinitesimal arcs, whose lengths in the standard position are ds_1 and ds_2, would, in any other position p, have lengths $f(p) . ds_1$ and $f(p) . ds_2$, so that their ratio would be unaltered. From this constancy of ratio, as we know through Riemann and Helmholtz, the above proposition follows. Hence all that Geometry requires, it would seem, as a basis for measurement, is an axiom that the alteration of shapes during motion follows a definite known law, such as that assumed above.

147. There is, however, in such a view, as I remarked above, a logical error as to the nature of magnitude. This error has been already pointed out in dealing with Erdmann[2], and need only be briefly repeated here. A judgment of magnitude is essentially a judgment of comparison: in unmeasured quantity, comparison as to the mere more or less, but in measured mag-

[1] The view of Helmholtz and Erdmann, that mechanical experience suffices here, though geometrical experience fails us, has been discussed above, Chapter II. §§ 73, 82.

[2] Chapter II. § 81.

nitude, comparison as to the precise how many times. To speak of differences of magnitude, therefore, in a case where comparison cannot reveal them, is logically absurd. Now in the case contemplated above, two magnitudes, which appear equal in one position, appear equal also when compared in another position. There is no sense, therefore, in supposing the two magnitudes unequal when separated, nor in supposing, consequently, that they have changed their magnitudes in motion. This senselessness of our hypothesis is the logical ground of the mathematical indeterminateness as to the law of variation. Since, then, there is no means of comparing two spatial figures, as regards magnitude, except superposition, the only logically possible axiom, if spatial magnitude is to be self-consistent, is the axiom of Free Mobility in the form first given above.

148. Although this axiom is *à priori*, its application to the measurement of actual bodies, as we found in discussing Helmholtz's views, always involves an empirical element[1]. Our axiom, then, only supplies the *à priori* condition for carrying out an operation which, in the concrete, is empirical—just as arithmetic supplies the *à priori* condition for a census. As this topic has been discussed at length in Chapter II., I shall say no more about it here.

149. There remain, however, a few objections and difficulties to be discussed. First, how do we obtain equality in solids, and in Kant's cases of right and left hands, or of right and left-handed screws, where actual superposition is impossible? Secondly, how can we take congruence as the only possible basis of spatial measurement, when we have before us the case of time, where no such thing as congruence is conceivable? Thirdly, it might be urged that we can immediately estimate spatial equality by the eye, with more or less accuracy, and thus have a measure independent of congruence. Fourthly, how is metrical Geometry possible on non-congruent surfaces, if congruence be the basis of spatial measurement? I will discuss these objections successively.

150. (1) How do we measure the equality of solids? These could only be brought into actual congruence if we had

[1] Chapter II. § 72.

a fourth dimension to operate in[1], and from what I have said before of the absolute necessity of this test, it might seem as though we should be left here in utter ignorance. Euclid is silent on the subject, and in all works on Geometry it is assumed as self-evident that two cubes of equal side are equal. This assumption suggests that we are not so badly off as we should have been without congruence, as a test of equality in one or two dimensions; for now we can at least be sure that two cubes have all their sides and all their faces equal. Two such cubes differ, then, in no sensible spatial quality save position, for volume, in this case at any rate, is not a sensible quality. They are, therefore, as far as such qualities are concerned, indiscernible. If their places were interchanged, we might know the change by their colour, or by some other non-geometrical property; but so far as any property of which Geometry can take cognisance is concerned, everything would seem as before. To suppose a difference of volume, then, would be to ascribe an effect to mere position, which we saw to be inadmissible while discussing Free Mobility. Except as regards position, they are geometrically indiscernible, and we may call to our aid the Identity of Indiscernibles to establish their agreement in the one remaining geometrical property of volume. This may seem rather a strange principle to use in Mathematics, and for Geometry their equality is, perhaps, best regarded as a definition; but if we demand a philosophical ground for this definition, it is, I believe, only to be found in the Identity of Indiscernibles. We can, without error, make our *definition* of three-dimensional equality rest on two-dimensional congruence. For since direct comparison as to volume is impossible, we are at liberty to *define* two volumes as equal, when all their various lines, surfaces, angles and solid angles are congruent, since there remains, in such a case, no *measurable* difference between the figures composing the two volumes. Of course, as soon as we have established this one case of equality of volumes, the rest of the theory follows; as appears from the ordinary method of integrating volumes, by dividing them into small cubes.

Thus congruence *helps* to establish three-dimensional equality,

[1] Contrast Delboeuf, L'ancienne et les nouvelles géométries, II. Rev. Phil. 1894, Vol. xxxvii. p. 354.

though it cannot directly *prove* such equality; and the same philosophical principle, of the homogeneity of space, by which congruence was proved, comes to our rescue here. But how about right-handed and left-handed screws? Here we can no longer apply the Identity of Indiscernibles, for the two are very well discernible. But as with solids, so here, Free Mobility can help us much. It can enable us, by ordinary measurement, to show that the internal relations of both screws are the same, and that the difference lies only in their relation to other things in space. Knowing these internal relations, we can calculate, by the Geometry which Free Mobility has rendered possible, all the geometrical properties of these screws—radius, pitch, etc.—and can show them to be severally equal in both. But this is all we require. Mediate comparison is possible, though immediate comparison is not. Both can, for instance, be compared with the cylinder on which both would fit, and thus their equality can be proved. A precisely similar proof holds, of course, for the other cases, right and left hands, spherical triangles, etc. On the whole, these cases confirm my argument; for they show, as Kant intended them to show[1], the essential relativity of space.

151. (2) As regards time, no congruence is here conceivable, for to effect congruence requires always—as we saw in the case of solids—one more dimension than belongs to the magnitudes compared. No day can be brought into temporal coincidence with any other day, to show that the two exactly cover each other; we are therefore reduced to the arbitrary assumption that some motion or set of motions, given us in experience, is uniform. Fortunately, we have a large set of motions which all roughly agree; the swing of the pendulum, the rotation and revolution of the earth and the planets, etc. These do not exactly agree, but they lead us to the laws of motion, by which we are able, on our arbitrary hypothesis, to estimate their small departures from uniformity; just as the assumption of Free Mobility enabled us to measure the departures of actual

[1] Prolegomena, § 13. See Vaihinger's Commentar, II. pp. 518—532 esp. pp. 521—2. The above was Kant's whole purpose in 1768, but only part of his purpose in the Prolegomena, where the intuitive nature of space was also to be proved.

bodies from rigidity. But here, as there, another possibility is mathematically open to us, and can only be excluded by its philosophic absurdity; we might have assumed that the above set of approximately agreeing motions all had velocities which varied approximately as some arbitrarily assumed function of the time, $f(t)$ say, measured from some arbitrary origin. Such an assumption would still keep them as nearly synchronous as before, and would give an equally possible, though more complex, system of Mechanics; instead of the first law of motion, we should have the following: A particle perseveres in its state of rest, or of rectilinear motion with velocity varying as $f(t)$, except in so far as it is compelled to alter that state by the action of external forces. Such a hypothesis *is* mathematically possible, but, like the similar one for space, it is excluded logically by the comparative nature of the judgment of quantity, and philosophically by the fact that it involves absolute time, as a determining agent in change, whereas time can never, philosophically, be anything but a passive form, abstracted from change. I have introduced this parallel from time, not as directly bearing on the argument, but as a simpler case which may serve to illustrate my reasoning in the more complex case of space. For since time, in mathematics, is one-dimensional, the mathematical difficulties are simpler than in Geometry; and although nothing accurately corresponds to congruence, there is a very similar mixture of mathematical and philosophical necessity, giving, finally, a thoroughly definite axiom as the basis of time-measurement, corresponding to congruence as the basis of space-measurement[1].

152. (3) The case of time-measurement suggests the third of the above objections to the absolute necessity of the axiom of Free Mobility. Psycho-physics has shown that we have an approximate power, by means of what may be called the sense of duration, of immediately estimating equal short times. This establishes a rough measure independent of any assumed uniform motion, and in space also, it may be said, we have a similar power of immediate comparison. We can see, by im-

[1] On the subject of time measurement, cf. Bosanquet's Logic, Vol. i. pp. 178—183. Since time, in the above account, is measured by motion, its measurement presupposes that of spatial magnitudes.

mediate inspection, that the sub-divisions on a foot rule are not grossly inaccurate; and so, it may be said, we both have a measure independent of congruence, and also could discover, by experience, any gross departure from Free Mobility. Against this view, however, there is at the outset a very fundamental psychological objection. It has been urged that all our comparison of spatial magnitudes proceeds by ideal superposition. Thus James says (Psychology, Vol. II. p. 152): "Even where we only feel one sub-division to be vaguely larger or less, the mind must pass rapidly between it and the other sub-division, and receive the immediate sensible shock of the more," and "so far as the sub-divisions of a sense-space are to be *measured* exactly against each other, objective forms occupying one subdivison must be directly or indirectly superposed upon the other[1]."

Even if we waive this fundamental objection, however, others remain. To begin with, such judgments of equality are only very rough approximations, and cannot be applied to lines of more than a certain length, if only for the reason that such lines cannot well be seen together. Thus this method can only give us any security in our own immediate neighbourhood, and could in no wise warrant such operations as would be required for the construction of maps &c., much less the measurement of astronomical distances. They might just enable us to say that some lines were longer than others, but they would leave Geometry in a position no better than that of the Hedonical Calculus, in which we depend on a purely subjective measure. So inaccurate, in fact, is such a method acknowledged to be, that the foot-rule is as much a need of daily life as of science. Besides, no one would trust such immediate judgments, but for the fact that the stricter test of congruence to some extent confirms them; if we could not apply this test, we should have no ground for trusting them even as much as we do. Thus we should have, here, no real escape from our absolute dependence upon the axiom of Free Mobility.

153. (4) One last elucidatory remark is necessary before our proof of this axiom can be considered complete. We spoke above of the Geometry on an egg, where Free Mobility does not hold. What, I may be asked, is there about a thoroughly non-

[1] Cf. Stumpf. Ursprung der Raumvorstellung, p. 68.

congruent Geometry, more impossible than this Geometry on the egg? The answer is obvious. The Geometry of non-congruent surfaces is *only* possible by the use of infinitesimals, and in the infinitesimal all surfaces become plane. The fundamental formula, that for the length of an infinitesimal arc, is only obtained on the assumption that such an arc may be treated as a straight line, and that Euclidean Plane Geometry may be applied in the immediate neighbourhood of any point. If we had not our Euclidean measure, which could be moved without distortion, we should have no method of comparing small arcs in different places, and the Geometry of non-congruent surfaces would break down. Thus the axiom of Free Mobility, as regards three-dimensional space, is necessarily implied and presupposed in the Geometry of non-congruent surfaces; the possibility of the latter, therefore, is a dependent and derivative possibility, and can form no argument against the *à priori* necessity of congruence as the test of equality.

154. It is to be observed that the axiom of Free Mobility, as I have enunciated it, includes also the axiom to which Helmholtz gives the name of Monodromy. This asserts that a body does not alter its dimensions in consequence of a complete revolution through four right angles, but occupies at the end the same position as at the beginning. The supposed mathematical necessity of making a separate axiom of this property of space has been disproved by Sophus Lie (v. Chap. I. § 45); philosophically, it is plainly a particular case of Free Mobility[1], and indeed a particularly obvious case, for a translation really does make some change in a body, namely, a change in position, but a rotation through four right angles may be supposed to have been performed any number of times without appearing in the result, and the absurdity of ascribing to space the power of making bodies grow in the process is palpable; everything that was said above on congruence in general applies with even greater evidence to this special case.

155. The axiom of Free Mobility involves, if it is to be true, the homogeneity of space, or the complete relativity of

[1] As is Helmholtz's other axiom, that the possibility of superposition is independent of the course pursued in bringing it about.

position. For if any shape, which is possible in one part of space, be always possible in another, it follows that all parts of space are qualitatively similar, and cannot, therefore, be distinguished by any intrinsic property. Hence positions in space, if our axiom be true, must be wholly defined by external relations, *i.e. Position is not an intrinsic, but a purely relative, property of things in space.* If there could be such a thing as absolute position, in short, metrical Geometry would be impossible. This relativity of position is the fundamental postulate of all Geometry, to which each of the necessary metrical axioms leads, and from which, conversely, each of these axioms can be deduced.

156. This converse deduction, as regards Free Mobility, is not very difficult, and follows from the argument of Section A[1], which I will briefly recapitulate. In the first place, externality is an essentially relative conception—nothing can be external to itself. To be external to something is to be an other with some relation to that thing. Hence, when we abstract a form of externality from all material content, and study it in isolation, position will appear of necessity as purely relative—it can have no intrinsic quality, for our form consists of pure externality, and externality contains no shadow or trace of an intrinsic quality. Hence we derive our fundamental postulate, the relativity of position. From this follows the homogeneity of our form, for any quality in one position, which marked out that position from another, would be necessarily more or less intrinsic, and would contradict the pure relativity. Finally Free Mobility follows from homogeneity, for our form would not be homogeneous unless it allowed, in every part, shapes or systems of relations, which it allowed in any other part. Free Mobility, therefore, is a necessary property of every possible form of externality.

157. In summing up the argument we have just concluded, we may exhibit it, in consequence of the two preceding paragraphs, in the form of a completed circle. Starting from the conditions of spatial measurement, we found that the comparison, required for measurement, could only be effected by superposition. But we found, further, that the result of such

[1] Cf. §§ 129, 130.

comparison will only be unambiguous, if spatial magnitudes and shapes are unaltered by motion in space, if, in other words, shapes do not depend upon absolute position in space. But this axiom can only be true if space is homogeneous and position merely relative. Conversely, if position is assumed to be merely relative, a change of magnitude in motion—involving as it does, the assertion of absolute position—is impossible; and our test of spatial equality is therefore adequate. But position in any form of externality must be purely relative, since externality cannot be an intrinsic property of anything. Our axiom, therefore, is *à priori* in a double sense. It is presupposed in all spatial measurement, and it is a necessary property of any form of externality. A similar double apriority, we shall see, appears in our other necessary axioms.

II. *The Axiom of Dimensions*[1].

158. We have seen, in discussing the axiom of Free Mobility, that all position is relative, that is, a position exists only by virtue of relations[2]. It follows that, if positions can be defined at all, they must be uniquely and exhaustively defined by some finite number of such relations. If Geometry is to be possible, it must happen that, after enough relations have been given to determine a point uniquely, its relations to any fresh known point are deducible from the relations already given. Hence we obtain, as an *à priori* condition of Geometry, logically indispensable to its existence, the axiom that *Space must have a finite integral number of Dimensions.* For every relation required in the definition of a point constitutes a dimension, and a fraction of a relation is meaningless. The number of relations required must be finite, since an infinite number of dimensions would be practically impossible to determine. If we remember our axiom of Free Mobility,

[1] This deduction is practically the same as that in Sec. A, but I have stated it here with more special reference to space and to metrical Geometry.

[2] The question: "Relations to what?" is a question involving many difficulties. It will be touched on later in this chapter, and answered, as far as possible, in the fourth chapter. For the present, in spite of the glaring circle involved, I shall take the relations as relations to other positions.

and remember also that space is a continuum, we may state our axiom, for metrical Geometry, in the form given by Helmholtz (v. Chap. I. § 25): "In a space of n dimensions, the position of every point is uniquely determined by the measurement of n continuous independent variables (coordinates).[1]"

159. So much, then, is *à priori* necessary to metrical Geometry. The restriction of the dimensions to three seems, on the contrary, to be wholly the work of experience[2]. This restriction cannot be logically necessary, for as soon as we have formulated any analytical system, it appears wholly arbitrary. Why, we are driven to ask, cannot we add a fourth coordinate to our x, y, z, or give a geometrical meaning to x^4? In this more special form, we are tempted to regard the axiom of dimensions, like the number of inhabitants of a town, as a purely statistical fact, with no greater necessity than such facts have.

Geometry affords intrinsic evidence of the truth of my division of the axiom of dimensions into an *à priori* and empirical portion. For while the extension of the number of dimensions to four, or to n, alters nothing in plane and solid Geometry, but only adds a new branch which interferes in no way with the old, *some* definite number of dimensions is assumed in all Geometries, nor is it possible to conceive of a Geometry which should be free from this assumption[3].

160. Let us, since the point seems of some interest, repeat our proof of the apriority of this axiom from a slightly different point of view. We will begin, this time, from the most abstract conception of space, such as we find in Riemann's dissertation, or in Erdmann's extents. We have here, an ordered manifold, infinitely divisible and allowing of Free Mobility[4]. Free Mobility involves, as we saw, the power of passing continuously from any one point to any other, by any course which may seem pleasant to us; it involves, also, that, in such a

[1] Wiss. Abh. Vol. II. p. 614.

[2] Cp. Grassmann, Ausdehnungslehre von 1844, 2nd ed. p. XXIII.

[3] Delboeuf, it is true, speaks of Geometries with m/n dimensions, but gives no reference (Rev. Phil. T. XXXVI. p. 450).

[4] In criticizing Erdmann, it will be remembered, we saw that Free Mobility is a necessary property of his extents, though he does not regard it as such.

course, no changes occur except changes of mere position, *i.e.*, positions do not differ from one another in any qualitative way. (This absence of qualitative difference is the distinguishing mark of space as opposed to other manifolds, such as the colour- and tone-systems: in these, every element has a definite qualitative sensational value, whereas in space, the sensational value of a position depends wholly on its spatial relation to our own body, and is thus not intrinsic, but relative.) From the absence of qualitative differences among positions, it follows logically that positions exist only by virtue of other positions; one position differs from another just because they are two, not because of anything intrinsic in either. Position is thus defined simply and solely by relation to other positions. Any position, therefore, is completely defined when, and only when, enough such relations have been given to enable us to determine its relation to any new position, this new position being defined by the same number of relations. Now, in order that such definition may be at all possible, a finite number of relations must suffice. But every such relation constitutes a dimension. Therefore, if Geometry is to be possible, it is *à priori* necessary that space should have a finite integral number of dimensions.

161. The limitation of the dimensions to three is, as we have seen, empirical; nevertheless, it is not liable to the inaccuracy and uncertainty which usually belong to empirical knowledge. For the alternatives which logic leaves to sense are discrete—if the dimensions are not three, they must be two or four or some other number—so that *small* errors are out of the question[1]. Hence the final certainty of the axiom of three dimensions, though in part due to experience, is of quite a different order from that of (say) the law of Gravitation. In the latter, a small inaccuracy might exist and remain undetected; in the former, an error would have to be so considerable as to be utterly impossible to overlook. It follows that the certainty of our whole axiom, that the number of dimensions is three, is almost as great as that of the *à priori* element,

[1] Cf. Riemann, Hypothesen welche der Geometrie zu Grunde liegen, Gesammelte Werke, p. 266; also Erdmann, op. cit. p. 154.

since this element leaves to sense a definite disjunction of discrete possibilities.

III. *The Axiom of Distance.*

162. We have already seen, in discussing projective Geometry, that two points must determine a unique curve, the straight line. In metrical Geometry, the corresponding axiom is, that two points must determine a unique spatial quantity, distance. I propose to prove, in what follows, (1) that if distance, as a quantity completely determined by two points, did not exist, spatial magnitude would not be measurable; (2) that distance can only be determined by two points, if there is an actual curve in space determined by those two points; (3) that the existence of such a curve can be deduced from the conception of a form of externality, and (4) that the application of quantity to such a curve necessarily leads to a certain magnitude, namely distance, uniquely determined by any two points which determine the curve. The conclusion will be, if these propositions can be successfully maintained, that the axiom of distance is *à priori* in the same double sense as the axiom of Free Mobility, *i.e.* it is presupposed in the possibility of measurement, and it is necessarily true of any possible form of externality.

163. (1) The possibility of spatial measurement allows us to infer the existence of a magnitude uniquely determined by any two points. The proof of this depends on the axiom of Free Mobility, or its equivalent, the homogeneity of space. We have seen that these are involved in the possibility of spatial measurement; we may employ them, therefore, in any argument as to the conditions of this possibility.

Now to begin with, two points must, if Geometry is to be possible, have *some* relation to each other, for we have seen that such relations alone constitute position or localization. But if two points have a relation to each other, this must be an intrinsic relation. For it follows, from the axiom of Free Mobility, that two points, forming a figure congruent with the given pair, can be constructed in any part of space. If this were not possible, we have seen that metrical Geometry could not exist. But both the figures may be regarded as composed of two points and their relation; if the two figures are congruent, therefore, it follows that the relation is quantitatively the same for both figures, since congruence is the test of spatial equality. Hence the two points have a quantitative relation, which is such that they can traverse all space in a combined motion without in any way altering that relation. But in such a general motion, any external relation of the two points, any relation involving other points or figures in space, must be altered[1]. Hence the relation between the two points, being unaltered, must be an intrinsic relation, a relation involving no other point or figure in space; and this intrinsic relation we call distance[2].

164. It might be objected, to the above argument, that it involves a *petitio principii*. For it has been assumed that the two points and their relation form a figure, to which other figures can be congruent. Now if two points have no intrinsic relation, it would seem that they cannot form such a figure. The argument, therefore, apparently assumes what it had to prove. Why, it may be asked, should not three points be required, before we obtain any relation, which Free Mobility allows us to construct afresh in other parts of space?

The answer to this, as to the corresponding question in the first section of this chapter, lies, I think, in the passivity of space, or the mutual independence of its parts. For it follows, from this independence, that any figure, or any assemblage of points, may be discussed without reference to other figures or points. This principle is the basis of infinite divisibility, of

[1] This is subject, in spherical space, to the modification pointed out below, in dealing with the exception to the axiom of the straight line. See §§ 168—171.

[2] In speaking of distance at once as a quantity and as an intrinsic relation, I am anxious to guard against an apparent inconsistency. I have spoken of the judgment of quantity, throughout, as one of comparison; how, then, can a quantity be intrinsic? The reply is that, although measurement and the judgment of quantity express the result of comparison, yet the terms compared must exist before the comparison; in this case, the terms compared in measuring distances, *i.e.* in comparing them *inter se*, are intrinsic relations between points. Thus, although the *measurement* of distance involves a reference to other distances, and its expression as a magnitude requires such a reference, yet its existence does not depend on any external reference, but exclusively on the two points whose distance it is.

the use of quantity in Geometry, and of all possibility of isolating particular figures for discussion. It follows that two points cannot be dependent, as to their relation, on any other points or figures, for if they were so dependent, we should have to suppose some action of such points or figures on the two points considered, which would contradict the mutual independence of different positions. To illustrate by an example: the relation of two given points does not depend on the other points of the straight line on which the given points lie. For only through their relation, *i.e.* through the straight line which they determine, can the other points of the straight line be known to have any peculiar connection with the given pair.

165. But why, it may be asked, should there be only one such relation between two points? Why not several? The answer to this lies in the fact that points are wholly constituted by relations, and have no intrinsic nature of their own[1]. A point is defined by its relations to other points, and when once the relations necessary for definition have been given, no fresh relations to the points used in definition are possible, since the point defined has no qualities from which such relations could flow. Now one relation to any one other point is as good for definition as more would be, since however many we had, they would all remain unaltered in a combined motion of both points. Hence there can only be one relation determined by any two points.

166. (2) We have thus established our first proposition—two points have one and only one relation uniquely determined by those two points. This relation we call their distance apart. It remains to consider the conditions of the measurement of distance, *i.e.*, how far a unique value for distance involves a curve uniquely determined by the two points.

In the first place, some curve joining the two points is involved in the above notion of a combined motion of the two points, or of two other points forming a figure congruent with the first two. For without some such curve, the two point-pairs cannot be known as congruent, nor can we have any test by which to discover when a point-pair is moving as a single

[1] See the end of the argument on Free Mobility, § 155 ff.

figure[1]. Distance must be measured, therefore, by some line which joins the two points. But need this be a line which the two points completely determine?

167. We are accustomed to the definition of the straight line as the *shortest* distance between two points, which implies that distance might equally well be measured by curved lines. This implication I believe to be false, for the following reasons. When we speak of the length of a curve, we can give a meaning to our words only by supposing the curve divided into infinitesimal rectilinear arcs, whose sum gives the length of an equivalent straight line; thus unless we presuppose the straight line, we have no means of comparing the lengths of different curves, and can therefore never discover the applicability of our definition. It might be thought, perhaps, that some other line, say a circle, might be used as the basis of measurement. But in order to estimate in this way the length of any curve other than a circle, we should have to divide the curve into infinitesimal circular arcs. Now two successive points do not determine a circle, so that an arc of two points would have an indeterminate length. It is true that, if we exclude infinitesimal radii for the measuring circles, the lengths of the infinitesimal arcs would be determinate, even if the circles varied, but that is only because all the small circular arcs through two consecutive points coincide with the straight line through those two points. Thus, even with the help of the arbitrary restriction to a finite radius, all that happens is that we are brought back to the straight line. If, to mend matters, we take three consecutive points of our curve, and reckon distance by the arc of the circle of curvature, the notion of distance loses its fundamental property of being a relation between *two* points. For two consecutive points of the arc could

[1] In Frischauf's "Absolute Geometrie nach Johann Bolyai," Anhang, there is a series of definitions, starting from the sphere, as the locus of congruent point-pairs when one point of the pair is fixed, and hence obtaining the circle and the straight line. From the above it follows, that the sphere so defined already involves a curve between the points of the point-pair, by which various point-pairs can be known as congruent; and it will appear, as we proceed, that this curve must be a straight line. Frischauf's definition by means of the sphere involves, therefore, a vicious circle, since the sphere presupposes the straight line, as the test of congruent point-pairs.

not then be said to have any corresponding distance apart—three points would be necessary before the notion of distance became applicable. Thus the circle is not a possible basis for measurement, and similar objections apply, of course, with increased force, to any other curve. All this argument is designed to show, in detail, the logical impossibility of measuring distance by any curve not completely defined by the two points whose distance apart is required. If in the above we had taken distance as measured by circles of *given radius*, we should have introduced into its definition a relation to other points besides the two whose distance was to be measured, which we saw to be a logical fallacy. Moreover, how are we to know that all the circles have equal radii, until we have an independent measure of distance?

168. A straight line, then, is not the *shortest* distance, but is simply *the* distance between two points—so far, this conclusion has stood firm. But suppose we had two or more curves through two points, and that all these curves were congruent *inter se*. We should then say, in accordance with the definition of spatial equality, that the lengths of all these curves were equal. Now it might happen that, although no one of the curves was uniquely determined by the two end-points, yet the common length of all the curves was so determined. In this case, what would hinder us from calling this common length the distance apart, although no unique figure in space corresponded to it? This is the case contemplated by spherical Geometry, where, as on a sphere, antipodes can be joined by an infinite number of geodesics, all of which are of equal length. The difficulty supposed is, therefore, not a purely imaginary one, but one which modern Geometry forces us to face. I shall consequently discuss it at some length.

169. To begin with, I must point out that my axiom is not quite equivalent to Euclid's. Euclid's axiom states that two straight lines cannot enclose a space, *i.e.*, cannot have more than one common point. Now if every two points, without exception, determine a unique straight line, it follows, of course, that two different straight lines can have only one point in common—so far, the two axioms are equivalent. But it may happen, as in spherical space, that two points *in general* determine a unique straight line, but fail to do so when they have to each other the special relation of being antipodes. In such a system every pair of straight lines in the same plane meet in two points, which are each other's antipodes; but two points, *in general*, still determine a unique straight line. We are still able, therefore, to obtain distances from unique straight lines, except in limiting cases; and in such cases, we can take any point intermediate between the two antipodes, join it by the *same* straight line to both antipodes, and measure its distance from those antipodes in the usual way. The sum of these distances then gives a unique value for the distance between the antipodes.

Thus even in spherical space, we are greatly assisted by the axiom of the straight line; all linear measurement is effected by it, and exceptional cases can be treated, through its help, by the usual methods for limits. Spherical space, therefore, is not so adverse as it at first appeared to be to the *à priori* necessity of the axiom. Nevertheless we have, so far, not attacked the kernel of the objection which spherical space suggested. To this attack it is now our duty to proceed.

170. It will be remembered that, in our *à priori* proof that two points must have one definite relation, we held it impossible for those two points to have, to the rest of space, any relation which would be unaltered by motion. Now in spherical space, in the particular case where the two points are antipodes, they *have* a relation, unaltered by motion, to the rest of space—the relation, namely, that their distance is half the circumference of the universe. In our former discussion, we assumed that any relation to outside space must be a relation of position—and a relation of position must be altered by motion. But with a finite space, in which we have absolute magnitude, another relation becomes possible, namely, a relation of magnitude. Antipodal points, accordingly, like coincident points, no longer determine a unique straight line. And it is instructive to observe that there is, in consequence, an ambiguity in the expression for distance, like the ordinary ambiguity in angular measurement. If $1/k^2$ be the space constant, and d be one value for the distance between two points, $2\pi kn \pm d$, where n is any integer, is an equally good value.

Distance is, in short, a periodic function like angle. Thus such a state of things rather confirms than destroys my contention, that distance depends on a curve uniquely determined by two points. For as soon as we drop this unique determination, we see ambiguities creeping into our expression for distance. Distance still has a set of *discrete* values, corresponding to the fact that, given one point, the straight line is uniquely determined for all other points but one, the antipodal point. It is tempting to go on, and say: If through *every* pair of points there were an infinite number of the curves used in measuring distance, distance would be able, for the same pair of points, to take, not only a discrete series, but an infinite *continuous* series of values.

171. This, however, is mere speculation. I come now to the *pièce de résistance* of my argument. The ambiguity in spherical space arose, as we saw, from a relation of *magnitude* to the rest of space—such a relation being unaltered by a motion of the two points, and therefore falling outside our introductory reasoning. But what is this relation of magnitude? Simply a relation of the *distance* between the two points to a *distance* given in the nature of the space in question. It follows that such a relation *presupposes* a measure of distance, and need not, therefore, be contemplated in any argument which deals with the *à priori* requisites for the possibility of definite distances[1].

172. I have now shown, I hope conclusively, that spherical space affords no objection to the apriority of my axiom. Any two points have one relation, their distance, which is independent of the rest of space, and this relation requires, as its measure, a curve uniquely determined by those two points. I might have taken the bull by the horns, and said: Two points *can* have no relation but what is given by lines which join them, and therefore, if they have a relation independent of the rest of space, there must be one line joining them which they completely determine. Thus James says[2]:

[1] Nor in any argument which, like those of projective Geometry, avoids the notion of magnitude or distance altogether. It follows that the propositions of projective Geometry apply, without reserve, to spherical space, since the exception to the axiom of the straight line arises only on metrical ground.

[2] Psychology, Vol. II. pp. 149—150.

"Just as, in the field of quantity, the relation between two numbers is another number, so in the field of space the relations are facts of the same order with the facts they relate....... When we speak of the relation of direction of two points towards each other, we mean simply the sensation of the line that joins the two points together. *The line is the relation*...... The relation of position between the top and bottom points of a vertical line is that line, and nothing else."

If I had been willing to use this doctrine at the beginning, I might have avoided all discussion. A unique relation between two points *must* in this case, involve a unique line between them. But it seemed better to avoid a doctrine not universally accepted, the more so as I was approaching the question from the logical, not the psychological, side. After disposing of the objections, however, it is interesting to find this confirmation of the above theory from so different a standpoint. Indeed, I believe James's doctrine could be proved to be a logical necessity, as well as a psychological fact. For what sort of thing can a spatial relation between two distinct points be? It must be something spatial, and it must, since points are wholly constituted by their relations, be something at least as real and tangible as the points it relates. There seems nothing which can satisfy these requirements, except a line joining them. Hence, once more, a unique relation must involve a unique line. That is, linear magnitude is logically impossible, unless space allows of curves uniquely determined by any two of their points.

173. (3) But farther, the existence of curves uniquely determined by two points can be deduced from the nature of any form of externality[1]. For we saw, in discussing Free Mobility, that this axiom, together with homogeneity and the relativity of position, can be so deduced, and we saw in the beginning of our discussion on distance, that the existence of a unique relation between two points could be deduced from the homogeneity of space. Since position is relative, we may say, any two points must have *some* relation to each other: since

[1] This step in the argument has been put very briefly, since it is a mere repetition of the corresponding argument in Section A, and is inserted here only for the sake of logical completeness. See § 137 ff.

our form of externality is homogeneous, this relation can be kept unchanged while the two points move in the form, *i.e.*, change their relations to other points; hence their relation to each other is an intrinsic relation, independent of their relations to other points. But since our form *is* merely a complex of relations, a relation of externality must appear in the form, with the same evidence as anything else in the form; thus if the form be intuitive or sensational, the relation must be immediately presented, and not a mere inference. Hence the intrinsic relation between two points must be a unique figure in our form, *i.e.* in spatial terms, the straight line joining the two points.

174. (4) Finally, we have to prove that the existence of such a curve necessarily leads, when quantity is applied to the relation between two points, to a unique magnitude, which those two points completely determine. With this, we shall be brought back to distance, from which we started, and shall complete the circle of our argument.

We saw, in section A § 119, that the figure formed by two points is projectively indistinguishable from that formed by any two other points in the same straight line; the figure, in both cases, is, from the projective standpoint, simply the straight line on which the two points lie. The difference of relation, in the two cases, is not qualitative, since projective Geometry cannot deal with it; nevertheless, there is some difference of relation. For instance, if one point be kept fixed, while the other moves, there is obviously some change of relation. This change, since all parts of the straight line are qualitatively alike, must be a change of quantity. If two points, therefore, determine a unique figure, there must exist, for the distinction between the various other points of this figure, a unique quantitative relation between the two determining points, and therefore, since these points are arbitrary, between only two points. This relation is *distance*, with which our argument began, and to which it at least returns.

175. To sum up: If points are defined simply by relations to other points, *i.e.*, if all position is relative, *every point must have to every other point one, and only one, relation independent of the rest of space. This relation is the distance between the* *two points.* Now a relation between two points can only be defined by a line joining them—nay further, it may be contended that a relation can only *be* a line joining them. Hence a unique relation involves a unique line, *i.e.*, a line determined by any two of its points. Only in a space which admits of such a line is linear magnitude a logically possible conception. But when once we have established the possibility, *in general*, of drawing such lines, and therefore of measuring linear magnitudes, we may find that a certain magnitude has a peculiar relation to the constitution of space. The straight line may turn out to be of finite length, and in this case its length will give a certain peculiar magnitude, the space-constant. Two antipodal points, that is, points which bisect the entire straight line, will then have a relation of magnitude which, though unaltered by motion, is rendered peculiar by a certain constant relation to the rest of space. This peculiarity presupposes a measure of linear magnitude in general, and cannot, therefore, upset the apriority of the axiom of the straight line. But it destroys, for points having the peculiar antipodal relation to each other, the argument which proved that the relation between two points could not, since it was unchanged by motion, have reference to the rest of space. Thus it is intelligible that, for such special points, the axiom breaks down, and an infinite number of straight lines are possible between them; but unless we had started with assuming the general validity of the axiom, we could never have reached a position in which antipodal points could have been known to be peculiar, or, indeed, a position which would have enabled us to give any quantitative definition whatever of particular points.

Distance and the straight line, as relations uniquely determined by two points, are thus *à priori* necessary to metrical Geometry. But further, they are properties which must belong to any form of externality. Since their necessity for Geometry was deduced from homogeneity and the relativity of position, and since these are necessary properties of any form of externality, the same argument proves both conclusions. We thus obtain, as in the case of Free Mobility, a double apriority: The axiom of Distance, and its implication, the axiom of the Straight Line, are, on the one hand, presupposed in the possibility of spatial magnitude, and cannot, therefore, be contradicted by any experience resulting from the measurement of space; while they are consequences, on the other hand, of the necessary properties of any form of externality which is to render possible experience of an external world.

176. In connection with the straight line, it will be convenient to discuss the conditions of a metrical coordinate system. The projective coordinate system, as we have seen, aims only at a convenient nomenclature for different points, and can be set up without introducing the notion of spatial quantity. But a metrical coordinate system does much more than this. It defines every point quantitatively, by its quantitative spatial relations to a certain coordinate figure. Only when the system of coordinates is thus metrical, *i.e.*, when every coordinate represents some spatial magnitude, which is itself a relation of the point defined to some other point or figure—can operations with coordinates lead to a metrical result. When, as in projective Geometry, the coordinates are not spatial magnitudes, no amount of transformation can give a metrical result. I wish to prove, here, that a metrical coordinate system necessarily involves the straight line, and cannot, without a logical fallacy, be set up on any other basis. The projective system of coordinates, as we saw, is entirely based on the straight line; but the metrical system is more important, since its quantities embody actual information as to spatial magnitudes, which, in projective Geometry, is not the case.

In the first place, a point's metrical coordinates constitute a complete quantitative definition of it; now a point can only be defined, as we have seen, by its relations to other points, and these relations can only be defined by means of the straight line. Consequently, any metrical system of coordinates must involve the straight line, as the basis of its definitions of points.

This *à priori* argument, however, though I believe it to be quite sound, is not likely to carry conviction to any one persuaded of the opposite. Let us, therefore, examine metrical coordinate systems in detail, and show, in each case, their dependence on the straight line.

We have already seen that the notion of distance is impossible without the straight line. We cannot, therefore, define our coordinates in any of the ordinary ways, as the distances from three planes, lines, points, spheres, or what not. Polar coordinates are impossible, since,—waiving the straightness of the radius vector—the length of the radius vector becomes unmeaning. Triangular coordinates involve not only angles, which must in the limit be rectilinear, but straight lines, or at any rate some well-defined curves. Now curves can only be metrically defined in two ways: *Either* by relation to the straight line, as, *e.g.*, by the curvature at any point, *or* by purely analytical equations, which presuppose an intelligible system of metrical coordinates. What methods remain for assigning these arbitrary values to different points? Nay, how are we to get any estimate of the difference—to avoid the more special notion of distance—between two points? The very notion of a point has become illusory. When we have a coordinate system, we may define a point by its three coordinates; in the absence of such a system, we may define the notion of point *in general* as the intersection of three surfaces or of two curves. Here we take surfaces and curves as notions which intuition makes plain, but if we wish them to give us a precise numerical definition of *particular* points, we must specify the kind of surface or curve to be used. Now this, as we have seen, is only possible when we presuppose either the straight line, or a coordinate system. It follows that every coordinate system presupposes the straight line, and is logically impossible without it.

177. The above three axioms, we have seen, are *à priori* necessary to metrical Geometry. No others can be necessary, since metrical systems, logically as unassailable as Euclid's, and dealing with spaces equally homogeneous and equally relational, have been constructed by the metageometers, without the help of any other axioms. The remaining axioms of Euclidean Geometry—the axiom of parallels, the axiom that the number of dimensions is three, and Euclid's form of the axiom of the straight line (two straight lines cannot enclose a space)—are not essential to the possibility of metrical Geometry, *i.e.*, are not deducible from the fact that a science of spatial magnitudes is possible. They are rather to be regarded as empirical laws, obtained, like the empirical laws of other sciences, by actual investigation of the given subject-matter—in this instance, experienced space.

178. In summing up the distinctive argument of this Section, we may give it a more general form, and discuss the conditions of measurement in any continuous manifold, *i.e.,* the qualities necessary to the manifold, in order that quantities in it may be determinable, not only as to the more or less, but as to the precise *how much.*

Measurement, we may say, is the application of number to continua, or, if we prefer it, the transformation of mere quantity into number of units. Using *quantity* to denote the vague more or less, and *magnitude* to denote the precise number of units, the problem of measurement may be defined as the transformation of quantity into magnitude.

Now a number, to begin with, is a whole consisting of smaller units, all of these units being qualitatively alike. In order, therefore, that a continuous quantity may be expressible as a number, it must, on the one hand, be itself a whole, and must, on the other hand, be divisible into qualitatively similar parts. In the aspect of a whole, the quantity is *intensive*; in the aspect of an aggregate of parts, it is *extensive.* A purely intensive quantity, therefore, is not numerable—a purely extensive quantity, if any such could be imagined, would not be a single quantity at all, since it would have to consist of wholly unsynthesized particulars. A measurable quantity, therefore, is a whole divisible into similar parts. But a continuous quantity, if divisible at all, must be *infinitely* divisible. For otherwise the points at which it could be divided would form natural barriers, and so destroy its continuity. But further, it is not sufficient that there should be a possibility of division into mutually external parts; while the parts, to be perceptible as parts, must be mutually external, they must also, to be knowable as *equal* parts, be capable of overcoming their mutual externality. For this, as we have seen, we require superposition, which involves Free Mobility and homogeneity—the absence of Free Mobility in time, where all other requisites of measurement are fulfilled, renders direct measurement of time impossible. Hence infinite divisibility, free mobility, and homogeneity are necessary for the possibility of measurement in *any* continuous manifold, and these, as we have seen, are equivalent to our three axioms. These axioms are necessary, therefore, not only for spatial measurement, but for all measurement. The only manifold given in experience, in which these conditions are satisfied, is space. All other exact measurement—as could be proved, I believe, for every separate case—is effected, as we saw in the case of time, by reduction to a spatial correlative. This explains the paramount importance, to exact science, of the mechanical view of nature, which reduces all phenomena to motions in time and space. For number is, of all conceptions, the easiest to operate with, and science seeks everywhere for an opportunity to apply it, but finds this opportunity only by means of spatial equivalents to phenomena[1].

179. We have now seen in what the *à priori* element of Geometry consists. This *à priori* element may be defined as the axioms common to Euclidean and non-Euclidean spaces, as the axioms deducible from the conception of a form of externality, or—in metrical Geometry—as the axioms required for the possibility of measurement. It remains to discuss, in a final chapter, some questions of a more general philosophic nature, in which we shall have to desert the firm ground of mathematics and enter on speculations which I put forward very tentatively, and with little faith in their ultimate validity. The chief questions for this final chapter will be two: (1) How is such *à priori* and purely logical necessity possible, as applied to an actually given subject-matter like space? (2) How can we remove the contradictions which have haunted us in this chapter, arising out of the relativity, infinite divisibility, and unbounded extension of space? These two questions are forced upon us by the present chapter, but as they open some of the fundamental problems of philosophy, it would be rash to expect a conclusive or wholly satisfactory answer. A few hints and suggestions may be hoped for, but a complete solution could only be obtained from a complete philosophy, of which the prospects are far too slender to encourage a confident frame of mind.

[1] Cf. Hannequin, Essai critique sur l'hypothèse des atomes, Paris, 1895, passim.

CHAPTER IV.

PHILOSOPHICAL CONSEQUENCES.

180. In the present chapter, we have to discuss two questions which, though scarcely geometrical, are of fundamental importance to the theory of Geometry propounded above. The first of these questions is this: What relation can a purely logical and deductive proof, like that from the nature of a form of externality, bear to an experienced subject-matter such as space? You have merely framed a general conception, I may be told, containing space as a particular species, and you have then shown, what should have been obvious from the beginning, that this general conception contained some of the attributes of space. But what ground does this give for regarding these attributes as *à priori*? The conception Mammal has some of the attributes of a horse; but are these attributes therefore *à priori* adjectives of the horse? The answer to this obvious objection is so difficult, and involves so much general philosophy, that I have kept it for a final chapter, in order not to interrupt the argument on specially geometrical topics.

181. I have already indicated, in general terms, the ground for regarding as *à priori* the properties of any form of externality. This ground is transcendental, *i.e.* it is to be found in the conditions required for the possibility of experience. The form of externality, like Riemann's manifolds, is a general class-conception, including time as well as Euclidean and non-Euclidean spaces. It is not motived, however, like the manifolds, by a *quantitative* resemblance to space, but by the fact that it fulfils, if it has more than one dimension, all those functions which, in our actual world, are fulfilled by space. But a form of externality, in order to accomplish this, must be, not a mere conception, but an actually experienced intuition. Hence the conception of such a form is the general *conception*, containing under it every logically possible *intuition* which can fulfil the function actually fulfilled by space. And this function is, to render possible experience of diverse but interrelated things. Some form in sense-perception, then, whose conception is included under our form of externality, is *à priori* necessary to experience of diversity in relation, and without experience of this, we should, as modern logic shows, have no experience at all. This still leaves untouched the relation of the *à priori* to the subjective: the form of externality is necessary to experience, but is not, *on that account*, to be declared purely subjective. Of course, necessity for experience can only arise from the nature of the mind which experiences; but it does not follow that the necessary conditions could be fulfilled, unless the objective world had certain properties. The *ground* of necessity, we may safely say, arises from the mind; but it by no means follows that the *truth* of what is necessary depends only on the constitution of the mind. Where this is not the case, our conclusion, when a piece of knowledge has been declared *à priori*, can only be: Owing to the constitution of the *mind*, experience will be impossible unless the *world* accepts certain adjectives.

Such, in outline, will be the argument of the first half of this chapter, and such will be the justification for regarding as *à priori* those axioms of Geometry, which were deduced above from the conception of a form of externality. For these axioms, and these only, are necessarily true of any world in which experience is possible.

182[1]. The view suggested has, obviously, much in common with that of the Transcendental Aesthetic. Indeed the whole of it, I believe, can be obtained by a certain limitation and interpretation of Kant's classic arguments. But as it differs, in many important points, from the conclusions aimed at by Kant, and as the agreement may easily seem greater than it is, I will begin by a brief comparison, and endeavour, by reference

[1] Compare, with the following paragraphs, the admirable discussion in Mr Hobhouse's Theory of Knowledge (Methuen 1896), Part I. Chapter II.

to authoritative criticisms, to establish the legitimacy of my divergence from him.

183. In the first place, the psychological element is much larger in Kant's thesis than in mine. I shall contend, it is true, that a form of externality, if it is to do its work, must not be a mere conception or a mere inference, but must be a given element in sense-perception—not, of course, originally given in isolation, but discoverable, through analysis, by attention to the object of sense-perception[1]. But Kant contended, not only that this element is given, but also that it is subjective. Space, for him, is, on the one hand, not conceptual, but on the other hand, not sensational. It forms, for him, no part of the data of sense, but is added by a subjective intuition, which he regards as not only logically, but psychologically, prior to objects in space[2].

This part of Kant's argument is wholly irrelevant for us. Whether a form of externality be given in sense, or in a pure intuition, is for us unimportant, since we neglect the question as to the connection of the *à priori* and the subjective; while the temporal priority of space to objects in it has been generally recognized as irrelevant to Epistemology, and has often been regarded as forming no part of Kant's thesis[3]. If we call intuitional whatever is given in sense-perception, then we may contend that a form of externality must be intuitional; but whether it is a pure intuition, in Kant's sense, or not, is irrelevant to us, as is its priority to the objects in it.

That the non-sensational nature of space is no essential part of Kant's *logical* teaching, appears from an examination of his argument. He has made, in the introduction, the purely logical distinction of matter and form, but has given to this distinction, in the very moment of suggesting it, a psychological implication. This he does by the assertion that the form, in which the matter of sensations is ordered, cannot itself be sensational. From this assumption it follows, of course, that space cannot be sensational. But the assumption is

[1] I speak of sense-perception instead of sensation, so as not to prejudge the issue as to the sensational nature of space,

[2] See Vaihinger's Commentar, II. pp. 86—7, 168—171.

[3] See Caird, Critical Philosophy of Kant, Vol. I. p. 287.

totally unsupported by argument, being set forth, apparently, as a self-evident axiom; it has been severely criticized by Stumpf[1] and others[2], and has been described by Vaihinger as a fatal *petitio principii*[3]; it is irrelevant to the logical argument, when this argument is separated, as we have separated it, from all connection with psychological subjectivity; and finally, it leaves us a prey to psychological theories of space, which have seemed, of late, but little favourable to the pure Kantian doctrine.

184. We have a right, therefore, in an epistemological inquiry, to neglect Kant's psychological teaching—in so far, at any rate, as it distinguishes spatial intuition from sensation—and attend rather to the logical aspect alone. That part of his psychological teaching, which maintains that space is not a mere conception, is, with certain limitations, sufficiently evident as applied to actual space; but for us, it must be transformed into a much more difficult thesis, namely, that *no* form of externality, which renders experience of diversity in relation possible, can be merely conceptual. This question, to which we must return later, is no longer psychological, but belongs wholly to Epistemology.

185. What, then, remains the kernel, for our purposes, of Kant's first argument for the apriority of space? His argument, in the form in which he gave it, is concerned with the eccentric projection of sensations. In order that I may refer sensations, he says, to something outside myself, I must already have the subjective space-form in the mind. In this shape, as Vaihinger points out (Commentar, II. pp. 69, 165), the argument rests on a *petitio principii*, for only if sensations are necessarily non-spatial does their projection demand a subjective space-form. But, further, is the logical apriority of space concerned with the externality of things to ourselves?

Space *seems* to perform two functions: on the one hand, it reveals things, by the eccentric projection of sensations, as external to the self, while, on the other hand, it reveals simultaneously presented things as mutually external. These

[1] Ursprung der Raumvorstellung, pp. 12—30.

[2] See the references in Vaihinger's Commentar, II. p. 76 ff.

[3] Commentar, II. p. 71 ff.

two functions, though often treated as coordinate and almost equivalent[1], seem to me widely different. Before we discuss the apriority of space, we must carefully distinguish, I think, between these two functions, and decide which of them we are to argue about.

Now externality to the Self, it would seem, must necessarily raise the whole question of the nature and limits of the Ego, and what is more, it cannot be derived from spatial presentation, unless we give the Self a definite position in space. But things acquire a position in space only when they can appear in sense-perception; we are forced, therefore, if we adopt this view of the function of space, to regard the Self as a phenomenon presented to sense-perception. But this reduces externality to the Self to externality to the body. The body, however, is a presented object like any other, and externality of objects to it is, therefore, a special case of the mutual externality of presented things. Hence we cannot regard space as giving, primarily at any rate, externality to the Self, but only the mutual externality of the things presented to sense-perception[2].

186. This, then, is the kind of externality we are to expect from space, and our question must be: Would the existence of diverse but interrelated things be unknowable, if there were not, in sense-perception, some form of externality? This is the crucial question, on which turns the apriority of our form, and hence of the necessary axioms of Geometry.

187. The converse argument to mine, the argument from the spatio-temporal element in perception to a world of interrelated but diverse things, is developed at length in Bradley's Logic. It is put briefly in the following sentence (p. 44, note): "If space and time are continuous, and if all appearance must occupy some time or space—and it is not hard to support both these *theses*—we can at once proceed to the conclusion, no mere particular exists. Every phenomenon will exist in more times or spaces than one; and against that diversity will be itself an universal[3]." The importance of this fact appears, when we

[1] *E.g.* by Caird, *op. cit.* Vol. I. p. 286.

[2] I have no wish to deny, however, that space is essential in the subsequent distinction of Self and not-Self.

[3] See also Book I. Chap II. passim; especially p. 51 ff. and pp. 70–1.

consider that, if any *mere* particular existed, all judgment and inference as to that particular would be impossible, since all judgment and inference necessarily operate by means of universals. But all reality is constructed from the *This* of immediate presentation, from which judgment and inference necessarily spring. Owing, however, to the continuity and relativity of space and time, no *This* can be regarded either as simple or as self-subsistent. Every *This*, on the one hand, can be analyzed into *Thises*, and on the other hand, is found to be necessarily related to other things, outside the limits of the given object of sense-perception. This function of space and time is presupposed in the following statement from Bosanquet's Logic (Vol. I. pp. 77—78): "Reality is given for me *in* present sensuous perception, and *in* the immediate feeling of my own sentient existence that goes with it. The real world, as a definite organized system, is *for me* an extension of this present sensation and self feeling by means of judgment, and it is the essence of judgment to effect and sustain such an extension... The subject in every judgment of Perception is some given spot or point in sensuous contact with the percipient self. But, as all reality is continuous, the subject is not *merely* this given spot or point."

188. This doctrine of Bradley and Bosanquet is the converse of the epistemological doctrine I have to advocate. Owing to the continuity and relativity of space and time, they say, we are able to construct a systematic world, by judgment and inference, out of that fragmentary and yet necessarily complex existence which is given in sense-perception. My contention is, conversely, that since all knowledge is necessarily derived by an extension of the *This* of sense-perception, and since such extension is only possible if the *This* has that fragmentary and yet complex character conferred by a form of externality, therefore some form of externality, given with the *This*, is essential to all knowledge, and is thus logically *à priori*. Bradley's argument, if sound, already proves this contention; for while, on the one hand, he uses no properties of space and time but those which belong to every form of externality, he proves, on the other hand, that judgment and inference require the *This* to be neither single nor self-subsistent. But I will endeavour, since the point is of fundamental importance, to reproduce the proof, in a form more suited than Bradley's to the epistemological question.

189. The essence of my contention is that, if experience is to be possible, every sensational *This* must, when attended to, be found, on the one hand, resolvable into *Thises*, and on the other hand dependent, for some of its adjectives, on external reference. The second of these theses follows from the first, for if we take one of the *Thises* contained in the first *This*, we get a new *This* necessarily related to the other *Thises* which make up the original *This*. I may, therefore, confine myself to the first proposition, which affirms that the object of perception must contain a diversity, not only of conceptual content, but of existence, and that this can only be known if sense-perception contains, as an element, some form of externality.

My premiss, in this argument, is that all knowledge involves a recognition of diversity in relation, or, if we prefer it, of identity in difference. This premiss I accept from Logic, as resulting from the analysis of judgment and inference. To prove such a premiss, would require a treatise on Logic; I must refer the reader, therefore, to the works of Bradley and Bosanquet on the subject. It follows at once, from my premiss, that knowledge would be impossible, unless the object of attention could be complex, *i.e.* not a *mere* particular. Now could the mental object—*i.e.*, in this connection, the object of a cognition—be complex, if the object of immediate perception were always simple?

190. We might be inclined, at first sight, to answer this question affirmatively. But several difficulties, I think, would prevent such an answer. In the first place, knowledge must start from perception. Hence, either we could have no knowledge except of our present perception, or else we must be able to contrast and compare it with some other perception. Now in the first case, since the present perception, by hypothesis, is a mere particular, knowledge of it is impossible, according to our premiss. But in the second case, the other perception, with which we compare our first, must have occurred at some other time, and with time, we have at once a form of externality. But what is more, our present perception is no longer a mere particular. For the power of comparing it with another perception involves a point of identity between the two, and thus renders both complex. Moreover, time must be continuous, and the present, as Bradley points out, is no mere point of time[1]. Thus our present perception contains the complexity involved in duration throughout the specious present: its mere particularity and its simplicity are lost. Its self-subsistence is also lost, for beyond the specious present, lie the past and the future, to which our present perception thus unavoidably refers us. Time at least, therefore, is essential to that identity in difference, which all knowledge postulates.

191. But we have derived, from all this, no ground for affirming a multiplicity of real things, or a form of externality of more than one dimension, which, we saw, was necessary for the truth of two out of our three axioms. This brings us to the question: Have we enough, with time alone as a form of externality, for the possibility of knowledge?

This question we must, I think, answer in the negative. With time alone, we have seen, our presented object must be complex, but its complexity must, if I may use such a phrase, be merely adjectival. Without a second form of externality, only one thing can be given at one moment[2], and this one thing, therefore, must constitute the whole of our world. The object of past perception must—since our one thing has nothing external to it, by which it could be created or destroyed—be regarded as the same thing in a different state. The complexity, therefore, will lie only in the changing states of our one thing—it will be adjectival, not substantival. Moreover we have the following dilemma: Either the one thing must be ourselves, or else self-consciousness could never arise. But the chief difficulty of such a world would lie in the changes of the thing. What could cause these changes, since we should know of nothing external to our thing? It would be like a Leibnitzian monad, without any God outside it to prearrange its changes. Causality, in such a world, could not be applied, and change would be wholly inexplicable.

[1] Logic, p. 51 ff.

[2] For the *This*, on such a hypothesis, has a purely temporal complexity, and is not resolvable into coexisting *Thises*.

Hence we require also the possibility of a diversity of simultaneously existing things, not merely of successive adjectives; and this, we have seen, cannot be given by time alone, but only by a form of externality for simultaneous parts of one presentation. We could never, in other words, infer the existence of diverse but interrelated things, unless the object of sense-perception could have substantival complexity, and for such complexity we require a form of externality other than time. Such a form, moreover, as was shown in Chapter III., Section A (§ 135), can only fulfil its functions if it has more than one dimension. In our actual world, this form is given by space; in any world, knowable to beings with our laws of thought, some such form, as we have now seen, must be given in sense-perception.

This argument may be briefly summed up, by assuming the doctrine of Bradley, that all knowledge is obtained by inference from the *This* of sense-perception. For, if this be so, the *This*—in order that inference, which depends on identity in difference, may be possible at all—must itself be complex, and must, on analysis, reveal adjectives having a reference beyond itself. But this, as was shown above, can only happen by means of a form of externality. This establishes the *à priori* axioms of Geometry, as necessarily having existential import and validity in any intelligible world.

192. The above argument, I hope, has explained why I hold it possible to deduce, from a mere conception like that of a form of externality, the logical apriority of certain axioms as to experienced space. The Kantian argument—which was correct, if our reasoning has been sound, in asserting that real diversity, in our actual world, could only be known by the help of space—was only mistaken, so far as its purely logical scope extends, in overlooking the possibility of other forms of externality, which could, if they existed, perform the same task with equal efficiency. In so far as space differs, therefore, from these other conceptions of possible intuitional forms, it is a mere experienced fact, while in so far as its properties are those which all such forms must have, it is *à priori* necessary to the possibility of experience.

I cannot hope, however, that no difficulty will remain, for

the reader, in such a deduction, from abstract conceptions, of the properties of an actual *datum* in sense-perception. Let us consider, for example, such a property as impenetrability. To suppose two things simultaneously in the same position in a form of externality, is a logical contradiction; but can we say as much of actual space and time? Is not the impossibility, here, a matter of experience rather than of logic? Not if the above argument has been sound, I reply. For in that case, we infer real diversity, *i.e.* the existence of different things, only from difference of position in space or time. It follows, that to suppose two things in the same point of space and time, is still a logical contradiction: not because we have constructed the data of sense out of logic, but because logic is dependent, as regards its application, on the nature of these data. This instance illustrates, what I am anxious to make plain, that my argument has not attempted to construct the living wealth of sense-perception out of "bloodless categories," but only to point out that, unless sense-perception contained a certain element, these categories would be powerless to grapple with it.

193. How we are to account for the fortunate realization of these requirements—whether by a pre-established harmony, by Darwinian adaptation to our environment, by the subjectivity of the necessary element in sense-perception, or by a fundamental identity and unity between ourselves and the rest of reality—is a further question, belonging rather to metaphysics than to our present line of argument. The *à priori*, we have said throughout, is that which is necessary for the possibility of experience, and in this we have a purely logical criterion, giving results which only Logic and Epistemology can prove or disprove. What is subjective in experience, on the contrary, is primarily a question for psychology, and should be decided on psychological grounds alone. When these two questions have been separately answered, but not till then, we may frame theories as to the connection of the *à priori* and the subjective; to allow such theories to influence our decision, on either of the two previous questions, is liable, surely, to confuse the issue, and prevent a clear discrimination between fundamentally different points of view.

194. I come now to the second question with which this chapter has to deal, the question, namely: What are we to do with the contradictions which obtruded themselves in Chapter III., whenever we came to a point which seemed fundamental? I shall treat this question briefly, as I have little to add to answers with which we are all familiar. I have only to prove, first, that the contradictions are inevitable, and therefore form no objection to my argument; secondly, that the first step in removing them is to restore the notion of matter, as that which, in the data of sense-perception, is localized and interrelated in space.

195. The contradictions in space are an ancient theme—as ancient, in fact, as Zeno's refutation of motion. They are, roughly, of two kinds, though the two kinds cannot be sharply divided. There are the contradictions inherent in the notion of the continuum, and the contradictions which spring from the fact that space, while it must, to be knowable, be pure relativity, must also, it would seem, since it is immediately experienced, be something more than mere relations. The first class of contradictions has been encountered more frequently in this essay, and is also, I think, the more definite, and the more important for our present purpose. I doubt, however, whether the two classes are really distinct; for any continuum, I believe, in which the elements are not data, but intellectual constructions resulting from analysis, can be shown to have the same relational and yet not wholly relational character as belongs to space.

The three following contradictions, which I shall discuss successively, seem to me the most prominent in a theory of Geometry.

(1) Though the parts of space are intuitively distinguished, no conception is adequate to differentiate them. Hence arises a vain search for elements, by which the differentiation could be accomplished, and for a whole, of which the parts of space are to be components. Thus we get the point, or zero extension, as the spatial element, and an infinite regress or a vicious circle in the search for a whole.

(2) All positions being relative, positions can only be defined by their relations, *i.e.* by the straight lines or planes

through them; but straight lines and planes, being all qualitatively similar, can only be defined by the positions they relate. Hence, again, we get a vicious circle.

(3) Spatial figures must be regarded as relations. But a relation is necessarily indivisible, while spatial figures are necessarily divisible *ad infinitum*.

196. (1) *Points.* The antinomy of the point—which arises wherever a continuum is given, and elements have to be sought in it—is fundamental to Geometry. It has been given, perhaps unintentionally, by Veronese as the first axiom, in the form: "There are different points. All points are identical" (*op. cit.* p. 226). We saw, in discussing projective Geometry, that straight lines and planes must be regarded, on the one hand as relations between points, and on the other hand as made up of points[1]. We saw again, in dealing with measurement, how space must be regarded as infinitely divisible, and yet as mere relativity. But what is divisible and consists of parts, as space does, must lead at last, by continued analysis, to a simple and unanalyzable part, as the unit of differentiation. For whatever can be divided, and has parts, possesses some thinghood, and must, therefore, contain two ultimate units, the whole namely, and the smallest element possessing thinghood. But in space this is notoriously not the case. After hypostatizing space, as Geometry is compelled to do, the mind imperatively demands elements, and insists on having them, whether possible or not. Of this demand, all the geometrical applications of the infinitesimal calculus are evidence[2]. But what sort of elements do we thus obtain? Analysis, being unable to find any earlier halting-place, finds its elements in points, that is, in zero quanta of space. Such a conception is a palpable contradiction, only rendered tolerable by its necessity and familiarity. A point must be spatial, otherwise it would not fulfil the function of a spatial element; but again it must contain no space, for any finite extension is capable of further analysis. Points can never be given in intuition, which has no concern with the infinitesimal: they are a purely conceptual construction, arising

[1] Chapter III. Section A, (§ 131).

[2] Cf. Hannequin, Essai critique sur l'hypothèse des atomes, Paris 1895, Chap. I. Section III.; especially p. 43.

out of the need of terms between which spatial relations can hold. If space be more than relativity, spatial relations must involve spatial relata; but no relata appear, until we have analyzed our spatial data down to nothing. The contradictory notion of the point, as a thing in space without spatial magnitude, is the only outcome of our search for spatial relata. This *reductio ad absurdum* surely suffices, by itself, to prove the essential relativity of space.

197. Thus Geometry is forced, since it wishes to regard space as independent, to hypostatize its abstractions, and therefore to invent a self-contradictory notion as the spatial element. A similar absurdity appears, even more obviously, in the notion of a whole of space. The antinomy may, therefore, be stated thus: Space, as we have seen throughout, must, if knowledge of it is to be possible, be mere relativity; but it must also, if *independent* knowledge of it, such as Geometry seeks, is to be possible, be something more than mere relativity, since it is divisible and has parts. But we saw, in Chap. III., Section A (§ 133) that knowledge of a form of externality must be logically independent of the particular matter filling the form. How then are we to extricate ourselves from this dilemma?

The only way, I think, is, not to make Geometry dependent on Physics, which we have seen to be erroneous[1], but to give every geometrical proposition a certain reference to matter in general. And at this point an important distinction must be made. We have hitherto spoken of space as relational, and of spatial figures as relations. But space, it would seem, is rather relativity than relations—itself not a relation, it gives the bare possibility of relations between diverse things[2]. As applied to a spatial figure, which can only arise by a differentiation of space, and hence by the introduction of some differentiating matter, the word relation is, perhaps, less misleading than any other; as applied to empty undifferentiated space, it seems by no means an accurate description.

But a bare possibility cannot exist, or be given in sense-perception! What becomes, then, of the arguments of the

[1] See Chapter II. § 69 ff.

[2] See third antinomy below, § 201 ff.

first part of this chapter? I reply, it is not empty space, but spatial figures, which sense-perception reveals, and spatial figures, as we have just seen, involve a differentiation of space, and therefore a reference to the matter which is in space. It is spatial figures, also, and not empty space, with which Geometry has to deal. The antinomy discussed above arises then—so it would seem—from the attempt to deal with empty space, rather than with spatial figures and the matter to which they necessarily refer.

198. Let us see whether, by this change, we can overcome the antinomy of the point. Spatial figures, we shall now say, are relations between the matter which differentiates empty space. Their divisibility, which seemed to contradict their relational character, may be explained in two ways: first, as holding of the figures considered as parts of empty space, which is itself not a relation; second, as denoting the possibility of continuous change in the relation expressed by the spatial figure. These two ways are, at bottom, the same; for empty space is a possibility of relations, and the figure, when viewed in connection with empty space, thus becomes a *possible* relation, with which other possible relations may be contrasted or compared. But the second way of regarding divisibility is the better way, since it introduces a reference to the matter which differentiates empty space, without which, spatial figures, and therefore Geometry, could not exist. It is empty space, then—so we must conclude—which gives rise to the antinomy in question; for empty space is a bare possibility of relations, undifferentiated and homogeneous, and thus wholly destitute of parts or of thinghood. To speak of parts of a possibility is nonsense; the parts and differentiations arise only through a reference to the matter which is differentiated in space.

199. But what nature must we ascribe to this matter, which is to be involved in all geometrical propositions? In criticizing Helmholtz (Chap. II. § 73), it may be remembered, we decided that Geometry refers to a peculiar and abstract kind of matter, which is not regarded as possessing any causal qualities, as exerting or as subject to the action of forces. And this is the matter, I think, which we require for the needs of the moment. Not that we affirm, of course, that actual matter can be destitute of the properties with which Physics is cognizant, but that we abstract from these properties, as being irrelevant to Geometry. All that we require, for our immediate purpose, is a subject of that diversity which space renders possible, or terms for those relations by which empty space, if space is to be studied at all, must be differentiated. But how must a matter, which is to fulfil this function, be regarded?

Empty space, we have said, is a possibility of diversity in relation, but spatial figures, with which Geometry necessarily deals, are the actual relations rendered possible by empty space. Our matter, therefore, must supply the terms for these relations. It must be differentiated, since such differentiation, as we have seen, is the special work of space. We must find, therefore, in our matter, that unit of differentiation, or atom[1], which in space we could not find. This atom must be simple, *i.e.* it must contain no real diversity; it must be a *This* not resolvable into *Thises*. Being simple, it can contain no relations within itself, and consequently, since spatial figures are mere relations, it cannot appear as a spatial figure; for every spatial figure involves some diversity of matter. But our atom must have spatial relations with other atoms, since to supply terms for these relations is its only function. It is also capable of having these relations, since it is differentiated from other atoms. Hence we obtain an unextended term for spatial relations, precisely of the kind we require. So long as we sought this term without reference to anything more than space, the self-contradictory notion of the point was the only outcome of our search; but now that we allow a reference to the matter differentiated by space, we find at once the term which was needed, namely, a non-spatial simple element, with spatial relations to other elements. To Geometry such a term will appear, owing to its spatial relations, as a point; but the contradiction of the point, as we now see, is a result only of the undue abstraction with which Geometry deals.

200. (2) *The circle in the definition of straight lines and planes.* This difficulty need not long detain us, since we have already, with the material atom, broken through the relativity which caused our circle. Straight lines, in the purely geometrical

[1] This atom, of course, must not be confounded with the atom of Chemistry.

procedure, are defined only by points, and points only by straight lines. But points, now, are replaced by material atoms: the duality of points and lines, therefore, has disappeared, and the straight line may be defined as the spatial relation between two unextended atoms. These atoms have spatial adjectives, derived from their relations to other atoms; but they have no *intrinsic* spatial adjectives, such as could belong to them if they had extension or figure. Thus straight lines and planes are the true spatial units, and points result only from the attempt to find, within space, those terms for spatial relations which exist only in a more than spatial matter. Straight lines, planes and volumes are the spatial relations between two, three or four unextended atoms, and points are a merely convenient geometrical fiction, by which possible atoms are replaced. For, since space, as we saw, is a possibility, Geometry deals not with actually realized spatial relations, but with the whole scheme of possible relations.

201. (3) *Space is at once relational and more than relational.* We have already touched on the question how far space is other than relations, but as this question is quite fundamental, as *relation* is an ambiguous and dangerous word, as I have made constant use of the relativity of space without attempting to define a relation, it will be necessary to discuss this antinomy at length.

202. Now for this discussion it is essential to distinguish clearly between empty space and spatial figures. Empty space, as a form of externality, is not actual relations, but the possibility of relations: if we ascribe existential import to it, as the ground, in reality, of all diversity in relation, we at once have space as something not itself relations, though giving the possibility of all relations. In this sense, space is to be distinguished from spatial order. Spatial order, it may be said, presupposes space, as that in which this order is possible. Thus Stumpf says[1]: "There is no order or relation without a positive absolute content, underlying it, and making it possible to order anything in this manner. Why and how should we otherwise distinguish one order from another?...To distinguish different orders from one another, we must everywhere recognize a

[1] Ursprung der Raumvorstellung, p. 15.

particular absolute content, in relation to which the order takes place. And so space, too, is not a mere order, but just that by which the spatial order, side-by-sideness (*Nebeneinander*) distinguishes itself from the rest."

May we not, then, resolve the antinomy very simply, by a reference to this ambiguity of space? Bradley contends (Appearance and Reality, pp. 36–7) that, on the one hand, space has parts, and is therefore not mere relations, while on the other hand, when we try to say what these parts are, we find them after all to be mere relations. But cannot the space which has parts be regarded as empty space, Stumpf's absolute underlying content, which is not mere relations, while the parts, in so far as they turn out to be mere relations, are those relations which constitute spatial order, not empty space? If this can be maintained, the antinomy no longer exists.

But such an explanation, though I believe it to be a first step towards a solution, will, I fear, itself demand almost as much explanation as the original difficulty. For the connection of empty space with spatial order is itself a question full of difficulty, to be answered only after much labour.

203. Let us consider what this empty space is. (I speak of "empty" space without necessarily implying the absence of matter, but only to denote a space which is not a mere order of material things.) Stumpf regards it as given in sense; Kant, in the last two arguments of his metaphysical deduction, argues that it is an intuition, not a concept, and must be known before spatial order becomes possible. I wish to maintain, on the contrary, that it is wholly conceptual; that space is given only as spatial order; that spatial relations, being given, appear as more than mere relations, and so become hypostatized; that when hypostatized, the whole collection of them is regarded as contained in empty space; but that this empty space itself, if it means more than the logical possibility of space-relations, is an unnecessary and self-contradictory assumption. Let us begin by considering Kant's arguments on this point.

Leibnitz had affirmed that space was only relations, while Newton had maintained the objective reality of absolute space. Kant adopted a middle course: he asserted absolute space, but regarded it as purely subjective. The assertion of absolute space is the object of his second argument; for if space were mere relations between things, it would necessarily disappear with the disappearance of the things in it; but this the second argument denies[1]. Now spatial order obviously does disappear with matter, but absolute or empty space may be supposed to remain. It is this, then, which Kant is arguing about, and it is this which he affirms to be a pure intuition, necessarily presupposed by spatial order[2].

204. But can we agree in regarding empty space, the "infinite given whole," as really given? Must we not, in spite of Kant's argument, regard it as wholly conceptual? It is not required, in the first place, by the argument of the first half of this chapter, which required only that every *This* of sense-perception should be resolvable into *Thises*, and thus involved only an order among *Thises*, not anything given originally without reference to them at all. In the second place, Kant's two arguments[3] designed to prove that empty space is not conceptual, are inadequate to their purpose. The argument that the parts of space are not contained *under* it, but *in* it, proves certainly that space is not a general conception, of which spatial figures are the instances; but it by no means follows that empty space is not a conception. Empty space is undifferentiated and homogenous; parts of space, or spatial figures, arise only by reference to some differentiating matter, and thus belong rather to spatial order than to empty space. If empty space be the pre-condition of spatial order, we cannot expect it to be connected with spatial relations as genus with species. But empty space may nevertheless be a universal conception; it may be related to spatial order as the state to the citizens. These are not instances of the state, but are contained in it; they also, in a sense, presuppose it, for a man can only become a citizen by being related to other citizens in a state[4].

[1] See Vaihinger's Commentar, II. pp. 189—190.

[2] See ibid. p. 224 ff. for Kant's inconsistencies on this point.

[3] The fourth and fifth in the first edition, the third and fourth in the second.

[4] Cf. Vaihinger's Commentar, II. p. 218.

The uniqueness of space, again, seems hardly a valid argument for its intuitional nature; to regard it as an argument implies, indeed, that all conceptions are abstracted from a series of instances—a view which has been criticized in Chapter II. (§ 77), and need not be further discussed here[1]. There is no ground, therefore, in Kant's two arguments for the intuitional nature of empty space, which can be maintained against criticism.

205. Another ground for condemning empty space is to be found in the mathematical antinomies. For it is no solution, as Lotze points out (Metaphysik, Bk. II. Chap. I., § 106), to regard empty space as purely subjective: contradictions in a necessary subjective intuition form as great a difficulty as in anything else. But these antinomies arise only in connection with empty space, not with spatial order as an aggregate of relations. For only when space is regarded as possessed of some thinghood, can a whole or a true element be demanded. This we have seen already in connection with the Point. When space is regarded, so far as it is valid, as only spatial order, unbounded extension and infinite divisibility both disappear. What is divided is not spatial relations, but matter; and if matter, as we have seen that Geometry requires, consists of unextended atoms with spatial relations, there is no reason to regard matter either as infinitely divisible, or as consisting of atoms of finite extension.

206. But whence arises, on this view, the paradox that we cannot but regard space as having more or less thinghood, and as divisible *ad infinitum*? This must be explained, I think, as a psychological illusion, unavoidably arising from the fact that spatial relations are immediately presented. They thus have a peculiar psychical quality, as immediate experiences, by which quality they can be distinguished from time-relations or any other order in which things may be arranged. To Stumpf, whose problem is psychological, such a psychical quality would constitute an absolute underlying content, and would fully justify his thesis; to us, however, whose problem is epistemological, it would not do so, but would leave the *meaning* of the spatial element in sense-perception free from any implication

[1] Cf. Vaihinger's Commentar, II. p. 207.

of an absolute or empty space[1]. May we not, then, abandon empty space, and say: Spatial order consists of *felt* relations, and *quâ* felt has, for Psychology, an existence not wholly resolvable into relations, and unavoidably *seeming* to be more than mere relations. But when we examine the information, as to space, which we derive from sense-perception, we find ourselves plunged in contradictions, as soon as we allow this information to consist of more than relations. This leaves spatial order alone in the field, and reduces empty space to a mere name for the logical possibility of spatial relations.

207. The apparent divisibility of the relations which constitute spatial order, then, may be explained in two ways, though these are at bottom equivalent. We may take the relation as considered in connection with empty space, in which case it becomes more than a relation; but being falsely hypostatized, it appears as a complex thing, necessarily composed of elements, which elements, however, nowhere emerge until we analyze the pseudo-thing down to nothing, and arrive at the point. In this sense, the divisibility of spatial relations is an unavoidable illusion. Or again, we may take the relation in connection with the material atoms it relates. In this case, other atoms may be imagined, differently localized by different spatial relations. If they are localized on the straight line joining two of the original atoms, this straight line appears as divided by them. But the original relation is not really divided: all that has happened is, that two or more equivalent relations have replaced it, as two compounded relations of father and son may replace the equivalent relation of grandfather and grandson. These two ways of viewing the apparent divisibility are equivalent: for empty space, in so far as it is not illusion, is a name for the aggregate of possible space-relations. To regard a figure in empty space as divided, therefore, means, if it means anything, to regard two or more other possible relations as substituted for it, which gives the second way of viewing the question.

The same reference to matter, then, by which the antinomy of the Point was solved, solves also the antinomy as to the relational nature of space. Space, if it is to be freed from

[1] Cf. James, Psychology, Vol. II., p. 148 ff.

contradictions, must be regarded exclusively as spatial order, as relations between unextended material atoms. Empty space, which arises, by an inevitable illusion, out of the spatial element in sense-perception, may be regarded, if we wish to retain it, as the bare principle of relativity, the bare logical possibility of relations between diverse things. In this sense, empty space is wholly conceptual; spatial order alone is immediately experienced.

208. But in what sense does spatial order consist of relations? We have hitherto spoken of externality as a relation, and in a sense such a manner of speaking is justified. Externality, when predicated of anything, is an adjective of that thing, and implies a reference to some other thing. To this extent, then, externality is analogous to other relations; and only to this extent, in our previous arguments, has it been regarded as a relation. But when we take account of further qualities of relations, externality begins to appear, not so much as a relation, but rather as a necessary aspect or element in every relation. And this is borne out by the necessity, for the existence of relations, of some given form of externality.

Every relation, we may say, involves a diversity between the related terms, but also some unity. Mere diversity does not give a ground for that interaction, and that interdependence, which a relation requires. Mere unity leaves the terms identical, and thus destroys the reference of one to another required for a relation. Mere externality, taken in abstraction, gives only the element of diversity required for a relation, and is thus more abstract than any actual relation. But mere diversity does not give that indivisible whole of which any actual relation must consist, and is thus, when regarded abstractly, not subject to the restrictions of ordinary relations.

But with mere diversity, we seem to have returned to empty space, and abandoned spatial order. Mere diversity, surely, is either complete or non-existent; degrees of diversity, or a quantitative measure of it, are nonsense. We cannot, therefore, reduce spatial order to mere diversity. Two things, if they occupy different positions in space, are necessarily diverse, but are as necessarily something more; otherwise spatial order becomes unmeaning.

Empty space, then, in the above sense of the possibility of spatial relations, contains only one aspect of a relation, namely the aspect of diversity; but spatial order, by its reference to matter, becomes more concrete, and contains also the element of unity, arising out of the connection of the different material atoms. Spatial order, then, consists of relations in the ordinary sense; its merely spatial element, however—if one may make such a distinction—the element, that is, which can be abstracted from matter and regarded as constituting empty space, is only one aspect of a relation, but an aspect which, in the concrete, must be inseparably bound up with the other aspect. Here, once more, we see the ground of the contradictions in empty space, and the reason why spatial order is free from these contradictions.

Conclusion.

209. We have now completed our review of the foundations of Geometry. It will be well, before we take leave of the subject, briefly to review and recapitulate the results we have won.

In the first chapter, we watched the development of a branch of Mathematics designed, at first, only to establish the logical independence of Euclid's axiom of parallels, and the possibility of a self-consistent Geometry which dispensed with it. We found the further development of the subject entangled, for a while, in philosophical controversy; having shown one axiom to be superfluous, the geometers of the second period hoped to prove the same conclusion of all the others, but failed to construct any system free from three fundamental axioms. Being concerned with analytical and metrical Geometry, they tended to regard Algebra as *à priori*, but held that those properties of spatial magnitudes, which were not deducible from the laws of Algebra, must be empirical. In all this, they aimed as much at discrediting Kant as at advancing Mathematics. But with the third period, the interest in Philosophy diminishes, the opposition to Euclid becomes less marked, and most important of all, measurement is no longer regarded as fundamental, and space is dealt with by descriptive rather than quantitative methods. But nevertheless, three axioms, substantially the same as those retained in the second period, are still retained by all geometers.

In the second chapter, we endeavoured, by a criticism of some geometrical philosophies, to prepare the ground for a constructive theory of Geometry. We saw that Kant, in applying the argument of the Transcendental Aesthetic to space, had gone too far, since its logical scope extended only to some form of externality in general. We saw that Riemann, Helmholtz and Erdmann, misled by the quantitative bias, overlooked the qualitative substratum required by all judgments of quantity, and thus mistook the direction in which the necessary axioms of Geometry are to be found. We rejected, also, Helmholtz's view that Geometry depends on Physics, because we found that Physics must assume a knowledge of Geometry before it can become possible. But we admitted, in Geometry, a reference to matter—not, however, to matter as empirically known in Physics, but to a more abstract matter, whose sole function is to appear in space, and supply the terms for spatial relations. We admitted, however, besides this, that all *actual* measurement must be effected by means of *actual* matter, and is only empirically possible, through the empirical knowledge of approximately rigid bodies. In criticizing Lotze, we saw that the most important sense, in which non-Euclidean spaces are possible, is a philosophical sense, namely, that they are not condemned by any *à priori* argument as to the necessity of space for experience, and that consequently, if they are not affirmed, this must be on empirical grounds alone. Lotze's strictures on the mathematical procedure of Metageometry we found to be wholly due to ignorance of the subject.

Proceeding, in the third chapter, to a constructive theory of Geometry, we saw that projective Geometry, which has no reference to quantity, is necessarily true of any form of externality. Its three axioms—homogeneity, dimensions, and the straight line—were all deduced from the conception of a form of externality, and, since some such form is necessary to experience, were all declared *à priori*. In metrical Geometry, on the contrary, we found an empirical element, arising out of the alternatives of Euclidean and non-Euclidean space. Three *à priori* axioms, common to these spaces, and necessary conditions of the possibility of measurement, still remained; these were the axiom of Free Mobility, the axiom that space has a finite integral number of dimensions, and the axiom of distance. Except for the new idea of motion, these were found equivalent to the projective triad, and thus necessarily true of any form of externality. But the remaining axioms of Euclid—the axiom of three dimensions, the axiom that two straight lines can never enclose a space, and the axiom of parallels—were regarded as empirical laws, derived from the investigation and measurement of our actual space, and true only, as far as the last two are concerned, within the limits set by errors of observation.

In the present chapter, we completed our proof of the apriority of the projective and equivalent metrical axioms, by showing the necessity, for experience, of some form of externality, given by sensation or intuition, and not merely inferred from other data. Without this, we said, a knowledge of diverse but interrelated things, the corner-stone of all experience, would be impossible. Finally, we discussed the contradictions arising out of the relativity and continuity of space, and endeavoured to overcome them by a reference to matter. This matter, we found, must consist of unextended atoms, localized by their spatial relations, and appearing, in Geometry, as points. But the non-spatial adjectives of matter, we contended, are irrelevant to Geometry, and its causal properties may be left out of account. To deal with the new contradictions, involved in such a notion of matter, would demand a fresh treatise, leading us, through Kinematics, into the domains of Dynamics and Physics. But to discuss the special difficulties of space is all that is possible in an essay on the Foundations of Geometry.

LIST OF TABLES

LIST OF DIAGRAMS

Preface

The unprecedented and unexpected development of suicide by individuals belonging to all age, income, social, educational, cultural, demographic, linguistic, religious and other groups in the Kashmir valley stands bewildering, catastrophic and devastating. It seems really a great tragedy which destroys two or more individuals every day, morning, evening or day time. It has eaten up 2700 humans in just 27 months from 2009 to 2011. These are the surprising reports in the local print media published with continuity, care and patience.

Suicides are the essential facts of life in the Kashmiri society today. There are several explanations to these acts in compulsion or desperation: sociological, economic, political, religious, psychological and so on. But, the basic fact reflects without least amount of doubt that while the Kashmiri society represented a non-violent social ethos and ideal peaceful environment, the present day situation represents violent behaviour and depressive environment. This has happened in the last 23 years in which the armed conflict took place between the Kashmiri militants and Indian security forces. Thus militancy and concomitant militarisation created a social situation radically different from the previous pattern. In this type of social situation, what one expects at the social scene, tension, depression, crime, drug abuse, disorganisation, deviance, delinquency, violation of norms and values, rejection of the authority of family, religion and school. The previous two decades social events are full of these and other such social acts and crimes which cut from the basis the level of human culture and civilisation.

In this type of mass depression, perpetual tension, ideological crisis, social anarchy and economic underdevelopment, we experience the phenomenon of suicide every day, every month and every year. Even the violators of human dignity and human rights abusers commit this deadly act.

This study was aimed at to portray this tragic reality in its sociological form. So, a 'suicide diary' was compiled for three years of 2009, 2010 and 2011 and the number of suicides committed effectively during this period were entered in it on day to day basis as reported in the local English and Urdu print media, popular throughout Kashmir. This became the base for developing propositions and conclusions through the scientific methodology and sociological framework. Thus this study defines, identifies, explains and interprets the mass of suicides in the sociological theoretical perspective.

Lastly, this book does not cover all suicides committed in Kashmir during last 23 years. In actuality, it is a specific study of specific number of such acts committed in a specific period and reported in the local daily newspapers. It follows that the total number of suicides during last two decades plus period goes above 20,000. We have taken a limited number for sociological analysis and conclusions.

Last, but not the least, though suicides represent a great tragedy, no serious governmental or non-governmental effort is on to control or to end this trend. There also is not any serious effort to study this significant trend. In this background, this study represents an initiation for a serious, scientific and comprehensive study of suicides in the present day Kashmir. I sincerely hope that many such initiatives will follow. Inshaullah.

B.A. Dabla

1 Introduction: Suicides at the Global Level

1. The Act of Suicide

Suicide means 'to kill oneself'. It generally refers to the act of intentionally causing one's own death or conditions of death. It is often committed by individual out of despair, *i.e.,* it has a certain particular cause attributed generally to abnormal condition of mental health. In other words, it may be characterised as the condition of mental disorder which includes depression, bipolar disorder, schizophrenia, alcoholism or drug abuse. The stress factors such as financial difficulties or troubles with interpersonal relationships often play a significant role.[1]

2. Social Phenomenon of Suicide

In general, suicide means a conscious, deliberate and intentional act of killing oneself due to set social factors. It has been defined as "conscious act of self-induced annihilation but understood malaise in a needful individual who defines an issue for which the suicide is perceived as the best solution.[2] The eminent classical sociologist, Emile Durkheim, in his classic book entitled *Suicide*, defined suicide as "every case of death which results directly or indirectly from a positive or negative act, accomplished by the victim himself which he knows must produce this result".[3] It has been argued that he did feel it necessary for suicide act to be intentional and to be extremely conscious. It was because he felt that intentions were very hard to identify and determine exactly. So, he broadened his definition of suicide where there is no chance of survival but no specific intention to kill oneself.

3. The Contribution of Emile Durkheim

Emile Durkheim made greatest contribution to the concept of suicide in which he developed its features of social determinism and social nature in comparison to mental or psychological factors. He chose to study suicide because it illustrated perfectly the necessity for a value of sociological explanation. He clearly maintained that the "tendency to commit suicide depended not on individual psychology or features of the physical environment but on the nature of individual's relations to society."[4]

So, he explained the act of suicide in terms of socially-determined feature than psychologically-determined forces or factors. In his view "suicide as an individual action represented the failure of social solidarity and was indicator of the ineffectiveness of social bonds."[5]

Thus he clearly preferred the social causation in comparison to psychological causation in the explanation of social phenomenon of suicide.

Emile Durkheim upheld that the individual conduct in society is always influenced by 'collective currents' and the best a sociologist can do is to record its effect in the form of a statistical rate. That is what he did in his historic work *Suicide.* He studied the variations in suicide rates between different groups and sects to which individuals are subject. Thus the frequency of suicides amongst soldiers than among artisans and among officials than other lower ranks leads him to conclude that this altruistic suicide in which the individual sees his life less important than conformity to group norms.

In this way, Durkheim provided an alternative explanation and perspective according to which suicide is not a process but an accident of the social standing of the individual. It is not correlated with different forms of mental disorder nor is there any clear relationship with mental make-up.

After giving the acts of suicide the absolute social character, he categorised all suicides in three distinctive types. The first and second types, altruistic and egoistic suicides, as the individual's relations to social ideals and purposes. In altruistic suicide, the individual is not strongly integrated into society which encourages and requires the individual to sacrifice his or her own life. Conversely, in the egoistic suicide, the individual is insufficiently integrated into society and so is not subject to the collective forces that prevent committing suicide and individual experiences a violation and detachment conducive to it. The third type of suicide, anomic suicide, depends on the social regulation of the individual's aims and ambitions and appetites are increased to a level where they cannot find satisfaction. This non-satisfaction of individual's desires of functional needs lead him to this type of suicide.

The typology of suicides given by Durkheim has been characterised and given the paradigms as mentioned below:

Table 1.1

Durkheim's Typology of Suicides (Pure type), their Characteristics and Paradigms

S.No.	*Basic Type*	*Characteristics*	*Paradigms*
1.	Egoistic suicides	Excessive individuation	with religious family & politics
		apathy results from men no longer Finding a basis for existence in life	-
2.	Altruistic Suicides	in sufficient individuation energy of person or will activity basis for existence appears Situated beyond life Eastern-like asceticism tend to achieve moksha or Nirvana heroic suicide	lower societies soldiers religious matters *harakiri* *sutee* *kanikari*
3.	Anomic suicides	literally deregulation lack of normative restraint	economic crisis sudden social change
		irritation, disgust, anger and Weariness often violence and murder always accompanied by a Desire for infinite lack of proper control abrupt social changes	widowhood divorce liberal occupations

3.1. Other Views About Suicides

After Durkheim presented his particular views, these were responded by other sociologists and professionals. Some of these critical points are explained below:

(a) for his definition of suicide and the mismatch between this definition and that embodied in the suicide situations, he used to substantiate his argument. This goes theoretically to opposite direction;

(b) for his classification of three types of suicides in terms of cause [so called actionological classification] which incorporates into the classification the very casual links he is seeking to establish;

(c) for his extreme polarisation of social and psychological explanations wherein complimentarity should be assured; and

(d) for using aggregate data to make inferences about individuals and their acts of suicide.[6]

Subsequently, the sociological concerns were related to the limitations of the official statistics about suicides. Jack D. Douglas, who was influenced by interactionists and ethno-methodologists, argued that suicides were defined or treated differently as they differed culture to culture, thereby calling into question cross-cultural and historical comparisons of suicides [which Durkheim had done in his work] or data/rates generated by different corners. However, it does not follow the suicide statistics have no value in analysing the social sources of suicide. These were to be treated with exceptional care and taking into consideration the variety of cultures. One needs to assess the impact of social and cultural factors as the construction of suicide statistics as well as the emerging trends of committing suicide. However, it must be noted, the tradition developed by Emile Durkheim continued in a range of studies which have provided an empirical support for his ideas and evidence of the impact of the said factor on the levels and trends of suicides.

4. Other Features of Suicide

In addition to the above-explained aspects, the concept of suicide has other sociological features which are mentioned below:

(i) the 'suicide continuum' includes competition, non-total attempts, gestures, partial self-destruction, indirect suicide, and ideation;[7] and

(ii) suicide prediction scales, psychological tests, situation procedures are usually not flexible, individualised, specific or thought enough. So, all these techniques have some degree of limitation in the explanation of suicide acts.

The common single predictors are as follows:

- Depressive illness,
- Alcoholism, mental disorder,

- Suicide ideation, talk, preparation, religious ideas,
- Prior suicide attempt,
- Lethal methods,
- Isolation, living alone, loss of support,
- Hopelessness, cognitive rigidity,
- Being an elder white male,
- Modeling, suicide in the family, genetics,
- Work problems, economics and occupations,
- Marital problems, family pathology,
- Stress, life events,
- Anger, aggression, irritability,
- Physical illness,
- Repetition and consorbidity of factors; and
- Suicidal career[8]

There are different settings or contexts for committing suicides, some of which are as mentioned below:

- Outpatient therapy,
- Jails, prisons, correctional facilities,
- Hospitals,
- Public buildings, skyscrapers, bridges,
- Homes,
- Work places or jobs,
- Life insurance companies,
- Drug companies,
- The law,
- Public health, government, and
- Survivors[9]

There are various types of suicides. First, Euthanasia: individuals who wish to end their own lives may enlist the assistance of another party to achieve death. The person, usually member of physician, may help to carry out the act when the individual lacks the physical capacity to do so alone, even if supplied with the means. Assisted suicides are contentious, moral and political issue in many countries of the world. Second, murder-suicide: it is an act in which an individual him/her and kills other persons. The motivation for this murder can be purely criminal in nature or be perceived by the perpetrator as an act of care for loved ones in the context of severe depression. Third, suicide attack: it is an act in which an attacker perpetrates an act of violence against others to achieve a military or political goal, which simultaneously results in his/her death. Suicide bombings are often considered as an act of terrorism by the targeted community. Fourth, mass suicide: these suicides are performed under social pressure or coordinated among a group of individuals. Mass suicides can take place with as few as two people, often referred to as suicide pact. Fifth, suicide pact: it explains the act of suicide of two or more individuals in pre-determined plan which may be aimed at to die together of separately or closely timed. This suicide is different from mass suicide in that the latter refers to a larger number of people who kill themselves together for a common ideological reason, often within a religious, political or military context. In contrast, suicide pacts usually involve small groups of more intimately related people whose motivations are personal and individual. Sixth, defiance or protest: sometimes suicides are committed as acts of defiance or political protest. Seventh, dutiful suicide: it refers to an act of fatal self violence at one's own hands done in the belief that it will secure a greater good, rather than to escape harsh or impossible conditions. This act can be voluntary to relieve some dishonour or punishment or imposed by threats of death or reprisals on one's family. Eighth, escape suicide: in situations where continuing to live would be intolerable, some individuals use suicide as a means of escape. Farmers suicides in India can be the extreme case in this regard.[10]

List of personal factors which compel an individual to commit suicide:

- age,
- sex,
- race,
- marital status,
- living arrangements,
- employment status,
- physical health,

- mental condition including alcoholism and drug addiction,
- medical aid within a limited time,
- previous suicide attempt threat,
- recent loss,
- separation,
- family history of mental illness, and
- history of physical, sexual and emotional health.[11]

The following can be considered as 10 commonalities of suicide:

- The common purpose of suicides is to seek a solution;
- The common goal of suicides causation of consumerism;
- The common stumuli in suicide is intolerable;
- The common stressor in suicides is frustrated psychological needs;
- The common emotion in suicides is hopelessness and helplessness;
- The common cognitive state in suicides is ambivalence;
- The common perpetual state in suicides is constriction;
- The common action in suicides is aggression;
- The common inter-personal act in suicides is communication of intention; and
- The common consistency in suicides is with lifelong coping pattern.[12]

The risk factors of suicides have generally been identified as follows:

(a) Clinical studies have revealed that underlying mental disorders are present in 87% to 98% of suicides. However, there are a number of other factors correlated with suicide risk, including drug addiction, family history of suicide or previous head injury;

(b) Socio-economic factors such as unemployment, poverty, homelessness and discrimination may trigger suicide thoughts. Poverty may not be a direct cause, but it can increase the risk of suicides, as impoverished individuals are a major risk group of depression;

(c) Hopelessness, the feeling that there is no prospect of improvement or progress in one's situation, is a strong indicator of suicide with the result of positive nature. Perceived burdensomeness—a feeling that one's existence is a burden to others such as family members or relatives is also coupled with hopelessness as are the feelings of loneliness,

(d) Advocacy of suicide has been cited as a contributing factor. Intelligence may also be a factor. Initially proposed as a part of an evolutionary psychology explanation, which posited a minimum intelligence required for one to commit suicide , the positive correlation between IQ and suicide has been replicated in a number of studies; and

(e) One study found that a lack of social support, a deficit in feelings of belongingness and living alone were crucial predictors of a suicide attempt.[13]

There are several precipitating circumstances and risk factors for suicide which include the following:

(a) Medical conditions: In various studies a significant association was found between suicidality and underlying medical conditions including chronic pain, mild brain injury (MBI) or traumatic brain injury (TBI). The prevalence of increased suicidality persisted after adjusting for depressive illness and alcohol abuse. In patients with more than one medical condition the risk was particularly high, suggesting a need for increased screening for suicidality in general medical setting. Sleep disturbances such as insomnia and sleep apnea have been cited in various studies as risk indicators for depression and suicide.[14]

(b) Mental disorders: These are often present at the time of suicide. It is estimated that from 87 % to 98 % of suicides are committed by people with some type of mental disorder broken down by type: mood disorders are present in 30 %, substance abuse in 18 %, schizophrenia in 14 %, and personality disorders in 13 % of suicides.[15] Major depression and alcoholism are the specific disorders most strongly correlated with suicide risk.

(c) Biology: Some mental disorders identified as risk factors for suicide often may have an underlying biological basis. Serotonin is a vital neurotransmitter in those who have attempted suicide, it has been found that they have lower serotonin levels and individuals who have completed suicide have the lowest levels.[16]

(*d*) Perceived burdensomeness to others: Several studies have revealed perceived burdensomeness to others to be a particularly strong risk factor. It also differentiates between attempted Vs completed suicide and predicts lethality of suicide method unlike feelings of hopelessness and emotional pain. Likely related to this, completed suicides are characterised by altruistic feelings while non-lethal self-injuries are characterised by feelings of anger or self-punishment.[17]

(*e*) Substance abuse: It is second most common risk factor after major depression and bipolar disorder. Both chronic substance misuse as well as substance abuse are associated with suicide. This is attributed to the intoxicating, disinhibiting and dissociative effects of many psychoactive substances. When combined with personal grief, such as bereavement, the risk of suicide is greatly increased. More than 50 % suicides have some relation to alcohol or drug use and up to 25 % of suicides are committed by drug addicts and alcoholics. The figure is even higher with alcohol or drug use among adolescents, playing a role in up to 77.00 % of suicides.[18]

The substances abused in the act of suicide include mainly the following:

- Cocaine: It has the highest correlation with suicides. An estimate revealed that 1 in 5 people who commit suicides uses this substance.
- Methamphetamine: It has a strong association with depression and suicides. Heroin users have a death rate nearly 13 times than that of their non-using peers.
- Opioids: Chronic use or abuse of prescribed benzodiazepines is associated with depression as well as increased suicide risk.
- Benzodiazepines: Dependence on it often results in a deteriorating clinical picture which includes social deterioration leading to comorbid alcoholism and drug abuse. Suicide stands as a common outcome of chronic misuse of this substance.

- Cigarettes: Various studies show a positive link between smoking, suicidal ideation and suicide attempts. In a study, it revealed that those smoking between 1 to 24 cigarettes per day had twice the suicide risk; 25 cigarettes or more, 4 times the suicide risk, as compared with those who had never smoked.
- Alcohol: Its use or misuse is directly associated with a number of mental health disorders and alcoholics have generally high suicide rate. It has been found that acute drinking, 6 drinks or more per day, leads to a sixfold increased risk of suicide.
- Media coverage: Various studies have suggested that how the media presents depictions of suicides may have a negative effect and trigger the possibility of suicide contagion. This risk is greater in adolescents who may romanticise death through the act of suicide.[19]

Methods of Committing Suicides

The leading methods of suicide varies dramatically between countries and cultures. The leading methods in different regions include hanging, pesticide poisoning and firearms. A 2008 review of 56 countries based on WHO mortality data found that hanging was the most common method in most of the countries, accounting 53 % of the male suicides and 39 % of the female suicides. Worldwide 30 % suicides are from pesticides. Asphyxiation and poisoning are fairly common as well. Together they comprised about 40 % of the US total suicides. Other methods include blunt force trauma, or car collision. Bloodletting, intentional drowning, self immolation, electrocution and intentional starvation are other suicide methods.[20]

Prevention of the Suicides

Suicide prevention is a term used for the collective efforts to reduce the incidence of suicides through preventive measures. Various strategies restrict access to the most common methods of suicide, such as firearms or toxic substances like pesticides and have proved to be effective in reducing suicide rates. Studies supported by empirical data have indicated that adequate prevention, diagnosis and treatment of depression and alcohol and substance abuse can reduce suicide rates, as does follow-up contact with those who have made a suicide attempt. Although crisis hotlines are common, there is little evidence to support or refute their effectiveness.[21]

The Best Practices Registry [BRP] for Suicide prevention is a formal effort of various suicide intervention programmes with those listing evidence-based programmes: interventions which have been subjected to indepth review and for which evidence has demonstrated positive outcomes.

Different types of suicidologists include the following professionals:

- Psychiatrists, physicians,
- Psychologists,
- Sociologists,
- Biologists, biostatisticians,
- Nurses,
- Social workers,
- Epidemiologists, demographers,
- Philosophers,
- Lawyers,
- Theologians,
- Politicians, and
- Educators.[22]

The typology of suicides as suggested by J. Baechler is as follows:

(a) Escapist	-	flight
	-	grief
	-	punishment
(b) Aggressive	-	vengeance
	-	crime
	-	blackmail
	-	appeal
(c) Oblative	-	sacrifice
	-	transformation
(d) Ludic	-	ordeal
	-	game[23]

Various studies of 'suicide notes' left by suicide-makers have identified the following relevant factors:

- Psychic tension,
- Depression,
- Mental confusion,
- Unfulfillable desires,
- Hostility,
- Positive effect,
- Heightened dependency needs,
- A view of the act is justified,
- Involvement with fantasy,
- Inability to distinguish between positive and negative,
- Constrictions,
- Ambivalence,
- Ideosyncrases in ideation,
- Cognitive impacement in positive enduration,
- Negating specific people, places and things fatalistic attitude, amd
- Ambivalent attachment to the person.[24]

5. Suicides at the Global Level

The fact stands with a lot of evidence that suicides are committed in every human society with certainty. At the same time, the associated fact is that suicides in different societies of the world occur differently. It has been explained in terms of differences in region, religion, culture, economy, polity, psychology, demography and so on. Thus different suicide rates have been associated with different countries, sub-regions and regions and the world at large. In this background, it may be argued, suicides occur in all societies of the world in different contexts due to variety of factors.

The preceding sociological propositions reflect completely in the statistical details released by international organisations, especially the World Health Organisation (WHO). Here we present the relevant statistical report released by WHO in 2009:

Table 1.2

Suicide Rate in Countries of the World, 2009

(per 1,00,000)

S.No.	*Country*	*Year*	*Total*	*Male*	*Female*
1.	Belarus	2003	36.80	63.30	10.30
2.	Lithuania	2007	31.85	53.90	09.80
3.	Russia	2006	31.70	53.90	09.50
4.	Sri Lanka	1991	30.70	44.60	16.80
5.	Kazakhstan	2007	27.60	46.20	00.09
6.	Hungary	2005	26.75	42.30	11.20
7.	Japan	2007	24.75	35.80	13.70
8.	Ukraine	2005	23.95	40.90	07.00
9.	Guyana	2005	22.70	33.80	11.60
10.	Korea, North	—	21.85	29.60	14.10
11.	Slovenia	2007	21.70	33.70	09.07
12.	Estonia	2005	21.40	35.50	07.03
13.	Lavia	2007	20.90	34.10	07.70
14.	Serbia	2006	19.75	28.40	11.10
15.	Finland	2007	18.95	28.90	09.00
16.	Belgium	1999	18.35	27.20	09.50
17.	Croatia	2006	18.30	26.90	09.70
18.	Switzerland	2006	17.60	23.50	11.70
19.	France	2006	17.25	25.50	09.00
20.	Uruguay	2004	16.15	26.00	06.30
21.	Moldova	2007	16.15	26.80	04.30
22.	Poland	2006	15.60	26.80	04.40
23.	Austria	2007	15.60	23.80	07.40
24.	Hong Kong	2006	15.40	19.30	11.50
25.	Suriname	2005	14.35	23.90	04.80
26.	China	1999	13.90	13.00	14.80
27.	Czech Republic	2007	13.50	22.70	04.30
28.	Sweden	2006	13.20	18.10	08.30

29. Bulgaria	2004	13.20	19.70	06.70
30. Slovakia	2005	12.85	22.30	03.40
31. New Zealand	2005	12.60	18.90	06.30
32. Cuba	2006	12.25	19.60	04.90
33. Trinidad & Tobago	2002	12.20	20.40	04.00
34. Germany	2006	11.95	17.90	06.00
35. Denmark	2006	11.95	17.50	06.40
36. Bosnia & Herze	1991	11.80	20.30	03.30
37. Iceland	2007	11.75	18.90	04.60
38. Portugal	2004	11.70	17.90	05.50
39. Romania	2007	11.45	18.90	04.00
40. Norway	2006	11.40	16.80	06.00
41. Canada	2004	11.35	17.30	05.40
42. United States	2005	11.10	17.70	04.50
43. Luxembourg	2005	11.00	17.70	04.30
44. India	1998	10.65	12.20	09.10
45. Ireland	2007	10.60	17.40	03.80
46. Australia	2004	10.55	16.70	04.40
47. Mauritius	2007	10.40	16.00	04.80
48. Chile	2005	10.40	17.40	03.40
49. Singapore	2006	10.30	12.90	07.70
50. Kyrgyzstan	2006	09.05	14.40	03.70
51. Turkmenistan	1998	08.65	13.80	03.50
52. Netherlands	2007	08.30	11.60	05.00
53. Argentina	2005	08.05	12.70	03.40
54. Zimbabwe	1990	07.90	10.60	05.20
55. Thailand	2002	07.90	12.00	03.80
56. Spain	2005	07.09	12.00	03.80
57. Costa Rica	2006	07.85	13.20	02.50
58. Saint Lucia	2002	07.70	10.40	05.00
59. Pureto Rico	2005	07.06	13.20	02.00
60. Belize	2001	07.50	13.40	01.60
61. Nicaragua	—	07.20	11.10	03.30

62. El Salvador	2006	06.95	10.20	03.70
63. Ecuador	2006	06.80	09.10	04.50
64. Mecedonia	2003	06.75	09.50	04.00
65. United Kingdom	2007	06.45	10.10	02.80
66. Malta	2007	06.40	12.30	00.50
67. Italy	2006	06.35	09.90	02.80
68. Israel	2005	06.00	08.70	03.30
69. Grenada	2005	05.85	09.80	01.90
70. Panama	2006	05.60	10.40	00.80
71. Colombia	2005	04.95	07.80	02.10
72. Uzbekistan	2005	04.65	07.00	02.30
73. Brazil	2005	04.60	07.30	01.90
74. Seychelles	1987	04.55	09.10	00.00
75. Paraguay	2004	04.10	05.50	02.70
76. Mexico	2006	04.05	06.80	01.30
77. Albania	2003	04.00	04.70	03.30
78. Venezuela	2005	03.75	06.10	01.40
79. Saint Vincent…	2004	03.65	07.30	00.00
80. Greece	2006	03.55	05.90	01.20
81. Bahrain	1988	02.70	04.90	00.50
82. Tajiskistan	2001	02.60	02.90	02.30
83. Cyprus	2006	02.50	03.20	01.80
84. Armenia	2006	02.45	03.90	01.00
85. Guatemala	2006	02.35	03.60	01.10
86. Georgia	2001	02.25	03.40	01.10
87. Philippines	1993	02.10	02.50	01.70
88. Kuwait	2002	01.95	02.50	01.40
89. Dominican Rep.	2004	01.60	02.60	00.60
90. Bahamas	2002	00.95	01.90	00.00
91. Sao Tome…	1987	00.90	00.00	01.80
92. Peru	2000	00.85	01.10	00.60
93. Barbados	2001	00.70	01.40	00.60
94. Azerbaijan	2007	00.65	01.00	00.30

95. Maldives	2005	00.35	00.70	00.00
96. Iran	1991	00.20	00.30	00.10
97. Jamaica	1990	00.15	00.30	00.00
98. Syria	1985	00.10	00.20	00.00

Source: World Health Organisation, Geneva, 2009.

The above Table reveals that while majority of developing and under-developed countries of the world had highest rates of suicide, the developed and under-developed countries had lowest rates of suicides in the world. In this regard, Belarus had 36.80 per 1,00,000 suicide rate, while Syria had 01 per 1,00,000 suicide rate in that rate.[25] Moreover, the suicide rates among the males in the developing and under-developed countries in were more comparison to lower or lowest suicide rates among females in the developed countries. In reality, there are many developed countries in which there are zero or near zero suicide rates among females than among males.

It has been found that over one million people die by suicide every year. While the WHO estimated that it stands as the 13th leading cause of death worldwide, it is rated sixth in the United States.[26] It is a leading cause of death among teenagers and adults under 35. The rate of suicide is far higher in men than in women, with males worldwide 3 to 4 times more likely to kill themselves than females.[27] There are an estimated 10-20 million non-fatal attempted suicides every year at the global level.[28]

It is also revealed from the Table that most of the countries had suicide rates ranging between 20s and 30s per 1,00,000. At the same time, lesser number of countries [four in total] had the suicide rates ranging between 30s per 1,00,000. Other countries of world, not majority in number, had the suicide rate below 10 per 1,00,000. It may be noted here that India had the suicide rate of 10.65 per 1,00,000 in the year 1998.

In the context of statistical details of suicide at the global level, based on WHO sources, we may infer the worldwide suicide increase has been experienced up to 60 per cent of the total, while global suicide rate has been fixed at 16 per 1,00,000, *i.e.,* 01 suicide per forty seconds. Again, it has been established that countries in the European continent have experienced lower suicide rates, the countries in the continents of Asia and Latin America have seen higher suicide rates. The suicide rates in religion-dominated Muslim countries were lower or lowest, as the suicide data support this proposition supported by experts. It may not be out of place to mention that the highly monotheistic religion of Islam has strongly condemned and prohibited and characterised as the sin to commit suicide. It has also been estimated that while 80 per cent of all suicides committed the world-over belong to the Asian countries, the Asian countries of China, Japan and India jointly commit 40 per cent of total suicides in the world.[29]

It has been found that deaths for self inflicted injuries per 1,00,000 inhabitants in the year 2004 was as mentioned below:

Number per 1,00,000	Age groups
-less than 03	18 - 21
-03 – 06	21 – 24
-06 – 09	24 – 27
-09 – 12	27 – 30
-12 – 15	30 – 33
-15 – 18	33 and above [30]

Thus worldwide suicide rates have increased by 60 % in the past 45 years, mainly in the developing countries and is currently the tenth leading cause of death with about a million people dying by suicide annually, a global mortality rate of 16 suicides per 1,00,000 people, or a suicide every 40 seconds.[31] According to 2007 data, suicides in the US outnumber homicides by nearly 2 to 1. Suicide ranks as the 11th leading cause of death in that country, ahead of liver disease and Parkinson's.[32]

The gender composition of suicide makers at the global level can be imagined/estimated from the following relevant statistics:

Suicide rate per 1,00,000 males and females from 1978-2008

Number	males	females
No data	05.80 – 08.50	22.50 – 26.00
Less than 01	08.50 – 01.20	26.00 – 29.50
01 – 05	12.00 – 19.00	29.50 – 33.00
05 –05.80	19.00 – 22.50	33.00 – 36.50[33]

In this statistics taken from the Western context, males die much more often by means of suicide than do female counterparts, although females attempt more than males. Some medical professionals argued that this difference stems from the fact that males are more likely to end their lives through effective means, while females primarily use less severe methods such as overdosing on medications. In most countries, drug overdoses account for about 2/3 of suicides among females and 1/3 among males.[34]

Alcoholics are 5 to 20 times more likely to kill themselves, while the misuse of other drugs increases the risk to 10 to 20 times. About 15 % alcoholics commit suicide and about 33 % of suicides in the under 35 age group have a primary diagnosis of alcohol or other substance abuse or drug misuse plays a role in up to 70 % of suicides.[35]

National suicide rates differ significantly between countries and among ethnic groups within national boundaries. For example, in the US, non-Hispanic Caucasians are nearly 2.5 times more likely to kill themselves than African Americans or Hispanics. In the UK, suicide rates vary significantly between different regions/parts of the country. In Scotland, the suicide rate is double than that of England.[36]

In some jurisdictions of some countries, the act or incomplete act of suicide is generally considered to be a crime. More commonly, a surviving party member who assisted in the suicide attempt will face criminal charges. In Brazil, if the help is directed to a minor, the penalty is applied in its double and not considered as homicide. In Italy and Canada, instigating another to suicide is also a criminal offence. In Singapore, assisting in the suicide of a mentally handicapped person is a capital offence. In India, abetting suicide of a minor or a mentally challenged person can result in a maximum one year prison term with a possible fine. Switzerland has taken steps recently to legalise assisted suicide for the chronically mentally ill.[37]

Most of the world religions have upheld the views which are extremely opposite to the act of suicide. All forms of Christianity considered suicide a sin. They held that life is a gift given by God which should not be spurned and that suicide is against the natural order and thus interferes with God's master plan for the entire world and its people. Judaism focuses on the importance of valuing this life in this world, and as such, suicide is tantamount to denying God's goodness in the world. Despite this, under extreme circumstances when there has seemed no choice but to either be killed or forced to betray their religion. Thus jews have committed individual suicide or mass suicide. Third, Islam has categorically condemned and banned the act of suicide. While Quran, the sole guiding source in Islam, clearly criticises suicide because it goes against the God's creation, planning and nature of life. The Prophet Mohammad too considered it the most illegal act in the religion of Islam. So, the Islamic law characterised it 'haram' and condemnable and illegal. In general, Hinduism too frowned upon suicide and considered it equally sinful as murdering another in contemporary Hindu society. Hindu scriptures state that one who commits suicide will become part of the spirit world, wandering earth until the time one would have otherwise died, had one not committed suicide. However, Hinduism accepts a man's right to end one's life through the non-violent practice of fasting to death, termed 'prayopavesa'. Finally, Jainism has a similar practice named 'santhara'. Sati or self-immolation by widows was prevalent in Hindu society during the Middle Ages.[38]

Some scholars see suicide as a legitimate matter of personal choice and a human right. These people work in the 'right to die' movement. Supporters of this position maintain that no one should be forced to suffer against their will, particularly from conditions such as incurable disease, mental illness and old age that have no possibility of improvement. Proponents of this view reject the belief that suicide is always irrational, arguing instead that it can be a valid last resort for those enduring major pain or trauma. This perspective is most popular and has a good deal of support in continental Europe, where euthanasia and other such topics are commonly discussed in parliament and public. Thus the advocacy of suicide has occurred in many countries, cultures and subcultures. For example, the Japanese military during World War II encouraged and glorified 'kamikaze' attacks and Japanese society as a whole has been described as 'suicide tolerant'.[39]

Some landmarks have become known for high levels of suicide attempts. The four most popular locations in the world are San Francisco's Golden Gate Bridge, Toronto's Bloor Street Viaduct, Japan's Aokigahara Forest and England's Beachy Head. In 2005, the Golden Gate Bridge had a count exceeding 1,200 jumpers since its construction in 1937. In 1997, the Bloor Street Viaduct had one suicide every 22 days, and in 2002, Aokigahara had a record of 78 bodies found within the forest, replacing the previous record of 73 in 1998. The suicide rate of these places is so high that numerous signs, using potential victims of suicide to seek help, have been posted.[40]

Views on suicide have been influenced by broader cultural views on existential themes such as religion, honour and meaning of life. The Abrahamic religions, especially Islam, Christianity and Judaism, traditionally consider suicide an 'offence towards God' due to the belief in the sanctity of life. It was always considered as a serious crime. Conversely, in Japan, 'seppuku' was respected as a means of atonement for failure or as a form of protest. 'Sati' in a Hindu funeral practice, now outlawed, in which the widow was expected or compelled to immolate herself on her husband's pyre either willingly or under pressure of the family.[41]

6. Suicides in the Indian Society

It has been experienced that certain degree of pathology and certain rate of suicides has emerged in the broader Indian society. Again, while the nature and methods of committing suicide are similar as well as dissimilar with other societies of the world, the magnitude are high and low as in the case of other societies. Multiplicity of factors are also same as in other societies of the world. Thus we argue that the Indian society, which represents continent of cultures, religions and ethnicities, has experienced different trends/rates of suicide. The plurality and diversity of the Indian society reflect in different numbers, rates, and trends of suicides.

The Statistical Support: As has been experienced in other societies, suicides in India, especially in South India, were in vogue from early times. In the recent past, these have increased tremendously due to various voluntary and involuntary factors. In the early 1960s, it was estimated that there were about 05 suicides per 1,00,000 people in different parts, regions and states of India.[16] However, other estimates in 1985 were 06 per 1,000 population, while it had gone up to 12 per 1,000 population in 1998.[42] In the previous years, *i.e.,* 2009-2010, the suicide rate in India was estimated at 10.50 per 1,00,000 population. It was also found that the southern states of Kerala, Tamil Nadu and Andhra Pradesh were quite ahead in committing suicides in comparison to the northern states of U.P., Bihar, Haryana and Himachal Pradesh.

The National Crime Records Bureau [NCRB] , Ministry of Home Affairs, Government of India, New Delhi is the sole official national level professional institute which provides the actual data about suicides in the country in previous few decades without any break. According to its reports released in 2009, the number of suicides in India was as follows:

Table 1.3

Incidence and Rate of Suicides in India

	Suicide Incidence		*Suicide Rate*	
Year	*Males*	*Females*	*Total*	*in lakhs*
1989	40212	28532	68744	08.47
1990	43451	30460	73911	08.94
1991	46324	32126	78450	09.23
1992	47481	32668	80149	09.24
1993	49851	34393	84244	09.53
1994	52752	34443	89195	09.91
1995	52357	36821	89178	09.74
1996	51206	37035	88241	09.47
1997	56281	39548	95829	10.03
1998	61686	43027	104713	10.79
1999	65488	45099	110587	11.21
2000	66032	42561	108593	10.80
2001	66314	42192	108506	10.60
2002	69332	41085	110417	10.50
2003	70221	40639	110851	10.40
2004	72651	41046	113697	10.50
2005	72916	40998	113914	10.30
2006	75702	42410	118112	10.50

Source: NCRB, 2009, New Delhi.

The above Table reveals that while 68,744 suicides [with 8.47 rate] were committed in 1989, it reached to the level of 1,18,532 suicides [with 10.50 rate] in 2006. In the former case, male-female composition was 40,212 and 28,532 in 1989, the same composition reached to 75,102 and 42,410 in 2006. Thus the number of suicide deaths has increased significantly. The rate has also increased concomitantly. However, the domination of males against females in suicide cases has always remained there. This increase in the incidence of suicides can be explained in terms of the degree of impact of the processes of modernisation, change and development in the post-independence period.

Again the NCRB, New Delhi published details about occurrence of suicides in all states/union territories of India in the same period. These details follow:

Table 1.4

Occurrence of Suicides in States/U.T.s

S.No	*State/U.T.*	*No. of Suicides*	*(per 1,00,000)*
1.	Pondicherry		48.60
2.	A & N Islands	38.50	
3.	D & N Haveli		29.60
4.	Kerala	26.30	
5.	Karnataka		21.60
6.	Tamil Nadu		20.90
7.	Chandigarh		20.70
8.	Sikkim	20.70	
9.	Tripura	20.30	
10.	Andhra Pradesh	18.20	
11.	West Bengal		17.00
12.	Goa		16.90
13.	Maharashtra	14.30	
14.	Orissa	10.90	
15.	Arunachal Pradesh		10.80
16.	Assam	10.30	
17.	Haryana		10.30
18.	Gujarat	10.00	
19.	Madhya Pradesh		09.20
20.	Delhi		08.90
21.	Damman and dia		08.20
22.	Chandigarh		07.80
23.	Rajasthan		06.90
24.	Himachal Pradesh		06.20
25.	Lakhshadeep	04.40	
26.	Jharkhand		04.30
27.	Meghalaya		03.50

28.	Punjab	03.20	
29.	Mizoram		02.90
30.	Uttrakhand		02.60
31.	Uttar Pradesh	02.10	
32.	Jammu and Kashmir	01.90	
33.	Manipur		01.50
34.	Nagaland		01.10
35.	Bihar		01.00

Source: NCRB, 2OO9, New Delhi.

The Table gives a clear picture about suicides in different states. U.T.s of India. While highest number of suicides occurred in

Pindicherry [48.60],
Kerala [26.30],
Karnataka [21.60],
Tamil Nadu [20.90],
Chattisgarh [20.70], and
Sikkim [20.70];

the least number of suicides were in the following states of

Bihar [01.00],
Nagaland [01.10],
Manipur [01.50],
Jammu and Kashmir [01.90],
Uttar Pradesh [02.10],
Uttrakhand [02.00], and
Mizoram [02.00];

The medium-range suicide states included the following:

Jharkhand [04.30],
Lakhadeep [04.40],
Himachal Pradesh [06.20],
Rajasthan [06.90],
Chandigarh [07.80],

Damman & Dev [08.20],
Delhi [08.90], and
Madya Pradesh [09.20].

Thus the preceding Tables and classified figures reveal that the broader and larger Indian society has experienced the phenomenon of committing suicide significantly at macro and micro levels. This clearly reveals in the occurrence of number of suicides, increasing rates of suicides, and direction of present-day incidence of suicides.

A recent report by NCRB released in 2008-09 revealed that there were 14 suicides per hour recorded, while a total number of 1,25,017 suicides were recorded throughout the year.[43] The number of suicide deaths, according to this report, was as mentioned below:

2004 1,13,697 suicides,

2005 1,13,914 suicides,

2006 1,18,112 suicides,

2007 1,22,637 suicides, and

2008 1,25,017 suicides.[44]

It follows that while 223 suicides were committed in one day on an average and 14-15 suicides were committed in an hour on an average at the national level.[45] This report had and supported by data many aspects of these suicides which we explain in the following:

(a) Though the year reported an increase of 1.9 % over the last year's %age, there was a marginal decline in suicides among farmers which decreased to 17,060 in 2006 from 16,632 in 2007 from 16,196 in 2008.[46] However, it goes in consonance with the general trend of increasing suicides among farmers in the country, especially Mahashtra. According to another report published in a national daily, the total number of suicides in Bundelkahnd [Uttar Pradesh] decreased to 519 in 2011 from 566 in 2009.[47]

(b) Five states in the country have emerged as 'sensitive states' for senior citizens. These states are Kerala, Karnataka, Maharashtra, Andhra Pradesh, and West Bengal. At the same time, the following metropolitan cities had experienced the incidence of suicides in that year as under:

Banglore	2.396,
Chennei	1,300,
Mumbai	1,100,
Delhi	1.107, and
Hyderabad	743.[48]

In terms of factors, the report divulged the information mentioned below:

- 82 people per day committed suicide due to family problems;
- 07 people per day committed suicide due to some kind of illness;
- 10 persons per day committed suicide due to reasons related to poverty;
- 19 persons per day committed suicide due to unemployment reasons; and
- 15 persons per day committed suicide due to profession-career related problems.[49]

It was also found that in a particular survey according to which social and economic causes led most of the male suicides, while emotional and personal causes compelled to most of the women suicides.[50] The student suicides in that year were recorded as mentioned below:

Delhi	150,
Mumbai	80,
Bangalore	84,
Chennai	77, and
Kanpur	65.[51]

It was also observed that while 20 students committed suicide every day in 2010, the total number of student suicides jumped to 7,379.[52]

6. Jammu and Kashmir situation of Suicides

The societies in J&K are comparatively tradition bound. So, till the recent past, these societies had not generally reflected significant proportions/trends of committing suicides. In the post-independence period, like other societies in the country, J&K societies too underwent processes of change and development and their large-scale implications.

Thus these societies faced social and economic development qualitatively as well as quantitatively. In this way, these societies joined the mainstream of social transformation. This macro and micro social transformation had more or less same factors, trends, characteristics, features, degrees, directions and so on.

However, there was an added factor, that was the armed conflict between Kashmiri militants and Indian security forces from 1989. This deeper and larger impact of this situation over the period of 21 years has given highest rise in the number of suicides and highest rates of suicides in the entire region of Kashmir and some districts in the Jammu region. That made the impact on suicides different from rest of India.

7. Statement of the Problem

As mentioned in the previous section, the armed conflict in Kashmir and some parts of Jammu region from 1989 had multi-dimensional, deepest, comprehensive and extensive impact on the societies in J&K month by month and year by year. This 21 year long and continuous impact proved long-term, totalistic, grand and large-scale. It was experienced in all fields of life, especially economic, political, cultural, social, cultural, demographic, educational, linguistic, psychological and other fields and all attitudes and behaviour-patterns in the broader society. The deeply-felt impact was experienced in all sectors and segments of society, particularly women, children, youth, disabled and diseased. In actuality, the whole life became the target of this forceful impact of militancy and militarisation which brutalised and dehumanised the entire environment in the state.

The most devastating effect of this abnormal and dangerous situation was felt on the psychology and personality of vulnerable segments of society such as women, children, elderly and disabled. This psychological-sociological situation was responsible for the emergence of social pathology in the life which resulted in the rise of psychological and phychiatric problems. These problems revealed in the occurrence of serious diseases and problems like PTSD, hypertension, depression, and threat-insecurity.

In this series of problems, the unprecedented emergence of suicidal tendencies, had dangerous and devastating effect on the Kashmiri society. This tendency, it was observed, was experienced in large number of suicides and in highest rate of suicides in all classes, groups, communities, and other groups. Over a period of decades, the number and rate have increased to such a level which the experts and professionals characterise as dangerous pattern that has posed potential threat to the social-cultural-ethical fabric of the Kashmiri society.

This situation of committing suicides in huge number reached to the alarming level. That has happened mainly because of non-availability of expertise, technology, and other facilities. The government too has not been able to provide all necessary and required tools, techniques and infrastructure. One can imagine about this situation because there exists a lone psychiatric hospital in the entire Kashmir region coping with heavy rush of about 250 OPD patients per day with a few qualified doctors and para-medical staff members. As the reports reveal, this sole hospital too lack latest technology, expert-experienced personnels, and necessary medical and other facilities. In this situation, most of the mental health patients could not get proper treatment and some of them could not get treatment at all. Some of these patients opted to go outside the state, especially to Delhi, Mumbai and Chennai, for treatment. But, they usually belonged to affluent sections of society. The common people can never think in terms of this type of treatment. Thus a large number of mental health cases continue to suffer and some of them have opted for committing suicide.

8. Objectives of the Study

In the context of the theoretical-thematic propositions mentioned in all above sections, this empirical study about suicides in the Kashmir region in J&K state reported in local print media in previous three years was aimed at to follow the general and particular objectives as follows:

(i) to collect the statistical information about nature, numbers, and variety of suicides committed in Kashmir region in the state during last three years of 2009-2011 as were reported in the local daily newspapers during that period;

(ii) to develop an objective and scientific understanding and sociological critique of the occurrence of the incidents of suicides in the present-day Kashmiri society;

(iii) to identify and investigate about nature, patterns, types and other classificatory factors of suicides in the valley of Kashmir repcrted in the local print media during last three years;

(iv) to carry out the sociological analysis of multi-dimensional factors responsible for causes, consequences and constant increase in the number and rate of suicides in the Kashmir region; and

(v) to draw a sociological scenario of suicides in totality in the Kashmiri society and compare it with suicides occurring in other states/regions in the country.

REFERENCES

1. Ronald W. Maris, Alan L. Berman, John T. Maltsberger and Robert I. Yufit, Editors, *Assessment and Prediction of Suicide* (New York, 1992, Guilford), p. 4.
2. *Ibid.*, p. 5.
3. Gordon Marshall, editor, *Oxford Dictionary of Sociology* (New Delhi, 1998, Oxford University Press), p. 175.
4. *Ibid.*
5. Maris and others, *op. cit.*
6. *Ibid.*
7. *Ibid.*
8. *Ibid.*
9. *Ibid.*
10. See Hawton K. Van Heeringen K. (2009), "Suicide", *Lanset* 373 (9672):1372-81.
11. See *op. cit.*, no. 1.
12. *Ibid.*
13. Indiana University, Centre for Disease Control and Prevention: Suicide: Data Sources.
14. Druss B., Pincus H. [2000], *Suicide ideation and suicide attempts in general medical illnesses, Arch. Inter. Med 160* [10] 1522-26 and Braden JB, Sullivan MD (2008), *Suicidal thoughts and behaviour among adults with self-reported pain conditionsn in the national comorbidity survey replication,* J. Pain 9 [12]: 1106-15.
15. Arsenault-Lapierre G., Kim C., Turecki G. (2004), *Psychiatric diagnosis and suicide—a meta analysis, BMC Psychiatry* 4; 37.
16. Bertolote J.M., Fleischmann A., De Leo D., Wasseman,

"Psychiatric diagnoses and suicide: revisiting the evidence", *Crisis* 25 [4], 147-55.

17. Joiner T.T., Brown L.R. (2005), "The psychology and neurobiology of suicidal behaviour", *Annual Review of Psychology,* 56, 287-314.
18. Miller N. S., Malher J.C., Gold M.S., "Suicide risk associated with drug and alcohol dependence", *Journal of addictive diseases,* 10 [3], 49-61.
19. *Ibid.*
20. Ajdacic-Gross V., Weiss M.G., ring M *et al.,* (2008), "Methods of suicide: International suicide patterns derived from the WHO mortality database", *Bull World Health Organ,* 86 [9], 726-32.
21. O'Connor, Rory C., Platt, Stephen, Gordon, Jacki, eds., *International Handbook of Suicide Prevention: Research, Policy and Practice*, John Wiley, p. 34.
22. See *op. cit.,* no. 1.
23. *Ibid.*
24. *Ibid.*
25. See WHO Report, 2009, *op. cit.*
26. See CIS, UN Body, Takes on Rising Suicide Rates-2006.
27. *Ibid.*
28. *Ibid.*
29. WHO, Geneva, *op. cit.*
30. See WHO (2002), "Mortality and burden of disease estimates for WHO Member states in 2002, 12-13.
31. "Suicide Prevention", *WHO Sites: Mental Health,* WHO, 2006.
32. "2007 Data", *Suicide Prevention,* Suicidology org., 2007.
33. See *op. cit.,* no. 30.
34. *Ibid.*
35. See Centre for Disease Control and Prevention (2006), "Homicides and Suicides—2003-2004", *MMWR Morb Mortal Wkly Rep., 55 []26], 721-24.*
36. *See Hoyert D.L., Heron M.P., Murphy H.L., Kung* H.C. (2006),

"Deaths: Final data for 2003", *Natl Vital Stat Rep., 54 [13], 53-64.*

37. *See ibid.*

38. "The Sin of Suicide, Aquinas", Clusb. Edu., 1996. See also authentic and primary sources of religions, especially of Christianity, Islam, Judaism, Hinduism and Jainism, which all criticise the concept of suicide.

39. See Simon Robinson (2005), "Europe's Way of Death", TIME.

40. See "Jumpers: The fatal grander of the Golden Gate Bridge", *new Yorker,* 2003.

41. See *op. cit.,* no. 38

42. WHO Report, *op. cit.*

43. NCBR Report, *op. cit.,* also quoted in *The Times of India,* New Delhi, 13.02.2010.

44. *Ibid.*

45. *Ibid.*

46. *Ibid.*

47. *Ibid.*

48. *Ibid.*

49. *Ibid.*

50. *Ibid.*

51. *Ibid.,* also TOI, 13.11.2011.

52. *Ibid.*

2 Methodology of the Study

1. The Empirical Study

At the initial stage, it must be noted here that this study represents primarily an empirical study based on statistical information collected from the local print media published from Srinagar. No particular theoretical or ideological framework was adopted to explain and analyse the suicides. But, at the same time, a thematic-ideational framework was selected for academic clarity, relevance and authenticity. The crucial sociological concepts and theories related to suicides were utilised in the study contextually in order to provide a sociological explanation of this social phenomenon in the existing Kashmiri society.

In this regard, special mention may be made about the contribution of famous sociologist, Emile Durkheim, to the concerned subject. His trend-setting book –*Suicide*- still stands unparalleled in the related academic speciality of Sociology. It still maintains the top academic value in the classical Sociology literature. His concept, classification, typology, explanation and other features of the social phenomenon of suicide have been used universally for the occurrence of suicide in every human society.

2. Innovative Methods

Since the incidence and study of suicides in the Kashmiri society stands completely unparalleled, it needs necessarily unprecedented tools and techniques and unconventional-innovative methods. These methods and techniques will divulge the reality of the incidence/occurrence of suicides and their related social dynamics. So, innovative and unconventional methods were consciously adopted in this empirical study.

3. Hypothesis

The major hypothesis about suicides in Kashmir has to be developed in the relevant context and portray the reality of this phenomenon. Generally, we can make the major hypothesis as follow:

(a) Like other societies in the world in modern times, the social phenomenon of suicide has emerged significantly in the Kashmiri society in present-day times;

(b) While the social phenomenon of suicide in present-day Kashmir can be related to the implications of the processes of change and development in this society, it can also be related to the perpetual continuation of the conflict situation in the previous two decades continuously;

(c) An observation of this pathological situation reveals clearly that there are set sociological causes and consequences for this phenomenon, as has been experienced and observed in similar other societies; and

(d) the number of suicides has increased tremendously in the past two decades. These suicides have increased qualitatively and quantitatively and among all groups, communities and classes of society.

4. Universe of the Study

The universe of this study is the Kashmir province in the J&K state. It is composed of ten administrative districts which are

(a) Srinagar, *(b)* Baramulla, *(c)* Budgam,

(d) Anantnag, *(e)* Bandipora, *(f)* Kulgam,

(g) Shopian, and *(h)* Ganderbal.

All cases of committed suicides in the administrative unit were covered with specific concentration.

5. Suicide Diary

At the initial stage of research, this empirical study started with an unconventional and innovative method of preparing the "Suicide Diary" for the period of April 2009-June 2011. This diary was meant to record day-to-day and month by month account of suicides committed and printed in the local daily newspapers. In this way, a systematic and continuous record of suicides was made which was confirmed in the news items of local largest circulated daily newspapers in English and Urdu languages published from the summer capital of the state, Srinagar. These newspapers and their period of coverage are as mentioned below:

(a)	Greater Kashmir (English), Srinagar	04/2009 – 06/2011
(b)	Rising Kashmir (English), Srinagar	10/2009 – 03/2011
(c)	Srinagar Times (Urdu), Srinagar	04/2009 – 06/2011
(d)	Aftaab (Urdu), Srinagar	04/2009 – 06/2011

Some other local and national daily newspapers in English and Urdu, published from Srinagar, Delhi, Jammu and Chandigarh, were also consulted occasionally for getting the required information. But, it was mostly either in duplication or repetition which we avoided necessarily. These media agencies included the following:

(a)	Etlaat [Urdu], Srinagar	2009 – 2011
(b)	Kashmir Images [English], Srinagar	2009 – 2011
(c)	The Times of India, New Delhi	2009 - 2011
(d)	Kashmir Life [weekly], Srinagar	2009 – 2011
(e)	Indian Express, Chandigarh	2009 – 2011
(f)	Tribune, Chandigarh	2009 – 2011
(g)	Doordarshan Srinagar News	2009 – 2011
(h)	Radio Kashmir Daily News	2009 - 2011

The 'Suicide Diary' recorded all necessary social details given in news items usually on front page. In fact, the entire local media showed keen interest in highlighting the cases of suicide as this was qualitatively new phenomenon in the Kashmiri society, had disastrous effect on the traditional social fabric, and was increasing day by day. Though these details in news items were not sufficient from sociological point of view, the minimum information provided in the news reports was fully noted and recorded. On the whole, this information revolved around sociologically relevant themes covered in the columns of 'Suicide Diary' which are mentioned below:

(a) serial number,

(b) day-month-year of suicide committed,

(c) district/tehsil in which suicide was committed,

(d) male-female composition of suicide-makers,

(e) age group composition of suicide-makers,

(f) occupational composition of suicide-makers,

(g) literacy proportion of suicide-makers,

(h) religious composition of suicide composition,

(i) marital status of suicide-makers,

(j) methods used for committing suicides,

(k) apparent reasons quoted for committing suicides,

(l) hospital aid provided at the time of committing suicides,

(m) number of survivors of suicide attempts,

(n) police investigation after committing suicide, and

(o) sources of news reports about committing suicides.

All these sociological themes shaped the 16 columns of the 'Suicide Diary'.

6. Sample of the Study

The sample of this study composed of the entire lot of news reports about committing suicides during the period of three years. The details follow:

(a) 04/2009 – 12/2009 — 116 cases of suicide

(b) 01/2010 - 12/2010 — 90 cases of suicide

(d) 01/2011 – 06/2011 — 21 cases of suicide

All reports about suicide cases were published in the local media and these were covered in totality by us. Duplication and repetition of suicide cases were not considered for record or assessment. These suicides were committed in all districts of the Kashmir region, mentioned in the previous section. Some cases of suicides which were committed in Kashmir but suicide-makers belonged to Jammu region, especially Doda, Rajouri, Poonch, Jammu and Udhampur, were also included in the sample.

Other sociological variables were considered positively in order to make the sample more representative and sociological. The variables were as follows:

(a) Sex (male-female) composition,

(b) age group composition,

(c) literacy status,

(d) occupational status,

(e) religious status,

(f) marital status,

(g) methods used in suicides,

(h) proportion of survivals,

(i) medical aid at the time/after suicide, and

(j) police intervention in suicide cases.

7. Focus of the Study

Though this study covered all cases of suicide committed and reported in the local press, it had some focused aspects which are mentioned below:

(a) the entire focus of this study was on all cases of suicide committed and confirmed in the local print media during the specific period of 04/2009 – 06/2011. No case of confirmed suicide, successful or not successful, was ignored or dropped;

(b) the focus of this study was on suicide-makers who all belonged to Kashmiri society and were living in the valley;

(c) the study was aimed at to identify most active groups in suicide making in Kashmir in order to determine the nature and trends emerging in Kashmir; and

(d) the study carried out a detailed sociological analysis and explanation for all aspects of suicides and suicide-makers, particularly causation, implications and reformation, and to establish their sociological co-relation.

8. Methods and Techniques Adopted

As is clear from the previous sections, this study adopted the method of 'content study' followed by the relevant techniques. All cases of suicide were examined, recorded and assessed scientifically and sociologically. Their necessary contents were analysed seriously. All sociological details could not be recorded as these were lacking from the news reports. Nearly all these news reports were brief and very brief. We tried to get maximum sociological information from these brief/very brief news items and we succeeded. In this way, we were able to understand and explain the social dynamics related to suicides and suicide-makers.

9. Procedure Followed in the Study

In the process of carrying out this study scientifically and sociologically, it was initiated with recording of daily suicides in Kashmir in the register within pre-determined sociological columns for the entire period of three years. The recording of suicides reported in the press was done on daily basis. So, any news report about committing suicide was not missed. After three years of recording all cases of suicide, these were checked and arranged on date/month/year basis. However, in the final stage, cases of suicides were arranged on month/year basis.

Subsequently, all suicide records were calculated mathematically that led to sub-totals, totals and grand totals of all sociological variables included in the columns of 'Suicide Diary'. That exercise gave the exact number and percentage of all variables which reveal in every column. The calculation of all records in the 'Suicide Diary' enabled us to carry out aggregation, classification, tabulation of statistical data related to the sociological variables/columns.

Finally, description, explanation and analysis of the thematic tables led us to arrive at sociological propositions and conclusions about all variables. Thus this scientific investigation and critique contributed towards sociological understanding of the phenomenon of committing suicide.

10. Limitations of the Study

The most crucial limitation of this study is its lone source of information which is press reports published in the local newspapers. Other sources of this information, *i.e.,* police stations and health/medical centres at all levels and in all areas were not included in this study . It follows that this study is wholly based cn the cases of suicide reported in local newspapers, though other sources were equally important and relevant. In this context, it may be argued that this empirical study is based solely on 227 cases of suicide committed in the valley of Kashmir during the period 04/2009-06/2011 and reported in local daily newspapers during that period. It also follows that the number of suicides committed in

Kashmir may be more. In fact, it is. But, this study is concerned with 227 cases of suicide only, which forms the part of the total number of suicides committed in Kashmir.

3 Suicides in the Jammu and Kashmir State

1. The Kashmir Context

Though we are concerned about the whole state of J&K, this study has concentrated specifically on the Kashmir region. Some propositions and some data have been presented here which deal with the state as a whole, but all necessary theoretical and statistical details about suicides have been presented about the Kashmir region only. It has been done because of four contextual reasons which are:

(a) the traditional situation in Kashmir was such which had neither ideational nor functional character or existence about suicides;

(b) this dominant situation has experienced the processes of change and development in the modernisation context, which was associated with its pathology, which gave rise to the phenomenon of committing suicide in addition to other grave social problems;

(c) in the recent past, the introduction of the armed conflict and its necessary implications over a period of two long decades exposed the Kashmiri society at large to the extreme form of pathology which increased and intensified the acts of committing suicides. This didn't happen in any other region of the state, though some other implications were unavoidable for those regions; and

(d) now, in the present context, we face a society which has experienced the higher/highest number/rates of suicide in the country. Moreover, the emerging trend and direction of these suicides is towards their increase and intensity. Thus this social phenomenon stand unparalleled and unprecedented.

2. The Statistical Estimates

It must be noted here that there is no official statistics or any other record about the nature, number and rate of suicides in the present-day society in the state. The police stations and health/medical centres have not kept records fully, properly and at all levels. Even the local print media reports, on which this study is based, have not covered 100 per cent cases of suicides in the Kashmir region in last 21 years long period. The official statistics about suicides published by National Crime Record Bureau [NCRB], Ministry of Home Affairs, Government of India, New Delhi has not given statistical information about this pathological situation in the Kashmir region. It has not shown the number or rate of suicides in this particular unit. However, the Crime Branch of Jammu and Kashmir Police, Srinagar has issued the statistics regarding various crimes in J&K state in 2009 and 2010. According to these statistics, the registered cases [in the police stations] of abetment to suicide were 312 in 2009 and 296 in 2010 which shows higher number as well as higher rate of suicides in Kashmir.[1] This trend of high rate and increasing trend was confirmed by the statistics issued by Jammu and Kashmir Police [IGP Headquarters, Srinagar] in 2011. According to this source, the overall crime situation was as grave as revealed in the following Table:

Table 3.1

Registered and not registered cases of Crime in Srinagar District

Year	Cases Registered Normal Crime	Militancy-related Crimes	Total	Cases Registered Normal Crime	Militancy-related Crime
1989	3,479	264	3,743	559	05
2000	2,752	506	3,258	241	09
2010	2,817	63	2,880	157	02

Source: J&K Police (IGP Headquarters), Srinagar.[2]

It follows from the above statistical details that the overall trend of increasing number and rate of suicides in district Srinagar and the direction of suicides is also towards the same goal. This district-level data stand symbolic and representative. So, we can infer that with the overall trend of rising crime, there is every possibility of heavy increase in the incidence of suicide in the Kashmir region.

Though these statistical figures are partial, unrepresentative and not in totality, these figures the basic idea and minimum information that will enable us to know about trends and direction of suicides in the state. In this context, we can logically and realistically assume that there exists the comparatively higher rate of committing suicides in J&K state.

2. Higher Rates of Suicide

In the preceding context, we may validly argue the Kashmir and some districts in Jammu region experienced highest number and rate of suicides. The social observers, sociologists and other experts feel that the mass media agencies portray the higher/highest number/trends of suicides and specifically focus on most negative, damaging and disastrous implications, and emphasise strongly to control this problem effectively and immediately.

3. Report on Suicides in the Kashmir Valley

Keeping in view the emerging huge number of suicides, the author carried out a micro-level sociological study for the period of one year—1999-2000 entitled *Suicides in the Kashmir Valley.* A brief report of that sociological study was prepared by the author which is produced here in toto:

Introduction

Suicide in general means killing oneself intentionally. Sociologically, it refers to an act on the part of individual which is essentially subject to social forces. The tendency to suicide depends less on individual psychology or the physical environment and more on individual's relation to the broader society. Thus it follows that suicide primarily represents an individual action which necessarily reveals the failure of social solidarity and is indicative of the ineffectiveness of social bonds. One of the founding fathers of Sociology, Emile Durkhiem [who has produced the trend-setting sociological study on suicides in modern times], has developed the following typology of suicides:

(i) Altruistic Suicide: In this type of suicide, the individual is too strongly integrated into society—a society which encourages or even requires the individual to Sacrifice his or her own life.

(ii) Egoistic Suicide: In this type of suicide, the individual is insufficiently integrated into society, and so is not subject to the collective forces that prevent suicide and experiences an isolation and detachment conducive to it.

(iiii) Anomic Suicide: This type of suicide depends on the social regulation of the individual's desires and ambitions. Where anomie [normlessness] is heightened in society, the individua l's passions, ambitions and appetites are increased to a level where they cannot find satisfaction, so opts for suicide.

Moreover, sociologists have emphasised that one must assess the impact of social and cultural factors on the construction of suicide statistics as well as the tendency to commit suicide. A range of studies have provided some empirical support for the evidence of the impact of social factors on levels of suicide.

The number of suicides in present-day Kashmiri society has experienced a phenomenal growth in the recent years. In fact, the patterns of committing suicide has emerged as a significant trend in Kashmir. It is partly because of sudden rise *of* suicides and partly because of peaceful social situation in the traditional Kashmiri society in which suicides were either totally absent or very insignificant. Thus we may argue that a significant trend of suicides has emerged in present-day Kashmir.

The phenomenon of suicide in the valley needs to be observed/ analysed in the above-mentioned sociological framework. The global-oriented sociological propositions need to be utilised in order to explain causes, consequences, nature/pattern, solutions and other important features of the going-on trend of suicides. This may prove a serious academic exercise. But, there are some serious limitations which make this work very difficult, even impossible. These limitations include non-availability of relevant data from any source and any propositions [governmental sources] and any professional-academic study on suicides *in* Kashmir. In this context, this micro-level study stands highly relevant and badly needed. This study is an attempt to identify and explain major sociological features of the acts of suicides in Kashmir during the period of last one year.

The suicides in Kashmir may be observed in the broader context of total societal dynamics. Thus these may not be explained/analysed in relation to the development of militancy alone, but will be seen and co-related in the totality of social, cultural, economic, psychological, political, educational, demographic and other relevant factors. It follows that while basic societal factors have determined the occurrence of suicides; the militancy-related developments have accelerated and intensified the rate of suicide in Kashmir.

Methodology

It has been mentioned in the preceding section too that though there has been phenomenal growth in the suicides [with the concomitant social consciousness] in Kashmir, no minor or major study/survey has been carried out by the concerned experts. It is partly because of academic apathy towards the scientific study of this problem and partly because of non-availability of information/data and other source material on this problem. In this situation, the only source which provides some basic, but raw, information is the local press in Kashmir. The local newspapers publish daily the reports about suicides and give details about sex, age, area, cause, method, reaction of the people and so on. In the prevailing situation, this content study, which stands as one of the credible methods for scientific investigation of human behaviour, is based on the news items about suicides published in the local newspapers. Though with certain inherent limitations, this method proved relevant and meaningful in our case.

In this content study, the scientific investigations of news-reports were carried out during the period of one year, *i.e.,* from September 1999 to August 2000. The total cases of suicide reported in the local press during this period was 185. The month-wise details about suicide have been given in the previous section. The local newspapers which were studied for knowing about cases of suicide were as follows:

(i) Greater Kashmir (English daily), Srinagar,

(ii) Srinagar Times (Urdu daily), Srinagar, and

(iii) Aftab (Urdu daily), Srinagar.

Keeping in view the broader sociological propositions about suicide, this content study dealt with suicide cases in the Kashmir province [in the state] which was unit of analysis. At the initial stage, news items reported in the local press were collected for a year. Subsequently, the data was aggregated and tabulated which provided the base for explanation/analysis of the suicides in the valley. At this stage, discussion was held with some experts. That enabled us to formulate the sociological propositions about the topic.

Findings of the Study

3.1. Number and Occurance of Suicides

The phenomenon of 'suicide' was near-absent in the traditional

Kashmiri society. But, at present, it has emerged as a significant social phenomenon. Though this act on the part of individual has attained crucial importance in the valley, this phenomenon has not been studied seriously and academically by the social observers and other experts. Consequently, there is hardly any data, in terms of actual number or estimates, available on this topic.

There are two basic methods for getting the relevant data. These are *(i)* the empirical investigation and *(ii)* study of reports about suicides published in the local press. We opted for the second method. But, this method has certain limitations. It is because all cases of suicide have not been reported in the press. According to an unofficial estimate, about 40 per cent cases of suicide have been reported in the local press. I feel that about 50 per cent suicides in Kashmir have been reported in the local press.

On the basis of content study of suicide reports in the local press during the period September 1999 to August 2000, we are in a position to say that about 15 suicides were committed in a month on an average. More or less, the same estimate (30 suicides in 2 months) was made by a local English daily in July 2000. The details about suicides are as follow:

Table 3.2
Number of Suicides in Kashmir, 1999-2000

S.No.	Period	No. of Suicides
1.	September, 1999	17
2.	October, 1999	20
3.	November, 1999	18
4.	December, 1999	11
5.	January, 2000	13
6.	February, 2000	13
7.	March, 2000	14
8.	April, 2000	15
9.	May, 2000	12
10.	June, 2000	19
11.	July, 2000	17
12.	August, 2000	16
	Total (12 months)	185
	01 month	15.41 (average)

It follows that about 2000 persons have committed/attempted suicides in Kashmir during the last one decade starting from 1990. The content study also revealed that about 23 per cent persons were saved from death *by* their family members and in different health centers/hospitals.

As the local press reported, suicides were spread throughout the valley. The occurrence-pattern, especially rise and *fall* of suicides was determined *by* various factors. The occurrence-pattern of suicides covered in this study showed the up-down pattern revealing in figure 3.1 which follows:

Fig. 3.1

Suicides in the Kashmir Valley: 1999-2000

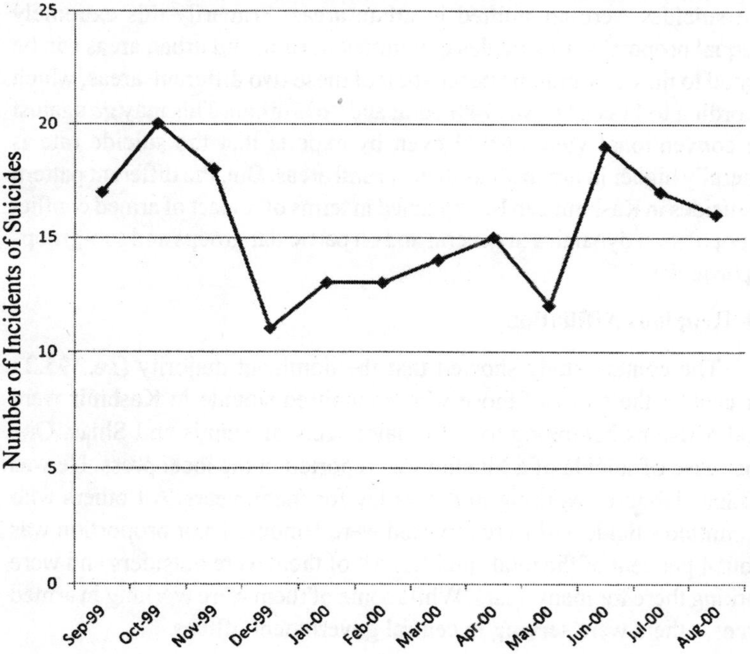

It may not be out of place to mention here, this content study is primarily sociological in nature. The major propositions developed in this report are fully supported by the relevant statistics. However, the arguments and figures are indicative, directional and revealing trends and patterns.

3.2. Male-Female Ratio

The cases of suicide reported in the local press were 77.4 I per cent females and 22.58 per cent males. It also revealed that about 70 per cent females were house-wives, while about 30 per cent females were working women. This huge number/proportion of females in comparison to the males was attributed to their [women's] lesser patience, lesser care inside and outside families, lesser exposure to unprecedented violent situation, discrimination and harassment.

3.3. Rural-Urban Ratio

The content-study divulged that among all reported cases of suicide, while 85.71 per cent suicides were committed in rural areas, 14.28 per cent suicides were committed in urban areas. Primarily this extremely unequal proportion of suicides committed in rural and urban areas can be related to the demographic population of these two different areas, which according to 11 census was 74% rural and 26% urban. This may *go* against the conventional view upheld even by experts that the suicide rate is generally higher in urban areas than in rural areas. But, the different pattern of suicides in Kashmir can be explained in terms of impact of armed conflict on population dynamics in general and on particular groups and sub-groups in particular.

3.4. Religious Affiliation

The content study showed that the dominant majority (*i.e.,* 95.23 per cent of the total) of those who committed suicide in Kashmir were local Muslims belonging to both major sects of Sunnis and Shias. One other case of suicide of a Muslim was reported in the local press. He was a Bihari labourer working in the valley for many years. All others who committed suicide and were reported were Hindus. Their proportion was about 4 per cent of the total suicides. All of them were outsiders and were working there for many years. While some of them were working in armed forces, others were serving in central government offices.

3.5. Age-Groups Ratio

Our study reflected the participation of different age-groups in committing suicides as follows:

Table 3.3

Age-Group Composition of Suicide-makers

S.No.	Age Group	Participation in Suicides (%)
1.	06-15 years	03.07
2.	16-25 years	76.92
3.	26-40 years	20.00
4.	41-years & above	00.00

The most active age group in committing suicide belongs to 16-25 years. This group of youngsters belonging to all demographic, economic, educational, social-cultural, occupational and other groups. They also have affiliation with all communities and castes. The second active age group in committing suicides belongs to 26-40 years. The members of this group are generally senior, matured and are settled in life comparatively. This group has more independence than the former group. The third group which has minor participation in suicides belongs to teen-agers. They are very young and mostly students in colleges. Some of them became suicide-squads against the enemy.

3.6. Married-Unmarried Ratio

The content study showed that there was significant degree of difference between married and unmarried people who committed suicide. While the proportion of the married was 40.32 per cent, the proportion of the unmarried was 59.67 per cent. The higher proportion of the unmarried in committing suicide (in comparison to the married) can apparently be related to younger age-groups, lesser experience of very complex problems, and extensive as well as intensive impact of the militancy situation. Moreover, in the psychological framework, unmarried people have shown more tendency to suicide in comparison to their married counterparts.

3.7. Literate0Illiterate Proportion

The news reports in local press gave no information about the literacy/illiteracy status of the people who committed suicide in the valley in the last one year. In general, there is a feeling that more literate and less illiterate people have committed suicide in the recent past. Our inference conveys while about 60 per cent people (who committed suicide) were literate, about 40 per cent were illiterate. There is also the feeling that literate people (who committed suicide) were more attached to social, economic, ideological and other related factors, while illiterate people were attached to marital, domestic and other related problems. It was also found that the literate's attempt to suicide led to sure death but the attempt of the illiterate didn't prove sudden death.

3.8. Occupational Composition

The suicide reports in the local press did not mention the occupation of individuals who committed suicide. Since less information is available in this regard, there is very less clarity about the occupational composition of those who committed suicide. However, our inference in this regard leads us to assume that most of the people who committed suicide in rural as well as urban areas were house-wives, even up to 65 per cent. The significant group composed of the employees working in governmental and non- governmental offices on lower/petty positions. The third group belonged to petty occupations and small business, especially in the urban areas.

3.9. Other Social Categories Ratio

In addition to the above mentioned groups and sub-groups of suicide-makers, other social categories composed of 27.41 per cent of the total.

(i) The first significant and distinctive group [in this series] composed of the students studying at pre-college and college level and their percentage was 72.17 per cent. They were very young (both boys and girls), belonging to the early and middle teens and showed desperation and frustration. Many of them committed suicide because they could not pass the examinations. Some of them were ideologically and religiously so committed that they [suicide squads] finished their lives for their cause. Some of them finished their lives simply because they had a dispute with their parents or other family members.

(ii) The second important group in the series composed of 'pregnant women' whose percentage was 11.96. Their compelling factors for taking extreme step of finishing their lives included marital disputes, economic compulsions and discrimination and harassment.

(iii) Another group, having the proportion of 5.88 per cent, composed of the personnels of the security forces/police. They belonged to other parts of the country and had come here for their official

work. It has been observed that living and service conditions are worse and they are not allowed even to proceed on leave. Moreover, they always live in fear. In this situation, they become frustrated and some of them ended their lives by committing suicide.

(iv) Still another group having 5.88 per cent proportion was of 'Bihari labourers' who have come here in recent years for work. This outside labour force, both skilled and unskilled, live in isolation but earn sufficient amount of money. Some of them have not been able to earn desired amount. Since they have come here with certain expectations which are not fulfilled in the prevailing conditions, 'they prefer the escape way' *i.e.,* the suicide.

(v) Another group which committed suicide was composed of the prisoners in the jails. Since the living conditions in the jails were worst and any protest meant dangerous consequences for the inmates' the jail prisoners preferred death through suicide.

3.10. Suicide Cases Registered by Police

Though the suicide rate in Kashmir is increasing fast, there has been no major, organised and continuous protest. The figures/percentage referred in this report are not more in comparison with the related situation prevailing in metropolitan areas, but even this number stands higher, even alarming, in the extremely traditional society of Kashmir. However, people feel about it at the individual and social levels. In some cases, this feeling reflected in their minor/peaceful protest followed by the registration of cases in police stations against persons considered responsible for compelling the persons to or creating the situation for committing suicide.

Among all cases of suicide, about 31 per cent cases were registered in local police stations against the following categories of people:

In-laws of the suicide-maker	22.58 per cent
Husbands of the suicide-maker	12.90 per cent
Family members & relatives	09.67 per cent
Others-Unknown	54.81 per cent

It was found that though the above-mentioned cases were registered neither relatives (of suicide-makers) nor the police were serious in pursuing/following these cases till their logical end. Moreover, the police delay and relatives' apathy made the situation more tragic. The analysis of the reports of suicide cases revealed that the police took some action only in 13.62 per cent cases and that also under compulsion.

3.11. Methods of Committing Suicide

The content study of news reports about suicide showed that it was committed by adopting the following methods:

(i)	Consuming poison	83.87 per cent
(ii)	Jumping in the river	06.45 per cent
(iii)	Self-immolation	04.83 per cent
(iv)	Hanging	03.22 per cent
(v)	Shooting with Gun	01.61 per cent

3.12. Apparent Reasons for Committing Suicide

The news in the local press about suicide in Kashmir reported the apparent reasons for committing suicide, which included the following reasons:

(i)	Extreme/heated arguments with parents/ relative over general/particular and personal issues	30.64 per cent
(ii)	Strained marital relations with husband/ disturbed marital life in the family/wrong expectations about post-marital life	20.96 per cent
(iii)	Extreme poverty/ very difficult economic conditions/unemployment	11.29 per cent
(iv)	Ill-treatment/discrimination/harassment of women by their in-laws	08.06 per cent
(v)	Father's/Guardian's death	06.45 per cent
(vi)	Psychological depression/pathology	06.45 per cent
(vii)	Compulsion for marriage with the parental choice	06.45 per cent
(viii)	To avoid rape by the security forces/ other armed groups	04.83 per cent
(ix)	Social factors	03. 22 per cent
(x)	Harassment/eve-teasing of young girls outside their homes	01.61 per cent.

3.13. Suicide Among Armed Forces

Like the phenomenon of suicide among the locals (civilians), it also exists among all sections of the armed forces, who all are outsiders and have been transferred here for a specific period. Though no exact figures about suicides among the security forces are available, the local press has reported several cases of suicide among them in last few years. During the period of this study, more than two cases of suicide were reported, one belonging to the officer cadre and other to the lower cadre. The reasons for their suicide cited in the press included perpetual fear of death, alienation, worst live-life conditions, no social-cultural life and refusal of leave. All suicides in the armed forces were committed by shooting themselves. In some cases, the individual armed person killed himself and his colleagues or officers.

3.14. Suicide Bombers

A new phenomenon emerged in the area of suicides in Kashmir in the context of armed conflict here in the last one decade. It was the emergence of 'suicide bombers' which refers to the local youths, belonging to the teen age group, who killed themselves by striking with the Indian security installations, campus and other related places.

3.15. Concluding Points

The preceding details of the cases of suicides prove that a high rate has been experienced in the Kashmir valley in the previous one decade. So, it has emerged as very significant phenomenon here qualitatively as well as quantitatively. It may be necessary to mention here that there is no information, especially in terms of statistics, available about suicides in Kashmir in the past. Same is the case about suicides at present. In this situation, it is impossible to have a comparison between the past and present. Only inferences and estimates can help in this regard.

In the above-mentioned situation, it seems really difficult to talk about proper/particular reasons of suicides in Kashmir. However, on the basis of scarse information which we got from the local newspapers, we may argue about the co-relation between the acts of suicide and various socio-economic and other factors. It follows that the incidence of suicides in the valley may be explained in terms of varying degrees of social, psychological, educational, political, economic and other relevant factors. These acts may also be explained partly in terms of implication of the on-going militancy in the valley. Thus the militancy has added certain other features to the acts of suicide in Kashmir such as their (suicides) peculiarities which include sudden and fast increase in the number of acts of suicide; more number of suicides committed by females than males; more acts of suicide committed in rural areas than in urban areas; no mass, organised and continuous protest against the increasing suicides here; extreme ups and downs in the trends of suicides here; and no official, formal and complete record of suicides.

Though it is absolutely desirable and functionally necessary that the incidence of suicide in Kashmir must be totally stopped and finally eliminated. But, the total elimination of this phenomenon in the valley seems difficult, even not possible. In actuality, this process seems irreversible in the social dynamics of our society. However, it may be controlled to the maximum extent by the prevailing active social forces/ factors. In order to make this control more realistic and effective, serious and long-term efforts have to be carried out at the psychological, family and broader social levels. In this regard, reference may be made to the social environment created during the month of *Ramadan,* which recorded the least number of suicides (11 in a month) during the previous year as well as this year.

Last, but not the least, it may be noted that there emerges an urgent and basic need to record all cases of suicides formally by the governmental and non-governmental organisations/ agencies and make detailed studies of suicides by the professionals, academicians and other experts. This will certainly help in the formulation and implementation of relevant policy/ programmes to control and eliminate suicides in Kashmir.

4. Other Features of Suicides in Kashmir

In the present study on suicides in Kashmir for the period 04/2009–06/2011, other sociological features were reflected in the press reports. Some of these distinctive features are explained below:

(i) *Higher/highest number and rate of suicide:* While the total number of suicides committed during 2009-2011 was 227 as per the reports published in the local daily newspapers, this number represented the part of the total number of suicides committed and recorded formally in health/medical centres and police stations in all areas. However, the number of suicides published in the local print media reveals categorically the higher/highest number and rate of suicides, and their direction is towards further increase.

(ii) *Women and Suicides:* It was reported repeatedly in the local press that females outnumber males in committing suicides in rural and urban areas in Kashmir. In fact, the press proved more conscious and alert in reporting the suicide incidents of females. It was generally assumed in the local media that suicide rate among females was higher than among males. It was consistently upheld that major causes of more suicides were related to family disorganisation, domestic problems, gender disputes, matrimonial matters, harassment by in-laws, dowry demand, and different kinds of discrimination. In actuality, the perpetual armed conflict and its non-stop implications effected adversely the family and its environment in such a way that hurt the female absolutely, especially after their marriage. So, they suffered in every field of life. It was in the context of these conflict and non-conflict determined factors which compelled necessarily the female of all age groups to opt for ending life miserably through committing suicides.

(iii) *Youth, Students and Suicides:*

(a) The local print media in Kashmir published regular reports about suicides among the youth, especially the students. Many newspapers published editorials repeatedly, in addition to daily news items on front/middle pages, about increasing trend of suicides among the youth (see *Srinagar Times,* Srinagar, 4th June, 2009 and 18th May, 2010). It was generally reported the youth composed of the most dominant and most active group among those who committed suicide in Kashmir and ended their lives voluntarily. A particular daily newspaper (*Srinagar Times,* Srinagar, 18th May, 2010) quoted a particular age group of 15–30 years which stands the most active group of suicide-makers. Other newspapers also cited more or less same age group for committing more suicides comparatively.

(b) The local media characterised this large number of suicides by youth as unprecedented. It put forward the idea that this type of situation never prevailed in the entire recorded history of Kashmir. The local media opined on the causation and implications of large number of 'youth suicides'. Every newspaper wrote several editorials and published many papers, articles and news-analysis on this topic. In general, the local media argued that this situation occurred in Kashmir mainly due to the environment of conflict in continuity for two long decades. That environment was characterised by highest degree of tension, depression, stress, anxiety, fear, threat, insecurity, etc. Moreover, the youth in Kashmir became the major target of security forces in this highly volatile environment. The longevity of the conflict situation added fuel to the fire and frustrated, brutalised and dehumanised the entire youth. In that situation, the youth felt that there was no alternative in life except to commit suicide. In this way, the act of suicide got wider social legitimacy and many youth ended their lives. Finally, the local print media argued that a full generation got lost and they lost everything from career to worldview and so need a radical change in order to save them.

(c) Among the youth, the dominant group composed of students, especially of medium and higher stages for one apparent reason or the other. According to a leading local daily newspaper (*Srinagar Times,* Srinagar, 4th June, 2009), one out of every five suicides belongs to the student community. They composed 33-36 per cent of the total number of youth who committed suicide (*Ibid.*) They belonged to school, college and university level institutions. The local media revealed that more literates than illiterates were involved in suicide-making. Thus a huge number of students lost their lives and their families had to face the pathetic impact. Most of the suicides among students occurred at the time of examination results. When students could not concentrate on studies due to widespread pathology, tension, depression, insecurity and physical threat, they perform miserably in the exams. And so become 'failures'. At that time, they get psychologically frustrated and dejected and thrown-out beings, so they feel about one escape route only, *i.e.,* suicide. When the number of failures remained constant or increased, the number of suicides too remained constant or increased heavily.

(c) According to the local press reports, the other major factor which compelled students to commit suicides was their

continuous harassment and torture inside as well as outside educational institutions on the part of security forces and local police. In fact, they remained one of the major targets of security agencies and forces in Kashmir, especially in the counter-insurgency operations. The added disadvantages were poverty, unemployment and corruption. With these major-minor sociological factors, which can directly be related to the long-term implications of the armed conflict in Kashmir, the local press analysed the problems faced by the students in the present-day conditions.

5. Religion and Suicide

An interesting topic touched by the local media in reporting suicide cases was the role of religion in the acts of committing suicides in Kashmir. These newspapers wrote many editorials, published many stories, articles and columns, and made several news-analysis about orientation and role of the dominant religion in Kashmir, *i.e.,* Islam, and the behaviour of its followers, *i.e.,* Muslims. It was clearly reported in all newspapers that in no way the religion has allowed committing suicide in any situation. In fact, Islam has completely forbidden it and considers it a 'sin'. Thus it in clear cut and absolute terms dubbed it as against religion and legally stopped its manifestations, tendencies and encouragement. The Islamic perception about life, as portrayed by the local media in English as well as Urdu languages, was presented as positive, purposeful and socially-naturally suitable.[3] According to this perception, human life is considered as the kindest and most valuable gift of God, which must neither be wasted nor finished purposelessly. It must be lived with proper identity, supreme dignity and live in consonance with laws-rules of the nature given by God in religious scriptures to all people of the world at different times and in different languages.

The local press also upheld the view that there must not be provided any justification even for the idea of suicide. The ideal position of Islam, mentioned above, was emphasised repeatedly by all newspapers. This media also upheld the view that all qualified and concerned scholars, *Ulema*, theologians and intellectuals have unanimously agreed that there can be no justification for committing suicides as Islam has categorically banned it. In fact, they considered it completely irreligious and totally un-Islamic. The media also presented the view that all authentic sources of Islam, especially *Quran* and *Hadith,* oppose or negate clearly and completely the act of suicide and characterise it as 'irreligious' and 'anti religious'.

In other words, the local media conveyed the message that every religion abhors suicide, so, it must be considered undesirable and must be necessarily condemned. The individual must not even think of committing these irreligious acts. On the one hand, the local media conveyed that suicide stands as the religious and legal offence. So, it must be avoided at all costs. On the other hand, it stressed on individuals, organisations and groups to resist it positively and strongly. It also called upon all social classes and communities to exert and resist actively the act of suicide. Finally, it appealed to the government and civil society to play a positive and active role in stopping the crime of suicide in Kashmir.

But, at the same time, the local press revealed the existing reality of everyday life in Kashmir. It was that despite the absolute religious opposition, suicides continue in Kashmir unabated. In fact, the reports reveal that the number and rate of suicides has increased continuously over last many years (The 'suicide diary' in this book established this point reasonably.) The religious condemnation of suicides seems to have no significant impact on the increasing trend of committing suicides. Thus this phenomenon expands and intensifies day by day in Kashmir. In actuality, it was found in the local press that in one case, a religious preacher (included in the 'suicide diary') himself committed suicide. In the second case (also included in 'suicide diary'), a young boy committed suicide by hanging from the fan just after he finished his evening prayers. In other cases, too, it was found that extremely religious persons committed suicide on one apparent reason or the other. Thus the religious attitudes and behaviour too could not change the direction of the tide of suicides in Kashmir.

6. The Reformative Campaignn

Out of the context of irreligiosity of suicide, a strong trend of campaign was born in Kashmir through the local media. Accordingly, while several editorials, columns, articles and news-analysis were published repeatedly to negate the concept and practice of suicides in Kashmir, many practical measures were suggested for the government and civil society for total elimination of this social problem. The local print media called upon the religious scholars and preachers to emphasise the irreligious character of suicide to distract the youth from these tendencies. It also stressed the role of intellectuals and scholars in this systematic and organised campaign. Finally, it also called on the government to solve core and crucial problems of youth, such as unemployment, poverty and corruption, so that they don't feel compelled to resort to this drastic and dreadful act.

But, as the fact stands, suicides in Kashmir have not stopped despite this continuous and sustained campaign against it. In reality, these have increased in numbers and rates despite reformative campaign. It may be argued that there are certain set factors, such as economic, psychological and political factors, which determine the nature and trends of suicide. These factors can not be ignored in the explanation of suicides. It follows that the act of suicide is not a religious act primarily, so it cannot be resolved totally by the religious persuation. Since it stands as the 'social act', it may be resolved through social efforts only. This approach towards suicides in Kashmir may prove more relevant, more useful and more productive.

7. The Suicide Note

A 'suicide note' of a person who commits a suicide or makes an attempt to suicide represents the real (and truthful) statements, emotions and compulsions. It also throws light on the complex factors or necessary causation about the 'successful act' of suicide. It becomes the base for post-suicide investigation and explanation of the deadly act. The local print media quoted partly or fully published from these 'suicide notes'. A local weekly newspaper published the full text of a 'suicide note' of a person who attempted suicide but failed.[5] This note throws light on various sociological aspects of this act of suicide. Sine this reveals comprehensively the social character of suicide, we present it here in original:

> "...It is limelight winter evening , I stand firm on my decision, while searching the deepest point in the Jhelum. I am not one of those water environmentalists nor a typical nature lover. I disown the paradox, world and this city. It has amplified my every effort into a debacle.
>
> I am fed up with this rat race and non-negotiable give ups. In fact, I may get at least some relaxation before being burnt in hell for eternity, as the common belief is. So, here am I, wishing good bye to the world of pain and only pain; saying that is it 'no more now.' By now your guess work is perfect; I am aspirant of suicide. Since afternoon I have been walking the streets of Lal Chowk waiting for the crowds to disperse, so that no one turns up to... save me! That's right!

Though today it appears like no one has a home or, like watchmen they will spend the night on the roads. While waiting, I have wasted enough energy to force myself to rest. Sitting alongside beggars on the bridge completely recognising the irony—'they are here begging for life and… I'. For a fraction of a minute I think good of life, then shake the thoughts out of my mind pondering at my own disastrous experiences. Eventually my eyes get heavier and my body becomes a little tipsy.

In no time… a man is standing on the bridge looking towards the sky , muttering something to himself. A tear rolls down his face plummeting into the muddy water. Steadily, he widens the distance between his arms, his heart pumps blood like a gush as he anticipates the outcome. Meanwhile he closes his eyes… and jumps!

My senses are choked from conveying anything. Somehow I titter to see him fall. Briefly I notice other faces in the same posture observing the same thing time and again till it all is a trite site. After that there is a lull but not before I witness trepidation. Some mob comes out from nowhere reaching the bridge and they act in congruence with the previous men. Again there is this killing silence followed by another kill. This cycle goes on, and on, till a conundrum of quietness comes into existence, an unpleasant calm overshadows everything! Now of course, it is no more a boring activity but full of apprehension and anxiety. It seems the city is nearly empty; none, nowhere.

I break into sweat—from my red, hot forehead, almost turning unconscious with fear. I think endlessly of what I an going to do? No people!!! No one! Completely frightened by the notion of total solitariness. The vacuous spaces and streets turn me into a statue, into a man who is suddenly transported to another world.

"This is the real hell, is it hell?" Hence I perform an involuntary action , in facme to do, only the purpose is an absolute contrast. Repeating the same old trick of stretching arms, a tear, closed eyes and not to forget, the jump!

As I am nearing the water, I become conscious of some known sounds, first from the near-by temple, then the invitation from the mosque, the muezzin crying, "Come towards God, come towards success". The moment I strike the water my hands start hurting me. My eye instantly opens up, I am on the bridge! On the footpath! Initially I felt I am dead. But seeing people coming out of their houses, with certainty I sum up, that for the whole night, I had been sleeping here. The most important part of it was only a nightmare! I walk to the edge of the bridge, observe the river punctiliously and smile!

As the sun rises, I journey back home. May be there are some interesting things stored in life."[6]

In response to this and other suicide notes [and attempts of committing suicide at large], there was a response from a reader of a local newspaper who wrote an open letter to all those who intend to commit suicide.[7] This letter was extremely emotional [but rational too] and religious in content. The reader made an argument that since the religion of Islam has prohibited suicide, there seems no ground or justification for committing this sinful act. Moreover, he continued, the suicide ruins the other world also as God is not happy with this act.[8] In this context, he appealed to all members of society, particularly the youth, to avoid killing themselves in all situations and live an honourable, religious, dignified and civilised life.

8. Potential Cases of Suicide in Kashmir

In the preceding sections of this chapter, we explained/analysed various sociological features of acts of suicide in Kashmir during last three years as reported in the local print media. In this section, we have identified many potential cases of suicide in Kashmir, whether successful or not, which were highlighted specifically by the local newspapers and gave sociological bits of information about these acts before or after this incident took place. In other words, the news items/stories convey details about social causation, social dynamics, social background and social implications which we intend to highlight here. In addition, it is the social relevance and particular context which provided the criteria for selecting these news items/reports/stories/analysis in this chapter. Here we present these news items, etc.

(a) An attendant of a patient admitted in SKIMS, Soura, Srinagar committed suicide by jumping from the window on Friday night. He was attending his father in ward no. 6A, jumped out at 1.30 a.m. He had a verbal duel with his father before committing suicide. Police has registered a case under FIR.[8]

(b) A girl, 23, tried to end her life after she found that her pre-paid mobile phone was not working while trying to reach out to her

friend. A resident of Chattergul in Ganderbal district, she had consumed some poisonous substance after she failed to connect with her friend on Sunday. However, she was discharged from the hospital on Monday after a stomach wash.[9]

(c) A young man hanged himself on a tree in Shopian district which sent a shockwave in the entire town. The concerned person, after evening prayers, went directly to his room for sleeping. When the family tried to wake him up in the morning, there was no response from inside. When the door was opened forcibly, they were shocked to see his body hanging from the room fan.[10]

(d) In newly-wed groom who had married only a month back was found hanged on the tree... In Kulgam district, 17-day old bride committed suicide and ended her life by consuming poison, the common method used for committing suicides in Kashmir... In Anantnag district, too, a young girl consumed poison and ended her life.[11]

(e) Not bearing the burden of this world, three women preferred consuming poison and ending their lives. The first consumed the gel poison and the second used the pesticides meant for horticulture purpose. The third hanged herself.[12]

(f) A student of 12th class committed suicide in Ganderbal district. People were shocked over this incident and they made a mass protest against government authorities and stoned all passing vehicles. He consumed poisonous substance in uncle's home. He was taken to the hospital where he could not be saved. No apparent reason/s has been quoted in this case. Police has started investigation officially.[13]

(g) S had left Kashmir in 2007 and Z in 2008. One had gone to Bangalore and the second to Delhi. When they met a week back in Kashmir on the banks of Dal, their thought went to two people, who were no longer in this world. S's thoughts went to his brother – M and Z's went to his girl friend, A. Both had committed suicide. "I see him in my dreams," says S. M was just 16 year old when he killed himself. "I sometimes still question myself why this happened? Why did I slap him that day?" says S with tears in his eyes. M had not been a good student and was not interested in studies. He preferred to spend most of his time at his father's

pharmaceutical shop. This worried his parents. "I wanted to become an engineer, and my brother wanted to become a salesman," says S who is in the final year of his engineering course. On the day M committed suicide, everything had seemed normal to the family. The family had to attend a get-together at a close relative's house who had returned from Hajj. Earlier M had failed in the exam. And he found little sense in continuing.[14]

(h) A on the contrary, had been brought up in a very understanding environment. She went to one of the best schools in the valley, had all the facilities, everything she desired. A met Z first at tuition class during class 11. The two started helping each other with studies and soon developed a good friendship. They fell in love. "She was very mild and she would even get angry at me" he says. Z is still at a loss to understand what happened. We met on the morning of that day and everything was okay. After the school, Z waited for her at the spot where they used to meet every day. But, she did not come. Z kept calling her phone, but it was switched off. He thought that she would turn up at tutors'. But, she did not. Z never saw her again.[15]

(i) R.S., 30, from Anantnag district is undergoing treatment in the hospital. He had attempted suicide by consuming pesticides. He was saved as his family took him to a hospital in time. He says he tried to commit suicide because of economic reasons. He is the only brother of four sisters and much is expected of him. His family is in shock but he is recovering.[16]

(j) B. A. too attempted suicide. He tried to cut his veins, but the timely intervention of his family saved him. He was unemployed for a long time. "For every case of suicide, there are around 8 cases of such attempted suicides", says his doctor.[17]

(k) R.B., a 20 year old girl from Bhaleesa (Jammu region), was pursuing her education in Kishtwar district. She was on her way to Ramban to meet her classmate who was also on his way to Kishtwar. Their buses stopped at pul-Doda for tea on a roadside stall. They were interrupted, the local SPO humiliated and beat Dar and threatened the girl for relationship with Dar. They were taken to the police station wherefrom girl's father was conveyed her alleged relationship with Dar. She ran away from the police

station and jumped into the nearby river wherefrom she could not be recovered.[18]

(l) On March17, 2009, S.B. who was in her 20s set herself afire and was admitted to a local hospital with 90 per cent burns. She died a day later. Resident of Kathua district (Jammu region), she in her dying statement accused the SPOs of exploiting her continuously. They were rounded up and investigation has started.[19]

REFERENCES

1. See M. Phil. Dissertation of Aijaz Ahmad Mir entitled *Trends of Crime in the Kashmir Valley: A Sociological Study in Srinagar District,* submitted in the Department of Sociology, University of Kashmir, Srinagar. The research was carried out under the supervision of the author, January 2012.
2. *Ibid.*
3. See local print media reports, analysis, articles, columns and editorials in this regard.
4. *Ibid.*
5. *Ibid.*
6. *Kashmir Life,* Srinagar, May 2010.
7. *Srinagar Times,* Srinagar, 03.07.2010.
8. *Ibid.*, 04.10.2010.
9. *Ibid.*, 03.04.2011
10. *Ibid.*, 31.09.2010.
11. *Ibid.*, 31.10.2010.
12. *Ibid.*, 23.09.2010.
13. *Ibid.*, 05.08.2010.
14. Kashmir Life, Srinagar, 19.06.2011.
15. *Ibid.*
16. *Ibid.*

17. *Ibid.*
18. *Ibid.*
19. *Ibid.*, 11.12.2011
20. *Ibid.*

4 Suicide Diary of Kashmir 2009-2011

S.No.	Date	Code No.	District	M/F	Age	Occupation	Literature Illetrate
(1)	(2)	(3)	(4)	(5)	(6)	(7)	(8)
1.	April, 2009	N-01	Srinagar	F	17-25	Employee	L
2.	April, 2009	N-02	Anantnag	M	17-25	Youth	ill
3.	April, 2009	N-03	Baramullah	M	26-35	Student	L
4.	April, 2009	N-04	Baramullah	M	Upto 16	Youth	ill
5.	April, 2009	N-05	Anantnag	F	17-25	House wife	NK
6.	April, 2009	N-06	Budgam	M	36-50	Lab.	NK
7.	April, 2009	N-07	Kupwara	F	26-25	Student	NK
8.	April, 2009	N-08	Shopian	M	17-25	Teacher	NK
9.	April, 2009	N-09	Srinagar	F	36-50	Youth	NK
10.	April, 2009	N-10	Anantnag	F	17-25	Student	L
11.	April, 2009	N-11	Anantnag	M	36-50	Youth	ill
12.	May, 2009	N-12	Kulgam	F	17-25	HW	L
13.	May, 2009	N-13	Baramullah	M	26-35	WW	NA
14.	May, 2009	N-14	Anantnag	F	17-25	GE	L
15.	May, 2009	N-15	Budgam	M	36-50	Youth	ill
16.	May, 2009	N-16	Srinagar	M	26-35	NK	L
17.	May, 2009	N-17	Srinagar	F	26-35	Student	NA
18.	May, 2009	N-18	Ganderbal	M	17-25	NK	L

(Contd...)

(Contd...)

(1)	(2)	(3)	(4)	(5)	(6)	(7)	(8)
19.	May, 2009	N-19	Anantnag	M	17-25	Youth	L
20.	May, 2009	N-20	Kupwara	F	10-16	NK	ill
21.	May, 2009	N-21	Srinagar	F	17-25	HW	L
22.	May, 2009	N-22	Budgam	M	26-35	Youth	L
23.	May, 2009	N-23	Baramullah	M	17-25	Student	L
24.	May, 2009	N-24	Baramullah	M	10-16	Youth	L
25.	May, 2009	N-25	Srinagar	M	26-35	NK	L
26.	May, 2009	N-26	Anantnag	F	17-25	Youth	L
27.	May, 2009	N-27	Srinagar	F	36-50	NK	NK
28.	May, 2009	N-28	Anantnag	F	50 +	Youth	NK
29.	May, 2009	N-29	Srinagar	F	17-25	Youth	L
30.	May, 2009	N-30	Ganderbal	F	17-25	Youth	L
31.	May, 2009	N-31	Budgam	M	17-25	GE	L
32.	June, 2009	N-32	Srinagar	F	17-25	Student	ill
33.	June, 2009	N-33	Anantnag	M	26-35	NK	NK
34.	June, 2009	N-34	Anantnag	M	36-50	Student	L
35.	June, 2009	N-35	Baramullah	M	17-25	Labour	NK
36.	June, 2009	N-36	Bandipora	F	26-35	HW	L
37.	June, 2009	N-37	Srinagar	F	36-50	Teacher	L

(Contd...)

(Contd...)

(1)	(2)	(3)	(4)	(5)	(6)	(7)	(8)
38.	June, 2009	N-38	Shopian	M	36-50	WW	ill
39.	June, 2009	N-39	Anantnag	F	26-35	HW	NK
40.	June, 2009	N-40	Srinagar	M	17-25	Student	NK
41.	Aug., 2009	N-41	Kupwara	F	10-16	youth	L
42.	Aug., 2009	N-42	Baramulla	M	26-35	Elder	L
43.	Aug., 2009	N-43	Baramulla	F	17-25	Youth	ill
44.	Aug., 2009	N-44	Anantnag	F	26-35	GE	ill
45.	Aug., 2009	N-45	Anantnag	F	17-25	Student	NK
46.	Aug., 2009	N-46	Anantnag	M	36-50	NK	NK
47.	Aug., 2009	N-47	Kupwara	F	17-25	Business man	NK
48.	Aug., 2009	N-48	Kulgam	M	36-50	NK	L
49.	Aug., 2009	N-49	Srinagar	M	17-25	Youth	ill
50	Aug., 2009	N-50	Anantnag	F	26-35	HW	L
51.	Aug., 2009	N-51	Budgam	M	10-16	Student	NK
52.	Sep., 2009	N-52	Anantnag	F	26-35	NK	NK
53.	Sep., 2009	N-53	Baramulla	M	17-25	Youth	L
54.	Sep., 2009	N-54	Srinagar	M	50 +	WK	L
55.	Sep., 2009	N-55	Srinagar	F	17-25	Youth	NK
56.	Sep., 2009	N-56	Budgam	F	10-16	Youth	NK

(Contd...)

(Contd...)

(1)	(2)	(3)	(4)	(5)	(6)	(7)	(8)
57.	Sep., 2009	N-57	Srinagar	F	17-25	Student	L
58.	Sep., 2009	N-58	Anantnag	F	17-25	Youth	L
59.	Sep., 2009	N-59	Budgam	M	36-50	NK	ill
60.	Sep., 2009	N-60	Srinagar	M	17-25	Youth	NK
61.	Sep., 2009	N-61	Anantnag	M	36-50	Student	L
62.	Sep., 2009	N-62	Anantnag	M	26-35	GE	L
63.	Sep., 2009	N-63	Kupwara	M	26-35	NK	NK
64.	Sep., 2009	N-64	Srinagar	M	17-25	Youth	NK
65.	Sep., 2009	N-65	Bandipora	F	36-50	HW	L
66.	Sep., 2009	N-66	Budgam	M	17-25	Youth	L
67.	Sep., 2009	N-67	Anantnag	F	26-35	HW	ill
68.	Sep., 2009	N-68	Budgam	F	17-25	Youth	L
69.	Sep., 2009	N-69	Ganderbal	M	36-50	NK	NK
70.	Sep., 2009	N-70	Srinagar	M	17-25	Youth	NK
71.	Sep., 2009	N-71	Kulgam	M	50 above	SPO	ill
72.	Sep., 2009	N-72	Srinagar	M	26-35	Student	L
73.	Sep., 2009	N-73	Baramulla	F	50 above	NK	NK
74.	Sep., 2009	N-74	Baramullah	M	17-25	Student	L
75.	Sep., 2009	N-75	Anantnag	F	26-35	Driver	NK

(Contd...)

(Contd...)

(1)	(2)	(3)	(4)	(5)	(6)	(7)	(8)
76.	Sep., 2009	N-76	Anantnag	M	17-25	Youth	L
77.	Sep., 2009	N-77	Srinagar	F	36-50	Teacher	NK
78.	Sep., 2009	N-78	Shopian	M	36-50	HW	NK
79.	Sep., 2009	N-79	Anantnag	F	26-35	NK	NK
80.	Sep., 2009	N-80	Kupwara	M	17-25	Student	NK
81.	Sep., 2009	N-81	Anantnag	F	17-25	Youth	L
82.	Sep., 2009	N-82	Srinagar	M	50 above	NK	NK
83.	Oct., 2009	N-83	Anantnag	M	17-25	Labour	L
84.	Oct., 2009	N-84	baramulla	F	26-35	NK	ill
85.	Oct., 20 09	N-85	Baramulla	F	17-25	Student	L
86.	Oct., 2009	N-86	Barramulla	M	10-16	Youth	NK
87.	Oct., 2009	N-87	Srinagar	M	26-35	SPO	NK
88.	Oct., 2009	N-88	Anantnag	M	26-35	NK	L
89.	Oct., 2009	N-89	Anantnag	M	17-25	Youth	iil
90.	Oct., 2009	N-90	Ganderbal	F	17-25	Youth	NK
91.	Oct., 2009	N-91	Pulwama	F	36-50	NK	L
92.	Oct., 2009	N-92	Budgam	M	17-25	Teacher	ill
93.	Oct., 2009	N-93	Srinagar	M	36-50	Student	L
94.	Oct., 2009	N-94	Srinagar	F	17-25	NK	NK

(Contd...)

(Contd...)

(1)	(2)	(3)	(4)	(5)	(6)	(7)	(8)
95.	Oct., 2009	N-95	Anantnag	M	26-35	NK	L
96.	Oct., 2009	N-96	Anantnag	F	17-25	Youth	L
97.	Oct., 2009	N-97	Shopian	M	10-16	NK	ill
98.	Oct., 2009	N-98	Kupwara	M	36-50	GE	NK
99.	Oct., 2009	N-99	Ganderbal	F	17-25	HW	NK
100.	Oct., 2009	N-100	Anantnag	M	10-16	Youth	NK
101.	Oct., 2009	N-101	Kupwara	F	26-35	Student	L
102.	Oct., 2009	N-102	Baramulla	F	26-35	NK	L
103.	Oct., 2009	N-103	Srinagar	M	17-25	Youth	L
104.	Nov., 2009	N-104	Kupwara	F	36-50	Labour	NK
105.	Nov., 2009	N-105	Budgam	M	17-25	Youth	NK
106.	Nov., 2009	N-106	Srinagar	F	36-50	Student	L
107.	Nov., 2009	N-107	Anantnag	M	17-25	NK	L
108.	Nov., 2009	N-108	Bandipora	M	26-35	Student	L
109.	Nov., 2009	N-109	Budgam	M	26-35	WW	N
110.	Nov., 2009	N-110	Anantnag	F	17-25	Youth	NK
111.	Nov., 2009	N-111	Srinagar	F	17-25	Youth	NK
112.	Nov., 2009	N-112	Srinagar	M	50 above	HW	ill
113.	Dec., 2009	N-113	Budgam	F	17-25	Youth	L

(Contd...)

(Contd...)

(1)	(2)	(3)	(4)	(5)	(6)	(7)	(8)
114.	Dec., 2009	N-114	Anantnag	F	50 above	Student	L
115.	Dec., 2009	N-115	Baramulla	F	17-25	Youth	L
116.	Dec., 2009	N-116	Srinagar	M	17-25	Student	ill
117.	Jan., 2010	N-117	Anantnag	F	10-16	Youth	NK
118.	Jan., 2010	N-118	Kupwara	M	26-35	GE	NK
119.	Jan., 2010	N-119	Srinagar	F	26-35	HW	L
120.	Jan., 2010	N-120	Srinagar	M	17-25	Student	L
121.	Jan., 2010	N-121	Ganderbal	M	36-50	HW	NK
122.	Feb., 2010	N-122	Anantnag	M	36-50	Labour	L
123.	Feb., 2010	N-123	Anantnag	F	17-25	Youth	ill
124.	Feb., 2010	N-124	Budgam	M	10-16	Youth	ill
125.	Feb., 2010	N-125	Pulwama	M	26-35	Teacher	NK
126.	Feb., 2010	N-126	Bandipora	F	17-25	Student	NK
127.	Feb., 2010	N-127	Anantnag	F	26-35	Service	L
128.	Feb., 2010	N-128	baramula	M	36-50	NK	NK
129.	Feb., 2010	N-129	Anantnag	F	26-35	NK	L
130.	Mar., 2010	N-130	Kulgam	M	17-25	Youth	NK
131.	Mar., 2010	N-131	Srinagar	M	17-25	NK	L
132.	Mar., 2010	N-132	Budgam	F	36-50	NK	L

(Contd...)

(Contd...)

(1)	(2)	(3)	(4)	(5)	(6)	(7)	(8)
133.	Mar., 2010	N-133	Shopian	M	36-50	Student	ill
134.	Mar., 2010	N-134	Kupwara	F	17-25	Youth	NK
135.	Mar., 2010	N-135	Anantnag	M	17-25	SPO	NK
136.	Mar., 2010	N-136	Baramula	F	26-35	NK	NK
137.	April, 2010	N-137	Anantnag	M	26-35	NK	NK
138.	April, 2010	N-138	Srinagar	M	17-25	Youth	NK
139.	April, 2010	N-139	Srinagar	F	17-25	NK	L
140.	April, 2010	N-140	Srinagar	M	10-16	GE	L
141.	April, 2010	N-141	Srinagar	F	17-25	Student	ill
142.	April, 2010	N-142	Srinagar	M	17-25	Labour	NK
143.	April, 2010	N-143	Budgam	F	26-35	NK	L
144.	April, 2010	N-144	Anantnag	M	36-50	NK	I
145.	April, 2010	N-145	Bermulla	F	10-16	Youth	L
146.	April, 2010	N-146	Ganderbal	F	17-25	GE	L
147.	April, 2010	N-147	Bandipora	M	10-16	Youth	ill
148.	April, 2010	N-148	Kupwara	F	26-35	NK	NK
149.	April, 2010	N-149	Anantnag	M	26-35	NK	NK
150.	April, 2010	N-150	Anantnag	F	17-25	Student	L
151.	April, 2010	N-151	Baramulla	M	36-50	NK	ill

(Contd..)

(Contd...)

(1)	(2)	(3)	(4)	(5)	(6)	(7)	(8)
152.	April, 2010	N-152	Srinagar	M	17-25	Youth	L
153.	April, 2010	N-153	Budgam	F	36-50	NK	NK
154.	April, 2010	N-154	Srinagar	F	26-35	Elder	NK
155.	May, 2010	N-155	Kulgam	M	26-35	Student	L
156.	May, 2010	N-156	Anantnag	M	17-25	Youth	ill
157.	May, 2010	N-157	Anantnag	F	36-50	Teacher	L
158.	May, 2010	N-158	Baramulla	M	36-50	Gujar	NK
159.	May, 2010	N-159	Srinagar	F	17-25	Youth	NK
160.	May, 2010	N-160	Budgam	M	10-16	Student	L
161.	May, 2010	N-161	Kupwara	M	26-35	SPO	L
162.	May, 2010	N-162	Anantnag	F	17-25	Youth	ill
163.	May, 2010	N-163	Srinagar	M	17-25	Student	NK
164.	May, 2010	N-164	Anantnag	F	26-35	HW	L
165.	May, 2010	N-165	Anantnag	M	17-25	Youth	l
166.	May, 2010	N-166	Srinagar	M	50 above	HW	NK
167.	May, 2010	N-167	Pulwama	M	17-25	Student	NK
168.	May, 2010	N-168	Ganderbal	M	17-25	Youth	NK
169.	May, 2010	N-169	Baramulla	F	17-25	Student	L
170.	May, 2010	N-170	Ganderbal	M	17-25	Youth	L

(Contd...)

(Contd...)

(1)	(2)	(3)	(4)	(5)	(6)	(7)	(8)
171.	May, 2010	N-171	Srinagar	M	36-50	NK	L
172.	May, 2010	N-172	Srinagar	F	17-25	Student	ill
173.	May, 2010	N-173	Anantnag	M	10-16	Youth	NK
174.	June, 2010	N-174	Budgam	M	36-50	GE	NK
175.	June, 2010	N-175	Bandipora	M	17-25	Youth	ill
176.	June, 2010	N-176	Anantnag	F	26-35	Service	NK
177.	June, 2010	N-177	Anantnag	M	26-35	Student	NK
178.	June, 2010	N-178	Budgam	M	17-25	HW	L
179.	June, 2010	N-179	Kulgam	F	36-50	Elder	L
180.	June, 2010	N-180	Baramula	M	17-25	Youth	L
181.	June, 2010	N-181	Kupwara	M	26-35	Youth	ill
182.	June, 2010	N-182	Kupwara	M	17-25	Youth	NK
183.	June, 2010	N-183	Ganderbal	F	17-25	Student	L
184.	June, 2010	N-184	Anantnag	M	26-35	SPO	L
185.	June, 2010	N-185	Anantnag	M	26-35	GE	NK
186.	June, 2010	N-186	Srinagar	F	17-25	Youth	NK
187.	July, 2010	N-187	Pulwama	M	26-35	Preacher	ill
188.	July, 2010	N-188	Baramula	M	17-25	NK	L
189.	July, 2010	N-189	Anantnag	F	17-25	Student	L

(Contd...)

(Contd...)

(1)	(2)	(3)	(4)	(5)	(6)	(7)	(8)
190.	July, 2010	N-190	Srinagar	M	10-16	Youth	NK
191.	July, 2010	N-191	Anantnag	F	26-35	Labour	NK
192.	July, 2010	N-192	Srinagar	F	17-25	H.master	NK
193.	July, 2010	N-193	Budgam	F	36-50	Doctor	L
194.	July, 2010	N-194	Srinagar	F	10-16	Youth	L
195.	July, 2010	N-195	Anantnag	M	17-25	HW	NK
196.	July, 2010	N-196	Srinagar	F	17-25	Student	NK
197.	July, 2010	N-197	Baramulla	F	17-25	Student	L
198.	Aug., 2010	N-198	Srinagar	M	26-35	HW	L
199.	Aug., 2010	N-199	Kupwara	M	10-16	Youth	ill
200.	Sep., 2010	N-200	Kulgam	M	26-35	SPO	NK
201.	Sep., 2010	N-201	Budgam	M	17-25	Student	NK
202.	Oct., 2010	N-202	Anantnag	F	26-35	Labour	NK
203.	Oct., 2010	N-203	Anantnag	M	26-35	Elder	NK
204.	Oct., 2010	N-204	Ganderbal	F	17-25	Youth	L
205.	Nov., 2010	N-205	Srinagar	M	26-35	NK	L
206.	Nov., 2010	N-206	Ganderbal	M	17-25	GE	L
207.	Nov., 2010	N-207	Srinagar	F	26-35	NK	NK
208.	Dec., 2010	N-208	Anantnag	M	17-25	Youth	L

(Contd...)

(Contd...)

(1)	(2)	(3)	(4)	(5)	(6)	(7)	(8)
209.	Dec., 2010	N-209	Baramula	F	17-25	Youth	NK
210.	Jan., 2011	N-210	Ganderbal	F	36-50	Student	L
211.	Jan., 2011	N-211	Ganderbal	M	17-25	HW	L
212.	Jan., 2011	N-212	Budgam	M	17-25	NK	ill
213.	Feb., 2011	N-213	Baramula	F	10-16	Youth	L
214.	Feb., 2011	N-214	Anantnag	M	17-25	Youth	L
215.	Mar., 2011	N-215	Anantnag	M	26-35	NK	ill
216.	Mar., 2011	N-216	Kupwara	F	17-25	NK	L
217.	April, 2011	N-217	Kulgam	M	36-50	B.Man	L
218.	May, 2011	N-218	Ganderbal	M	17-25	Youth	NK
219.	May, 2011	N-219	Baramula	F	36-50	NK	NK
220.	May, 2011	N-220	Anantnag	M	17-25	Youth	L
221.	May, 2011	N-221	Anantnag	M	17-25	Youth	L
222.	May, 2011	N-222	Pulwama	F	17-25	Student	ill
223.	June, 2011	N-223	Ganderbal	F	26-35	Student	NK
224.	June, 2011	N-224	Anantnag	F	26-35	Student	NK
225.	June, 2011	N-225	Kupwara	M	36-50	Labour	NK
226.	June, 2011	N-226	Kulgam	F	36-50	student	NK
227.	June, 2011	N-227	Srinagar	M	17-25	WW	L

(Contd...)

(Contd...)

S.No.	Religion	Married/ Unmarried	Method Used	Apparent Reason	Hospital Aid	Survival	Police Investigation	Source
(1)	(9)	(10)	(11)	(12)	(13)	(14)	(15)	(16)
1.	M	M	Poison	Family	Y	Y	Y	GK/ST/AF
2.	M	M	Poison	NR	Y	N	Y	GK/ST/AF/RK
3.	H	M	Poison	Dowry demand	Y	N	N	GK/ST/AF/RK
4.	M	Un	Poison	Poverty	Y	N	Y	GK/ST/AF/RK
5.	M	Un	Poison	Domestic problem	Y	N	Y	GK/ST/AF/RK
6.	M	M	Jumping	NK	Y	N	Y	GK/ST/AF/RK
7.	H	Un	Poison	Poverty	NK	N	Y	GK/ST/AF/RK
8.	M	Un	Hanging	Matrimonial disputes	Y	Y	NK	GK/ST/AF/RK
9.	H	M		DP	Y	NK	Y	GK/ST/AF/RK
10.	M	M	Poison	DP	NK	N	NK	GK/ST/AF/RK
11.	M	Un	Jumping	NK	Y	NK	Y	GK/ST/AF/RK
12.	M	M	Poison	Exam failure	Y	N	Y	GK/ST/AF/RK
13.	M	Un	Burnt	Tortured	Y	N	Y	GK/ST/AF/RK
14.	M	M	Poison	NK	NK	N	Y	GK/ST/AF/RK
15.	S	Un	Hanging	Poverty	N	NK	Y	GK/ST/AF/RK
16.	M	Un	Poison	Mental.health	Y	Y	Y	GK/ST/AF/RK
17.	M	M	Poison	MD	Y	N	Y	GK/ST/AF/RK

(Contd...)

(Contd...)

(1)	(9)	(10)	(11)	(12)	(13)	(14)	(15)	(16)
18.	M	Un	Jumping	Love	Y	NK	Y	GK/ST/AF/RK
19.	M	M	Burnt	DP	Y	N	Y	GK/ST/AF/RK
20.	M	M	Poison	DP	Y	N	N	GK/ST/AF/RK
21.	M	M	Poison	Poverty	Y	N	Y	GK/ST/AF/RK
22.	C	M	Hanging	Un-E-7	Y	NK	Y	GK/ST/AF/RK
23.	M	Un	Poison	DP	Y	Y	NK	GK/ST/AF/RK
24.	M	M	Jumping	MD	N	N	Y	GK/ST/AF/RK
25.	M	Un	Poison	MH	Y	N	NK	GK/ST/AF/RK
26.	M	M	Burnt	LA-7	Y	N	Y	GK/ST/AF/RK
27.	M	M	Burnt	NK	Y	NK	Y	GK/ST/AF/RK
28.	M	Widow	Shooting	poverty	NK	NK	NK	GK/ST/AF/RK
29.	M	M	Poverty	FC	Y	Y	Y	GK/ST/AF/RK
30.	M	M	Hanging	NK	Y	N	Y	GK/ST/AF/RK
31.	S	Un	Hanging	LA	NK	N	Y	GK/ST/AF/RK
32.	H	M	Jumping	LA	Y	N	NK	GK/ST/AF/RK
33.	M	Un	Jumping	DP	Y	NK	N	GK/ST/AF/RK
34.	M	M	Poison	NK	Y	Y	NK	GK/ST/AF/RK
35.	M	M	Burnt	DP	Y	Y	Y	GK/ST/AF/RK
36.	M	Un	Shooting	MD	Y	N	Y	GK/ST/AF/RK

(Contd...)

(Contd...)

(1)	(9)	(10)	(11)	(12)	(13)	(14)	(15)	(16)
37.	M	M	Poison	Poverty	Y	NK	Y	GK/ST/AF/RK
38.	M	M	Poison	DP	NK	N	Y	GK/ST/AF/RK
39.	M	Un	Poison	MH	Y	N	Y	GK/ST/AF/RK
40.	M	M	Poison	MD	Y	N	Y	GK/ST/AF/RK
41.	M	M	Burnt	Poverty	Y	N	Y	GK/ST/AF/RK
42.	N	M	Poison	DP	Y	NK	Y	GK/ST/AF/RK
43.	M	M	Jumping	Poverty	NK	N	NK	GK/ST/AF/RK
44.	M	Un	Poison	Un-E	Y	N	Y	GK/ST/AF/RK
45.	M	M	Hanging	DP	Y	N	N	GK/ST/AF/RK
46.	M	M	Poison	NK	Y	NK	Y	GK/ST/AF/RK
47.	M	M	Poison	MD	Y	N	Y	GK/ST/AF/RK
48.	M	Un	Poison	MH	N	NK	Y	GK/ST/AF/RK
49.	M	M	Burning	LA	Y	N	Y	GK/ST/AF/RK
50.	M	Un	Poison	Poverty	Y	N	NK	GK/ST/AF/RK
51.	M	Un	Poison	DP	Y	NK	Y	GK/ST/AF/RK
52.	H	Un	Jumping	—	Y	N	Y	GK/ST/AF/RK
53.	M	M	Hanging	NK	Y	Y	Y	GK/ST/AF/RK
54.	M	M	Poison	NK	Y	N	Y	GK/ST/AF/RK
55.	M	M	Poison	Poverty	N	N	Y	GK/ST/AF/RK

(Contd...)

(Contd...)

(1)	(9)	(10)	(11)	(12)	(13)	(14)	(15)	(16)
56.	M	Un	Burning	NK	Y	N	Y	GK/ST/AF/RK
57.	M	M	Poison	MH	Y	N	NK	GK/ST/AF/RK
58.	M	M	Poison	NK	Y	N	NK	GK/ST/AF/RK
59.	M	M	Poison	DP	Y	N	Y	GK/ST/AF/RK
60.	M	Un	Jumping	NK	Y	N	Y	GK/ST/AF/RK
61.	M	Un	Jumping	FC	Y	N	NK	GK/ST/AF/RK
62.	M	M	Poison	DP	Y	NK	Y	GK/ST/AF/RK
63.	M	M	Hanging	Poverty	Y	N	NK	GK/ST/AF/RK
64.	M	Un	Poison	Poverty	Y	Y	Y	GK/ST/AF/RK
65.	H	Un	Burning	MD	Y	NK	Y	GK/ST/AF/RK
66.	M	M	Hanging	NK	Y	N	N	GK/ST/AF/RK
67.	M	M	Poison	LA	Y	NK	Y	GK/ST/AF/RK
68.	H	Un	Poison	DP	N	N	N	GK/ST/AF/RK
69.	M	M	Poison	DD	NK	N	Y	GK/ST/AF/RK
70.	M	Un	Poison	Poverty	Y	Y	Y	GK/ST/AF/RK
71.	M	M	Poison	NK	Y	N	Y	GK/ST/AF/RK
72.	M	Un	Burning	NK	Y	NK	Y	GK/ST/AF/RK
73.	S	M	Jumping	Un-E	Y	N	Y	GK/ST/AF/RK
74.	M	Un	Burning	DP	N	N	Y	GK/ST/AF/RK

(Contd...)

(Contd...)

(1)	(9)	(10)	(11)	(12)	(13)	(14)	(15)	(16)
75.	M	M	Poison	MD	Y	NK	Y	GK/ST/AF/RK
76.	M	Un	Poison	P	Y	N	Y	GK/ST/AF/RK
77.	M	M	Burning	LA	Y	N	Y	GK/ST/AF/RK
78.	M	M	Poison	DP	Y	Y	Y	GK/ST/AF/RK
79.	M	M	Hanging	DP	Y	N	Y	GK/ST/AF/RK
80.	H	Un	Poison	NK	Y	Y	Y	GK/ST/AF/RK
81.	M	Un	Poison	P	NK	NK	Y	GK/ST/AF/RK
82.	M	Un	Jumping	NK	NK	N	Y	GK/ST/AF/RK
83.	M	M	Shooting	MH	Y	N	Y	GK/ST/AF/RK
84.	M	M	Poison	N	NK	NK	Y	GK/ST/AF/RK
85.	H	M	Poison	MD	Y	NK	Y	GK/ST/AF/RK
86.	M	Un	Poison	DP	Y	Y	Y	GK/ST/AF/RK
87.	M	M	Burning	DD	Y	N	Y	GK/ST/AF/RK
88.	M	Un	Hanging	LA	NK	NK	Y	GK/ST/AF/RK
89.	M	M	Hanging	NK	Y	N	Y	GK/ST/AF/RK
90.	M	Un	Poison	DP	Y	NK	Y	GK/ST/AF/RK
91.	M	M	Poison	DP	Y	N	Y	GK/ST/AF/RK
92.	M	Divorce	Jumping	—	Y	Y	Y	GK/ST/AF/RK
93.	M	M	Poison	NK	Y	NK	Y	GK/ST/AF/RK

(Contd...)

(Contd...)

(1)	(9)	(10)	(11)	(12)	(13)	(14)	(15)	(16)
94.	M	Un	Jumping	P	Y	Y	Y	GK/ST/AF/RK
95.	M	M	Poison	NK	Y	NK	Y	GK/ST/AF/RK
96.	H	Un	Poison	P	Y	N	Y	GK/ST/AF/RK
97.	M	M	Burning	NK	Y	Y	NK	GK/ST/AF/RK
98.	M	M	Poison	P	Y	N	Y	GK/ST/AF/RK
99.	M	M	Burning	NK	Y	N	Y	GK/ST/AF/RK
100.	H	M	Poison	DP	Y	N	N	GK/ST/AF/RK
101.	M	Un	Burning	Un-E	Y	NK	Y	GK/ST/AF/RK
102.	M	M	Poison	—	N	N	NK	GK/ST/AF/RK
103.	M	M	Shooting	DP	Y	N	Y	GK/ST/AF/RK
104.	M	Un	Poison	NK	Y	N	NK	GK/ST/AF/RK
105.	M	M	Poison	P	Y	N	Y	GK/ST/AF/RK
106.	M	M	Poison	MH	Y	NK	Y	GK/ST/AF/RK
107.	M	Un	Jumping	DP	Y	N	Y	GK/ST/AF/RK
108.	M	Un	Hanging	MD	Y	N	Y	GK/ST/AF/RK
109.	M	Un	Poison	NK	N	N	Y	GK/ST/AF/RK
110.	M	M	Poison	MH	NK	N	Y	GK/ST/AF/RK
111.	M	Un	Jumping	LA	NK	N	N	GK/ST/AF/RK
112.	M	M	Poison	P	Y	N	NK	GK/ST/AF/RK

(Contd...)

(Contd...)

(1)	(9)	(10)	(11)	(12)	(13)	(14)	(15)	(16)
113.	M	M	Poison	Poison	Y	N	Y	GK/ST/AF/RK
114.	H	M	Poison	MH	Y	N	NK	GK/ST/AF/RK
115.	H	M	Poison	DP	Y	N	Y	GK/ST/AF/RK
116.	M	Un	Poison	LA	Y	Y	NK	GK/ST/AF/RK
117.	M	M	Poison	DP	Y	NK	Y	GK/ST/AF/RK
118.	M	M	Poison	P	Y	Y	NK	GK/ST/AF/RK
119.	M	Divorce	Jumping	MD	Y	N	Y	GK/ST/AF/RK
120.	M	M	Jumping	MH	Y	Y	N	GK/ST/AF/RK
121.	M	M	Hanging	NK	Y	Y	Y	GK/ST/AF/RK
122.	M	Un	Poison	DP	Y	NK	NK	GK/ST/AF/RK
123.	M	M	Burning	Un-E	Y	NK	Y	GK/ST/AF/RK
124.	M	Un	Poison	P	Y	N	Y	GK/ST/AF/RK
125.	M	Un	Burning	IA	Y	NK	Y	GK/ST/AF/RK
126.	H	Un	Poison	FC	N	N	Y	GK/ST/AF/RK
127.	M	M	Burning	NK	Y	NK	Y	GK/ST/AF/RK
128.	M	m	Poison	NK	y	N	y	GK/ST/AF/RK
129.	M	Un	Jumping	LF	Y	N	Y	GK/ST/AF/RK
130.	M	M	Poison	EF	Y	N	Y	GK/ST/AF/RK
131.	M	M	Jumping	DP	Y	N	Y	GK/ST/AF/RK

(Contd...)

(Contd...)

(1)	(9)	(10)	(11)	(12)	(13)	(14)	(15)	(16)
132.	M	Un	Poison	P	Y	N	Y	GK/ST/AF/RK
133.	M	M	Burning	DFM	NK	N	Y	GK/ST/AF/RK
134.	M	Un	Poison	MD	Y	N	Y	GK/ST/AF/RK
135.	M	M	Poison	DP	Y	Y	Y	GK/ST/AF/RK
136.	M	M	Poison	P	Y	NK	Y	GK/ST/AF/RK
137.	M	Un	Poison	DP	NK	N	Y	GK/ST/AF/RK
138.	M	Un	Hanging	NK	NK	N	Y	GK/ST/AF/RK
139.	M	Un	Burning	NK	NK	N	Y	GK/ST/AF/RK
140.	S	M	Hanging	NK	Y	NK	N	GK/ST/AF/RK
141.	H	M	Hanging	P	Y	Y	NK	GK/ST/AF/RK
142.	M	M	Hanging	P	Y	N	Y	GK/ST/AF/RK
143.	M	Un	Hanging	Un-E	Y	N	NK	GK/ST/AF/RK
144.	M	Un	Hanging	NK	Y	NK	Y	GK/ST/AF/RK
145.	M	M	Hanging	DP	Y	Y	Y	GK/ST/AF/RK
146.	M	M	Jumping	NK	Y	NK	Y	GK/ST/AF/RK
147.	M	M	Hanging	DP	Y	N	Y	GK/ST/AF/RK
148.	M	M	Hanging	P	Y	Y	N	GK/ST/AF/RK
149.	M	Un	Burning	NK	Y	N	N	GK/ST/AF/RK
150.	M	M	Hanging	DD	N	N	Y	GK/ST/AF/RK

(Contd...)

(Contd...)

(1)	(9)	(10)	(11)	(12)	(13)	(14)	(15)	(16)
151.	M	M	Burning	NK	Y	N	Y	GK/ST/AF/RK
152.	M	M	Burning	DP	Y	NK	Y	GK/ST/AF/RK
153.	H	M	Hanging	NK	Y	N	Y	GK/ST/AF/RK
154.	M	Un	Hanging	DP	Y	N	Y	GK/ST/AF/RK
155.	M	M	Hanging	LF	Y	NK	Y	GK/ST/AF/RK
156.	M	Un	Hanging	MH	Y	N	Y	GK/ST/AF/RK
157.	M	M	Burning	P	Y	Y	Y	GK/ST/AF/RK
158.	M	Un	Burning	P	N	N	Y	GK/ST/AF/RK
159.	H	Un	Hanging	MD	N	N	Y	GK/ST/AF/RK
160.	M	M	Hanging	MH	Y	N	Y	GK/ST/AF/RK
161.	M	M	Jumping	NK	NK	N	Y	GK/ST/AF/RK
162.	M	M	Jumping	DP	NK	NK	Y	GK/ST/AF/RK
163.	M	Un	Jumping	FC	Y	N	Y	GK/ST/AF/RK
164.	M	Un	Jumping	MD	Y	N	Y	GK/ST/AF/RK
165.	m	un	Hanging	LA	Y	N	Y	GK/ST/AF/RK
166.	M	Un	Hanging	LA	Y	NK	Y	GK/ST/AF/RK
167.	S	M	Jumping	EF	N	N	NK	GK/ST/AF/RK
168.	M	Dir	Jumping	DP	Y	N	NK	GK/ST/AF/RK
169.	M	M	Hanging	DP	Y	N	Y	GK/ST/AF/RK

(Contd...)

(Contd...)

(1)	(9)	(10)	(11)	(12)	(13)	(14)	(15)	(16)
170.	M	M	Hanging	DP	Y	N	Y	GK/ST/AF/RK
171.	M	Un	Poison	Un-E	Y	N	Y	GK/ST/AF/RK
172.	M	M	Poison	P	Y	N	Y	GK/ST/AF/RK
173.	M	M	Poison	NK	Y	Y	N	GK/ST/AF/RK
174.	M	M	Burning	LA	y	NK	NK	GK/ST/AF/RK
175.	M	Un	Poison	P	NK	NK	Y	GK/ST/AF/RK
176.	M	M	Poison	DP	Y	N	Y	GK/ST/AF/RK
177.	M	Un	Jumping	MD	Y	NK	Y	GK/ST/AF/RK
178.	M	M	Poison	MD	NK	N	NK	GK/ST/AF/RK
179.	M	Un	Burning	P	Y	N	Y	GK/ST/AF/RK
180.	M	M	Poison	MH	Y	NK	Y	GK/ST/AF/RK
181.	H	M	Poison	DP	N	N	Y	GK/ST/AF/RK
182.	M	M	Poison	NK	Y	NK	Y	GK/ST/AF/RK
183.	H	Un	Poison	Exam failure	Y	Y	Y	GK/ST/AF/RK
184.	M	Un	Poison	NK	Y	N	Y	GK/ST/AF/RK
185.	H	M	Hanging	P	Y	N	N	GK/ST/AF/RK
186.	M	Un	Poison	D.F.N	Y	NK	Y	GK/ST/AF/RK
187.	M	Un	Poison	LA	Y	Y	Y	GK/ST/AF/RK
188.	M	M	Jumping	DP	Y	N	NK	GK/ST/AF/RK

(Contd...)

(Contd...)

(1)	(9)	(10)	(11)	(12)	(13)	(14)	(15)	(16)
189.	M	M	Poison	NK	Y	NK	Y	GK/ST/AF/RK
190.	M	Un	Poison	NK	Y	N	Y	GK/ST/AF/RK
191.	M	Un	Poison	NK	Y	N	Y	GK/ST/AF/RK
192.	S	Un	Hanging	DP	Y	Y	Y	GK/ST/AF/RK
193.	M	M	Burning	P	Y	N	NK	GK/ST/AF/RK
194.	M	Divorce	Jumping	Un-E	Y	N	Y	GK/ST/AF/RK
195.	M	M	Burning	NK	N	N	Y	GK/ST/AF/RK
196.	M	M	Jumping	MH	NK	N	Y	GK/ST/AF/RK
197.	M	M	Poison	NK	NK	N	Y	GK/ST/AF/RK
198.	M	M	Poison	MH	NK	N	Y	GK/ST/AF/RK
199.	M	M	Poison	MK	Y	N	Y	GK/ST/AF/RK
200.	M	M	Jumping	DP	NK	N	Y	GK/ST/AF/RK
201.	M	M	Burning	Un-E	Y	N	y	GK/ST/AF/RK
202.	m	M	Jumping	p	N	NK	Y	GK/ST/AF/RK
203.	M	Un	Poison	DP	Y	N	Y	GK/ST/AF/RK
204.	H	Un	Poison	NK	Y	NK	Y	GK/ST/AF/RK
205.	H	M	Poison	P	Y	N	N	GK/ST/AF/RK
206.	M	M	Hanging	P	Y	NK	Y	GK/ST/AF/RK
207.	M	M	Jumping	MD	N	N	Y	GK/ST/AF/RK

(Contd...)

(Contd...)

(1)	(9)	(10)	(11)	(12)	(13)	(14)	(15)	(16)
208.	M	Un	Poison	DP	Y	N	N	GK/ST/AF/RK
209.	M	M	Burning	NK	N	NK	Y	GK/ST/AF/RK
210.	M	Un	Poison	Un-E	Y	Y	Y	GK/ST/AF/RK
211.	M	Un	Burning	EF	Y	NK	N	GK/ST/AF/RK
212.	M	Un	Poison	NK	Y	N	Y	GK/ST/AF/RK
213.	H	Un	Poison	DL	Y	NK	Y	GK/ST/AF/RK
214.	M	Un	Poison	P	Y	Y	N	GK/ST/AF/RK
215.	M	M	Poison	P	Y	N	Y	GK/ST/AF/RK
216.	M	M	Hanging	LA	Y	NK	Y	GK/ST/AF/RK
217.	M	Un	Poison	DP	Y	N	NK	GK/ST/AF/RK
218.	M	Un	Hanging	MD	Y	N	Y	GK/ST/AF/RK
219.	M	M	Poison	NK	Y	Y	Y	GK/ST/AF/RK
220.	M	Widow	Hanging	MH	Y	N	Y	GK/ST/AF/RK
221.	M	M	Burning	DP	N	N	Y	GK/ST/AF/RK
222.	M	M	Shooting	LA	Y	N	NK	GK/ST/AF/RK
223.	M	Un	Poison	NK	y	Y	Y	GK/ST/AF/RK
224.	M	Divorce	Poison	NK	Y	N	Y	GK/ST/AF/RK
225.	M	Divorce	Poison	P	Y	N	N	GK/ST/AF/RK
226.	M	Divorce	Poison	NE	Y	N	N	GK/ST/AF/RK
227.	M	M	Poison	NK	Y	Y	Y	GK

5 Findings of the Study

1. Total Number of Suicides Committed

The number of suicides published in the local print media during the period of three years, 04/2009 – 06/2011, was 227. Some reports were repetitive or in duplication but those were dropped. It was attempted that one suicide case was recorded once only. So, the actual number of suicides covered in this study was 227. The multi-layer details of these suicides follow in Table No. 5.1:

The preceding table reveals that the year-wise and month-wise number of suicides published in the local print media was as mentioned below:

2009	(09 months)	116	(51.10 %) suicides
2010	(12 months)	90	(29.64 %) suicides
2011	(06 months)	21	(09.25 %) suicides

The highest number of suicides in a month during the period of 03 years was 30 in May 2009 followed by 19 in October 2010. At the same time, the lowest number of suicides committed in a month during this period was 01 in April 2011 and 02 each in August-September 2010, December 2010 and February-March 2011 respectively.

Again, the highest number of suicides in particular months during the period of 03 years was 44 in May and 32 in September [2011]. As against this, the lowest number of suicides in this entire period of study was 05 in December and 06 in November. These figures essentially conveyed the lowest or highest number of suicides in particular winter and summer months.

All different numbers and proportions, mentioned above, have been explained in different sections of this chapter. So, here the effort was limited to the presentation of the relevant data. The total number of suicides, given above, reflect in the diagrams nos. 01 and 02 below:

2. Number of Suicides in Three Particular Months

The total number of suicides in three particular months selected randomly, during 2009–2011 also reflect the same trend and direction of suicides in Kashmir. The Table 5.2 showing these details is given on next page:

The preceding Table reveals clearly the similar trend and direction of suicides in the study period of three years. These particular figures are mentioned below:

(a)	I month	09/2009	34 suicides per month
(b)	II month	06/2010	30 suicides per month
(c)	III month	04/2011	30 suicides per month

The dominant trend which reveals from the above statistical information shows that 30 suicides per month on an average were committed in Kashmir and were reported by the local print media. It follows that one suicide per day was committed in Kashmir that was reported by the press. Comparatively speaking, while highest number of suicides was recorded in September 2009, the related situation in other months/years was different, *i. e.,* higher or lower. The up/down trends of suicides have certain set social factors whose analysis has been carried out in following sections of this chapter.

These statistics also reflect in the following Table 5.3 on next page.

Grand Total Number of Suicides in Kashmir

The statistics presented in two preceding tables gave suicide data for three years period of 2009-2011 and for three particular months of 09/2009, 06/2010 and 04/2011, on number and rate of suicides about different periods. In this statistical framework, we make the following statistical estimates about suicides in the Kashmir region in the state:

(a)	Total number of suicides	03 years (27 months)	227
(b)	Total number of suicides	03 years (36 months)	303

Table 5.1

Actual Suicides in Kashmir for 3 Year (Pres Information) 2009-2011

Year	Jan.	Fab.	March	April	May	June	July	Aug.	Sep.	Oct.	Nov.	Dec.	Total	%
2009	x	x	x	11	20	10	9	11	30	19	3	3	116	51.1
2010	5	8	6	18	18	12	11	2	2	3	3	2	90	39.64
2011	3	2	2	1	6	7	x	x	x	x	x	x	21	9.25
Total	8	10	8	30	44	29	20	13	32	22	6	5	227	100.00

Table 5.2

No. of Suicides in Three Paticular Months in Three Years

Days	1	2	3	4	5	6	7	8	9	10	11	12	13	14	15	16	17	18	19	20	21	22	23	24	25	26	27	28	29	30	31	Total
Sep., 2009	2	X	X	3	X	2	X	1	X	1	2	X	2	3	X	X	3	2	2	X	1	X	2	X	3	X	1	1	X	2	1	34 % 36.17
June, 2010	2	X	1	X	2	X	1	1	X	2	X	3	X	1	1	X	2	1	X	2	X	1	X	2	X	3	X	1	1	2	1	30 % 31.19
April, 2011	2	X	1	2	X	1	X	1	X	1	1	X	2	X	1	2	1	X	2	X	1	2	2	1	1	X	2	X	1	1	2	30 % 31.19
Total	**6**	**X**	**2**	**5**	**2**	**3**	**1**	**3**	**X**	**4**	**3**	**3**	**4**	**4**	**2**	**2**	**6**	**3**	**4**	**2**	**2**	**3**	**4**	**3**	**4**	**3**	**3**	**2**	**2**	**5**	**4**	**94 % 100.00**

(c)	Total number of suicides	01 year (12 months)	101
(d)	Total number of suicides	01 month (30 days)	08.41
(e)	Total number of suicides	01 day	00.30
(f)	Grand total of suicides	21 years (1990-2011)	2,121

Thus we may argue that an overall/aggregated estimate of suicides reported in the local print media during 2009–2011 convey the total number of 2,121 suicides in 21 years. It is important to note here that this number [*i.e.*, 2,121] represents a portion and not the total number of suicides in Kashmir. These were the acts of suicides which were reported in the local print media. Some or many other suicides, not included in this study, have been registered in health-medical centres and police stations at the village, tehsil, block and district levels or not reported as well as registered anywhere. For our academic purpose within the sociological framework, we have taken the 227 cases which were individually and specifically published in the local print media during the period of 2009-2011. This method and perspective have served the purpose effectively and have enabled to understand and study the phenomenon of suicide in the Kashmir region.

3. Composition of Age Groups

It has been observed that age has emerged as one of the important contributing factors in forcing individuals and groups to attempt/commit suicide. Accordingly, different segments and sections of society responded differently to the conditions for compelling individuals to end their lives. These sociological factors establish positive or negative co-relation with the phenomenon of suicide. The role of the age factor is shown in the following statistical Table on next page.

The Table 5.4 conveys that most active group in suicide-committing belong to the age group of 17–25 years, the least active age group was 50 plus years. It follows that youngsters, males as well as females, commit more suicides than their elders. These groups shared unequal share of 45.87 per cent and 14.28 per cent of the total number of suicides. It seems that former group had lesser experience of life, had not faced earlier different complex problems and were emotional in their attitude. On the other hand, the elders had faced difficult and complex problems in life and were matured enough to respond to suicide compulsions. That is why they committed least number of suicides. Another group of minors had

Table 5.4

Age Group Composition of Suicide-Makers

Year/ month	Age Groups (years) Up to 16	17-25	26.35	36.50	50 plus	
2009/9m.	08 07.33	50 45.87	32 29.35	17 15.59	02 01.83	109 48.01
2010/12m.	12 14.28	40 47.61	15 18.48	14 17.85	03 03.57	84 37.00
2011/6m.	03 08.82	10 29..41	11 32.35	09 26.47	01 02.94	34 14.97
Total	23 10.13	100 44.05	58 25.55	40 17.62	06 02.64	227 100.00

also experienced comparatively lower number, *i.e.,* 23 out of 227 (10.13 per cent) suicides during last three years.

The trends of committing suicide, reflecting from the Table, shows positive and negative co-relation with main sociological variables. Thus minimum age groups' suicide rate was lowest (10.13 per cent) because of immature understanding of life and total dependency. The marriage emerged as a contributing factor among younger groups. So, a significant number and percentage of suicides (44.05 % and 25. 55 %) were committed in two age groups of 17-25 years and 26-35 years.

Thus the above Table reveals that while the rate of suicide stands lowest among up to 16 and 50 plus age groups, that of high and higher rates of suicide prevailed among 17-25 and 26-35 age groups.

The methods of committing suicides were also related to age groups. It was found that younger age groups committed suicides by consuming poison or jumping into river, while elder age groups consumed poison, burnt their bodies and hanged.

The apparent reason/s for ending their lives also varied. While the younger age groups ended their lives because of petty reasons such as quarrel with parents, exam failure, denial of mobile phone service, the elder age groups performed the dreaded act because of serious reasons like poverty, unemployment, matrimonial problems and family disputes.

Though police has shown positive response in dealing with the cases of suicide and carried out investigation in these cases formally. But, in reality, it was not serious about these cases as was reported in the local media.

4. Composition of Marital Groups in Suicide

The marital status of individuals and groups has definite relationship with age composition of suicide. In fact, this relationship is determined by two major factors, age and marriage. Sociologically, it has been observed that generally

(a) in traditional societies, more marriages are solemanised in early age groups;

(b) in modern societies, more marriages are materialise in later age groups; and

(c) in changing societies, marriages are carried out in both early and later age groups.

The case of Kashmiri society fits in all three situations because these exist simultaneously. It was found that this marriage situation has directly effected the nature and pattern on the act of suicide too. This relationship between marital status of an individual and suicides has been observed in Kashmir as is shown in the following Table:

Table 5. 5
Composition of Marital Groups in Suicides

Marital status	2009	2010	2011	Total
Married	19 15.07	70 55.55	37 29.36	126 55.50
Unmarried	11 12.50	42 47.72	35 39.77	88 38.76
Divorced	02 25.00	03 37.50	03 37.50	08 03.52
Widows	00 00.00	02 66.66	01 33.33	03 01.32
Others	00 00.00	01 50.00	01 50.00	02 00.88
Total	32 14.09	118 51.98	77 33.92	227 100.00

The Table clearly shows a relationship between marriage and suicide which can be explained as follows:

(a) highest number of committing suicides among married groups [55.50 %];

(b) high number of committing suicide among unmarried groups [38.76 %]; and

(c) lower number of committing suicide among divorcees and widows.

It was observed that married groups, which have the highest number of suicides, faced more problems like facing tough life and family conditions, more trouble with family and in-laws, difficult economic conditions and so on. This situation usually led to the crisis in family and made the conditions ripe for committing suicides by its members.

It is also revealed from the above Table that unmarried group had also high number of suicides, *i.e.,* 38.76 %. But, they have separate set of factors responsible for this condition. These include literacy, culture, economy and history. All these factors collectively create a depressive situation which leads to rise of suicidal tendencies that become the base for committing suicide. But, the number of unmarried suicide-makers is lesser than married suicide-makers. The former tries to compromise at the individual level, but becomes difficult for the latter do away with responsibility, especially of family members and relatives.

The above Table also shows lesser number of suicides (*i.e.,* 3.52 % and 1.32 %) among widows and divorcees, though the suicidal tendencies remain high in these troubled groups due to suffering. The Table gives least number of cases of suicide committed by recently married persons, particularly pregnant women. This type of suicide can be explained in terms of extreme form of discrimination, injustice, torture, harassment and so on imposed on them mostly in domestic context.

5. Composition of Litracy Groups in Suicides

It has been observed clearly that literacy and illiteracy contribute significantly to the occurrence of suicides, though in different ways. While the literate group has its own compelling reasons such as depression, unemployment, poverty, career failure and alienation, the illiterate group too has real factors like tension, depression, insecurity and family disputes. Both these trends reflect in our study as is shown in the following Table:

Table 5. 6

Literacy Status of Suicide-Makers

Status	2009 [6 m.]	2010 [12 m.]	2010 [9m.]	Total
Literate	14 14.14	55 55.55	30 30.30	99 43.61
Illiterate	08 22.85	17 48.57	10 28.57	35 15.41
Not Known	16 17.20	54 58.06	23 24.77	93 40.96
Total	38 16.74	186 55.50	63 27.75	227 100.00

The preceding Table shows clearly that there were 99 out of 227 (*i.e.,* 43.63 %) suicides committed by literate individuals, while 35 out of 227 (*i.e.,* 15.41 %) suicides were involved in the dreadful act. It follows that majority of those were educated and committed suicide did it consciously and deliberately. Many social, psychological, political, economic and health factors contributed to this situation. On the other hand, a significant illiterate group , *i.e.,* 15.40 %, opted for this type of death. This trend is more or less like the previous trend but due to opposite factors which include psychological, political and economic factors. Thus it is continuity in the trend of suicide even which is contributed due to different and opposite factors. The third trend, unknown, may also be considered in consonance with two trends mainly because both factors, literacy as well as illiteracy, lead to the occurrence of suicide.

In reality, the continuous trend of suicides in Kashmir has to be necessarily related to the strong factor of armed conflict and its long-term implications on local residents. Since education was the major victim of conflict, it suffered extremely which created a pathological situation conducive to committing suicide.

The press reports about suicides did not mention the literacy status of suicide-makers in many cases, *i.e.,* 40.96 %. But, in these cases also, either literacy or illiteracy directly contributed to the occurrence of suicides.

6. Composition of Sexual Groups in Suicides

It has been generally observed that suicides are committed more by females and less by males in the Kashmiri society. The psychological, emotional, health and other relevant factors are presented in favour of this argument. At times, it seems correct but not always. It may emerge rational but not always. In actuality, suicides maintain both characteristics. In one situation, men may emerge as the dominant group among suicide-makers. But, at other times, this role may be adopted by women. The same kind of situation can be thought in the Kashmiri society.

But, there is an added factor in the case of factors, *i.e.,* long-term implications of armed conflict situation in Kashmir. Traditionally, Kashmir was completely a non-violent society and hardly anybody committed or heard about the act of committing suicide. But, the conflict and post-conflict situation for more than 2 decades created many abnormal conditions in which a huge number of suicides , more among females than among males, was committed by different individuals and groups. Thus both sexes were actively involved in this criminal act. These details in statistical form reflect in the following Table:

Table 5. 7

Composition of Sexual Groups in Suicides

Year/months	Year	Male	Female	Total
2009/09m.	2009	10 21.73	36 78.26	46 20.26
2010/12m/.	2010	49 38.56	78 61.41	127 55.94
2011/06m.	2011	24 14.44	30 55..55	54 23.78
Total		83 36.56	144 63.46	227 100.00

The above Table reveals that the total estimated number of suicides in Kashmir during the period of last few decades has more share of females than that of males. In fact, the female share composed more than double of the males. In terms of statistics, it is 83 out of 227 (36.56 %) for males and 144 out of 227 (63.43 %) for females. The male-female composition in the incidence of suicides in Kashmir in all three years of study is mentioned below:

(*a*) 2009 21.73 % for males and 78.26 % for females,

(*b*) 2010 38.50 % for males and 61.41 % for females, and

(*c*) 2011 14.44 % for males and 55.55 for females.

It seems that the pattern of committing suicide go in consonance and dissonance of the global pattern. While all three years' suicides are similar to the pattern at the global level among females than males. On the other hand, this pattern reveals the dissimilarity because in this case females dominate than that of males. In the context of processes of modernisation, urbanisation, industrialisation, females dominate males in committing suicides. Several features of suicides were presented for this kind of suicides. The first important feature in this regard is weak psychological nature of females, which is not generally in a position to face acute problems repeatedly and courageously. Not facing these psychological challenges, they surrender and in many cases opt for the idea of ending life and that psychological mind leads to suicide among them. In comparison to this pattern, males either face these psychological challenges or some of them ignore these problems boldly and courageously. However, some of them with weak psychological power scummb to these pressures and problems.

7. Rural-Urban District-wise Composition of Suiciide-Makers

It has been observed in general that every human society has experienced one or other kind of suicide. It has also all types of suicide with certain background, cause and consequence. Thus suicides were also observed in the demographic background, *i.e.,* rural and urban areas. In societies which inhabit in hilly areas, suicides were recorded there also. Thus it may be assumed validly that are different patterns, types and kinds of suicides in different demographic areas.

In general societies, the normal scientific explanation of this social phenomenon (*i.e.,* suicide) is that in the context of the processes of modernisation, urbanisation and industrialisation, the following patterns of suicides were noticed:

(a) urban areas have higher rate of suicides;

(b) rural areas have lower rate of suicides;

(c) mixed areas have mixed rate of suicides; and

(d) hilly areas have high rate of suicides.

The explanation of these types of suicide can be made by the nature and implication of the related social dynamics of societies at different stages of change and development. Normally, it was found that suicides were of higher rate or lower rate depending upon the stage or level of development achieved by the society. Particular factors have played different role in determining the nature and rate of suicides in specific situations. These factors include social, cultural, religious and other factors. The same kind of situation must have prevailed in the Kashmiri society.

In the present-day context, different population data also show the trends of suicide. On the basis of official data, we can establish the co-relation between rural//urban areas and the degree of suicide rate. In the J&K context, we can establish two major propositions which follow:

(a) rural areas have generally lower suicide rates; and

(b) urban areas have comparatively higher suicide rates.

The logic of these grand propositions can be given by arguing that while rural areas [having lower suicide rates] have lesser impact of the processes of modernisation and urbanisation comparatively, the urban areas have greater impact of these processes. Our study about suicides in rural-urban context confirms these sociological propositions. It clearly reveals in the statistical Table presented below:

Table 5. 8

Rural-Urban District-wise Composition of Suicide-Makers

S. No.	District	Suicide Number	Suicide rate (%)	Rural/Urban character
1.	Srinagar	52	22.90	Urban+/Rural
2.	Budgam	23	10.13	Rural+/Urban
3.	Baramulla	28	12.33	Rural+/Urban
4.	Anantnag	64	28..19	Rural+/Urban
5.	Kupwara	17	07.48	Rural only
6.	Bandipora	07	03.08	Rural only
7.	Kulgam	10	04.40	Rural only
8.	Shopian	05	02.20	Rural only
9.	Pulwama	05	02.20	Rural only
10.	Ganderbal	16	07.04	Rural-Urban

The above Table reveals that the following districts were urban dominated (*i.e.,* majority of population was urban town-based. At the same time, these districts had experienced higher rate of suicides comparatively. The relevant statistics in this regard is presented below:

- *(a)* Anantnag district 28.19
- *(b)* Srinagar district 22.90
- *(c)* Baramulla district 23.13
- *(d)* Budgam district 10.30

All these districts reveal higher rate of suicides in urban dominated or significantly urban areas. The relevant reasons for higher rate of suicides may be related to urban environment, urban dynamics, urban life-style and more impact of processes of change and development. In brief, these higher rates can be traced in urban determined social melieu only. Since Srinagar district is more urban than Baramulla district, the former has higher rate of suicide than the latter. This can be explained in terms of more impact of armed conflict (and having the status of frontier district) in the Baramulla district in comparison to Srinagar district. Same explanation may be provided for different rates of suicide between Srinagar and Anantnag districts.

The above mentioned Table also reveals that rural dominated districts had generally lower suicide rates. The following details support this point:

- *(a)* Kupwara district 07.68 %
- *(b)* Bandipora district 03.08 %
- *(c)* Kulgam district 04.40 %
- *(d)* Pulwama district 02.20 %
- *(e)* Ganderbal district 07.04 %

All these districts have experienced lower rates of suicide even in single digits and lowest percentages. The reasons may be directly opposite to the reasons quoted in the higher rate of suicides. These reasons include lesser urban social dynamics, lesser degree of urbanisation, lesser impact of the processes of change and development and the impact of conflict situation. However, relatively higher rates in Ganderbal and Kupwara in terms of more urban impact in the former case and more conflict impact in the latter case are reported.

In totality, we may argue that different rural-urban composition of suicide-makers in last three years reflects in higher or lower rates of suicide for different reasons in different demographic areas. While in urban areas, the higher rates led to social quias, lesser social solidarity, valuelessness, anarchy, lesser personalised relationship and so on, and directly opposite and lesser effect in rural areas.

8. Occupational Composition of Suicide-Makers

It has been observed in many sociological studies at the global level that occupation and structure have effected the attitude and behaviour towards the acts of suicides in traditional as well as modern societies. This response reveals both positive and negative responses and both aspects have the support of social evidence. It follows that individuals and groups in all occupations develop particular attitudes and behaviour patterns towards occupational life and its chief characteristics. In this way, occupations shape the lives and attitudes towards life of those who work there. In this situation, they either develop depressive psychological traits and life-style or progressive framework and perspective of life.

All these sociological propositions can be validly applied to the occupational life in Kashmiri society. The present situation can be explained by most of these theoretical propositions. The Kashmiri society, though not changed extremely and didn't adopt all features of modern life, has adopted many basic features of modernity. At the same time, though the Kashmiri society doesn't stand for an extremely traditional society, it has left/dropped many of its basic features. In this half-changed and half-unchanged society, suicides were not much in vogue till recent past. But, the last two decades long conflict situation has demolished all limits and barriers of committing suicide, giving rise to a peculiar situation in which it was easy to think about and to make an act of suicide within minutes or seconds time. Many of the families, groups and communities in Kashmir face devastating and tragic situation today. The occupational participation in suicides in Kashmir reveals in the number of individuals associated to different occupations or occupational activities in these acts, which is shown in the following Table on next page:

The above Table clearly reveals that all occupational groups and communities had certain participation rate in suicides in Kashmir during last three years. It reflects in the higher participation rate of 20.95 % and 19.38 % youth and student respondents, and lesser rates of even 01 % participation rate for various occupational individuals and groups. In totality, our study reveals that these occupational groups and communities can be classified into three major categories. The first group-community has highest participation rate in suicides, *i.e.,* 299.25 % to 17.36 % belonging to youth and students. Most of these young groups have become

Table 5.9
Composition of Occupational Groups in Suicides

S.No.	Occupation/Occupl. Activities	2009 (6m.)	2010 (12m.)	2011 (9m.)	Total
1.	Govt. employees	02	07	03	12
		16.66	58.33	25.00	05.28
2.	Businessmen	00	01	01	02
		00	50.00	50.00	00.58
3.	Labourers	02	04	02	08
		25.00	50.00	25.00	03.52
4.	Students	07	24	13	44
		15.90	54.54	29.55	19.38
5.	Youth	10	38	20	68
		14.70	55.88	29.41	29.95
6.	Housewife	03	11	04	18
		16.66	61.11	22.22	07.92
7.	Elders	01	02	01	04
		25.00	50.00	25.00	01.76
8.	Teachers	01	03	02	06
		16.66	50.00	33.33	02.64
9.	Gujjars	00	01	00	01
		00	100.00	00	00.44
10.	SPOs	01	04	01	06
		16.66	66.66	16.66	02.64
11.	Driver	01	00	00	01
		100.00	00	00	00.44
12.	Working women	00	03	01	04
		00	75.00	25.00	01.76
13.	Servants	01	00	01	02
		50.00	00.00	50.00	00.88
14.	Preachers	01	00	00	01.00
		100.00	00.00	00.00	00.44
15.	Head Master	00	01	00	01
		00.00	100.00	00.00	00.44
16.	Doctor	00	00	00	01
		00.00	00.00	100.00	00.44
17.	Not Known	08	28	12	48
					21.14
	Total	39	126	62	227
		17.18	55.50	27.31	100.00

the prime victims of conflict situation in Kashmir, feeling situational compulsions imposed on them. In this situation, they preferred to end than to live torturous life conditions.

The second category of groups-communities which committed suicides in last three years, according to our empirical study, can be characterised as 'medium participation rate' in suicides. The social collectivities in this category with this participation rate are as follows:

(i)	House wives	07.42 %
(ii)	Government employees	05.28 %
(iii)	Labourers	03.52 %
(iv)	Teachers and policemen	02.61 %

The third category of groups-communities is characterised with the 'lowest participation rate' in the acts of suicides in last three years from 2009 to 2011. These social collectivities with their suicide participation rate are as follows:

(i)	Elderly people, working women	01.74 %
(ii)	Businessmen, servants	00.86 %
(iii)	Gujjars, doctor, driver, preacher, head master	00.44 %

In the preceding sections, we have classified the suicide groups on the basis of their participation rate in suicides. Though there are different participant groups with different participation rates but can be explained by similar factors /reasons which include the following:

- Impact of modernisation process
- Implications of the processes of change and development
- Specific occupations and their different responses to different challenges posed by the armed conflict
- Downward mobility of all occupations
- Upward mobility of some occupations
- Overall economic downfall and baselessness
- Torture and harassment of the youth by security forces and police
- Processes of militarisation and dehumanisation
- Mental health deterioration
- Emergence of deadly diseases

- Collective insecurity
- Social insecurity and social dependence
- Deviance and delinquency
- Social disorganisation and social crisis
- Crime and drug addiction
- Depression and tension

In the study, a significant degree of response, *i.e.,* 21.14 % [48 out of 227] showed that there was no response published by the local media. This can be explained in terms of non-publication of the relevant details related to committing of suicides.

9. Religious Composition of Suicide-Makers

Many sociological studies at the regional-global level and in cross-cultural context, have categorically revealed that the acts of suicide were committed in all societies irrespective of their differences in religious systems, religious beliefs, and religious practices. In fact, all monotheistic religions, especially Islam, Christianity and Judaism, oppose and negate the concept of suicide to be committed by their followers. But, the sociological fact stands that all religious groups-communities have experienced suicides in different proportions despite religious negation and opposition to suicides. Thus we may argue that suicides have been experienced in all religious societies irrespective of their difference and ideal opposition to the act. In this way, religion does not represent an independent or determining factor for committing suicides on the part of groups and individuals. However, we may infer that followers of all religions commit suicides though their rates vary, origins vary, justifications vary, dimensions vary, features vary, causes and consequences vary. These views go in consonance with the views held by eminent sociologist, Emile Durkheim.

In this broader theoretical background, we may validly assume that the Indian society too experienced suicides among all its religious communities, especially in the recent past. The fact of equal importance is that these acts of suicide differ in terms of different rates [lower, higher and medium], causes, consequences, methods and so on. Thus suicides have been experienced in all religious communities in the past and in the present times. More or less the same situation prevailed in the Kashmiri society in last three years which reflects in the Table 5.10:

Table 5.10

Religious Composition of Suicide-Makers

S.No.	*Religion*	*2009*	*2010*	*2011*	*Total*
1.	Muslims	36 18.36	99 50.51	61 31.12	196 86.34
2.	Hindus	05 21.73	10 43.47	08 34.78	23 10.13
3.	Sikhs	01 16.66	03 50.00	02 33.33	06 02.64
4.	Christians	00 00.00	01 100.00	00 00.00	01 00.44
5.	Bhuddists	00 00.00	00 00.00	01.00 00.44	01..00 000.44
	Total	42 18.50	113 49.77	72 31.71	227 100.00

The above table about suicides in different communities in Kashmir reveals that these acts were committed in all religious communities of Muslims, Hindus, Sikhs, Christians and Bhuddists. Though religions of all these communities, except Hinduism, have categorically opposed the acts of suicide, their societies have experienced these acts in the past and present and may continue in future.

Though suicides were experienced in all religious communities in Kashmir, their numbers, factors and patterns differed qualitatively and quantitatively. The suicide rates among different religious communities during 2009-2011, as per our investigation, were as mentioned below:

(i)	Muslims	196/227	(86.34%)
(ii)	Hindus	23/227	(10.13%)
(iii)	Sikhs	06/227	(02.64%)
(iv)	Christians	01/227	(00.44%)
(v)	Bhuddists	01/227	(00.44%)

The suicide rates among different religious communities vary extremely in terms of numbers and factors. It follows that the majority religious community has recorded 86.34 % of the total suicides in Kashmir during 2009-2011, the minority religious communities have recorded 13.86 % suicides jointly during the same period.

The factors responsible for different rates of suicide in religious communities vary. While the highest proportion of suicides in the Muslim community can be directly related more to conflict than other factors. In direct contrast to this, the social-psychological factors were more responsible than the conflict factor in the case of minority religious communities in Kashmir. The difference of factors can also be explained in terms of the involvement of the Muslim than the non-Muslim communities in the militancy activities during last two decades.

Finally, it was observed that impact of different suicide rates and different factors responsible was felt differently. While the majority religious community suffered a huge human and material loss, the minority religious communities faced material loss only.

10. Methods Used by Suicide-Makers

It has been observed that different methods are used in committing suicides in different societies. It has been observed in all societies that not one but many old and new methods are utilised to end lives due to social compulsions. Some of these methods are inhuman, brutal, painful, effective, time taking and cruel, while others are not. But, all methods of low or high intensity have the same destination, *i.e.,* death. Some of these suicide-makers do not reach to their destination, they survive. So, the rate of suicide is not determined by the total number of suicide attempts but by the number of those who don't survive.

The adoption of a particular method for committing suicide depends upon certain factors which include availability of resource of instrument, deadly material/substance, and environment for adopting the method. In this context, it may be argued that among regular armed forces, guns or pistols are most common weapon which they use during suicides for making a sure and confirmed death.

The adoption of a particular method for committing suicide can also be correlated with variables like age, sex, marital status, rural affiliation and psychology of the individual. It has been observed that early age groups generally prefer one set of methods, while elder age groups preferred another set of methods. Same is the situation among sex and economic groups. Finally, psychological attitude of the individual determine his/her method of committing suicide.

All above propositions can be applied to the situation of suicides in Kashmir. In this regard, our empirical investigation got the information noted in the Table 5.11:

Table 5.11

Methods adopted by Suicide-Makers

S.No.	Name of the Method	2009	2010	2011	Total
1.	Consuming poison	30 23.07	55 42.30	45 34.67	130 57.26
2.	Jumping in river	05 16.12	15 48.38	11 35.48	31 13.65
3.	Hanging from roof/tree	06 22.32	13 48.14	08 29.62	27 11.89
4.	Burnt on fire	07 21.87	18 56.25	07 21.87	32 14.09
5.	Shooting by gun	01 14.28	04 46.25	02 28.57	07 03.08
	Total	49 21.58	105 46.25	73 32.15	227 100.00

The above Table clearly reveals that the most common methods of committing suicide in our society were as mentioned below:

(a)	Consuming poison	130 / 227	(57.26 %)
(b)	Jumping in river	31 / 227	(13.68 %)
(c)	Hanging from roof/tree	27 / 227	(11.89 %)
(d)	Burnt on fire	32 / 227	(14.09 %)
(e)	Shooting with gun	07 / 227	(03.08 %)

It was found that common people, on the basis of general feelings, felt differently about different methods as soft or hard or crude. Thus all kinds of suicides were characterised as follows:

(a) Suicide by poisoning
- most common method
- available and cheapest form of substance
- easy to consume
- not a long pain
- most effective method

(b) Jumping in river
- common and most easy
- cost free method
- sufficient survival chances
- takes more time comparatively

(c) Hanging from roof - not so common and not so easy
- crude, hard, painful and torturous
- survival chances blight
- takes more time comparatively

(d) Burning on fire - not so common and not very easy
-needs certain degree of courage
- highly crude, painful and torturous
- survival chances blight

(e) Shooting with gun - not so common and not easily available
- sudden and fast death certain
- highly effective method among all methods of suicide
- survival chances minimum.

All above-mentioned methods for committing suicides in Kashmir represent completely a new social phenomenon which was non-existent in the traditional social environment, especially before 1947. In the absolute situation of peace and non-violence, the society hardly witnessed any act of suicide. However, various social, political, economic, cultural, educational and psychological developments in post-1947 era changed the social environment qualitatively as well as quantitatively which proved favourable to the conditions for suicide-making. In addition to these factors of change and development, the most important factor of militancy and resultant militarisation increased and enhanced the number and rate of suicide. In actuality, this situation gave boost to the occurrence of suicide here. In other words, the conflict proved fuel to the fire for increase in suicides in Kashmir. In this way, the suicides in Kashmir were multiplied by hundreds and thousands.

11. Police Investigation in Suicide Cases

The act of committing suicide was generally considered offensive, undesirable and condemnable, socially as well legally. In reality, suicide stands as the 'crime' according to the laws of the land and punishable under law. It follows that suicide as a crime is unlawful. Any direct or indirect involvement/encouragement in this act, inducing or compelling one commit this act, helping an individual in any way is all illegal and stood socially condemned. In this background, the police involvement in suicide cases is logical and natural because it is meant ensuring and implementing the relevant laws. So, when any case of suicide takes place, police get interested and involved in it, investigate it, try to reach at the root-cause and punish the culprit if any found. In this process, entire society supports the police operations.

In the preceding context, police get involved necessarily, carry out their investigation about the concerned case objectively in order to know the real cause of the act of suicide. But, at the same time, people in general try to hide the incident of suicide and try to hide its real motives in the families. This is done mainly due to the fear of prosecution or harassment on the part of the police, social taboos associated with the act of suicide, and negative social implications for other family members of suicide-maker. Despite this social opposition, open or hidden, police carry out its formal investigations to reach at logical and real conclusion. It has been observed that , in some cases, the police investigation gets complete and successful in reaching to the basic reality, while in other cases, it remains incomplete to divulge the concerned facts and truth. In both cases, police expose the real facts and their causation, though interpretation of these facts differ.

In our study about police investigation regarding suicides in Kashmir, we got the statistical information included in the following Table:

Table 5.12
Police Investigation in Suicide Cases

S. No.	Police Investigation	2009	2010	2011	Total
1.	Yes	25 14.28	95 54.28	55 31.42	1755 77.09
2.	No	04 20.00	10 50.00	06 30.00	20 08.81
3.	Not Known	04 12.00	20 62.50	08 25.00	32 14.09
	Total	33 14.53	125 55.06	69 30.39	227 100.00

This study reveals a particular social dynamics related to the police investigation of suicide cases. Normally, committing suicide was considered in the Kashmiri society as 'undesirable' and 'illegal'. It was also termed as *gunaahe kabira* (the bigger sin) in the religious context. So, all individuals tried to oppose and resist it. But, due to social compulsions, many suicides were committed and the trend goes on. When these acts are performed, the family members and other relatives try to hide these for the fear of social taboos and for negating social implications. But, at the same time, the news about suicide, whether successful or not, leaks and also reaches to the police stations in all villages, towns and cities. Immediately, they become alert and start investigating about this act on the part of any individual. Though investigation starts in all cases but succeeds in bringing out real facts in some cases only. Thus it is believed that in some cases, the police succeed, but in most of the cases, they fail. It was found that generally no individual was found culprit and punished also.

The above Table reveals that in 175/227 (77.09 %) cases of suicide, police carried out their investigation, according to our study. While all these cases were reported either by family members or relatives of the suicide-maker or were registered by the police on their own initiative. Even in this situation, it is believed that all cases of suicides in all areas were not reported to or registered by the police. So, in majority of the cases of suicide, FIR was not registered, while in minority of the cases, it was done due to some kind of compulsion or pressure. It was also found that in majority of the cases, the investigation was not completed or no conclusion was drawn. So, the police investigation had gone waste.

Against the preceding case, it was found in our study that 20/227 (08.31 %) cases were not touched at all in terms of investigation. These confirmed non-investigated cases generally belonged to socio-economically lower groups and classes which had not got proper attention by the police or there was no pressure or compulsion of inquiry in these cases. They die without any report or inquiry. This is their fate.

Finally, in 32/227 (14.09%), it was not known whether any investigation took place or not. In all possibilities, these cases of suicide were also not investigated by the police at all.

12. Medical Help at the Time of Suicide

As mentioned earlier, the acts of suicide are considered highly undesirable and condemned and legally banned in every human society. So, there prevails deeper antipathy towards suicide in societies. When an act of suicide takes place, people generally show sympathy towards the suicide-maker. There emerges a wave of sympathetic attitude and compel people to help, rather save, the suicide-maker. They try to provide any/every kind of medical help or immediately rush him/her to hospital to save his/her life. All these collective efforts result in saving the lives of some suicide-makers. Thus these efforts are directly related to the survival chances of suicide-makers. Some of them die while taking to the hospital or any health centre, especially these medical units are far away from the place of suicide.

The fact must be emphasised that a significant number of those who commit suicide die before they are taken to the nearby hospital or health centre at any level. Many also die after they reach to the hospital or medical centre. While some among them get the proper medical treatment, others among them are considered 'brought dead'.

In this context, we made a detailed inquiry in our study about the availability of medical help at the time of committing suicide by individuals, especially in non-urban areas. We got the relevant statistical information which has been shown in the following Table:

Table 5.13

Medical Help Provided at the Time of Suicide-Making

S.No.	Medical facility provided	2009	2010	2011	Total
1.	Yes	25 13.73	102 56.04	55 30.21	182 88.17
2.	No	04 20.00	10 50.00	06 30.00	20 08.81
3.	Not known	04 16.00	16 64.00	05 20.00	25 11.01
	Total	33 14.53	128 56.37	66 29.07	227 100.00

The above Table reveals that 182/227 [88.17 %] cases of suicide got the necessary medical help at village, tehsil, district or province level. In this way, many lives were saved from death. Thus we see a significant number of those who committed suicide but survived. But, at the same time, many others could not be saved despite providing them the necessary medical help.

The study also found that in this context, there were deaths due to suicides in three following patterns:

(a) if the suicide was committed by shooting oneself, the availability of medical help didn't prove effective;

(b) if the suicide was committed by jumping into the river, the medical aid proved helpful and effective; and

(c) if the suicide was committed by burning oneself, the medical aid proved helpful and saved them completely.

In our study, it was found that 20/227 (08.31 %) persons in context were not provided the necessary medical help at the time of suicides. These cases usually belonged to the areas which were not connected with roads and there was no medical facility available in those areas. The consequence of these conditions had to be paid in terms of human loss.

This study also revealed that in 25/227 (11.01) cases of suicide, it was not known whether they were provided necessary hospital aid or not after the crucial time of suicide-making. From the experience and practices in the field, it may be inferred that no proper health care must have been provided in these cases. So, in every possibility, they must have died. It is argued that if these cases were taken to the nearest health/medical centre for help, these would have been registered there.

13. Number of Suicide Survivals

It has been always observed that a certain number of suicide-makers survive certainly. This is determined mainly by three factors which are *(a)* the common sympathy wave in favour of suicide-makers, *(b)* particular method used in suicide leading to death or not, and *(c)* availability of medical help at the time of suicide. So, there is some certainty of survival which occurs in all conditions and situations.

It seems important to note here that, like suicide-makers [who die in these attempts], the suicide survivors too have to face social implications in all societies. In reality, they are supposed to face social as well as legal action on the part of society and police respectively. But, in actuality, neither the implementation of social implications is carried out by the societal members nor the legal action is initiated against the suicide survivors.

In the context of preceding complex situation, our study got the relevant statistical information included in the following Table on next page.

The succeeding table reveals that out of the total 227 suicides, only 32 (*i.e.,* 14.09 %) cases survived. Though this does not represent a significant number, the involved cases survived mainly because of the medical help provided immediately after committing suicides in the nearest health/medical centre in their respective areas. However, after they survived

Table 5.14

Number of Suicide Survivals

S.No.	Suicide Survival	2009	2010	2011	Total
1.	Yes	06 18.75	18 56.25	08 25.00	32 14.09
2.	No	30 22.05	54 39.70	52 38.23	136 59.91
3.	Not known	11 18.64	30 50.84	18 30.50	59 25.99
	Total	47 20.70	102 44.93	78 355.02	227 100.00

the suicide attempts, they and their family members faced negative social situation, especially in terms of negative social image and non-interaction.

Against the preceding trend, in 136 out of 227 (59.91 %) cases of suicide, nobody survived. All of them fell to the jaws of cruel death. In actuality, they did not survive mainly because of adopting most effective method of suicide or were not provided immediate medical aid after the attempt of committing suicide.

In our study, it was also found that in 59 out of 227 (*i.e.*, 25.99 %) cases, it was not known whether they survived or not. In actuality, the print media could not confirm about the death of the suicide-makers.

It is also revealed from the Table that there were two major trends of suicide survival during the period of study. These trends were

(*a*) 2009 — 20.70 % survival rate; and

(*b*) 2010 and 2011 — 44.93 % and 35.02 % survival rate.

14. Apparent Reasons for Committing Suicides

Generally, there are set social reasons for the acts of committing suicides. In reality, no act of suicide occur without a set reason. But, these real reasons are not necessarily conveyed and quoted after the act is performed by an individual, whether he/she dies or survives. At many times, the real reasons for suicides remain hidden or consciously thrown into the background and fake or apparent reasons are conveyed and quoted in the broader society. This is done consciously by all, family members, relatives, neighbours, police, people and print media. But, the fact must be emphasised that these apparent reasons are not always real, actual and truthful. Sometimes or many times, fictitious, false and baseless reasons are circulated in the whole society through the mass media agencies. This has emerged as an established trend in the society.

In this study, investigation about 'apparent reasons' conveyed to and quoted for others after commission or suicides gave the statistical information noted in the following Table:

Table 5.15
Apparent Reasons for Committing Suicides

S. No.	Apparent Reason	2009	2010	2011	Total
1.	Minor clash with parents	01 20.00	03 60.00	01 20.00	05 02.20
2.	Dowry demands	01 25.00	02 50.00	01 25.00	04 01.76
3.	Exam Failure	01 20.00	03 60.00	01 20.00	05 02.20
4.	Abnormal mental health	03 18.95	09 56.25	04 44.44	16 07.04
5.	Unemployment	01 10.00	05 50.00	04 40.00	10 04.40
6.	Family/domestic problems	09 18.75	25 52.08	14 29.16	43 21.14
7.	Poverty	06 15.00	20 50.00	14 35.00	40 17.62
8.	Love affairs	05 29.41	07 41.71	05 29.41	17 07.48
9.	Denial of mobile phone	00 0.00	02 66.66	01 33.33	03 01.32
10.	Torture by armed forces	02 40.00	02 40.00	01 20.00	05 02.20
11.	Matrimonial problems	02 11.11	10 55.55	06 33.33	18 07.92
12.	Not Known	13 19.69	39 59.09	14 21.21	66 29.07
	Total	35 15.40	127 55.91	65 28.63	227 100.00

The preceding Table reveals three distinct trends of apparent reasons which are mentioned below:

I Trend	-Family and domestic problems	46/227 (21.14%)
	-Poverty	40/227 (17.62%)

This trend stands as the most common category of apparent reasons which shows mostly the correct and real reasons. The huge number of suicides in this category reflects the extremely deteriorating social and economic conditions in Kashmir.

II Trend of apparent reasons is composed of the following:

- Marital problems	18/227 (0792%)
- Love affairs	17/227 (07.68%)
- Mental health deterioration	16/227 (07.07%)

This trend stands as the second list of different apparent reasons responsible for the acts of suicide in Kashmir. It seems clearly that the psychological, mental and marital health in the present-day situation is created by the conflict conditions in Kashmir.

III Trend of apparent reasons is composed of the following:

-Unemployment	10/227	(04.40%)
-Minor clash with parents	05/227	(02.20)
-Failure in exams.	05/227	(02.20)
-Harassment of armed forces	05/227	(02.20)
-Dowry demand	04/227	(01.76%)
-Denial of mobile phone	03/227	(01.32%)

The above trend of apparent reasons conveys necessarily the social, psychological, economic and general crisis prevailing in the Kashmiri society at present. While unemployment represents the serious aspects of the crisis, the denial of mobile phone as apparent reason reflects the petty dimension of the prevailing crisis.

Our study also revealed that in 66 out of 227 cases of suicide, there was no 'apparent reason' conveyed or quoted in the local print media or by police or by family-relatives. These cases were considered as 'suspicious' cases as there were many apparent reasons responsible for those suicides or there was no certainty about a particular reason for its role. There were many cases in this trend which can easily be characterised as fake, false and fictitious.

14. Primary Sources of the Study

This study of suicides in Kashmir in last three years, 2009-2011, was exclusively based on the day-to-day reports in English and Urdu daily newspapers, largest in circulation, published from Srinagar. These reports were published, televised and broadcast as follows:

(a) English	- *Greater Kashmir,* daily	2009-2011	227 reports
	- *Rising Kashmir,* daily	2009-2011	74 reports
	- *Kashmir Images,* daily	2009-2011	34 reports
	- *Kashmir Life,* weekly	2009-9011	32 reports
	- *The Times of India* , New Delhi	2009-2011	25 reports
(b) Urdu	- *Srinagar Times, daily*	2009-2011	227 reports
	- *Aftaab,* daily	2009-2011	117 reports
(c) English, Urdu & Kashmiri	- *Evening News,* Doordarshan *Srinagar*	2009-2011	100 reports
	- *Evening News,* Radio Kashmir, Srinagar.	2009-2011	100 reports

6 Critique and Conclusion

1. Emergence of Suicidal Tendencies

It has been established now repeatedly that committing suicide in large numbers has surely emerged as the fact of everyday life in Kashmir. Like other societies in India, the number and rate of suicides in Kashmir have increased heavily. While this number/rate was much lower in the past, it has increased significantly in the present day situation. This has happened in Kashmir in the context of multi-farious implications of large-scale transformation. Several processes of modernisation, especially urbanisation, industrialisation, secularisation, materialistic orientation, individualistic attitudes and behaviour, were introduced through the processes of change and development in all rural, urban and hilly areas and among all groups, classes and communities. This larger, deeper and greater effect of the processes of modernisation influenced the entire society and every section and sector of society felt its impact seriously.

In addition to alleviating influence on life conditions of most of the people in the state, these developments introduced an element of instability and pathology which was considered by the experts as the 'after-falls' and 'side effects' of the processes of modernisation. These implications, short-term as well as long-term in nature, were also considered as 'due' or 'expected' outcome. This situation gave rise to the phenomenon of 'social pathology' which engulfed the entire society as it reflected in many fields of life, especially related to the psychological attitudes and behaviour of individuals and groups. This 'psychological downfall' in the Kashmiri society crudely reflected in the following socially determined phenomena:

- Emergence of major and minor crimes
- Rise in social deviance and delinquency
- Heavy expansion of drug addiction

- Pattern of social disorganisation
- Lower degree of social solidarity and social cohesion
- Conflict and confrontation between various social collectivities at various levels
- Deviant attitudes and behaviour among children and youth
- Violence as a way of life and violent worldview
- Mass depression and large-scale tension
- Mental health deterioration
- Stress, anxiety, strain and PTSD
- Insecurity and dependence
- Helplessness and loneliness
- Threat perception.

In the social environment of above-mentioned problems, the rise of suicidal tendencies was considered as 'normal' and necessary. That is what is materialised in the emergence of suicides in large numbers in Kashmir.

2. Perspective on Suicide in Kashmir

But, at the same time, there stands another potential factor for explaining the increasing trend in committing suicides in Kashmir. This is the factor of the role of armed conflict between Kashmiri militants and Indian security forces for a long period of two decades from 1989. The continuous impact of this conflict led to its long-term implications in the society and gave rise to a situation characterised as 'conflict situation'. It was observed that this situation had necessary, dominant and devastating effect on all fields of life. The processes related to militancy and militarisation exposed the old stable society in Kashmir to all kinds of excesses, violations, brutalities, torture and harassment of people during anti-militancy operations carried out by the security forces for a long time. In short, the traditional society was exposed to the vagaries of social pathology which made Kashmir an 'inferno' and social life was polluted and degenerated.

On the whole, the whole psyche of the young generation was hurt and they emerged as the primary victims and sufferers. The entire womenfolk became psychologically sick and felt threatened because of the fear of rape, murder and molestation. The entire lot of elders was completely exposed to insecurity, dependence and helplessness. The entire generation of children has experienced psychological downfall and completely degenerated environment. They lost their entire childhood in the conflict situation. In totality, the Kashmiri society underwent the processes of dehumanisation, brutalisation and de-functionalisation. Every single individual was humiliated, hurt, tortured and harassed once or repeatedly during the 21 years of disturbed conditions. All cultural and civilised standards of social life were debased. All basic human rights violations by the armed forces beat all global records.

The preceding situation was characterised by mass depression, tension and apathy and had completely pathological impact on the social life. As a result, social life in itself became 'casualty' and 'liability' and everybody was concerned about security. It was full of pain, agony, tragedy, torture, misery and threat to life. At that time during last two decades, every individual wanted to die in order to avoid the sub-human threatening conditions. An individual wanted death in the morning than in the evening, because he/she wanted to leave this world early. An average person preferred death today than tomorrow than to face the wrath of forces. The collective sentiment too reflected these emotions by upholding the view it is better to die once collectively than to die in pieces and many times. Thus the suicidal tendencies were obvious in the individual and collective psychology of people mainly due to conflict situation.

In this socially deranged situation in Kashmir, certain degree of social pathology emerged and got established with the dynamics of day-to-day life. It follows that the nature and pattern of normal social life became totally impossible or was denied to vast majority of individuals and families. This social environment had nothing positive to offer to life. So, it gave rise to ethos characterised by pathological features which have been identified above. In other words, this environment gave rise to particular tendencies and trends of suicides, which all materialised in the occurrence of significant rate [of suicides] in Kashmir where these deadly acts were almost absent in the recent past. It was in this changing situation that people felt mentally pathological and unsatisfied with the ongoing events, which, in turn, provided the ideational, moral and social support to the acts of suicide. Thus the common pathological sentiments, attitudes and tendencies determined degree and rate of committing suicides. Since the conflict situation became intense and acute increasingly day by day, so was the number and rate of suicides in Kashmir.

3. Increasing Number and Rate of Suicides

The reality stands that no exact number of suicides in Kashmir is known to any authentic and credible source, official or unofficial. It is solely because no governmental or non-governmental organisation, agency, institution and association have carried out such an exclusive study or census. However, there are different estimates about total number of suicides in Kashmir during last two decades provided by different sources, official and unofficial. These estimates were presented mainly by academics, professionals, print media, health centres, and police records. These vary widely because *(a)* these originate from different sources with different focus and different objectives; *(b)* adoption of different mechanisms, procedures and methodology; and *(c)* prevalence of different places/environments, incidents and reasons of suicides.

Though the exact number of suicides committed in Kashmir in last 21 years is not available, the estimates provided by various individuals, organisations and agencies give us an idea about average number of suicide committed here, their causation, survival chances and some other related information. The medical and police sources have provided some estimated figures in this regard. But, these are neither complete nor representative. In these estimates, while some have concentrated on particular segment of suicide-makers, others have focused on other components. Again, the local print media in Kashmir has quoted figures which vary from 5,000 t0 30,000 in two decades time. In this context, there emerges the urgent need to carry out a comprehensive and scientific study/survey of suicides committed in Kashmir and Jammu regions by various official and unofficial organisations and institutions. This effort may provide the most authentic and realistic figures about suicides.

Our study concentrated on total number of suicides committed in Kashmir and Jammu [partly] regions during last three years of 2009-9011 which were published by four leading daily newspapers of Srinagar. According to this source, the total number of suicides committed during last three years was 227. This figure represents a part of the total figure of suicides committed during this period and 21 years long period. Rest of the suicides committed during this period were registered in health/medical centres and police stations in all areas. This study is actually based on

- Suicides committed during the year 2009;
- Suicides committed during the year 2010; and
- Suicides committed during the year 2011.

But, at the same time, it may be assumed on the basis of findings in this study, that these suicide rates stood much higher comparatively. It was much higher in comparison to the past records in the Kashmiri society and higher in comparison to such other societies in India. This seems logical, realistic and reasonable. The situation of high, higher and lower rates of suicide in Kashmir is portrayed in the following diagram:

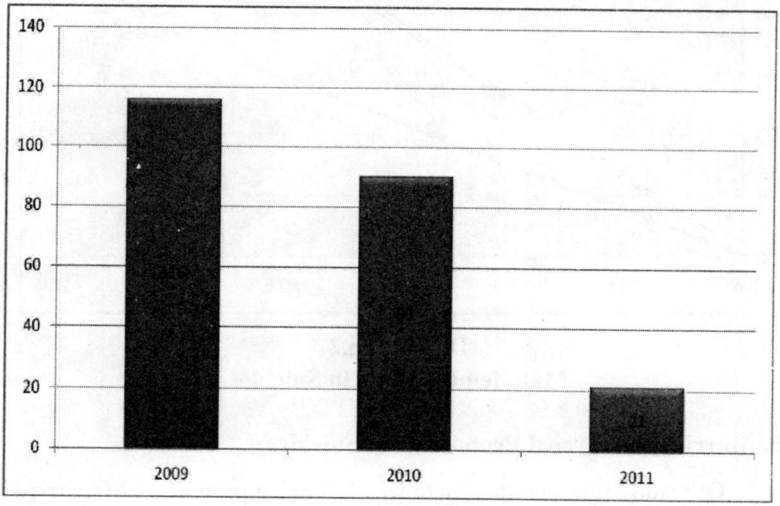

Diagram 6.1
High, higher and lower Suicide Rates in Kashmir

4. Male and Female Ratio in Suicides

Our study observed that the sex ratio in committing suicides was more females and less males [63.4323 % and 36.56 % respectively]. This pattern of suicide is generally against the common pattern of more suicides for males and less suicides for females, as was observed at all-India level. But, different pattern in Kashmir can be explained in terms of causation of suicides rooted with overall implications of armed conflict situation. Experts feel that lower percentage of males than females show more and sensitive exposure of the former than the later to the conflict. In that situation, women faced terrorised and faced more excesses and brutalities by the security forces. This male-female proportion is portrayed in the following diagram:

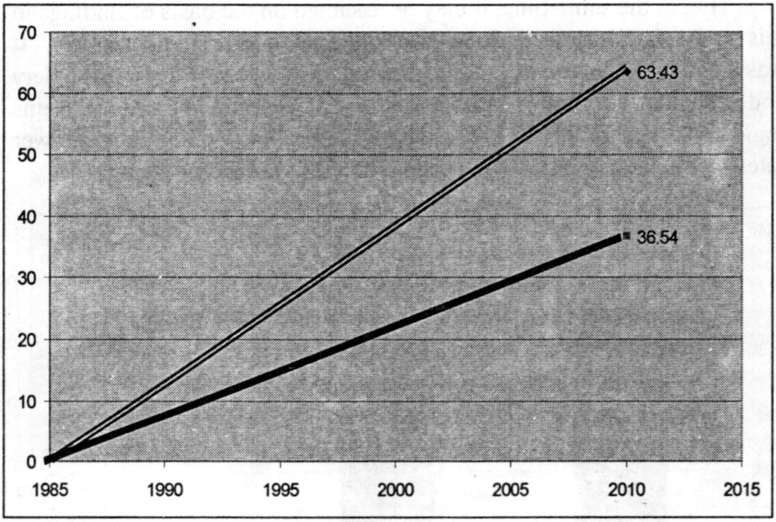

Diagram 6.2
Male-female Ratio in Suicides

5. Married-unmarried Proportion in Suicides

Our study revealed that there was following proportion of married and unmarried suicide-makers:

(a) suicides by married persons 55.50 %

(b) suicides by unmarried persons 35.76 %

The above figures clarify that married persons committed more suicides than the unmarried persons. It is believed that the latter have comparatively lesser number and degree of worldly problems. So, they in lesser number felt compelled to opt for ending their lives. When they marry, they add up new, hard and complex problems which compel them more to go for ending their lives. So, the former maintains higher number and rate of suicides. It was also observed that the married individuals face more serious, complex and socially more damaging problems than their unmarried people. These propositions related to the different proportion of the married and unmarried in committing suicides in Kashmir reflect in the following diagram:

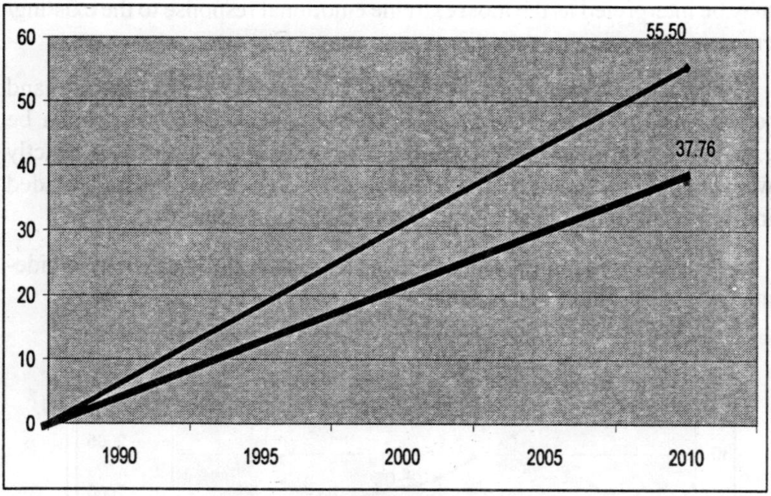

Diagram 6.3
Married-unmarried Proportion in Suicides

6. Age Groups Composition in Suicide

Our study showed the following ratio of different age groups in committing suicides:

(a)	Age group of – 16 years	10.13 % suicides
(b)	Age group of 17-25 years	44.25 % suicides
(c)	Age group of 26-35 years	25.05 % suicides
(d)	Age group of 36-50 years	17.22 % suicides
(e)	Age group of 50 + years	02.64 % suicides

The higher participation rate in committing suicides in the case of b, c and d groups can be explained in terms of having relatively younger age with lesser family responsibility, possessing higher degree of maturity and seriousness, living a purposeful life and maintain a particular life-style, and establish certain particular role and status in society. When any of or all of these social standards/interests are challenged extremely and from within the system, they feel threatened and, in extreme cases, opt for closing the last chapter of their life. The dominant younger age group at 'b' maintain the highest record in committing suicides primarily because it stands as most reactive and most responsive group. In other words, it may be interpreted as the most extreme emotional response to the existing/ emerging situation.

In direct contrast to 'b', 'c' and 'd' groups, the age groups at 'a' and 'e' showed different response, *i.e.,* lower suicide rates which can be explained in terms of being innocent, immature and not knowing exactly what suicide means or too much knowledge and awareness about dreaded impact of this horrible act held by elderly groups of 50 +.

These propositions related to the age groups composition in suicide-making reflect in the following diagram:

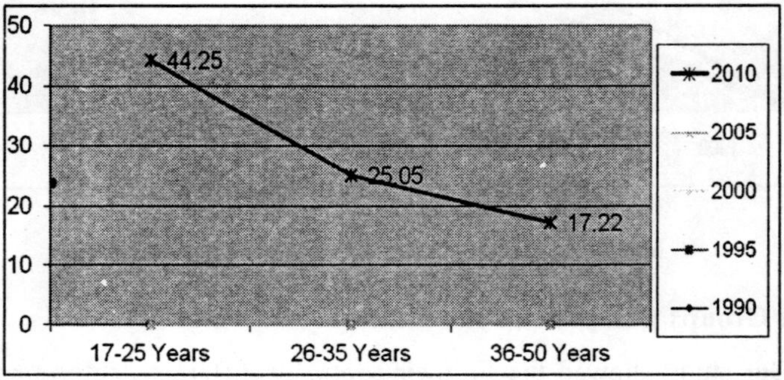

Diagram 6.4
Age Group Proportion in Suicides

7. Religious Proportion among Suicide-Makers

Our study established the point that dominant majority of suicide-makers was from the Muslim community, as they form the majority in J&K state. It had 86.34 % record suicides in the total number of such acts. This trend of suicides also reflects the demographic character of Kashmir region which has got 97 % Muslim population. Other religious communities in the state experienced incidence of suicides as mentioned below:

(a) Hindus — 10.13 % suicides

(b) Sikhs — 02.64 % suicides

(c) Christians — 02.44 % suicides

(d) Bhuddists — 00.44 % suicides

The preceding statistical figures essentially reveal the rates and trends in each case determined by the conflict factor. As the members of these communities are permanent members of the Kashmir society, they shared equally and qualitatively, the social dynamics related to the occurrence of suicide. Since they were essential part of this dynamics, they too suffered in human and material loss. But, the important fact is that they were not directly involved in the armed conflict with Indian security forces. They were also not considered as the 'enemy' of the country. So, they did not face the wrath and devastation on account of anti-insurgency operations. This whole situation explains their lowest suicide rates during the conflict period. But, the Muslims' case stands completely a different, rather opposite case.

The different suicide rates prevailing among Muslims, Hindus, Sikhs and Christians are portrayed in the diagram drawn below:

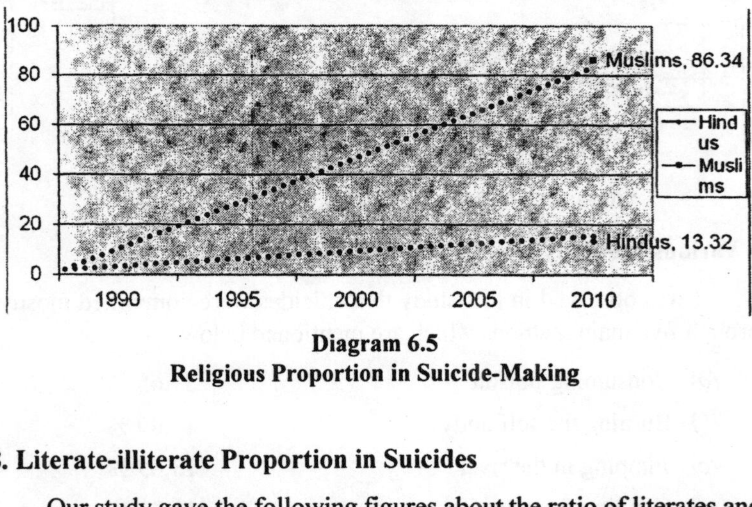

Diagram 6.5
Religious Proportion in Suicide-Making

8. Literate-illiterate Proportion in Suicides

Our study gave the following figures about the ratio of literates and illiterates among those who committed suicide:

(a)	Literates	43. 61 %
(b)	Illiterates	15. 41 %
(c)	Not Known	40. 96 %

While the dominant group of suicide-makers belonged to literates, the illiterates' share in this act was least. But, in a significant number of suicide cases, it was not reported in the local print media whether they belonged to the former or latter group. On the basis of partial evidence, trend and direction of suicides in Kashmir during the study period, we may infer that most of these suicides were committed by literate persons and some of suicide-makers were illiterates. It can be explained in terms of exposure, threats and challenges to the literates, more problems and their serious reaction, and ideological commitment and assertion. These two prominent trends of suicides committed by literate and illiterate persons are portrayed in the diagram which follows:

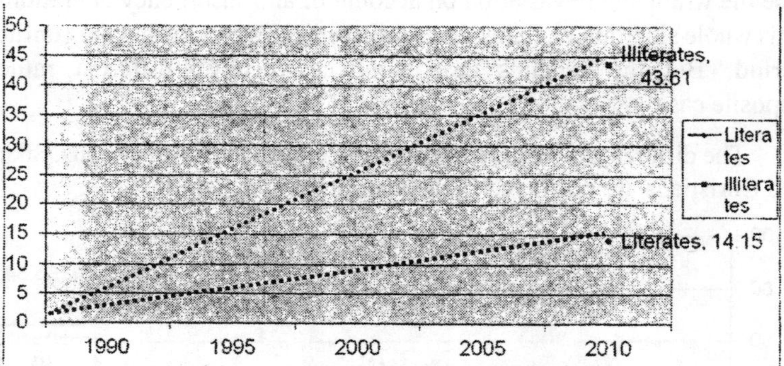

Diagram 6.6
Literates' and Illiterates, Share in Suicide-Making

9. Various Methods used in Suicides

It was observed in this study that suicides were committed mostly through five main methods which are mentioned below:

(a)	Consuming poison	57.65 %
(b)	Burning the self body	14.09 %
(c)	Jumping in the river	13.65 %
(d)	Hanging from roof/tree	11.89 %
(e)	Shooting oneself	03.08 %

The consumption of poison for sure suicide has emerged as most common method of committing suicides in Kashmir. It was mainly because it stands very cheap, sometimes free, always available in homes and ensures certain death. In rural areas, insecticides, used for horticulture purpose, was mostly used for committing suicide. The second dominant method used for effective suicides was burning one's body partly or fully, mostly after sprinkling kerosene on the body. This crude method was often used by women suicide-makers involved in matrimonial disputes, dowry demands, in-laws' torture and harassment and family mal-adjustment. The third major method used for effective suicide was jumping into the river and lake. It was often used by younger age groups and illiterates. They considered it as a simple way to finish their lives, but many of them survived because they were saved. The fourth main method for an effective suicide was hanging on the roof of house or tree in the open field. It is considered torturous and painful and is often used by younger elements. The fifth method , shooting one's head, is rare than common. While it is used only by those who possess this weapon legally or illegally, it mostly happens in the armed forces than among civilians. Proper shooting of one's head leads to sure and sudden death of a person.

The above propositions may lead to conclude that though no necessary co-relation can be established between the acts and methods of committing suicides, certain method/s may be seen as common or uncommon due to regional and cultural factors. Some methods can also be co-related with particular groups, classes, communities, associations and organisations. This co-relation can be established only after seeing the totality of the suicide situation.

The above five methods of committing suicide differently have been shown in the diagram as follows:

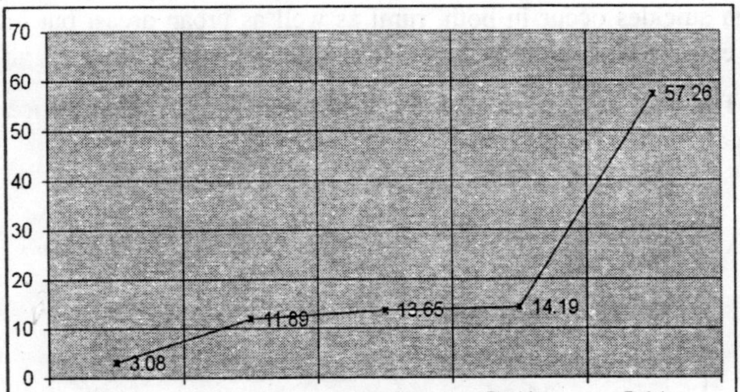

Diagram 6.7
Major Methods of Committing Suicides

10. Rural-Urban Proportion in Suicides

The rural-urban composition in suicides in this study revealed in the distribution of suicide cases in different districts which were characterised as rural, urban and significantly urban. These details follow:

(a)	I category	Urban	Srinagar	22.90 %
(b)	II category	Rural	Pulwama	02.20 %
			Shopian	02.20 %
			Kulgam	04.40 %
			Bandipora	03.08 %
			Kupwara	07.48 %
(c)	III category	Significantly urban	Anantnag	28.19 %
			Budgam	10.13 %
			Baramulla	12.33 %
			Ganderbal	07.05 %

It reveals that while urban district of Srinagar has 22.90 % suicides committed, significantly urban district of Anantnag has 28.19 % of the same, the highest percentage in all districts. Again, significantly urban districts of Baramulla and Budgam have 12.33 % and 10.13 % respectively, while rural districts of Kupwara and significantly urban district of Ganderbal have 07.48 % and 07.05 % respectively. It may be inferred that though suicides occur in both, rural as well as urban areas, but urban areas experience slightly higher than rural areas.

The suicide rates of each category, urban, rural and significantly urban are portrayed in the following diagram:

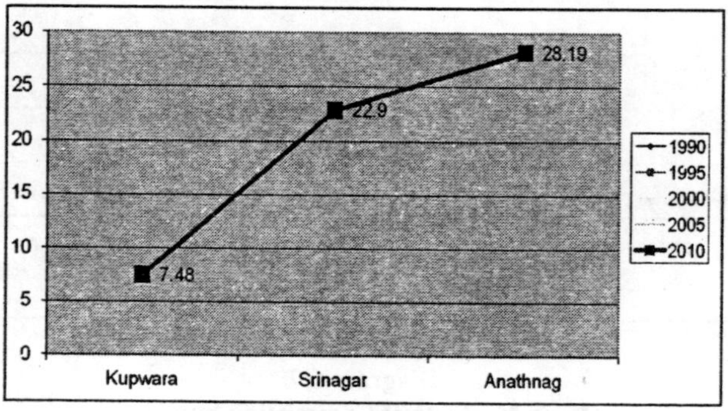

Diagram 6.8
Rural-Urban Composition of Suicide-Makers

11. Occupational Composition of Suicide-Makers

The suicide-makers in this study belonged to all occupations, irrespective of their similarities and dissimilarities. These can be classified as follows:

I category	19.00 – 30.00 %	-students -youth
II category	03.00 – 08.00 %	-government employees -labourers -housewives -teachers -SPOs
III category	01.00 – 02.00	- businessman -elderly -gujjar -driver -doctor -preacher

The above categories reveal that there prevails multiplicity of occupational participation in the acts of suicide. Most of the above mentioned occupations in the valley have been exposed to the damaging effect of conflict that created conducive environment for committing suicides in Kashmir. It may be argued that all occupations of low or high social-economic status have been involved in committing suicides continuously.

12. Apparent Reasons for Committing Suicides

In every case of suicide, successful or not, has a definite reason. If the suicide-maker hides it, others in the society raise it. These reasons may be different from the real and actual reasons. In our study, various apparent reasons were cited in the press reports which may be categorised as follows:

(a) I category	01 – 10 %	-minor clash with parents -dowry demand/torture -failure in exams -mental health deterioration -unemployment -love affairs

		-denial of mobile phone -torture of security forces -matrimonial problems
(b) II category	11 – 27 %	-domestic problems -poverty

These responses essentially represent primary and secondary reasons which compel individuals to commit suicides. While the primary reasons can be explained in terms of basic and important problems like poverty, unemployment, family disorganisation, marital disputes, and mental health deterioration, the secondary reasons include failure in exam denial of mobile phone and so on.

13. Hospitalisation and Survival of Suicide-Makers

The medical help provided to the suicide-maker at that very time stands crucial because it creates and enhances the chances of survival and saves the person from the jaws of death. In our study, it was divulged that the medical help at the time of suicide in the nearest area of residence was provided to 88.17 % suicide cases, while as it could not be provided to 05.88 % suicide cases. About 11.01 % suicide cases, the reports in the local print media was silent, *i.e.,* they had no knowledge whether medical help was provided or not at that crucial time.

These findings must be seen in the background of general 'sympathy wave' which is generated after this act is performed by the individual, and all other individuals want to help him in any way in order to save his life. This mass sentiment on the part of known and unknown people results in the immediate hospitalisation of the suicide-maker. In all possibilities, medical help leads to saving the human life.

In many other suicide cases, it was observed that many suicide-makers die before they are formally treated in the hospitals. These cases are called as 'brought dead' cases.

14. Police Investigation of Suicides

The police investigation about suicides was pure formality performed in the field by the police. While this is not objected by the society, police tries to know the compelling and complex reasons of suicides. In our study, it was found that in 77.09 % cases of suicide, the police investigation was carried out fully, while in 08.81 % cases it was not carried out at all.

These different trends in police investigation make it an issue of social responsibility of police. In this regard, the role of the local police has not been purposeful and appreciated. While in some cases, the police investigation was considered satisfactory, but in many cases the investigation was incomplete and not considered satisfactory. The former cases generally belonged to socially upper status families and groups, and the latter cases are from lower status families and groups. Thus the police investigation, though necessary for knowing the reality, hardly reaches to the root cause of suicides.

15. Suicides-Unprecedented and Dangerous Trend

The explanation and analysis of the phenomenon of committing suicides in Kashmir in the preceding chapters from I to V in this book, one can easily conclude, the suicides have emerged as the fact of everyday life in Kashmir which was never the case in the past. In actuality, it has risen as the crucial symbol or sign of mass social pathology that has developed through the implications of two decade long conflict situation. This huge number of suicide has been dealt scientifically and sociologically and explained their nature, patterns, trends, rates, features, dimensions, correlation, causation and implications.

A cursory view of the social situation in the entire past history of Kashmir suggests that this situation seems different and distinct qualitatively and quantitatively. Never in any period of history, Kashmiris had opted for such kind of deaths. They suffered extremely the cruelties and brutalities of their own and alien rulers but never lost the hope of life. They didn't live those days, they survived. But, they never opted for collective suicide and hope for life was never dashed. However, the present situation related to the armed conflict stands completely different. In this background, it may be argued that committing suicides in huge numbers stand unparalleled and unprecedented.

A cumulative view of this pathological and pathetic situation reveals a grave social scenario which had disastrous and dangerous consequences for the present and future generations. First, these trends with heavy number of suicides committed have eliminated the most dynamic, productive and empathic younger element in the population and in the society at large. Second, the widespread suicidal tendencies have generated and legitimised the social pathology and social crisis in terms of multitude of grave problems which resist the resolution, and which may be characterised as social devastation and social degeneration. Third, this socially deteriorating situation has effected at attitudinal and behavioural level, most of the individuals, groups, classes and communities and other social collectivities. Finally, all these and other dimensions of heavy numbers and higher rates of suicides committed in Kashmir have given rise to alarming and dangerous socially pathological trends which need to be controlled and eliminated immediately.

In this entire situational background, there emerges a basic and dire need to

(a) effectively and purposefully contains control and stop this mad rush for committing suicides through voluntary and involuntary efforts and formal and informal means; and

(b) to stop the practices of committing suicides necessarily and forcefully by the state organisations and agencies, especially the police force. But, at the same time, systematic and organised social efforts must be also initiated to stop (even) the occurrence of suicides in the Kashmiri society.

It must be understood clearly that the act of suicide is neither related to religion nor is it encouraged by religious attitudes. In fact, religion, particularly the religion of Islam, abhors, negates and condemns this in-human act on the part of its followers. So, essentially, it is not a religious issue. In this context, the preaching of religious principles, laws and orders cannot lonely solve this problem. In actuality, the total resolution of suicides needs the solutions of fundamental problems like poverty, unemployment, social mobility and alleviation, proper treatment of mental health deterioration, stopping of torture-harassment and so on, in addition to the propagation of anti-suicide ideology of the religion of Islam. This strategy may work as the realistic and scientific approach towards eliminating the problem of increasing suicides in Kashmir.

In regard to stopping of suicides in Kashmir, three main components of modern society, *i.e.,* government, NGOs and civil society, must work unitedly, systematically and in an organised-planned-co-ordinated way to control, negate and eliminate this highly undesirable act. Bold initiatives and continuous efforts by governmental as well as by non-governmental organisations must be jointly oriented towards achieving this particular goal. These efforts need to be institutionalised in order to make these more effective, contextual, purposeful and productive in stopping the acts of suicides.

بقیہ نمبر3

سے باندھا تھا اور خود کو اسی پردے کے سہارے پھانسی پر لٹکایا تھا۔ چنانچہ اس سلسلے میں پولیس کو فوری طور پر اطلاع دی گئی اور پولیس نے وسیم احمد کی لاش اپنی تحویل میں لیکر اس کا پوسٹ مارٹم کرایا جس کے بعد لوازمات پورے کئے گئے اور وسیم احمد کی لاش اس کے ورثا کے سپرد کی گئی ۔ کے ایم این نمائندے کے مطابق وسیم احمد طرے ڈگری کالج خونپاس میں بی اے فائنل ائر کا طالب علم تھا۔ اس کی خودکشی کی وجہ فوری طور پر معلوم نہیں ہوسکی تاہم پولیس اس سلسلے میں تحقیقات شروع کردی ہے اور دفعہ 174 سی آر پی سی کے تحت کیس رجسٹر کیا گیا ہے۔ وسیم احمد کی خودکشی کے نتیجے میں پورے قصبے میں غم والم کی لہر دوڑ گئی ہے اور اس کے گھر پر ہزاروں لوگ پرنم آنکھوں سے وسیم کی موت پر افسوس کر رہے ہیں۔

شہزادہ اور شکیلہ نے بھی اپنا کام تمام کیا

سرینگر /۲۱ جون/سی این ایس/کولگام اور قاضی گنڈ اننت ناگ میں خودکشی کے ۵، الگ الگ واقعات میں ۳ ہلاک جبکہ دیگر دو کو اسپتال میں داخل کئے گئے ہیں۔ اطلاعات کے مطابق آج کولگام کی ایک مضافاتی بستی میں اسوقت کہرام مچ گیا جب بستی کی دو جوان سال چچیری بہنیں شکیلہ زوجہ محمد الطاف ہلہ اور شہزادہ دختر غلام محمد ہلہ ساکنان کھری بٹہ پورہ کولگام کی لاشیں گاؤں میں پہنچادی گئیں۔ بتایا جاتا ہے کہ مذکورہ لڑکیوں نے اپنے والدین کے نصیحت کرنے پر غصے میں آکر کیڑے مار دوائی کھائی جسکے بعد دونوں کو اسپتال لے جایا گیا جہاں ڈاکٹروں کی بچاؤ کوششوں کے باوجود وہ دم توڑ بیٹھیں اور دونوں لڑکیوں کی لاشیں جب گاؤں میں پہنچادی گئیں تو وہاں کہرام مچ گیا دونوں لڑکیاں رشتے سے آپس میں چچیری بہنیں / 8

کوئی زہریلی چیز کھا کر اپنا کام تمام کیا

سرینگر /۱۱ جون/سی این ایس/کھنہ بل اننت ناگ کے دیہات میں ایک نوجوان نے زہر کھا کر خودکشی کرلی ہے۔ اطلاعات کے مطابق میر گنڈ کھنہ بل اننت ناگ کے رہنے والے ایک نوجوان ارشد احمد میر ولد محمد یوسف میر نے نامعلوم وجوہات کی بنا پر کوئی زہریلی شئے کھائی ہے جسکے بعد مذکورہ نوجوان کو اسپتال لے جایا گیا جہاں وہ اپنی زندگی سے ہاتھ دھو بیٹھا۔ ڈاکٹروں نے اسپتال میں مذکورہ نوجوان کو بچانے کی بہت سی کوششیں کیں لیکن وہ سب اس وقت بےکار ہوگئی ہیں جب نوجوان اسپتال انتقال کرگیا ہے تاہم یہ معلوم نہیں ہوسکا ہے مذکورہ نوجوان کن وجوہات کی بنا پر خودکشی کرلی ہے۔

فورسز میں خودکشی کے رجحان میں اضافہ

سرینگر: ریاست جموں وکشمیر میں تعینات فورسز اہلکاروں میں خودکشی کرنے کے واقعات میں روز بروز اضافہ ہوتا جارہا ہے گذشتہ چار ماہ کے دوران فورسز ایجنسیوں سے وابستہ ۱۶ اہلکاروں نے خودکشی کرکے اپنی جانیں گنوائیں۔ تفصیلات کے مطابق ریاست جموں وکشمیر میں رواں سال کے چار مہینوں کے دوران ۲۳ خودکشی کے واقعات رونما ہوئے ہیں جن میں سے ۱۶ اہلکاروں کی خودکشی کی کامیاب کوششیں ہوئی ہیں۔ تاہم ۷ اہلکاروں کو بچالیا گیا جن میں سے بی ایس ایف کے ۸ اہلکاروں نے اپنے آپ پر گولیاں چلائیں جن میں سے ۵ اہلکاروں کی موت واقع ہوئی جبکہ ۳ اہلکاروں/ ...

فوجی جوانوں کی طرف سے خودکشی کے واقعات میں بتدریج اضافہ

سرینگر/۶ مئی/ کشمیر میڈیا نیٹ ورک/ راجوری میں گذشتہ پندرہ روز کے عرصے کے دوران اپنی نوعیت کے تیسرے واقعہ میں ایک فوجی اہلکار نے اپنی سروس رائفل سے خود کو گولی مار کر موت کو گلے لگا لیا۔ فوج نے واقعہ کی کورٹ آف انکوائری کے احکامات صادر کیے ہیں جبکہ پولیس الگ سے معاملے کی چھان بین کر رہی ہے۔ پولیس ذرائع نے کے، ایم این کو بتایا کہ نوشہرہ راجوری میں لائن آف کنٹرول کے کیری سیکٹر میں تعینات فوج کی 8 مہار رجمنٹ سے وابستہ نائیک اے ج کمار نے بدھوار کی شب اُس وقت خود کو گولی ماردی جب وہ گارڈ ڈیوٹی دے رہا تھا۔ گولی کی آواز سنتے ہی اسکے ساتھی اسکی طرف دوڑ پڑے اور اسے خون میں لت پت پایا۔ ذرائع کے مطابق نائیک اے ج کمار کو اسپتال پہنچایا گیا جہاں ڈاکٹروں نے اسے مردہ قرار دیا، وہ راستے میں ہی زخموں کی تاب نہ لا کر دم توڑ گیا تھا۔ فوری طور پر مذکورہ اہلکار کی خودکشی کی وجہ معلوم نہیں ہو سکی اور اس کا پتہ لگانے کے لئے فوج نے معاملے کی کورٹ آف انکوائری کا حکم دیا ہے۔ اس دوران راجوری پولیس نے اس واقعہ کے بارے میں دفعہ 174 سی آر پی سی کے تحت کیس درج کر کے اپنی سطح پر تحقیقات کا آغاز کیا ہے۔ نائیک اے ج کمار کی لاش کا پوسٹ مارٹم کرانے کے بعد لاش اسکے ورثا کے سپرد کی گئی ہے۔ گذشتہ 15 دنوں کے دوران پیش آنے والا اپنی نوعیت کا تیسرا واقعہ ہے جس میں کسی فورسز اہلکار نے اپنی سروس رائفل سے اپنے آپ کو گولی مار کر خودکشی کی ہے۔ صرف تین روز قبل ریلوے پولیس سے وابستہ ایک ایس پی او نے اپنے سینئر افسر کو گولی مار کر ہلاک کرنے کے بعد خود کو بھی گولی سے اڑا دیا۔ دونوں کے درمیان کسی بات کو لیکر جھگڑا ہوا تھا جس کے نتیجے میں یہ واقعہ رونما ہوا۔ قابل ذکر ہے کہ جموں کشمیر میں تعینات فورسز کی مختلف ایجنسیوں سے وابستہ اہلکاروں کے ذریعے ذہنی تناؤ کا شکار ہو کر خودکشی کرنے کے واقعات میں گذشتہ چند برس سے مسلسل اضافہ دیکھنے کو ملا ہے۔

شوپیان میں نوجوان وسیم احمد نے اپنے آپ کو پھانسی پر لٹکا دیا

سرینگر/۳ ستمبر/ کشمیر میڈیا نیٹ ورک/ جنوبی قصبہ شوپیاں میں آج اس وقت غم واندوہ کی لہر دوڑ گئی جب بی اے فائنل ائر کے ایک طالب علم نے خود کو پھانسی پر لٹکا کر اپنی زندگی کا خاتمہ کر دیا۔ 20 سالہ وسیم احمد طرے ولد بشیر احمد گذشتہ شب نماز تراویح کے بعد اپنے کمرے میں سونے کیلئے گیا اور جب سحری کے وقت اسے معمول کے مطابق موبائل پر فون پہ کال کر کے جگانے کی کوشش کی گئی تو اس نے فون نہیں اٹھایا۔ بعد میں صبح ساڑھے سات بجے اس کی ماں اسے جگانے کیلئے کمرے میں گئی تو اس پر یہ دیکھ کر قیامت ٹوٹ پڑی کہ اس کا لخت جگر کمرے کی چھت سے لٹک رہا ہے۔ وسیم کی ماں کی دلدوز چیخیں سننے کے بعد وہاں پورے علاقہ کے لوگ جمع ہو گئے اور علاقہ میں سنسنی پھیل گئی۔ معلوم ہوا ہے کہ وسیم احمد نے کھڑکی کا پردہ نکال کر اپنی گردن

Suicide

Anantnag, June 2012: A twenty six year old youth ended his life by consuming some poisonous substance. Reports said that Irshad Dar, son of Yusof of Mirgund Khanabal consumed some poisonous substance. He was rushed to hospital and doctors failed to save him.

Detainee 'Commits Suicide' in Police Custody

Srinagar, Oct. 6: The government on Tuesday ordered a magisterial probe into the death of an accused, who allegedly committed suicide in police custody here.

"The accused Pawan Kumar Sharma and two others Koushal Sharma and Guru Dutt were arrested from Jammu last week in connection with the abduction of a girl from Srinagar," a police official told *Greater Kashmir.*

2 Commit Suicide

Islamabad: One person identfied as Mushtaq Ahmad Bhat s/o Muhammad Sultan Bhat of Devsar today commited suicide by hanging himself. The cause behind the extreme step was not known. Meanwhile, Shameema w/o Abdul Rashid of Qazigund today killed herself by consuming some poisonous substance.

Mandi Aftermath: Woman Attempts Suicide

Poonch, April 4: Shocked over the death of her husband in the recent road accident near Mandi, a woman tried to commit suicide after consuming some poisonous substance.

Police said that Shamshada Begum lost her husband, Muhammad Shabir, in the bus accident. Unable to bear the shock the woman tried to end her life by consuming poisonous substance. She was immediately rushed to Mandi hospital, where doctors washed her stomach. Her condition was stated to be out of danger.

Detainee 'Commits...

Sharma lodged in the police station Ram Munshi Bagh was found hanging with the grill of the bathroom window in the lock-up this morning. "He had cut the jute mat and made a noose out of it. He had then hanged himself from the window grill," the official said, adding that he was taken to a hospital where doctors declared him brought dead.

He said that the parents of the abducted girl had lodged a missing report in police post Nehru Park in August this year. "During investigations it was found that the accused had stayed put in their houseboat before abducting the victim," he added.

"The main accused, Rajneessh Sharma, who is also the brother of the deceased, is still absconding along with the girl," the official said.

He said the deceased detainee was remanded to police custody on Thursday by the district magistrate Srinagar for five days. "On Monday he was produced before the judicial magistrate who extended his remand by four days," he added.

Meanwhile, police said it had apprised the district magistrate about the matter and proceedings under section 176 CrPC had been initiated. Fllowing Sharma's death the district magistrate ordered a magisterial inquiry, and appointed the additional deputy commissioner Srinagar as the investigating officer.

خودکشی کرنے والوں سے ایک گزارش

ڈاکٹر مرزا ریاضت حسین

مجھے خودکشی کرنے والوں سے اس کے سوا اور کوئی ہمدردی نہیں کہ وہ مرنے سے پہلے اللہ کے نیک بندے اور نبی کریم صلی اللہ علیہ وآلہ وسلم کی شفاعت کا مدعا کے طلب گار تھے لیکن بخیتِ نفس کے سبب اپنی سانسوں پر اختیار کی اوندھی خواہش نے ان نادان براندازوں کو اس ذلت سے بچلا اور رگیدا ہے کہ قیامت تک قول توڑنے پر احتساب گناہ کا ارتعاش انہیں اذیت میں مبتلا رکھے گا... میں قطعاً اس فلسفے کا حامی نہیں کہ حکومت یا حکمران کلی طور پر ان خودکشیوں کے ذمے دار ہیں یا پھر اس طبقے کو مورد الزام ٹھیرا کر بارگاہ ایزدی میں ان کے خلاف ایک اور مقدمہ درج کرا دیا جائے... اقتدار کے سنگھاسن پر براجمان بے حسی کے اشلوک پڑھنے والی اس عجیب و غریب مخلوق کے گناہ تو پہلے ہی اتنے زیادہ ہیں کہ قبر کا منہ بھرا ہوا ہے مگر حقیقت تو یہ ہے کہ ہر انسان سے اس کے نفس کے متعلق دریافت کیا جائے گا... ماں کے پیٹ میں ذات بنتی ہے اور دنیا میں صفات بنتی ہیں، اگر صفات میں کمال ہے تو درجات میں بھی جمال ہے اور اگر صفات کمال سے خالی ہیں تو زوال جہنم کی طرف دھکیل دے گا جہاں عقوبت اور پکڑ کی عبرت انگیز شکل ہے یہ درست ہے کہ طبقاتی فرق، بے لگام اشتہا اور امرا کی عیاشیوں کے باعث زمین سے اگنے والی عدم توازن کی خودرو جھاڑیوں نے راستہ دشوار کر دیا ہے... اور یہ بھی سچ ہے کہ اصلیت اور ماہیت کے برخلاف ٹی وی اسکرینز پر ناچ گانوں کی یلغار، طلاق و خلا لے کی سرگزشت، حقائق کے برعکس محبت کی داستانوں اور مصنوعی چکاچوند نے احساسِ محرومی اور اشتعال کو ہوا دی ہے لیکن اس کا یہ مطلب ہرگز نہیں کہ اللہ کی عطا کردہ نعمت بے بہا پر اس کا غصہ نکالا جائے، اپنی ذات کو تو خون میں نہلایا ہی جائے مگر ساتھ ہی ساتھ معصوم بچوں کو بھی بے دردی سے قتل کر دیا جائے... تم مایوس، بے زار، بزدل، ڈرپوک اور کم ہمت ہو ٹھیک ہے مگر تمہارے بچے تو ابھی عقل کی اس سرحد تک پہنچے ہی نہیں جہاں سے شعور کی روشنی میں منزل کی سمت سفر کا آغاز کیا جاتا ہے پھر انہیں قتل کیوں کرتے ہو؟ اس ڈر سے کہ کہیں مفلسی کا اژدہا انہیں بھی نہ نگل لے؟... کیا تم (معاذ اللہ) خدا ہو؟ تم نے تقدیر لکھی ہے؟ تم نے رزق دینے کا وعدہ کر رکھا ہے؟ بھول گئے کہ تمہیں اور تمہارے بچوں کو رزق دینے والے رزاق کو بھی موت نہیں... اتنی آسانی سے فراموش کر دی سورۃ بنی اسرائیل کی یہ 31 ویں آیت کہ "اور اپنی اولاد کو مفلسی کے خوف سے قتل نہ کرنا، (کیونکہ) ان کو اور تم کو ہم ہی رزق دیتے ہیں، کچھ شک نہیں کہ ان کا مار ڈالنا بڑا سخت گناہ ہے"... کتنے کٹھور، سنگ دل اور ظالم ہو کہ اپنی اور اپنے جگر کے ٹکڑوں کی جانوں کو طعن و تشنیع کا لاوا اگلنے والے میڈیا کی کمائی کا ذریعہ بنا دیتے ہو ہم تمہاری لاش کو بیچتے ہیں، دلخراش مناظر اور روح فرسا چیخیں سن کر "سب پر بازی لے جانے" کا جشن مناتے ہیں، پھر کسی سرکاری اہلکار یا وزیر موصوف کو ٹیلیفون لائن پر لے کر اس کی کھال کھینچتے ہیں، اپنے آپ کو پارسا اور اسے انتہائی بدصفت اور ایک لایعنی وجود ثابت کرنے کی کوشش کرتے ہیں اور خبر کو انجام تک پہنچانے کے بعد پیچھے مڑ کر اپنے پروڈیوسر سے پوچھتے ہیں "اچھا رہا نا!" شاید میری برادری مجھ سے کچھ دیر کے لیے ناراض ہو جائے مگر دل میں سب ہی جانتے ہیں کہ میں جو کچھ لکھ رہا ہوں وہ ان کا بھی سچ ہے... یہ کامیاب زندگی نہیں ہے کہ آدمی چار پیسے بنائے اور مرے کی بے فکر حیات کا انتخاب کر لے، ذہن کی بے قراری اور بے چینی آ جائے تو سمجھ لیجیے کہ زندگی کامیاب ہے... میرے سرکار العالمین صلی اللہ علیہ وآلہ وسلم نے فرمایا ہے کہ "دنیا مردار ہے اور اس کے طلب کرنے والے کتے ہیں" یہ نہیں فرمایا کہ اس کے طلب کرنے والے گدھ اور کوے ہیں، کیونکہ مردار پر تو گدھ اور کوے بھی بیٹھتے ہیں مگر اس فرق کے ساتھ کہ کوے کو وہاں آنے سے نہیں روک سکتے اور گدھ دوسرے گدھوں کو بھنبھوڑنے سے منع نہیں کرتے مگر کتا اگر کسی مردار پر بیٹھا ہو اور دوسرا ابھی وہاں پہنچ جائے تو وہ شدید خفگی کے عالم میں بھونک بھونک کر اسے وہاں سے بھگا دیتا ہے... تو پھر ایسی دنیا کے لیے کیوں خودکشی کرتے ہو؟ یہ تو معین وقت تک جسم کو زندہ رکھنے کا صرف ایک ٹھکانہ ہے... بس چند روز ہی تو جینا اور اس کی سختیوں اور تکلیفوں کو جھیلنا ہے، ہماری طلب بھی نہیں تھی اور پروردگار نے ہمیں وجود عطا فرمایا جب وجود جیسی دولت خالقِ کائنات نے مانگے بغیر بخش دی تو بعد کی دولتوں کا سوال ہی کیا؟ اور پھر اسی مالکِ حقیقی نے محض اپنے فضل سے قلوب میں ایمان کی قندیلیں روشن کیں، عقل کا تحفہ دیا، آنکھوں کو نور سے سجایا، ہاتھوں اور پیروں میں حرکت دی، والدین، بہن بھائی، بیوی، بچوں، رشتے داروں اور احباب کے پیار سے نوازا، یہ حسن کیا کم ہے جو ہم دنیا کے زر و نقد میں الجھے ہوئے ہیں... اے خودکشیاں کرنے والو! شکر ادا کرو اس رب کا کہ جس نے تمہیں نماز، تلاوت، ذکر، علم اور نیک کاموں کی توفیق دی اپنے بچوں کو مارنے والو! سجدے کرو اس پروردگار کے حضور کہ جس نے تمہیں ماں اور باپ بنایا ورنہ تو سیدنا زکریا علیہ السلام اور سیدہ سارہ علیہا السلام جیسی عظیم ہستیاں بھی قرآن کے پاروں میں اولاد کے لیے تڑپتی نظر آتی ہیں... آج اگر تمہاری جیبوں میں کچھ سکے یا چھپے ہوئے نوٹ نہیں اور کوئی تم سے یہ پوچھ لے کہ "بھیا کیا حال ہیں؟" تو تم اکتاہٹ سے جل کر کہتے ہو کہ "جیب خالی ہے، مصیبت میں گرفتار ہوں، حال کیا خاک اچھے ہوں گے" یعنی میرے مولا کی عطا کردہ ساری نعمتیں ایک طرف اور جیب میں روپوں کا نہ ہونا ایک طرف! تم کو اس کی ترجیح ہو چلے، ملے تو بس یہی اس کا فضل نظر آتا ہے؟ ادھر ادھر سے لوٹ مار کے، رشوت اور سود کا تیزاب اپنی آخرت کے رخسار پر انڈیل کر اور یتیموں کی زمینوں پر قبضے کرنے کے بعد ان پر بلند تختیاں لگا کر "ھذا من فضل ربی" کا ورد لگا لینے سے اس کا فضل نہیں ہو جاتا بھائی! جس میں تقویٰ نہیں اور جسے ذکر و فکر کی توفیق نہیں اس پر فضلِ رب نہیں! ایمان، یقین، معرفت، بصیرت، علم اور آقا کریم صلی اللہ علیہ وآلہ وسلم سے نسبت کی دولت کی تمنا کرو تو بات ہے، اس دنیا کے سکوں کی جھنکار اور سانپ کی پھنکار میں زیادہ فرق نہیں... جس کو اللہ نے دیا ہے اس کے لیے دعا کرو کہ وہ غنی ہو جائے اور جسے نہیں دیا ہے اس سے کہو کہ وہ شکر کرے کہ قبر سے حشر کی منزلوں تک اس کا راستہ آسان کر دیا گیا ہے... مصائب و آلام میں پریشان نہ ہو بلکہ دل سے باتیں کیا کرو اس سے پوچھو کہ تو بے قرار تو نہیں ہے، اللہ کی رضا پر مطمئن ہے نا؟ اور اگر وہ "ہاں" کہے تو سمجھو کہ رب کو تم پر پیار آ گیا ہے اور وہ تمہیں آزما رہا ہے تاکہ اپنی رحمت کا خوان تمہارے آنگن میں اتارے اور اگر قلبِ مضطر کا جواب "نہیں" ہے تو استغفار کرو کہ رب نے تمہیں پکڑ لیا ہے مگر اللہ کے واسطے خودکشی نہ کرو! ہاں اپنے آپ کو دلدل میں مت ڈالو، جب گناہ نہیں چھوٹتے تو توبہ کیوں چھوڑتے ہو؟ گناہوں کے میل کچیل کو الحاح و زاری کے آنسوؤں سے دھو ڈالو، پھر میلا ہو جائے تو پھر دھو ڈالو اور پھر میلا ہو جائے تو پھر دھو ڈالو، کسی ایسے "عقلمند" کو دیکھا ہے کہ جس نے نہانا صرف اس لیے چھوڑ دیا ہو کہ بار بار پسینہ آ جاتا ہے یا کپڑے بدلنے اس وجہ سے ترک کر دیے ہوں کہ وہ میلے ہو جاتے ہیں؟ یقیناً نہیں! تو پھر اس کی بارگاہ میں بار بار معافی مانگنے میں شرم کیسی؟ اس کی قدرت کے CCTV پوری کائنات کا احاطہ کیے ہوئے ہیں اور بخشش کے باغ سے اس کا فضل دولت کے بل پر نہیں بلکہ ندامت کے آنسوؤں کے ہدیے سے حاصل کیا جاتا ہے

Why Isn't rising suicide rates in Kashmir anybody's concern?

729 suicide cases registered in SMHS in 2003

Srinagar, June 29: Sumaira (name changed), a 35-year-old woman belonged to a poor family in the city. Her brother was a militant and was killed in an encounter with the security forces. Being 35 and still un-married finally took a toll on her psyche. She suffered depression and ultimately ended her life by consuming a toxic substance.

Ayesha Akhtar of Kulgam ended her life after failing to find a job despite being a masters degree holder. Similarly a girl Saleema from Varmul district ended her life for the same reason.

Statistics reveal an enormous increase in the number of suicide cases in valley in last few years which is a matter of concern for all.

368 suicide attempt cases have been reported only at SMHS hospital from April 1, 2002 to March 31, 2003. The number rose to an alarming 729 in the following year which is an average of two cases of suicide everyday.

The trend is higher in females. Against 272 males, 457 females attempted suicide from April 1, 2003 to March 31, 2004. The actual number of cases is much higher as many cases go unreported due to the social and religious stigma attached to suicides. Usually, the report says, the families pass off their suicides as accidents.

The pattern of almost all the cases is same: consuming of different kinds of toxic substances. It has been observed that most cases coming from rural areas are of people who have consumed pesticides or insecticides, which is readily available in almost every home there.

According to Dr. Hamidullah Shah, HOD, Govt. Psychiatric Hospital, one of the main reasons for increase in suicides in valley is personality problems. Love affair in teen age, low tolerance, competition in all spheres of life, over-expectancy of parents of their wards and dejection are some of the other reasons.

"Potential warning signs can be identified. At least three quarters who commit suicide betray their intentions", says Dr. Hamidullah adding parents should take threat of suicide seriously and not just as a joke.

Two College Girls Commit Suicide in City

New Delhi: Two college girls committed suicide in New Delhi over the past two days — Shubhra Tanwar was reportedly driven to it because she was unable to tackle her obesity, while Arpita was suffering from depression for some months.

Shubhra, 19, was an undergraduate law student of Jamia Millia Islamia and was found dead in her parents' Sector 29 flat in Noida this week. While police are saying she committed suicide as she was depressed about being obese, the university, which held a condolence meeting on Thursday, says it was told the girl died of a brain tumour.

There is a conflict regarding the date too. As per the information received by the university, the girl died on Wednesday. But police officers in Noida say the girl committed suicide on Thursday morning. Noida's Sector 20 police chief Arjun Singh told *Times News Network*, Shubhra was depressed as she was overweight. The daughter of a serving Wing Commander in the IAF, she had tried virtually everything, including crash diets, to lose weight. After one of these 'crash diets', about a month ago, Shubhra had reportedly gone into a coma, and had to be hospitalised. But after recuperating from the trauma of the diet, she went back on a strict exercise regimen.

If what the police are saying is true, Shubhra's is the second suicide prompted by weight concerns in the district this year. In the first case, another 19-year-old student had shot herself with her father's licensed .32 calibre revolver at her Dadri residence.

According to Singh, Shubhra's suicide happened sometime between 10 am and 11 am on Thursday. Shubhra's father, Wing Commander B.K. Tanwar, was away at work. Shubhra's sister and brother were at school. Shubhra and her mother, Alka Tanwar, were at home, in separate rooms.

At about 12.30 pm, her mother found Shubhra's bedroom locked from inside.

Shubhra did not respond to shouts or knocking. So, the door was broken open by neighbours and she was found hanging from the ceiling fan. Her body was sent for an autopsy. But police said there did not, at first sight, appear to be any foul play.

Arpita, 20, was a final year BIT student of Acharya Narendra Dev College. The police said they received a call at 3 pm on Friday.

The victim was found hanging from the ceiling fan with her dupatta at her Nehru Apartments residence in Kalkaji.

Arpita was reportedly suffering from depression and had been undergoing treatment at VIMHANS. No suicide note has been found.

Hitting Rock Bottom

- 19-yr-old Shubhra Tanwar was unable to tackle her obesity.
- She tried everything, including crash diets, to lose weight.
- 20-yr-old Arpita was suffering from depression for some months.
- She had been undergoing treatment at VIMHANS.

ڈورو میں نئے نویلے دولہا کی لاش درخت سے لٹکتی ہوئی پائی گئی، دلہن بے ہوش

کولگام میں ایک اور دلہن کی پُراسرار موت، دونوں واقعات پُراسرار، گاؤں والے حیرت کا مجسمہ بن گئے ہیں

سرینگر ۱۳؍اکتوبر ا کے این ایس ا جنوبی کشمیر میں لرزہ خیز وارداتوں میں 4 ماہ کے دولہے کو بے دردی کے ساتھ پھانسی پر لٹکا کر موت کے گھاٹ اتار دیا گیا جبکہ کولگام میں 17 روز کی نئی نویلی دلہن نے زہریلی شئے کھا کر اپنی زندگی کا خاتمہ کر دیا۔ اس دوران اننت ناگ میں ایک دوشیزہ نے زہر کھا کر اپنا کام تمام کرنے کی کوشش کی۔ گذشتہ روز 24 سالہ محمد رفیق خان ولد عبدالغنی ساکن بشتر گام ڈورو اپنی بیوی 20 سالہ شمی جان کے ہمراہ ٹہلنے کیلئے گھر سے روانہ ہوا۔ نمائندے نے بتایا کہ جب میاں بیوی دیر گئے شام تک گھر واپس نہ لوٹے تو افراد خانہ نے اُن کی تلاش شروع کر دی تاہم بسیار تلاش کے باوجود بھی نوجوان جوڑے کا کوئی بھی اتہ پتہ نہیں چل سکا۔ چنانچہ کافی تھک ہار کے بعد افراد خانہ نے معاملے کی نسبت پولیس کو مطلع کیا اور اس سلسلے میں متعلقہ پولیس تھانے میں گمشدگی کی رپورٹ درج کرائی۔ نمائندے نے بتایا کہ آج صبح افراد خانہ پر اُس وقت قیامت ٹوٹ پڑی جب انہوں نے اسی علاقے میں محمد رفیق کھانڈے کی لاش سفیدے کے درخت سے لٹکی ہوئی پائی جبکہ شمی جان کو دوسرے درخت کے ساتھ رسیوں سے باندھ کر رکھا گیا تھا اور وہ نیم مردہ حالت میں تھی۔ چنانچہ پولیس نے فوری طور پر جائے وقوع پر پہنچ کر محمد رفیق کی لاش اپنی تحویل میں لی جبکہ شمی جان کو انتہائی نازک حالت میں علاج و معالجہ کی غرض سے نزدیکی اسپتال پہنچایا گیا۔ اگرچہ فوری طور پر یہ معلوم نہ ہو سکا کہ کن افراد نے محمد رفیق کھانڈے کا قتل کر دیا تاہم پولیس نے حقائق کا پتہ لگانے /2

دُنیا کے ستم سے دل برداشتہ خواتین نے ''زہر'' کو ہی غم سے نجات کا ذریعہ.

ایک عورت نے زہریلی شے پی کر اپنا کام تمام کیا، دوسری نے جراثیم کش دوا سے خودکشی کی، تیسری نے اپنے آپ کو پھانسی پر لٹکایا

Girl Attempts Suicide after pre-paid Mobile Goes Dead

Srinagar: Subreena Hakim, 23, tried to end her life after she found that her pre-paid mobile phone was not working while trying to reach out to her friend. A resident of Chattergul in Ganderbal district, she had consumed some poisonous substance after she failed to connect with her friend on Sunday sources said. However, she was discharged from the hospital on Monday after a stomach wash on Sunday. District SP Imtiyaz Hussian refused to admit that the girl might have consumed poison after finding her phone dead. Her father Ghulam Nabi Hakim, a head constable in Jammu and Kashmir police, presently posted in Doda, also rejected that Subreena consumed poison after finding her mobile phone dead. "She was depressed as she was not good at studies," Hakim said.

Interestingly, thousands of pre-paid mobile phone subscribers revalidated their SIM cards on Saturday for three months. There are three million pre-paid mobile connections in Jammu and Kashmir and home ministry had banned its use in the state after it found militants misusing the facility.

Meanwhile, Union minister for renewable energy Farooq Abdullah said that pre-paid facility will be resumed soon in the state. The state government has taken up the matter with the Centre, Farooq said here on Monday. Former chief minister Mufti Mohammad Sayeed also castigated the Centre for banning pre-paid mobile phone connections in the state.

"One fails to understand the logic behind banning the facility in Jammu and Kashmir," he said.

Nazima Bhat of Soura, a student, was equally angry with the ban and said, "The facility was cheap in terms of money while post-paid SIM card costs more as telecom companies also charge rent for the phone. I get limited pocket money from my parents and cannot afford to keep post-paid phone connection," she said. Meanwhile, telecom companies have started converting pre-paid connections into post-paid connections after proper verification of the subscriber by the police, a BSNL official said.

'Don't Pray for One Who Commits Suicide'

Srinagar, June 28: The Grand *Mufti* of Jammu and Kashmir, Mufti Muhammad Bashir-ud-Din Ahmad on Thursday issued *a fatwa* (religious order that is binding on Muslims) urging Muslims not to participate in the funeral prayers of a person who commits suicide. While announcing an important decision after a meeting of *ulema* on suicides in Kashmir he urged *Imams* to make people aware that suicide in Islam is forbidden.

"Islam strictly prohibits suicide and it is criminal act in our religion to commit suicide. *Imams* should make people aware about the importance of life," Mufti Bashir told *Greater Kashmir.*

While Urging the Imams of Valley to use their influence to eradicate obscenity and immorality in the society, the Grand *Mufti* said, "Our younger generation indulges in immoral and unethical activities due to which they suffer from mental agony. Later they end their lives to avoid mental disturbance."

The Grand *Mufti* said that committing suicide was against the teachings of Holy Quran and Prophet Muhammad (SAW).

"Depression, unemployment, drug abuse and late marriages are fast growing. We are on verge of disaster. Drugs are being sold to younger generation which will doom them," he said.

Mufti Bashir said that everybody has to take blame of it. "I hold everybody responsible including myself. I appeal *Imams* and religious scholars to take a lead and impart teachings of *Quran* to the people."

He also urged respectable citizens in society to come forward and play their role to stop these unislamic acts.

Mufti Bashir's *fatwa* came in the backdrop of rising rate of suicides in Kashmir over past some years. Statistics reveal that during last 12 years suicides have become second most common mode of unnatural death besides deaths caused by gunfire and blast injury.

The other alarming aspect of suicides and attempted suicides in Kashmir is that majority of those who commit suicide or attempt to end their lives are youth and in the age group of 15-25 years, statistics reveal.

Kashmir's leading psychiatrist Dr. Mushtaq Margoob had recently stated that there was need for an element of spirituality to stop the suicides.

"Religious leaders have a strong role to play to make the suffering society free from the miseries of depression, drug-abuse and other social ailments. The element of spirituality, which is almost inherent in everybody's life, is unfortunately not a priority in present day materialistic Kashmir. Clergy here has a role to play," Dr. Margoob, who has done pioneering work in the field of Psychiatry in Kashmir, had told *Greater Kashmir* in February this year.

"There are more than one million depression patients in Kashmir and more than a lakh of them think in terms of ending their lives which is a matter of great concern, rather a big challenge," he had added.

Last Friday, the *Imam* of Hamza Masjid in Lal Chowk also delivered a sermon on suicides.

"It is the duty of everyone to stop this unislamic act. Anyone who commits suicide will go to hell," the Imam said.

ولگام کی عورت نے زہریلی شے کھا کر خودکشی کی
2006ء میں 61 افراد نے اپنا کام خود تمام کیا

سرینگر/ ۲۹ جون/ یو این آئی/ جموں وکشمیر کے مفتی اعظم بشیر الدین احمد کے ذریعہ جاری کردہ ایک فتویٰ میں خودکشی کو غیر اسلامی فعل قرار دینے کے ایک دن بعد ہی آج ایک خاتون نے خودکشی کرلی۔ پولیس ترجمان کے مطابق ولگام کے ہردونا گاؤں کے رہنے والے خورشید احمد وار کی بیوی حسینہ بیگم نے آج صبح اپنے گھر میں کوئی زہریلی شے کھا کر خودکشی کرلی۔ کل ہی بہار کے رہنے والے دو مزدوروں نے خودکشی کرلی تھی جب کہ دیگر دو مقامی افراد نے بھی زہر کھا کر خودکشی کی تھی۔ اس سلسلہ میں یو این آئی کی ایک رپورٹ پر کارروائی کرتے ہوئے مفتی اعظم نے کہا تھا کہ خودکشی یا خود کو ہلاکت میں ڈالنے جیسے عمل کو اسلام میں سختی سے منع کیا گیا ہے۔ سرکاری اعداد وشمار کے مطابق 2006ء میں 61 افراد نے خودکشی کی تھی جب کہ رواں سال کے دوران خودکشی واقعات میں ڈرامائی انداز میں اضافہ ہوا ہے اور 6 ماہ کے اندر ہی خود/10

سرینگر ٹائمز

بروز سنیچروار 30 جون 2007ء

خودکشی کے واقعات کے اسباب

اس امر کے باوجود کہ اسلام نے خودکشی کو بزدلی کہا ہے اور اس کی سختی سے ممانعت کی ہے، عالمی سطح پر بالخصوص مسلم ممالک میں خودکشی کے واقعات بڑھ رہے ہیں۔

انسان کی سب سے پیاری چیز اس کی جان ہوتی ہے، ایک انسان زندگی کی آخری سانس تک زندہ رہنا چاہتا ہے، انہی دنوں جاپان میں 110 برس کے ایک بوڑھے نے اپنا جنم دن منایا، جب اسے پوچھا گیا کہ اسکی طویل العمری کا راز کیا ہے تو کہا میں نے عمر بھر شراب نہیں پی لی ہے، تمباکو سے میں نفرت کرتا ہوں، میں سبزی خور ہوں، جب اسے پوچھا گیا کہ وہ اور کتنے عرصہ تک زندہ رہنا چاہتا ہے تو کہا میں مرنا نہیں چاہتا، مجھے اپنی زندگی بڑی پیاری ہے۔

ایک انسان خودکشی کیوں کرتا ہے؟ ماہرین نفسیات کے مطابق اس کی کوئی ایک وجہ نہیں ہوتی؟ اگر ایک دن میں 10 انسان خودکشی کریں تو ہر خودکشی کے پیچھے اپنا اپنا کارن ہوسکتا ہے؟ ایک نوجوان محبت میں ناکامی پر اپنی زندگی کا خاتمہ کرتا ہے؟ کسی موزی اور لاعلاج مرض میں مبتلا ایک انسان موت کو گلے لگانے سے ہی اپنے لئے آرام آسودگی اور سکون مانتا ہے۔ خود کشی اُس کیفیت کا نام ہے جب انسان کسی بات پر انتہائی غمگین، بے حد خشمگین اور بہت زیادہ مایوس ہوجائے۔ ایسی حالت میں اس کے حواس کا توازن بگڑ جاتا ہے اور وہ موت کو گلے لگاتا ہے۔ اس عالم گونا گوں میں کئی لوگوں نے اپنے پالتو کتے کی موت پر اُس کے ساتھ ہی اپنی زندگی کا بھی خاتمہ کردیا۔ فٹ بال یا کرکٹ کی دو ٹیمیں کھیل رہی ہوتی ہیں ایک کی ہار اور

دوسری کی جیت ہوتی ہے؟ ہارنے اور جیتنے والے میچ کے آخر مین ایک دوسرے کے گلے مل جاتے ہیں لیکن تماشا بینوں میں سے ایک شخص اپنی من پسند ٹیم کی ہار برداشت نہیں کرتا اور وہ گول پوست پر رسی کا پھنداڈال کر اس پر اپنی گردن الکاتا ہے اور خودکشی کرتا ہے۔ تاریخ گواہ ہے کہ بادشاہ نے اپنی ملکہ کی موت پر اپنی زندگی کو بےکار سمجھا اور سلطنت کو لات مار کر خودکشی کی۔

کشمیر میں پچھلے ۱۸ برسوں کے نامساعد حالات میں سینکڑوں لوگوں نے زندگی کو اپنے کاندھوں اور اپنے کنبہ کے لوگوں پر بار سمجھ کر خود کو اس سے چھٹکارا پایا۔

جی ہاں! خودکشی بزدلی ہے اور اسلام خودکشی کی ممانعت کرتا ہے۔ جموں و کشمیر کے مفتی اعظم مفتی بشیر الدین نے فتویٰ جاری کیا ہے کہ خودکشی کرنا ایک غیر اسلامی حرکت ہے اور اس کا مرتکب شخص کبھی مسلمان نہیں ہوسکتا۔ آپ نے کہا ہے خودکشی کر کے اپنی زندگی کا خاتمہ کرنے والے کے جنازہ میں بھی شامل نہیں ہونا چاہیے۔ لیکن اس چیز کا کیا جواز کہ مسلم ممالک میں دشمن کو زیر کرنے کیلئے خودکشی کو موثر ہتھیار سمجھا جاتا ہے۔ خودکشی جہاد کا حصہ بن گیا ہے۔ عراق، لبنان، فلسطین، افغانستان اور خود ہمارے اپنے کشمیر میں خودکش بمبار اپنی زندگی کو داؤ پر لگا کر اور دوسرے کتنے لوگون کو موت کی نیند سلا دیتے ہیں۔

خودکشی کی وارداتیں زیادہ تر جیل خانوں میں ہوتی ہیں۔ طویل سزا پانے یا موت کی سزا کے انتظار میں قیدی زندگی سے جلد از جلد چھٹکارا پانے کیلئے پھانسی کے پھندے کا انتظار نہیں کرتے۔ وہ جیل کی کوٹھری میں ہی کسی طرح سے اپنے آپ کو زندگی کی آغوش میں سلا دیتے ہیں۔

ہمارے مولوی صاحبان ملا اور مفتی صاحبان خودکشی کو بزدلی تو بتا دیتے ہیں لیکن اس کی وجوہات بتانے اور اس کے پیچھے کارفرما جذبہ پر روشنی ڈالنے میں کیوں کتراتے ہیں؟ اس کی وجہ وہی بتا سکتے ہیں۔

یاس وناکامی اور تاریک مستقبل کا خوف،

وادی میں خودکشی کے واقعات میں روز افزوں اضافہ، دانشوروں کیلئے فکر وتشویش کا باعث

سرینگر/ نیوز ٹوڈے/ پچھلے کئی مہینوں سے پوری وادی میں جس تیزی سے خودکشی کا رجحان بڑھتا جارہا ہے اور آئے دن مختلف علاقوں سے خودکشی کے واقعات کے سلسلے میں اطلاعات موصول ہورہی ہیں اُس نے سنجیدہ اور ذی شعور حلقوں کو فکر وتشویش میں مبتلا کیا ہے۔ اگرچہ وادی کے طول و عرض میں پیش آنے والے خودکشی کے تمام واقعات منظر عام پر نہیں آتے تاہم جتنے بھی واقعات کی جانکاری موصول ہوتی ہے اُن سے سنجیدہ حلقے اپنے دانتوں تلے اُنگلی دبانے پر مجبور ہورہے ہیں۔ ماہرین نفسیات کے مطابق خواہشات کی اُونچی اڑان، گھریلو مسائل، پیار محبت میں ناکامی، مالی اور ذہنی پریشانیاں، امتحانات میں ناکامی، والدین یا پھر اپنے کسی قریبی رفیق کی اچانک بے رُخی، طویل بیماری اور مستقبل کی تاریکیوں کا خوف خودکشی کے بنیادی اسباب ہیں۔ گوکہ عام طور پر یہی کہا جارہا ہے کہ خودسوزی کرنے والا شخص انتہائی بزدل ہوتا ہے اور وہ زندگی کی تلخیوں اور ناکامیوں کا مقابلہ کرنے کی جرأت نہیں کر سکتا لیکن جب اُس کی زندگی موت سے بھی بدتر ہوجاتی ہے اور اُس کی اُمیدوں کی روشن دنیا اچانک معدوم ہوجاتی ہے تو وہ اپنی دانست میں انتہائی جرأت مندی کا مظاہرہ کرکے خود پر مٹی کا تیل چھڑک کر آگ لگاتا ہے اور تڑپ تڑپ کر دم توڑ بیٹھتا ہے، یا پھر پھانسی لگا کر اپنا کام تمام کر بیٹھتا ہے۔ اکثر حالات میں خودسوزی کرنے والے جراثیم کش ادویات کا استعمال کرتے ہیں کیونکہ اُن کی نظروں میں قفس دنیا سے نجات پانے کا یہ سب سے آسان راستہ ہے۔ مافوق الفطرت والے ایسے لوگوں کی تعداد اگرچہ پہلے انتہائی کم تھی تاہم موجودہ حرص و ہوس کے اس دور میں ان کی تعداد میں حیرت انگیز حد تک اضافہ ہورہا ہے۔ سماج میں قوت برداشت ختم ہورہی ہے۔ ہر شخص کامیابیوں کی نئی اُفق کو چھونا چاہتا ہے۔ حصول دھن دولت اور زندگی کے تمام آرام اور آسائش انسان کا واحد مقصد بن گیا ہے۔ زندگی میں کوئی شخص کس قدر کامیاب و کامران ہے اُس کا اندازہ اُس کی عقل و دانش سے نہیں بلکہ اُس کی مالی آسودگی سے لگایا جاتا ہے اور یہاں صرف مالی اعتبار سے کامیاب اشخاص کو ہی قدر و منزلت کی نگاہوں سے دیکھا جارہا ہے جس کے نتیجہ میں وہ قابل قدر افراد انتہائی مایوسیوں کا شکار ہوجاتے ہیں جو لگن اور قابلیت کے باوجود دھن دولت حاصل کرنے کی دوڑ میں بچھڑ جاتے ہیں اور سماج میں اپنی قدر و قیمت کھونے کے بعد اس حد تک مایوسیوں کا شکار ہوجاتے ہیں کہ وہ انتہائی قدم اُٹھا کر موت کو گلے لگا کر اپنے والدین یا عزیز و اقارب کو تاعمر نوحہ کناں ہونے پر مجبور کرتے ہیں۔ زندگی سے زیادہ اُمیدیں لگانا موت کو گلے لگانے کے مترادف بن گیا ہے۔ چھوٹے سے دل میں بڑے بڑے ارمان مچلنے اور رنگین دنیا کا شیدائی ہونے سے نوجوانوں کے دل و دماغ میں انتشاری کیفیت پیدا ہوجاتی ہے اور یوں وہ صحیح سمت میں زندگی کا تعین کرنے کے بجائے ایسے اقدام اُٹھاتا ہے جو بلاآخر اُس کے لئے گرداب فنا ثابت ہوتے ہیں۔ ایسا برسوں سے ہوتا آیا ہے اور آئیندہ بھی ایسا ہی ہوگا۔ کیونکہ فی الوقت عام لوگوں کے لئے یہ کوئی سنگین مسئلہ نہیں یہ مسئلہ صرف اُن کنبوں کے لئے فکر وتشویش کا باعث ہے جن کے بچے مقدر کی ناکامیوں کا شکار ہیں اور جو اپنی تمام تر کوششوں کے باوجود زندگی کی تلخیوں کے حصار سے بچ نکلنے میں کامیاب نہیں ہورہے ہیں۔ انسان کی کامیابیوں کو اگر دھن دولت کے ترازو میں تولا نہ جاتا تو شاید یہاں خودسوزی کے واقعات میں کمی آنے کی اُمید بن جاتی ہے۔

☆☆☆

وادی میں خودکشی کا بڑھتا رجحان...لمحہ فکریہ!

رواں سال میں 35 واقعات رونما، 19 افراد موت کے شکار، 16 کو بچالیا گیا، فوج بھی محفوظ نہیں 7 نے جان دے دی

سرینگر/۱۶/مئی// وادی میں یکم جنوری 2007 سے 15 مئی تک خودکشی کے 35 واقعات رونما ہوئے جن میں 19 افراد موت کی ابدی نیند سو گئے جبکہ 16 افراد کو فوری طبی امداد پہنچا کر بچالیا گیا۔ خودکشی کرنے والوں میں زیادہ تعداد جواں سال خواتین کی ہے جو گھریلو پریشانیوں اور محبت میں ناکامی کے بعد اپنی جان دینے پر آمادہ ہوگئیں۔ نیوز ٹوڈے کے ایک جائیزے کے مطابق اس عرصہ میں 6 خواتین نے زہریلی شے کا استعمال کیا۔ جن میں سے تین خواتین لقمہ اجل بن گئیں۔ جبکہ باقی تین کی جان بچائی گئی۔ امتحان میں ناکامی کی وجہ سے دو طالبات نے اپنا کام تمام کرنا چاہا اور اُنہوں نے جراثیم کش دوا پی لی۔ لیکن دونوں طالبات کو بروقت طبی امداد سے موت کے منہ سے واپس نکالا گیا۔ من پسند نوجوان کے ساتھ شادی رچانے کے سلسلے میں والدین کے انکار اور پیار محبت میں ناکامی کی وجہ سے 10 دوشیزاوں نے زہریلی دوا پی لی جن میں سے 4 کی موت واقع ہوئی۔ جبکہ ایک خاتون نے طویل بیماری سے تنگ آکر اپنی زندگی کا خاتمہ کرلیا۔ دہال ہانجی پورہ میں ایک خاتون رہبر تعلیم نے اپنے کپڑوں پر مٹی کا تیل چھڑک کر آگ لگادی جو کہ بعد میں صورہ میڈیکل انسٹیچوٹ میں دم توڑ بیٹھی۔ تین اشخاص نے گھریلو مسائل سے پریشان ہوکر موت کو گلے لگالیا۔ جبکہ شیر باغ اننت ناگ میں مقامی مندر کے پجاری کے بیٹے نے خودسوزی کرنے کے لئے اپنے کپڑوں میں آگ لگادی۔ اُدھر اسی عرصہ میں بی۔ ایس۔ ایف کے 2، سی۔ آر۔ پی۔ ایف کے 2 اور راشٹریہ رائفلز کے ایک اہلکار نے اپنی سروس رائفل سے اپنا کام تمام کرلیا۔ فوجی ذرایع کے مطابق یہ لوگ ذہنی پریشانیوں اور حکام کی طرف سے رخصت نہ ملنے پر اپنی زندگی کا خاتمہ کرنے پر مجبور ہوگئے۔ کاڈی پورہ اننت ناگ میں ایک شخص نے تیز دھار والے ہتھیار سے اپنی گردن کاٹنے کی کوشش کی۔ زونی مر میں ایک شخص نے محض اس وجہ سے خودکشی کرلی کیونکہ اُس کی بیوی اُسے اکثر و بیشتر روپے پیسے کا تقاضا کرتی رہتی تھی۔ جبکہ عشمقام اننت ناگ میں گورنمنٹ مڈل سکول میں تعینات ایک رہبر تعلیم نے ایک کمسن لڑکی کے پیار محبت میں اپنے جذبات پر قابو نہ پاتے ہوئے جراثیم کش دوا پی کر اپنا کام تمام کرنا چاہا۔ وادی میں خودکشی کے بڑھتے ہوئے واقعات سے ہر مکتب فکر سے تعلق رکھنے والے افراد اپنے دانتوں تلے اُنگلی دبانے پر مجبور ہورہے ہیں۔ ماہرین نفسیات کے مطابق موجودہ جدید دور میں لوگوں کی قوت برداشت کم ہورہی ہے جبکہ اُن کی خواہشات کا دائیرہ وسیع تر ہوتا جارہا ہے اور جب لوگوں کو اُمید سے بہت زیادہ کم حاصل ہوتا ہے تو وہ موت کو ہی گلے لگانا پسند کرتے ہیں تاکہ اُنہیں مستقبل کے انتشار کے دور سے نجات حاصل ہوسکے۔ ماہرین نفسیات نے کہا ہے کہ اُمیدوں اور توقعات کا دائیرہ جس قدر چھوٹا ہوگا اُس قدر آدمی چین اور سکون کی زندگی گزار سکتا ہے۔

2 سال : جھڑپوں میں 282 فوجی ہلاک

برادرکشی اور خود کشی وارداتوں میں 408 جوانوں کی جانیں تلف

2006 میں ہزار فوجیوں نے نوکری چھوڑنے کی درخواست دی، پارلیمنٹ میں وزیر دفاع کا انکشاف

[illegible]

تھی۔اس حوالے سے ماہر نفسیات ڈ.
ارشد حسین نے الصفا کو بتایا کہ صد
اسپتال سرینگر کے میڈیکل ریکارڈ کے
مطابق گذشتہ 3 سال کے دوران 14,
830 افراد نے خودکشی کی۔ڈاکٹر ارشد
کے مطابق گذشتہ 3 سال کی تحقیق سے
ثابت ہے کہ 3.5 افراد روزانہ خودکشی
کر لیتے ہیں جو صدر اسپتال میں داخل
ہوتے ہیں۔تین سالہ تحقیق سے پتہ چلا
ہے کہ خودکشی کے ان واقعات میں جو لوگ
اپنی جان گنوا دیتے ہیں ان میں مردوں کی
تعداد زیادہ ہے جن کی عمر 25 سے
34 سال ہے جبکہ خودکشی کی اکثر کوششیں
خواتین سے ہوتی ہے جن کی عمر 19 سے
24 سال ہوتی ہے۔ڈاکٹر ارشد کے
مطابق تشویشناک پہلو یہ ہے کہ خودسوزی
کے واقعات میں روز افزوں اضافہ ہو رہا
ہے جبکہ خودکشی کے واقعات میں اب گلا
کاٹنے کا سلسلہ بھی پروان چڑھ رہا
ہے۔ڈاکٹر ارشد کہتے ہیں کہ ذہنی پریشانی
اور گھریلو معاملات سے دوچار اکثر لوگ
خودکشی پر مائل پائے جاتے ہیں تاہم
انہوں نے کہا کہ خودکشی کرنے والوں میں
مواضعات سے تعلق رکھنے والے افراد کی
تعداد زیادہ ہے۔اسپتال ذرائع کے
مطابق سال 2010ء میں 3.4 افراد
کے یومیہ اقدام خودکشی کے مقابلے میں یہ
تناسب بڑھ کر 4.5 ہو چلا ہے۔ڈاکٹر
ارشد کا کہنا ہے کہ مردوں میں خودکشی کی
وجہ نفسیاتی وباؤ جیسے ذہنی اضمحلال، غربت
اور بیروزگاری کا عنصر پایا جا رہا ہے جبکہ
خواتین میں خانہ فساد، تنگ طلبی ان کے
محرکات ہیں۔ بڑھتے ہوئے خودکشی
کے رجحان کے متعلق ملکی نفسیات کی
ماہر ڈاکٹر شیبا محی الدین کا کہنا ہے کہ
کو خودکشی کرنے کے کئی ایک وجوہات
ہو سکتے ہیں اور نوجوان طبقے میں سب سے
بڑی وجہ identity crises کا ہے
۔ڈاکٹر شیبا نے الصفا کو بتایا کہ بچوں کی
جسمانی نشوونما تو صحیح انداز سے ہوتی ہے
لیکن ان میں ذہنی نشوونما اس ڈھنگ سے
نہیں ہوتی جس کا نتیجہ یہ ہوتا ہے کہ ایسے
بچے والدین کی معمولی ڈانٹ ڈپٹ بھی

خودکشی
کہ سابق دستیاب ریکارڈ کے مقابلے میں
ان واقعات میں 50 فیصد اضافہ ہوا ہے
جو کہ باعث تشویش ہے اور رواں جد و جہد
کی بھینٹ چڑھنے والوں کا بعد دوسرا نمبر
خودکشی کرنے والے لوگوں کا ہے۔ایک
تازہ اندازے کے مطابق ہر ماہ قریب
11 اقدام خودکشی کے واقعات ہوتے ہیں
۔ [illegible]

خودکشی: لاکھ دکھوں کی ایک دوا

وادی میں بڑھتے واقعات سنجیدہ طبقے کیلئے باعث تشویش، ماہرین پریشان

سال 2011

ماہ	خودکشی کے واقعات	مرنے والوں کی تعداد
جنوری	3	1
فروری	8	3
مارچ	9	6
اپریل	9	5
مئی	12	7
جون	19	8

امتیاز خان

سرینگر// 90 کی دہائی سے قبل خودکشی کا لفظ بولنا بھی حرام سمجھا جاتا تھا لیکن چند برسوں کے دوران اس میں بے پناہ اضافہ ہوا ہے۔ رواں سال خودکشی کے 60 واقعات رونما ہوئے ہیں جن میں 30 افراد نے جان گنوادی ہے جبکہ سال 2010 میں 76 واقعات پیش آئے تھے جن میں 39 افراد کی موت واقع ہوئی تھی۔ تحقیقی رپورٹ کے مطابق گذشتہ 3 سال کے دوران 830 ,14 افراد نے خودکشی کی ۔ماہرین طب کے مطابق وادی میں روزانہ 4 سے 5 اقدام خودکشی کے واقعات رونما ہوتے ہیں۔ اگرچہ خودکشی کے بڑھتے واقعات کے بعد اس کے خلاف فتویٰ بھی جاری کیا گیا تھا، تاہم اس کے باوجود بھی خودکشی کے رجحان میں تشویشناک اضافے سے سنجیدہ طبقہ متفکر نظر آرہا ہے۔ اعداد وشمار سے پتہ چلتا ہے۔

صفحہ 6/خودکشی

12ویں جماعت کے طالب علم کی خودکشی

ہیلتھ سینٹر، تحصیل آفس اور دیگر سرکاری عمارتوں پر پتھراؤ

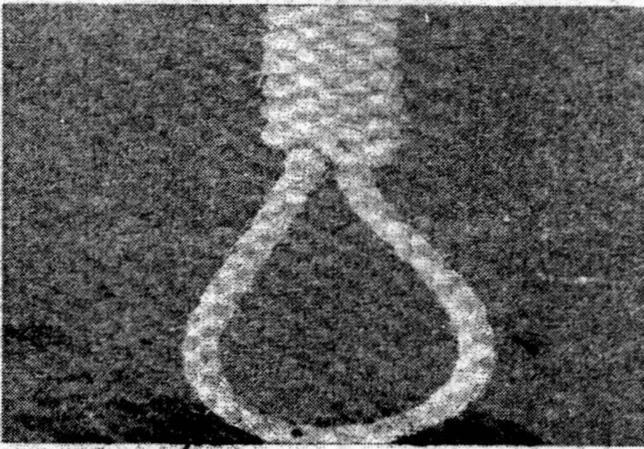

سرینگر// گاندربل کے علاقہ لار میں 12ویں جماعت کے طالب علم کی خودکشی کے ایک معاملے کو سیاسی رنگ دیتے ہوئے درجنوں لوگوں نے پرائمری ہیلتھ سینٹر لار، تحصیل آفس لار و دوسری سرکاری عمارتوں، دکانوں اور گاڑیوں پر پتھراؤ کیا اور حکومت کے خلاف نعرے بازی کی۔ اس دوران اس معاملے پر پورے لار علاقے میں ہڑتال کی گئی۔ ادھر لار اور اس کے آس پاس کے لوگوں نے اس معاملے پر سیاست کھیلنے پر افسوس ظاہر کرتے ہوئے کہا کہ جو لوگ پتھراؤ بازی میں ملوث ہیں ان کے خلاف سخت کارروائی کی جائے۔ ادھر لار میں پتھراؤ بازی کے دوران 6 افراد بھی زخمی ہوئے ہیں۔ قیصر احمد وانی ساکن بٹرن ککن گذشتہ کئی سالوں سے اپنے ماما نثار احمد ماگرے ولد غلام محمد ماگرے ساکنہ لار گاندربل کے پاس رہتا تھا اور وہ 12ویں جماعت میں زیر تعلیم تھا۔ گاندربل سے اطلاع فراہم کرتے ہوئے بتایا گیا کہ مذکورہ لڑکے نے کسی بات پر گذشتہ روز اپنے ماما کے گھر میں موجود کوئی زہریلی شے کھائی جس کے نتیجے میں وہ بے ہوش ہو گیا۔ مذکورہ لڑکے کو فوری طور علاج و معالجے کیلئے پرائمری ہیلتھ سینٹر لار لے جایا گیا جہاں قیصر احمد کے ماما اور اس کے گھر والوں کے مطابق لار ہسپتال میں کوئی بھی ملازم موجود نہیں تھا جس کے بعد اس کو شیر کشمیر میڈیکل انسٹی چیوٹ صورہ لے جانے کی کوشش کی گئی تاہم وہ دم توڑ بیٹھا۔ اس کے مطابق اگرچہ مذکورہ لڑکے کو گذشتہ رات 11 بجے اپنے آبائی علاقے بٹرن میں دفن کیا گیا تاہم جمعرات کی صبح لار علاقے میں درجنوں افراد اپنے گھروں سے باہر آئے اور انہوں نے جبراً دکانیں بند کروائیں اور گاڑیوں و دکانوں پر پتھراؤ کیا۔ اس دوران احتجاجی لوگ پرائمری ہیلتھ سینٹر لار کی عمارت کے پاس پہنچے اور انہوں نے ہسپتال کی عمارت پر چاروں طرف سے اندھادھند پتھراؤ کیا جس کے نتیجے میں مذکورہ ہسپتال عمارت کے شیشے چکنا چور ہو گئے اور عمارت کی کھڑکیوں و دروازوں کو خاصا نقصان پہنچا۔ پتھراؤ کی واردات کے دوران ہسپتال میں موجود عملے کی بھی مشتعل ہجوم نے پٹائی کی۔ ہجوم میں شامل لوگوں نے بعد میں تحصیل آفس لار کی عمارت پر زبردست پتھراؤ کیا جس کی وجہ سے مذکورہ آفس کی عمارت کو بھی خاصا نقصان پہنچا۔ ہجوم میں شامل لوگوں نے حکومت اور ضلع انتظامیہ گاندربل کے خلاف زوردار نعرے بازی کی۔ ان لوگوں کے بقول جب زہر کھانے والے لڑکے قیصر احمد وانی کو لار پرائمری ہیلتھ سینٹر لے جایا گیا تو وہاں کوئی عملہ موجود نہیں تھا جس کی وجہ سے اس کی موت ہوئی۔ ہجوم نے بعد میں لار چوک میں پہنچ کر نعرے بازی کی۔ پتھراؤ کی وجہ سے پورے لار علاقے میں مکمل ہڑتال رہی۔ اس دوران لار اور اس کے آس پاس علاقوں کے لوگوں نے بتایا کہ قیصر احمد کی خودکشی پر سیاست کی جا رہی ہے جبکہ علاقے کے ایک سیاسی کارکن کے بیٹے نے جان بوجھ کر اپنے ساتھیوں کو لیکر ہسپتال و تحصیل آفس کی عمارتوں پر پتھراؤ کروایا۔ ادھر خودکشی کی اس واردات کے سلسلے میں پولیس نے ایک کیس درج کر لیا ہے۔ ذرائع کے مطابق پتھراؤ کی وارداتوں میں کئی افراد بھی زخمی ہو گئے ہیں۔ جبکہ کئی گاڑیوں کے شیشے بھی چکنا چور ہو گئے اور کئی دکانوں کو بھی نقصان پہنچا۔

7 Three Sets of Suggestions

1. Suggestions for Jammu and Kashmir Government

To carry out a formal and official survey or census by professional experts about mental health problems in general and suicides committed in particular in J&K state, particularly the Kashmir region. Its objective must be partly for the investigation about exact number of suicides committed in the Kashmir valley and partly knowing about causes and consequences of the trend. After knowing about these dimensions of the social phenomenon of suicides, the state can formulate its policy subsequently.

Since the trend of committing suicides in Kashmir has reached to an alarming level, the state government must show serious concern and proper response to this problem. After formulating state's social policy towards suicides, it must take effective means and measures to arrest and control and finally negate completely this abnormal trend through initiation of specific programmes with proper planning and implementation mechanism.

After formulating policy and inclusion in the social planning, special programmes and schemes must be started to control and negate totally this increasing trend of suicides in Kashmir. Since a large number of youth in thousands of numbers have become victims of phenomenon, more emphasis must be laid on the practical aspects, *i.e.,* to take effective measures through which this problem can be resolved in a reasonable manner.

The state government must immediately provide all necessary help to the victims of mental health deterioration, especially suicidal tendencies. This help can be explained in terms of establishing needed medical centres, professional expertise, experienced technical manpower, and specialised services and facilities, including costly drugs. All affected people from all groups and classes must be included in these operations.

To sponsor, establish and maintain centres, institutions and agencies to work seriously and in academic and academic framework for the predetermined objectives related to mental health deterioration in general and committing suicides in large numbers in particular, experts, technology and facilities must be borrowed from outside the state as per national standards.

The state government must also try to make available at very cheaper rates all standard expertise, technology, services and facilities. These must be made cheaper items by subsidising all these facilities.

The government must shun its apathetic attitude and develop a liberal and sympathetic attitude towards those who survive the suicide attempts. In fact, they need proper health care and counseling practices, which must be provided to them. At the same time, the family members of suicide-makers must be suitably compensated and helped due to this heavy loss of human life to the family.

Last, but not the least, in order to establish the environment of peace, stability, harmony, solidarity and cooperation (to discourage the rise of suicidal tendencies), the government and its concerned agencies and authorities must stop the offences, excesses, threats, violations, molestation, harassment and torture carried out repeatedly by the security and armed forces in Kashmir.

2. Suggestions for Non-Governmental Organisations

An independent, comprehensive and professional survey or census about total number of patients involved in different mental health problems and cases of attempting suicides and successful suicides must be carried out in order to get exact number and enormity of this dangerous trend in the Kashmir region. This document must be different and better than the official document in terms of quality as well as quantity. The NGOs at the international, national and local status are in a better position to collect these figures and maintain and portray these figures.

Since a huge number of suicides, even in thousands, have occurred in the valley, the entire social environment has been polluted. So, there is the need for evolving friendly environment and providing helping hand by the NGOs by various means, especially expertise, facilities, technology and condusive social and psychological environment.

All NGOs must initiate and must work for long time on specific, focused and end-oriented programmes to eradicate the problem of committing suicides in all relevant fields and in all areas of the region in consultation and coordination with each other.

Continuous professional assessment of suicidal tendencies and committing suicides and the formal-informal medical care provided in this regard must be carried out periodically and reports must be circulated and advertised/broadcast/telecast regularly. Professional diagnosis and controlling mechanism must also be highlighted in this regard.

Statistical and descriptive reports about occurrence of suicides and prevalence of suicidal tendencies must be carried out and circulated among professional-technical groups regularly.

The NGOs of all status must sponsor or organise formally the training programmes and orientation courses for the medical and para-medical personnel involved in the official services to control mental health problems in general and phenomenon of suicides in particular. It is because these organisations are better suited and well equipped with the required talent, infrastructure and services.

These organisations, especially those of the local status, must organise on regular basis seminars, workshops and counseling sessions for different segments of society. While the seminars and workshops must be meant for technical and professional personnels involved in controlling these mental health problems, the counseling sessions must be oriented towards the past and present patients of mental health diseases. The local NGOs are most relevant organisations to pursue these aims and objectives effectively and purposefully. However, the colloberation may be provided by the national and international NGOs for financial and academic reasons.

In order to carry out mass level campaign against mental health problems and suicidal tendencies and attempts in particular, a mass level organisation of conferences, camps, meetings and other informal sessions must be organised, especially by the local NGOs and preferably in local medium and in the local suitable environment. This campaign must cover the common people as well as particular segments of population. In totality, these activities are required for all groups, sub-groups, classes and communities.

The international NGOs must work specially for quality treatment of the affected people of these diseases and problems and would be affected groups. It is because these organisations maintain world-class expertise, global technology and experienced personnels in all fields of mental health diseases and problems, including the problem of committing suicides.

National level NGOs must work among all groups, classes and communities of society on the mass level in the fields of coordination, cooperation, mutual support and reciprocal help. It is mainly because the national level organisations have enough experience in these fields at the national level and in culturally different context.

The local NGOs must emerge as the most effective and most potential source in the formation and implementation of various programmes and schemes to eradicate the problem of committing suicides. So, these must emerge strong instruments of accessibility in availing the available facilities and information.

3. Suggestions for Civil Society

Formal as well as informal efforts must be carried out for initiating a broad-based social movement for creating an environment in which it becomes extremely difficult, even impossible, to carry out or think about committing suicide by highlighting disastrous consequences for him and his family.

All major and minor social and cultural activities must be performed so as to control and arrest the increasing trend of suicidal tendencies and acts of committing suicides through various organisations, agencies, institutions, forums and social connections. In most of the cases, these social instruments may prove to be highly relevant, effective and purposeful.

All professionals and status groups in the society, especially doctors, engineers, lawyers, academicians, journalists, officers, bureaucrats, teachers, experts, scientists, businessmen, politicians, researchers, intellectuals and others must work consciously and with commitment against the problems of tendencies and committing of suicides. As these groups form the public opinion, these can prove most effective agents for convincing the groups and sub-groups which are prone to commit suicide.

The primary institutions of family, school and religion must be systematically and effectively used in all situations and in all cases to debunk and discredit the act of suicide and to promote the positive view of life. This will certainly help in rooting out the very ideational basis of suicide and its ideology.

There is a need of organising on permanent basis social, cultural, religious, literary and other programmes in different areas and sections of society for recreational and entertainment purpose, so that the pathological and depressed conditions, which provide the basis for committing suicides, are negated completely. These programmes will also generate the positive, productive and realistic ideological views about life and society.

It seems necessary that all folk as well as formal notions, ideas, institutions and practices necessarily associated with the dominant religion to reduce and finally eliminate the trends of suicide tendencies and acts of committing suicides.

It has been felt that a systematic, organised and sustainable social campaign against the problem of suicides by identifying its damaging, disastrous and disorganising implications can certainly help its restriction and control.

A planned, rational and well-thought policy campaign in higher-secondary schools, colleges, universities and technical-professional institutions will certainly discredit and delegitimise the act of suicide on the part of educated segment population, which constitutes the majority of suicide-makers, and develop positive ideology and positive worldview.

All agencies of mass media, print as well as electronic media, must be utilised in a purposeful and effective manner for portraying realistically the causes and consequences of committing suicides.

Last, but not the least, there seems basic and urgent need to form and activate the social activities and social activist groups to keep social vigil on the attempts of suicides and give rise to positive views about life and society.

INDEX